erica hannickel

Melodramatic Formations

tallmen
can men
+ painted ?

1820

1870

patrician theatres
paternalism
elite
1830s

waning republican
paradigm

→ bourgeois
cultural authority

1830-55
"Jacksonian
yeoman independence"

liberal capitalism:
male individualism
female domesticity
social respectability

even more class stratified

(causes:
economic change, new
class formation, major
political shifts, new
theatrical practices)

hero worship

STUDIES IN THEATRE HISTORY

AND CULTURE

Edited by Thomas Postlewait

MELODRAMATIC

FORMATIONS

AMERICAN THEATRE

AND SOCIETY, 1820 – 1870

BY BRUCE A. McCONACHIE

UNIVERSITY OF IOWA PRESS ꙮ IOWA CITY

University of Iowa Press,
Iowa City 52242

Printed in the
United States of
America

Design by Richard Hendel

Printed on acid-free paper

Library of Congress
Cataloging-in-
Publication Data
McConachie, Bruce A.
Melodramatic formations:
American theatre and
society, 1820–1870
/ by Bruce A. McConachie.—
1st ed.
p.   cm.—(Studies in theatre
history and culture)
Includes bibliographical
references and index.
ISBN 0-87745-359-4,
ISBN 0-87745-360-8 (pbk.)
1. Theater—United States—
History—19th century.
2. Theater and society—
United States.   3. Melo-
drama, American—History
and criticism.   4. American
drama—19th century—His-
tory and criticism.
I. Title.   II. Series.
PN2248.M34   1992   91-44085
792'.0973'09034—dc20   CIP

97 96 95 94 93 92 C 1 2 3 4 5 6
03 02 01 00 99   P   2 3 4 5 6

Contents

Acknowledgments

One of the pleasant consequences of taking a long time to write a book is an increase in the number of people who helped make possible its publication. I have benefited from the financial aid, research assistance, and scholarly advice of numerous institutions and individuals, some of whose names I have probably overlooked in the listing which follows.

A National Endowment for the Humanities fellowship got me started several years ago on what I hoped would be a simple revision and extension of my dissertation from the University of Wisconsin. Several summer grants and a semester sabbatical from the College of William and Mary kept me going. A final semester leave paid for by the Commonwealth Center for the Study of American Culture allowed me to finish the project.

Along the way, librarians at several theatre collections, including those at the New York Public Library, Brown University, the Hoblitzelle in Austin, Texas, Columbia University, and the Harvard Theatre Collection, guided me to troves of documents, pictures, programs, and scripts. Deborah Taylor, Ilona Koren-Deutsch, Monica Maillot, Alexandra Michos, and other graduate students in American Studies at William and Mary and in the Interdisciplinary Theatre program at Northwestern University also assisted my research efforts. Before I learned to fumble at word processing, Linda Williams, Phyllis Leffler, and Deborah Buchman helped me to compile early chapters of the manuscript.

Professors Daniel T. Rodgers, Walter Meserve, and Alan Woods gave me important advice on an early draft of *Melodramatic Formations*. Over the course of writing several conference speeches, journal articles, and essays in anthologies—all of which helped me to put the book together—I have benefited immensely from the insights of Rosemarie Bank, Thomas Postlewait, John Steven Paul, Richard John, Cynthia Jenner, Alan Wallach, and Richard Butsch.

I'm also happy to thank Stephanie McConachie for her sensitivity to unnecessary jargon and ponderous rhetoric and for her patience and faith in my ability to finish The Book That Swallowed a Family. Thanks, too, to Chris and Andrew McConachie for tolerating a father who occasionally spent more time on his scholarly child than on his teenage sons. Finally, I'm grateful to my father and mother, Don and Audrey McConachie, for their encouragement and support over the years.

Preliminary versions of portions of *Melodramatic Formations* appeared in the following journals and anthologies: *Theatre for Working-Class Audiences in the United States, 1830–1980* (Greenwood, 1985), *Theatre Survey, Journal of Dramatic Theory and Criticism, When They Weren't Doing Shakespeare: Actors and Culture on the Nineteenth-Century Stage* (University of Georgia Press, 1989), *For Fun and Profit: The Transformation of Leisure into Consumption* (Temple, 1990), *Journal of American Drama and Theatre*, and *The American Stage: Social and Economic Issues from the Colonial Period to the Present* (Cambridge, 1992).

In my Marxian musings (Groucho, not Karl), I had always hoped to read a sentence at the end of the acknowledgments section, following lavish thanks to numerous scholars, which stated: "Of course, the blame for any mistakes in the book rests entirely with them, not me." But having written such a sentence myself, I am no more able to endorse its wise crack than any other scribbling pedant. My mistakes, alas, are my own.

Introduction

The most interesting and difficult part of any cultural analysis, in complex societies, is that which seeks to grasp the hegemonic in its active and formative but also its transformational processes. Works of art, by their substantial and general character, are often especially important as sources of this complex evidence.

—*Raymond Williams,* Marxism and Literature

Always historicize!

—*Fredric Jameson,* The Political Unconscious

The Prophet!

Melodrama was ubiquitous in American culture between 1820 and 1870. Spectators as diverse as Philip Hone, mayor of New York, John Commerford, cabinetmaker and union activist, Margaret Fuller, feminist writer, and Abraham Lincoln, president, applauded, wept over, and laughed with actors depicting heroism, villainy, and innocence on American stages. Different types of melodrama appealed to a range of audiences, from elite males to urban workers and business-class women, by the time of the Civil War. And these nineteenth-century Americans took their melodramas just as seriously as most citizens today take their adventure programs and soap operas on television.

The relevant issue for theatre historians is not whether these diverse melodramas were any good. Judging plays solely on the basis of such formalistic concepts as complexity, style, and naturalness merely backs the historian into what Terry Eagleton has called "the ideology of the aesthetic." Unfortunately, as theatre historian Joseph R. Roach notes, many theatre scholars unthinkingly accept this ideology and its consequent assumption, "derived from German idealist philosophy and eighteenth-century theories of art, that the aesthetic exists as an autonomous category, transcending the sublunary sphere of power relations and ideologies."[1] Nor is it particularly helpful to rail against melodrama for encouraging its spectators to escape from reality. All successful fiction, whatever its aesthetic merit, induces its audience to temporarily leave behind the workaday world for an imagined one. As a "symbolic act," however, melodramatic performance, like all cultural behavior, was not only an imagined representation but also a social event involving the interaction of people in a specific place and time— an event as real as making love or mining coal.[2]

Rather, the question is what types of melodramatic experiences did nineteenth-century theatregoers participate in and what meanings did they construct from them. In a sense, we need to understand not what audiences were escaping from, but what they escaped to, and what impact this willing suspension of disbelief may have had on their lives. When theatrical communication succeeds, spectators identify with and affirm certain roles, values, and assumptions represented on the stage. These identifications and affirmations, like all ideologies, both limit and sustain the beliefs and behaviors of their historical subjects. Consequently, theatre historians need to explore what the experience of melodrama did with, for, and to their willing participants.

No investigation of this problem is possible, of course, without locating the dynamics of melodramatic production, formulaic diversity, and audience reception within the context of social history. But how is this to be done? Since empirically based research has yet to verify—and may be incapable of ascertaining—the general relationship between performances and the historical culture of which they are a part, the theatre historian needs some guidance in framing questions and pursuing leads when investigating this issue. More than that, she or he needs some definitions and assumptions, since writing history without these foundations is impossible.[3]

My own predilections in this regard are eclectic. Although the traditions of western Marxism provide the framework and most of the foundational metaphors for this study, I also borrow from the constructions of Meadian sociology, materialist feminism, new historicism, and the rhetoric of Kenneth Burke. Indeed, my scholarly debts are more numerous than these since, as Fredric Jameson remarks, "the sociologist of literature or culture is absolutely dependent on the paradigms of social history and class relations furnished him by the specialists in the field."[4] My reconstructions of historical audiences and melodramatic ideologies lean heavily on the formulations and evidence provided by Robert Wiebe, Mary Ryan, Sean Wilentz, John Kasson, and the many other historians cited in my notes. Without the work of these scholars, the social contours and dynamics of nineteenth-century theatre history in the United States would be indecipherable.

The concept of a "reading formation," as outlined by neo-Marxist theorist and historian Tony Bennett, provides a cogent framework for relating the repetition of a type of theatrical performance to its wider historical context. Bennett proposes

> a way of rethinking context such that, ultimately, neither text nor context are conceivable as entities separable from each other. According to most formulations, context is social; that is, a set of extra-discursive and extra-textual determinations to which the text is related as an external backdrop or set of reading conditions. The concept of reading formation, by contrast, is an attempt to think of context as a set of discursive and intertextual determinations, operating on material and institutional supports, which bear in upon a text not just externally, from the outside in, but internally, shaping it—in the historically concrete forms in which it is available as a text-to-be-read—from the inside out.[5]

Bennett's formulation has clear implications for the analysis of theatrical events and their historical contexts. Play performance and spectator response may be looked at together as mutually interactive elements of a single phenomenon. Audiences shape performances over time, encouraging or discouraging elements of dramatic style, certain character types, and various acting conventions. At the same time, similar performances are shaping the audience, driving away some spectators from the theatre and pulling in others eager to be entertained and persuaded in ways specific to these productions. In effect, groups of spectators and theatre performers produce each other from the inside out as artists-to-be-experienced and audiences-to-be-entertained in a given historical period. The result is what may be termed a theatrical formation, the mutual elaboration over time of historically specific audience groups and theatre practitioners participating in certain shared patterns of dramatic and theatrical action. Employing the concept of theatrical formation, then, requires the historian to dive into the apparent chaos of theatrical events and to emerge with regularities of production, genre, and audience over a significant stretch of time.

Between 1820 and 1870 audiences and theatre people in the United States constructed and maintained a variety of these formations. Different groups enjoyed and produced specific types of comedy, opera, farce, minstrelsy, and melodrama over periods ranging from fifteen to forty years. The formations centering on various melodramatic productions and responses, however, encompassed a greater diversity of social experience than other confluences of productive modes, audience groups, and theatrical genres. Elite males enjoyed fairy-tale melodramas produced by paternalistically run stock companies between 1820 and 1835. From 1830 into the mid 1850s, stars combined with stock companies to entertain male Jacksonians of all classes with heroic melodramas. In a subformation of this historical type, native-born workers supported apocalyptic melodramas between 1835 and 1850. Beginning about 1845, a new formation emerged centering on moral reform melodramas and an audience of respectable Protestant families, most of whose female and youthful auditors were new to theatregoing. In the mid 1850s, many in this group merged with business-class spectators to applaud sensation melodramas produced by companies controlled by capitalist-managers. These melodramatic formations, then, provide a logical focus for investigating the ways in which contextual social realities shaped the nineteenth-century American theatre "from the inside out."

The narrative thread stitching together *Melodramatic Formations* traces the decline of one type of cultural hegemony and the gradual rise of another.[6] Differences in the ideology of various kinds of melodramatic performances, coupled with shifts in audiences and pressures on the stock company mode of production, helped to facilitate a sea change in cultural domination from the elite paternalism of the 1820s to business-class respectability in the 1860s. Raymond Williams' notions of "residual" and "emergent" culture are useful in charting this transformation. "The residual, by definition, has been effectively formed in the past, but it is still active in the cultural process . . . as an effective element in the present," states Williams. For the most part, the traditions of agrarianism, male honor, and republicanism constituted Jacksonian melodramatic theatre as residual culture. The production and reception of moral reform melodrama, on the other hand, contained elements which were "substantially alternative or oppositional" to the earlier hegemonic; hence, Williams would term the culture of this theatrical formation "emergent."[7] *Melodramatic Formations* concludes on the eve of the Panic of 1873, which led to the destruction of American stock companies, the productive base of theatrical culture in the 1820–70 period.

Because of my interest in charting this transformation over fifty years, I am limiting this study to melodramatic formations in the northeastern United States, the region which experienced the most wrenching social and economic changes in the 1820–70 period. Confining my discussion to the Northeast also means looking mostly at urban theatrical formations. This limitation, however, limits very little: well over eighty percent of midcentury theatres in the United States served urban audiences; the West (New Orleans excepted) imported nearly all of its theatre from the Northeast; and theatres in the South grew slowly, retained the elite as their core audience, and rarely produced apocalyptic or moral reform melodrama. In short, audiences and theatre artists in the Northeast needed new melodramatic forms to project their newfound hopes and assuage their modern fears. Theatre participants in other regions could wait for these melodramatic formulae to be developed in the Northeast or could do without them.

Theoretically, there is nothing in the definition of a theatrical formation that requires the theatre historian to look only at dramas written by playwrights sharing the same nationality as the audience. On the nineteenth-century American stage, popular British melodramas, often derived from French originals, outnumbered successful American ones by perhaps 5 to 1. (The ratio for popular social comedies was probably 12 to 1.)[8] More significantly, French and English culture generated nearly all the formulaic conventions used by most American playwrights to structure their melodramas. The one important exception was the formula for heroic melodrama which, because it legitimated Jacksonian ideology, confounded British audiences. Nonetheless, I will be looking almost exclusively at American plays, partly because of the Jacksonian exception, but mostly because there were minor differences, despite their derivative form, which put an American spin on their ideological meanings. The Jacksonian plays aside, however, there was little that was uniquely American about these texts and their ideologies. The theatrical formations of which they were a part were simply one more reality in the complex dynamic of Anglo-American social and cultural history, itself a part of the history of the modern West.

PART I

The Waning of Paternalistic Theatre

for the Elite, 1820–1835

During the first third of the nineteenth century, theatre in northeastern cities maintained the dominance of elite male culture. Theatre architects provided commodious spaces for patricians to discuss business affairs, parade their status, and arrange for assignations as well as to enjoy their plays. Managers, eager to please the class that employed them, sought the approbation of the house in their choice of plays and actors. Among the most popular entertainments with elite audiences in the 1820s and early 1830s were fairy-tale melodramas, a type of performance which spoke directly to upper-class male fears of losing control over their children, their cities, and their nation. Given the rapid pace of social change in the 1820s, patrician worries were justified. Even within their theatres, actors and managers were beginning to challenge the institutional structures of traditional elite authority.

The ideology of paternalism, which legitimated patrician hegemony in the Northeast, suffused most of the plays and practices of the theatre in this era. Paternalism centers authority in upper-class, mature males; it defines them as protectors, judges, and benefactors, and those under their control as socially irresponsible children. For most of the eighteenth century, paternalism provided much of the moral justification for familial, economic, and political forms of authority, binding wives to husbands, servants to masters, and colonists (later citizens) to local elites. Even into the early nineteenth century, paternalistic belief and behavior retarded the development of more democratic and competitive social relations. As social historian Richard Sennett notes, merchants, philanthropists, and wealthy landowners assuming the persona of the benevolent father toward their social subordinates were often "motivated by a desire to make personal, face-to-face contacts—to make a community—in an economic system always pulling people into paths of individual striving and mutual competition." But the paternalism of the urban patriciate, especially in its melodramatic manifestations, rested on an "authority of false love," in Sennett's apt phrase—false because the paternalists had no intention of fulfilling their implicit "promise of nurturance." At a time when most fathers envisioned their control over their children as gradually lessening to enable them to establish independent lives of their own, paternalistic father figures, having cast their charges as victims, had no intention of relaxing their benevolent grip.[1]

For paternalism to work—for it to grease effectively the many points of friction in a social system perpetuating inequality—both parties to the paternalistic relationship must accept its definitions, norms, and values. If the paternalists were to feel justified in their benevolence, servants, wives, children and other social inferiors had to acknowledge their fatherly concern with respect, gratitude, and even affection. The lack of such emotionally charged reciprocity would strip paternalistic behavior of its mythos and reveal the manipulative self-interest at its core.

By the late 1820s, the pressures of free market capitalism and egalitarian democracy had undermined paternalistic relations in the theatre to such an extent that traditional practices began collapsing of their own weight. Theatre historians have long understood the revolutionary impact of itinerant starring on acting companies and playwrighting, but they have not seen this change as part of a larger transformation of American culture linked to the rise of laissez-faire capitalism. Star performers in the 1820s and early 1830s were entrepreneurs of their own careers who avoided the hierarchical restraints of local acting companies for the freedom of an emerging national market of talent. Traditional paternalists like William B. Wood, co-manager of the Chestnut Street Theatre in Philadelphia for most of the teens and twenties, struggled in vain to incorporate the stars within traditional controls, only to watch helplessly as paternalistically managed theatres foundered on the rocks of competition in the late 1820s. Working-class assertions of egalitarianism also corroded paternal prerogatives in the theatre. As the northeastern elite discovered that it could no longer "control the opinions and direct the judgment" of their social inferiors in their playhouses, they gradually withdrew from public theatregoing to exercise more modern means of cultural influence.[2]

1. "A Spirit of Locomotiveness"

T he intertwining of paternalism and mercantile capitalism which had structured the economic and social relations of the stage since before the Revolution continued into the 1820s. In part because elite stockholders owned the prestigious theatres of New York, Philadelphia, and Boston, individual enjoyment and social control joined with profit taking as the primary goals of theatre ownership. Patrician theatrical corporations employed a manager or two co-managers who were accorded relatively free rein in hiring actors, playwrights, machinists, and others to produce theatrical entertainment. Stability as well as profitability organized the employment and remuneration of these theatre artists. Managers regularly awarded actors who had worked with the troupe for several years a "permanent" place in the company hierarchy, thus protecting them from the vagaries of the labor market among actors. More important, the direct patronage of the patriciate through "benefits" given to the manager and the actors was nearly as crucial as the profits of the theatre in determining the yearly remuneration received by company members. As long as upper-class males regarded playgoing as a both enjoyable and necessary extension of their power and status in local public affairs, paternalistic theatre in the Northeast would continue to amble these traditional paths. Capitalist competition, however, transformed these mercantilist roadways into the train tracks of the star network, leaving theatre managers like William B. Wood blinded by the smoke.

Not all of the patriciate went to the theatre in the 1820s and 1830s, but enough of them did and with enough frequency to keep most theatres in the Northeast under elite influence. Some of the upper class condemned theatregoing in the same breath with prostitution and gambling. The Reverend Lyman Beecher thundered that the theatre was "the center of the Valley of Pollution," and Timothy Dwight found "player, vagabond, and maximum of vice and wickedness [to] be only different names for the same thing." Other ministers sermonized against the immorality of the plays, the amount of money and time wasted in playhouses, the presence of prostitutes, and the occasional scantiness of female costumes on stage.[1] Such clerical condemnation, little different from the antitheatrical prejudices of ministers in earlier decades, continued throughout the period. Few in the elite, however, seem to have heeded their advice. To be sure, some evangelical merchants like Arthur and Lewis Tappan of New York City shunned the theatre as the house of the devil, but many others saw no contradiction between spending money on church-supported moral uplift groups and buying a box seat at the playhouse.

Evidence abounds on the popularity of theatregoing among the upper class. One visitor to America in 1838 noted that the audience for a play he witnessed consisted mainly of "young men engaged in trade . . . and rich merchants and their families whose tastes are, to a certain extent, intellectual, but whose mental resources are not very extensive." An Italian actor who toured American theatres in the 1830s complained:

> It is well known that, in large cities, a considerable portion of those who frequent the boxes of a theatre on *great occasions* go there to show themselves, or to meet with their friends, or to escape from their common enemy *ennui* or because they have nothing else to do, or because, if they do not go, they cannot have to say tomorrow that they were at the theatre last night (and if they had not this to say, what could they say?), or they go for any reason the reader may please to imagine except to see and attend to what is going forward on the stage.

Such socialite *arrivés* at elite status went to the theatre in increasing numbers after 1820.[2]

Upper-class predominance in the playhouses of northeastern cities during the twenties and early thirties is not surprising. Wealthy shareholders and property owners financed the construction and controlled the leasing of all theatres during the period. When the Park Theatre in New York burned in 1820, it was quickly rebuilt and leased back to the previous managers by John Jacob Astor and John K. Beekman, two of the richest men in the city. General Charles W. Sandford, a prominent lawyer and businessman, financed much of the construction of the Lafayette Theatre in an uptown section of New York in 1825. He did so primarily to induce the patriciate to build houses nearby so that his real estate would climb in value. Real estate speculation also led some of the Philadelphia rich to build the Arch Street Theatre in 1828, despite the fact that the city's other two theatres were barely surviving on their portion of elite patronage. In Boston, "gentlemen of wealth and influence" established the Tremont Street Theatre in 1827. According to mid nineteenth-century theatre historian William W. Clapp, Jr., these upper-class theatregoers had no difficulty securing a grant of incorporation from the state legislature.[3]

The urban elite did not sit alone in their theatres, of course, their numbers being too small to sustain an ongoing professional company and, hence, to pay back their investment in the property. Theatre managers could count on substantial patronage from wealthy visitors to their cities: country merchants and gentry farmers, sea captains and merchants from other ports, and a variety of other well-to-do travelers, some of whom were already coming to the city simply "to see a show." As the transportation revolution created several northeastern cities as the nuclei for trade with their surrounding countrysides, it also brought more travelers to city theatres. Even less populous centers benefited. One Englishman visiting the theatre in Providence, Rhode Island, in 1841 noted that the audience was "composed mostly of strangers passing through the city on their way to and from New York and Boston." Of all the theatres in the Northeast, those in New York City—by 1825 the terminus of the Erie Canal and the busiest port in the nation—benefited the most from increased travel. In 1832, the *New-York Mirror* reported that "the invigorating influence of the [spring] season is visible in the theatrical as well as the vegetable world. . . . The country folks crowd into town to buy goods, and of course, go to the theatres."[4] Already, theatres in the Big Apple were profiting from the out-of-town trade.

Sitting apart from the urban elite and well-to-do travelers at fashionable playhouses were other social groups and classes. Male apprentices, journeymen, servants, and African-Americans generally congregated in the gallery, the rear balcony containing the lowest-priced seats. The "middling classes," to use the designation of a journalist in 1825, usually sat on wooden benches in the pit, that area of the theatre below the boxes roughly corresponding to the present-day orchestra. The pit also held some of the better-off workers, as an English visitor in 1818 was surprised to learn. Expecting the pit audience to "resemble the same department [as that] in an English establishment," he found, instead, "men that, if in London, could hardly buy a pint of porter—and should they ever think of seeing a play, must take up their abode among the upper gallery."[5] Working-class attendance at fashionable playhouses began to decline in the 1830s as workers shifted their patronage to other theatres offering plays more appealing to their aesthetic and social values.

Apart from prostitutes, who inhabited the third tier of side boxes in virtually all playhouses until the 1840s, few women attended elite theatres with any regularity. "Ladies are rarely seen there, and by far the larger proportion of females deem it an offense against religion to witness the representation of a play," reported the renowned English visitor Mrs. Trollope. Comic actor Tyrone Power noted that the "well-filled house" at the Tremont Theatre in Boston in 1833 was composed "chiefly of men, as on my debut at New York." When respectable women did put in an appearance, they generally sat with their husbands or fathers in the boxes. The English actress Fanny Kemble, performing with her father at the Park Theatre in 1832, reported in her journal that there were scarce "twenty women in the dress circle" to witness her father's American debut. Whenever word spread that there might be a riot or even a minor disturbance at one of the playhouses—a not infrequent occurrence until the 1850s—the women stayed away. In 1825, Edmund Kean's appearance touched off a riot in Baltimore, and "the greatest portion of the female auditors," not having received advance warning of possible trouble, "retired in disgust from the disgraceful scene."[6] Discouraging "ladies" from theatrical attendance and restricting them primarily to the boxes when they did arrive were customs inherited from the British during colonial times. Thus traditional patriarchy combined with female reticence to keep theatregoing a predominantly male activity in the 1820s and 1830s.

The patriciate paid for their status when they purchased a box seat in one of their theatres. Prices for each seating area in the playhouse paralleled the rough hierarchy of classes of spectators to be found in the box, pit, and gallery. At the Walnut and Chestnut Street theatres in the early 1820s, the upper class paid a dollar for a seat in a theatre box, compared to seventy-five cents for the pit and fifty cents for the gallery. In the 1830s, most managers kept the box price the same but lowered the pit and gallery rates to fifty and twenty-five cents respectively, probably to encourage flagging working-class attendance.

Occasional experimentation with ticket prices confirmed the management's belief that a hierarchical ordering of prices and classes was necessary. Taking advice which he later regretted, manager William B. Wood at the Chestnut Street Theatre lowered prices to seventy-five, fifty, and twenty-five cents in 1823, but found no increase in patronage. Wood concluded that "a slight inclination to exclusiveness" for the elite must be built into ticket prices. When the Bowery Theatre opened in New York, the price of admission to the boxes and the pit was the same—fifty cents—with twenty-five cents charged for the gallery. But, notes nineteenth-century theatre historian Joseph N. Ireland, "a few nights' experience proved that to keep a portion of the house free from admixture with the vulgar and unrefined, it would be necessary to dis-

Interior of the Park Theatre, New York City, *watercolor on paper, 1822, by John Searle (New-York Historical Society). The painting showcases many of the New York male elite, shown seated in the pit, and also depicts prostitutes and their johns, standing in the doorways, in the third tier.*

criminate between the box and the pit." Accordingly, the management altered its initial prices to 75¢ for the boxes and 37½¢ for the pit.[7]

Upon entering the theatre, the businessman of the time found himself in a spacious lobby, well suited for greeting friends, conducting business, displaying the latest in fashionable attire and, in general, for confirming his status as a member of the elite. After the old Park Theatre burned down in 1820, proprietors Astor and Beekman took the opportunity to enlarge the lobby when they rebuilt their playhouse, making the new one "sufficiently spacious to contain the whole audience," as the *Evening Post* commented in 1821. The managers of the new Chestnut Street Theatre, which had also burned in 1820, boasted on the reverse of the opening bill in 1822 that their new furnace-heated lobby held over a thousand people. Other theatre owners in the 1820s also found occasion to mention newly installed furnaces or fireplaces, a significant advance over previously unheated entries. The lobby of the newly redecorated Chatham Garden Theatre, a predominately spring- and summertime playhouse in New York, featured a fountain with "a refreshing column of pure water" to delight the eye and cool the senses in 1827. The reporter added that "every attention has been paid to render the house as cool and pleasant as possible."[8]

Eclipsing all previous theatrical lobbies and saloons in New York were those of the second Bowery Theatre of 1828. The dazzled reporter for the *New-York Mirror*, probably copying a press release from the manager's new press agent, devoted the entire front page of the weekly journal to its description. Among other delights was a saloon open only to patrons of the dress circle:

> It is a commodious and well-arranged apartment, richly furnished and ornamented, the furniture being of blue, to correspond with the ground of the boxes, and the ornaments also the same style with those of the interior, which we shall presently describe. Two rooms close the extremities, the one being a retiring-room for ladies, and the other the coffee room. The whole suite is sumptuously lighted with gas lamps of an antique fashion.[9]

In the constant effort to attract elite patronage to their theatres, owners and managers, especially in New York City, played a never-ending game of refurbishment leapfrog, jumping over the competition in spaciousness and luxury only to be surpassed, the next year, by more lavish displays elsewhere. This expensive game helped to ruin more than one manager in the late 1820s and encouraged others to seek new ways of attracting the elite or even of abandoning them for a different audience.

The extravagant lobbies and saloons served as more than pleasant passageways for entering and leaving the theatre or for grabbing a quick drink at intermission. Elite theatres of the twenties and thirties pampered the active entrepreneur of the period by providing semiprivate coffee rooms and saloons where business could be discussed, friends met, and assignations with the women of the third tier discreetly arranged. During an evening's entertainment, the typical businessman might spend almost as much time chatting with friends as he would watching the performers, especially when, as often happened, the actors were doing a show he had seen a few times before. The Chatham Garden Theatre, for example, boasted "a spacious balcony" where "the sentiments of friendship may be interchanged or any topic discussed, without molestations or interruptions."[10] Managers of the Chatham Garden and other upper-class playhouses could guarantee that elite conversations would remain uninterrupted because theatre patrons sitting on the benches in the pit or the gallery generally had no access to the lavish retreats of the patricians.

Throughout the 1820s, theatre owners in the urban Northeast usually provided separate entrances and lobbies for each class of patron, with the degree of spaciousness and decoration improving as the patron moved up the social ladder. For the most part, such architectural discrimination passed without comment, but occasionally those having some grudge against a theatre manager used it as an excuse to foment a disturbance. William B. Wood noted that "some of the persons connected with the McKenzie riot" involving his company put out the following handbill when the new Chestnut Street Theatre opened in 1822:

EQUALITY,

OR THE

NEW THEATRE

AS IT SHOULD BE.

To the independent citizens, who, from a long experience and due appreciation
of their rights in the great charter of citizenship can well understand their relations,

and spurn at any indignities in the social compact, the following limits may not be unnecessarily offered:—

You, citizens, whose patronage the drama is proud to acknowledge, and whose inclination, taste, or means may lead to the Pit or Gallery, why subject you at an entrance comparatively less respectable than what has been assigned to those whose *assumed* superiority has led to distinctions wherein *no* distinctions are at all justifiable?

The national spirit of America has triumphed over the pride of European armies; shall that spirit slumber under the degradation of European distinctions? [11]

Apparently, such "European distinctions" were not enough to animate the McKenzie rioters to a second disturbance. At the Chestnut Street Theatre, as elsewhere, the "slumber" of the "national spirit" with regard to antidemocratic entrance and seating arrangements continued until the 1840s. The "gallery gods" and "pittites" might annoy the elite by shouting and throwing food at the actors, but by themselves they had little real power in the theatres of the 1820s.

Theatre boxes confirmed elite hegemony in the playhouses of the time. Box seats outnumbered all other types of seating combined in almost all theatres built in the 1820s. The 1822 Chestnut Street Theatre, for instance, accommodated over two thousand spectators, but of that number only three hundred could sit in the gallery and four hundred in the pit, leaving about thirteen hundred in the boxes. In financial terms, the predominance of the boxes was even more staggering. At 1822 prices, the Chestnut gallery had a potential nightly yield of $150, the pit $300, and the boxes $1,300, almost triple the combined revenue of the other two. Not surprisingly, some theatre builders in the 1820s did away with gallery seating completely in an effort to squeeze in more box seats. This strategy was risky, however, as the managers of the Chatham Garden and Lafayette theatres in New York learned when their abolition of gallery seating helped to bring about the closing of their theatres in the highly competitive period of the late 1820s. Elsewhere, some theatre managers suffered from too few box seats. At the 1828 Tremont Street Theatre, reports Clapp, "the house was too small, or rather the dress circle would not contain those who would not take seats in the second tier." [12] At the Arch in Philadelphia, the large proportion of pittites and gallery gods to those in box seats (roughly 1,100 to 900 on full-house nights) proved a distinct liability in the 1820s, but became an asset later on when different managers strove to attract predominantly working-class audiences.

Sitting above the pit and protected from the vulgarity of the gallery, the elite came to the theatre as much to be seen as to see. This was especially true of the nouveau riche. Apparently the boxes at the new Chatham Garden Theatre in 1824 had been built deeply in order to pack in the elite, with the consequence that not enough light from the auditorium illuminated the few ladies who sat there. "What is the use of spending two hours at the toilet," complained a sympathetic newspaper editor on the ladies' behalf, "if no one can perceive the improvement?"[13] The managers took the hint and promptly increased the lighting.

At the Chatham Garden and virtually all other theatres before the early 1850s it was customary to leave audience lights undimmed during the performance, partly to increase spectator visibility of the stage but mostly to allow the audience to see one another. Indeed, the technology of gas illumination—first tried at the Chestnut in 1816 and in general theatrical use in the Northeast by the mid 1820s—made full houselights during the show increasingly obsolete from an aesthetic point of view. Socially, though, gas was a big improvement over the typically "cracked and dingy" oil lights previously used, providing enough illumination to distinguish friends in an opposite box, or, occasionally, to signal one of the "ladies of the night" in the third tier. One of the boasts of the new Lafayette Theatre, for instance, was "a superb gas chandelier . . . suspended from the center, directly under the ventilator, shedding a light over the whole audience like the splendor of the midday sun."[14] (Mention of the ventilator in the same breath with the chandelier, by the way, was not accidental: the new gaslights had smelled like rotten eggs when first introduced.)

The *New-York Mirror* puff for the Bowery Theatre of 1828 made much of the advantages of gas lighting. "On entering the box circle," gushed the reporter, "the spectator is dazzled with the blaze of light that suddenly bursts upon him; and it is some time before he can ascertain the particulars of the commingled splendor and beauty which the hand of liberality and taste has spread here with unsparing luxuriance." Further, the back walls of the Bowery boxes were "painted of the apple-blossom colour, as being most favourable to display the spectators to advantage."[15] In effect, each box of these theatres became a mini-stage designed to frame the elite spectators within small prosceniums—stages which often competed successfully with the actors for audience attention. Competition between actors and spectators in the theatre, of course, was nothing new. The American patriciate followed in the tradition of Renaissance princes, Restoration rakes, and eighteenth-century patriarchs in performing socially sanctioned roles for all to see when they went to the playhouse.

What explains this elite need for social performance and display? Apart from the satisfaction of personal vanity, upper-class males maintained the legitimacy of their domination through such rituals of theatregoing. The editor of the *Columbian Sentinel*, for instance, could appeal to "the liberality, taste and discrimination of those elevated classes of society who are the 'makers of manners,' and to whom talent and worth have a right to look up to for a generous countenance and patronage" in his plea for potential shareholders to support the rebuilding of the Park Theatre. Mayor Philip Hone, a regular theatregoer himself, put the matter bluntly in an 1826 speech celebrating the opening of the first Bowery Theatre: "It is therefore incumbent upon those whose standing in society enables them to control the opinions and direct the judgment of others, to encourage, by their countenance and support, a well-regulated theatre."[16] Paternalistic dominance may not have been the conscious motive of most of the elite shareholders and theatregoers, as it was with Hone, but it was certainly the result, intended or not. When upper-class merchants, brokers, and professional men looked down from their box seats at the pittites, many of them must have met the eyes of those below looking up at them, searching for their "countenance and support." How easy and how thoroughly appropriate in such circumstances for patrician males to play the role of beneficent father figures to other spectators in their theatres.

The architectural interiors of most 1820s theatres also facilitated the elite's paternalistic gaze at the players. Performing well in front of the proscenium on an apron stage jutting into the house, the actors were surrounded on three sides by patrician spectators, some of whom were only a few feet away. From this superior position easily seen by the rest of the audience, upper-class males could ignore, harass, or applaud the performers, actions well within the accepted norms of spectator behavior at the theatre.

The notion that going to the theatre meant arriving before the entertainment began, staying seated until a designated intermission, and remaining silent unless induced by the performers to respond—these conventions taken for granted by auditors in the twentieth century—would have been ridiculously abnormal in the 1820s. Spectators arrived at the theatre and left their seats whenever they wished, regardless of what was occurring on stage. Actors sometimes had to shout to make themselves heard above the small talk which often filled the theatre, especially during the first half-hour or so of the entertainment. Critics complained of "the titter of the impure, and the dull chatter of her stupid wooer" from the third tier, "the din of oaths" from the gallery, and "the loud conversation . . . in the midst of a soliloquy" from the elite in the boxes.[17] Ignoring the drama on stage for the show in the audience was made all the easier because the stock system of repertory production guaranteed the frequent repetition of familiar pieces by familiar players. Why watch attentively if you already know the play and perhaps even the reading the stock actor would give to his next line?

Spectator attention to the show could be just as nerve-racking for the performers as their indifference. Audiences yelled at singers and musicians, sometimes pelting them with fruit, when they performed classical pieces rather than patriotic or popular tunes for entre'acte music. Actors badly imperfect in their lines, especially in a well-known play, might be hooted or even egged off the stage. "The egg as a vehicle of dramatic criticism came into early use in this continent," noted one playgoer. Even when they liked the show, the audience might distract the actors with frequent applause. New York performer James Fennell, for a short time the editor of a theatre magazine, politely reminded his auditors that "the merits of an actor can be sufficiently rewarded by the public . . . by applause bestowed on him at his exit" or during appropriate pauses; they needn't applaud whenever their enjoyment prompted it. But audiences resisted all suggestions designed to curb their "rights." Commenting on the disturbance following an 1817 performance of *The Beggars' Opera*, one magazine critic observed: "In speaking of the rights of the public in the theatre, no one who knows what he is talking about has any reference to the statute book. There is a tacit convention between the managers and the audience, which an intelligent public knows how to enforce. Custom and common sense regulate the understanding."[18] Custom gave spectators the rights to

Interior of the Chatham Theatre, New York, *lithograph, 1825, by H. A. Thomas from a drawing by A. J. Davis (Museum of the City of New York). Bench seating throughout most theatres during the first third of the century facilitated sociality and frequent movement among playgoers.*

chat during performances, move around the theatre at any time, hiss inferior actors, and applaud lustily whenever they wished.

Upper-class playgoers in the 1820s justified their control of the theatre, and their domination of the actor-audience relationship, on paternalistic grounds. Men of character and wealth, it was believed, had a public responsibility to exercise their power for the benefit of all. Drawing little distinction between public and private institutions, most U.S. urbanites saw the theatre as a public gathering place for entertainment and communication, not as a private business organized for individual recreation. As historian Peter Buckley notes, the theatre was public in a second sense as well: box, pit, and gallery were viewed as a "corporate body which represented the totality of class relations and the structures of power" in a city. Although this homology between the classes of the urban body politic and the distribution of audience members in the theatre was never wholly accurate, belief in its symbolic reality allowed upper-class theatregoers to exercise their prerogatives in the theatre in the name of the "public."[19]

Successful theatre managers understood their "public" responsibilities and strove to operate their companies in a manner which would guarantee the approbation of the patriciate. William B. Wood, for example, practiced a managerial paternalism with his company in Philadelphia clearly modeled on the social beliefs and behaviors of his betters. Born the son of a New York goldsmith, Wood climbed the hierarchy of the Chestnut company slowly, gaining co-managerial authority through deference and patience. Wood's memoirs, published in 1855 after his retirement from the stage, recount his paternalistic policies in the teens and twenties, and express as well his frustration and bitterness with their eventual failure. From Wood's perspective, a well-organized and well-regulated theatre company should be a kind of conservative microcosm for society as a whole: firm but fair paternalists should maintain a traditional hierarchy of talent and status to oversee the gradual progress and enlightenment of humanity.

Looking back from 1855, Wood continued to champion the fixed ranking of actors in a theatre company, the same kind of hierarchy prevalent in the Chestnut company in the eighteenth century during his theatrical apprenticeship and common, too, in most other professional companies of the era. Consequently, Wood favored unambiguous, long-term "lines of business": the "permanent" assignment of specific kinds of roles to certain actors or actresses by the manager. Thus, if a new play were to be mounted, the actor who usually performed the male lead would step into that role again, while the character of the comic maid stayed with the actress of soubrette parts, and the "walking gentlemen" took whatever male roles remained after the men above them in the company hierarchy were cast. This system, inherited from a long tradition in the English theatre, insured company stability but sometimes at the cost of frustrating younger talent and, occasionally, of undermining dramatic credibility. More than one middle-aged actress, having gained some status in an acting company primarily through longevity, performed Rosalind or Juliet on the antebellum stage. Yet Wood, like most other managers of the early nineteenth century, insisted that premiere actors should not be made to play secondary roles, whatever the consequences.[20]

From Wood's point of view, an acting company was like an extended family with a father-manager at its head and the actors occupying various niches in the family hierarchy. Indeed, several of the permanent members of the Chestnut company in the early twenties were related to each other, a situation common in many traditional businesses of the period. Wood had married into the company in 1804, and his wife's sister also performed on the Chestnut Street stage. Wood's partner, William Warren, married the sister-in-law of Joseph Jefferson, both of whom performed with the company. The Jeffersons, in turn, were united through marital ties to the Burkes, another theatrical family in the troupe. When Warren and Wood opened the rebuilt Chestnut Street Theatre in 1822, the cast consisted mainly of family members: two Wallacks, two Darleys, two Hathwells, and three Jeffersons. By that time, the actor on the Chestnut Street boards who was not a permanent member of the company was the exception rather than the rule. When Wood left the Chestnut Street Theatre in 1826 to manage the rival Arch, he recalled later, "I felt somewhat as if I was abandoning my own offspring."[21]

This paterfamilias of the Chestnut company evinced high regard for paternalistic justice, hierarchical order, and artisanal duty. Company actors drunk on stage or imperfect in their lines for a role they had been given ample time to study, for instance, were to be fined or, in extreme cases, fired. Wood disliked producing shows like *Tom and Jerry*, an English favorite centering on London lowlife and requiring that supers be cast in speaking roles, because it upset the regimen needed to keep such apprentice performers in their place. Wood counseled actors and managers always to defer to the wishes of the theatre spectators when they demanded, as they often did, that a speech be repeated, a song sung again, or a scene enacted once more. On one occasion, the audience insisted that the Chestnut company repeat an entire play, and Wood reported that he instructed his weary actors to comply. "An honorable feeling of duty to the public" and their employers was a necessary attribute of the actor, Wood believed. Even his wife was little above the status of theatrical servant in her husband's eyes. In his memoirs, he eulogized Mrs. Wood, who died in 1836, for her "active theatrical service of thirty-five years."[22] As an artisan dependent upon patrician favor, Wood knew that his wife's and his company's failure to please the public could have dire consequences.

The Kean riots of 1825 forcibly demonstrated the sovereignty of the public in the theatre. In 1821, the English star Edmund Kean had insulted American patriotism by refusing to perform for a small audience in Boston. The *Boston Gazette* published a letter from "Peter Public" which castigated the "run away" and called for revenge against the "stage player calling himself Kean": "As he has violated his pledged faith to me, I deem it my duty to thus put my neighbors on guard against him." Theatregoers hoping for a riot rejoiced when Kean returned to the United States in 1825, his infamy in the eyes of Americans having increased by his well-publicized drubbing in the English courts from a cuckolded husband. When Kean appeared at the Park Theatre in New York, the audience refused to allow him to perform. Elite men in side boxes shouted obscenities; some in the pit and gallery threw fruit and denounced the seducer; others outside the theatre lobbed rocks through the windows. Kean struggled vainly to be heard above the din, but finally abandoned the stage and sneaked out the back door. The next day he published an apology in the papers:

> That I have committed an error appears too evident from the all decisive voice of the public; but it is but justice to the delinquent (whatever may be his enormities) to be allowed to make reparation where the offenses were committed. My misunderstandings took place in Boston. To Boston I shall assuredly go, to apologize for my indiscretions.[23]

Despite Kean's contrition, a Boston mob treated him no better. Many in the packed house at the Federal Street Theatre may have been willing to forgive his indiscretions but those who had planned a riot were "so loud, that whether they were more numerous or not, they carried their point." Kean soon withdrew "amid a shower of nuts, almonds, cake and other inoffensive missiles" from all parts of the house. Returning with the manager who sought to placate the mob, Kean was greeted next with a hail of metal balls and beat a hasty retreat. The rioters, joined by others previously outside the theatre, let the manager know what they thought of his policies by taking apart his theatre. "The chandeliers were wantonly broken, some of the iron railings torn from their positions, the seats in some of the boxes and in the pit were torn up, [and] some of the box doors removed from their hinges."[24] Kean left for England, nevermore to return.

In the Kean riots, as in similar public disturbances, the mob, the managers, the elite, and the civil authorities stayed within the generally accepted boundaries of traditional rioting behavior. Rioters (which included members of the patriciate) planned their actions beforehand, determined the placement of their leaders inside and outside the theatre, and passed the word that women should stay away from the theatre for that evening. In the Kean riots, the managers of the Park and Federal Street theatres did not call in the constabulary until after the mob began breaking windows, even though all knew a riot was planned. By common consent, the rioters limited their fury to the destruction of property. Usually, a cadre of upper-class males not in the mob took it as their responsibility to restrain over-eager rioters, though property damage was more excessive than normal in the Kean riots. Elite success in restraining the mob had more to do with traditional habits of deference than with upper-class manipulation of the constabulary, which, in both cases, were too few to stop the riot. In New York and Boston, the constables merely read the riot act from the stage and then departed, knowing that a riot was a public matter for the elite, the mob, and the manager to negotiate. One of the distinguishing features of hegemonic culture is its ability to contain disturbances within boundaries that do not threaten the power of the dominant social group. The Kean riots, like most theatre riots before 1830, demonstrated patrician hegemony in the theatre.[25]

I keep thinking of Foucault— what if we talked about disciplining?

Occasional riots forcibly reminded managers that they might ply their trade only so long as they did not violate the public trust. If riots were sticks, however, theatrical benefits were carrots, rewarding all theatre artists for pleasing upper-class tastes. The pit and gallery might enforce its wishes (within boundaries generally set by the elite) in a riot, but the price of theatre boxes insured that upper-class males would control benefits. Once a year, each member of the stock company, the manager included, "took a benefit," performing a leading role in a play of his or her choice and pocketing the box-office proceeds minus house expenses. Receipt of the profits from the third performance of a new play was the traditional benefit accorded a playwright and might, in fact, be the only payment he or she received for the effort. If a new show ran only two nights, the playwright generally got nothing. Popular theatre artists in stock companies might make nearly half as much from their benefit as they could from their generally meager salaries over an entire season. Most actors preferred to take their benefits in the spring to provide themselves with income over the summer when theatres were dark and company members unemployed. As one of them noted, actors "must either depend on a successful benefit night or have to struggle with poverty from the time their engagements cease, until nearly the commencement of winter."[26] Consequently, winning the favor of the fashionable in the boxes was the best way for theatre artists to guarantee themselves a modest livelihood and a successful career. Reliance upon benefits meant that the stock company incorporated elements of traditional patronage in its mode of economic production. Although mostly dependent on the market, theatre artisans could not cut their traditional ties to elite support as long as the sale of tickets generated insufficient income to maintain their companies.

Patrician patronage through benefits did nothing to help theatre artisans when their companies went bankrupt, however. In the late 1820s, several stock companies in Philadelphia, New York, and Boston collapsed, casualties chiefly of the greed of local elites who had built more theatres and stocked them with more companies than their class could support. In Boston, the opening of the Tremont Theatre in 1827 led to competition between its company and the established troupe at the Federal Street playhouse. Both companies lowered ticket prices and hired more stars but fared poorly, the Federal Street company closing shop in 1829. With the remodeling for year-round entertainment of Niblo's Garden Theatre, elite New Yorkers had six theatres to choose from in 1827: the Park, Niblo's, the Lafayette, Chatham Gardens, the Richmond Hill, and the Bowery. By 1832, only the Park, Niblo's, and the Richmond Hill remained as houses of upper-class entertainment. Managers at the Lafayette and Chatham Gardens tried lower prices, equestrian shows, and more stars but could not buck the competition. At the Bowery, Thomas Hamblin ignored elite tastes and cultivated a working-class audience by featuring American stars and sensational melodramas.

Caught in similar crises of competition and failure in the late 1820s in Philadelphia, William B. Wood struggled vainly to maintain paternalistic control against the incursions of ruinous competition and rapacious stars. Some theatre managers thrived under the new conditions. Stephen Price at the Park Theatre had already established a near monopoly on transatlantic star traffic and continued to profit from the American public's hunger for British luminaries. And Hamblin's switch to working-class entertainment made him rich in the thirties and forties. But Wood resisted adapting his eighteenth-century managerial strategies and habits of deference to the changing realities of theatre in the Age of Jackson. Though caused partly by conditions beyond his control, Wood's failure as a manager was also his own fault, blinded as he was, even in retrospect, by the narrowness and inflexibility of his own ideology. His problems point up the shortcomings of managerial mercantilism in the new era of theatrical capitalism.

Under the co-management of Wood and William Warren, the Chestnut Street Theatre had nearly monopolized theatrical entertainment in Philadelphia from 1794 until the early 1820s. Even with the addition of competition from a company under the indirect management of Stephen Price at the Walnut Street Theatre in 1822, Warren and Wood's company remained the favorite of the Philadelphia elite. But the storm clouds were already gathering. Internally, Wood's heavy-handed paternalism was alienating several members of his troupe, especially those who, like actor Francis Wemyss, were hired to perform certain roles but whom Wood relegated to a status far inferior to their promised line of business. Externally, Warren and Wood were paying Stephen Price for many more British stars than they had imported during the decade of the teens. Along with the increased cost of stars (without, usually, any increase in profit) came rising costs for spectacular productions of fairy-tale melodramas, pantomimes, and operas, and increases in their rent for using the theatre. Warren and Wood's most profitable season had been 1815–16, palmy days of stock rather than star performances, low rent, and little company strife, which showed no prospect of returning in the mid 1820s.[27]

Believing that he was losing control of the Chestnut's future, Wood decided to abrogate the joint management with Warren and to make himself sole manager. He had grown perturbed at Warren for occasionally assenting to the advice of their stockholders concerning the operation of the theatre. The stockholders had gained a reduction in ticket prices for the 1824–25 season, for example, and were requesting changes in seating and casting policies. Wood won the battle to restore the old prices for 1825–26, but he feared that his genial co-manager would capitulate again and undermine their control of the company. "I therefore told my old friend in the summer of 1825," wrote Wood in his memoirs, "that the joint management, if it was about to be conducted on any judgment not his own—irresponsible and unknown to me—must end. I offered to buy him out myself, and so become sole manager." Evidently, this was Wood's underlying intention since, as

Warren noted in his journal, Wood did "everything he could to destroy the [1825–26] season—he wanted to make matters so uncomfortable that he thought I would throw up the concern in a pet and he might get it on any terms." But Wood's stratagem backfired. Warren took him at his word to quit the partnership, bought him out on easy terms, and arranged for Wemyss to take his place as manager for the next season. Wishing to continue their friendship, Warren also guaranteed Wood and his wife permanent places in the acting company. Wood's desire to become the sole reigning father figure at the Chestnut Street Theatre had cost him his co-management.[28]

Wood continued to perform with the Chestnut company through April 14, 1828, when he took a farewell benefit. By that time, he had accepted an offer from several of the city elite to manage a new company in a new theatre on Arch Street. Thinking that the Chestnut under Warren could not survive and also assuming, as did many Philadelphians, that the Walnut Street Circus, the only other competition, would soon be torn down, Wood hoped to establish his paternalistic control over a new, more promising venture. By the end of the summer, Wood and his agents had put together what he remembered as "in all respects a good theatrical community." It seemed to Wood that he had found a second theatrical family to father.[29]

In the late 1820s, however, managerial mercantilism fell apart in the Philadelphia theatre. "Battle—battle—battle," remembered Wood's former antagonist Francis Wemyss in his biography, explaining, "We now approach the season 1828 and '29 in Philadelphia, where we shall find three theatres and a circus [the Pavilion] struggling for existence where, heretofore, one was deemed sufficient." Warren and Wood, now competitors, cut admission prices, sold entire boxes for the season, and hired a bevy of stars—all in an attempt to catch the public fancy and undermine the other theatres. Attendance at the Chestnut, promising at the start of the season, fell off rapidly in November. Business is "horrible, most horrible," wrote Warren in his journal on December 6, 1828, adding, with evident satisfaction, "Mr. Wood at his new Arch Street concern does worse then we." Wood was the first to succumb, closing the Arch on December 22. Warren, now sixty-one years old and eager to retire, sold out to Wemyss and a partner and took his final benefit on December 30. By the end of May 1829, Wemyss and his partner had gone bankrupt, following by about a month the failure of the Walnut Street management. The 1829–30 Philadelphia season was even harder on managers, involving the dissolution of partnerships at all three theatres almost as quickly as they were drawn up. Competition had vanquished the long monopoly of the Chestnut Street Theatre, helped to destroy the managerial careers of Warren and Wood, and driven theatre in Philadelphia to the point where, in Wood's words, everything "was at sixes and sevens."[30]

Clearly, the biggest blow to traditional modes of producing theatre was the victory of acting stars over company managers. This shift in the balance of power in the Philadelphia theatre can be pinpointed with some precision. In 1827, Warren, fearing a loss of business to the increasingly aggressive management of the Walnut Street Theatre, capitulated to the demands of a ballet company that the gross receipts of all performances be divided equally between them. In the past, Warren and Wood had exerted some leverage over the stars by insisting, in most instances, that only the net profits from each performance be divided. If the profits were meager, the star could lose money (though, in practice, this rarely occurred). After giving in to the ballet company, Warren was forced to accede to the same demands made by stars Thomas A. Cooper and Edwin Forrest in 1828, remarking, distastefully, that he wouldn't have taken "those Hard Conditions but that Cowell who opened the [Walnut] Circus Theatre . . . would have given it most gladly." With the dike thus breached through competition, stars swamped the 1828–29 season in all three Philadelphia theatres, charging what the market would bear and leaving managers to sink when operating expenses could not be met. By 1831, one group of managers at the Arch Street Theatre, following the lead of Tom Hamblin, had discovered that many working-class Americans who had not regularly attended the theatre in the past would do so if the price was right and American stars in American plays were the featured attraction. In the meantime, Maywood and Company gained control of the Walnut and Chestnut Street theatres, restored the old prices and some of the old policies, and attempted, through monopolistic practices, to control Philadelphia playgoing. But the floodgates had been washed away by the tide of stars; restoration of the Warren and Wood days was no longer possible.[31]

Wood's reaction to the debacle of mercantilist theatre in the late 1820s reflected his stubborn attachment to paternalistic ways. From his point of view, he had lost his theatrical family in the crosscurrents of change. His desire to banish the villainous stars from the theatrical firmament and to restore the permanency of traditional stock companies to their rightful place in the heavens motivated the publication of his *Personal Recollections* in 1855. Though Wood found minor villains among amateur managers and theatregoing socialites caught up in "ostentatious exhibition," he reserved most of his scorn for the stars, especially the second-rate luminaries whom he saw as mere money-grubbers and "pretenders." He began his analysis of "the system of stars" with an opening sentence, which, despite its length and convolution, reveals the connections Wood perceived between stars and other threatening innovations:

> The breaking up of the great English theatres [i.e., the Chestnut and Walnut]—a season of general inflation and excitement in all things (brought about, I suppose, by a commercial season of great excess, and, as was then supposed, of high prosperity)—a spirit of locomotiveness hitherto unexampled, and incident, I suppose, to our feeling, as we then first fairly did, that we could annihilate time and space by the use of steam vessels across the Atlantic, and railroads over our continent—the total break-up with Warren of the old management and of its system, in short a spirit of change—of exhilaration—of excitement, incident to an end of the older order of things, and the advent of some new and undefined ones—all these with some other causes, had now made the system of stars the order of 1835.[32]

Wood correctly linked the triumph of stars to the building of railroads; the new transportation network made extensive starring economically feasible. But the manager was hardly neutral, seeing in the "annihilating" victory of steam-driven starring the cause of all the faults of theatrical production and operation since the early 1830s. According to Wood, the success of itinerant stars led to mediocre performances by stock actors, mismanaged casting of actors to play opposite the stars, negligent scenic effects, more benefit performances than economically feasible, newspaper puffing, and lack of variety in the overall season. These charges were simplifications and exaggerations. Stock company acting without stars had had a high tolerance for mediocrity, as Wood's faltering early career attested. On the other hand, the lack of rehearsal time when a star came to town probably did lead to a lessening of the ensemble effect in performances of good stock companies like the Chestnut. Concerning poor casting and neglected scenery, actors at the Chestnut in the mid twenties accused Wood of both, grumbling especially about the built-in nepotism of established lines of business. Newspaper puffery started well before the early 1830s, though Wood was probably correct in correlating its increase with the rise of the starring engagements. Wood's assertion that stars cut into the variety a manager could offer his patrons was the exact opposite of the truth. Stars rose in public esteem in part *because* they offered the public a change from the same actors and plays that local stock companies had been putting before them for decades. Wood's complaint about too many benefits was true only from the perspective of traditional modes of theatrical operation. Other managers were able to fashion successful strategies to accommodate the stars' hunger for wealth and fame and to accumulate some profit for themselves. Finally, Wood's belief that starring constituted a new system was off the mark. The emerging star network was an important change within the stock company structure, but it did not alter the fundamental relations of production between businesspeople and theatre workers in that system.

Underlying much of Wood's melodramatic analysis was the assumption that the break-up of permanent companies and the rise of the stars victimized stock actors. While there was some truth to this charge, Wood ignored the new economic freedom for the better actors that competitive capitalism in the theatre helped to foster. To insure the security of stock actors and to keep opportunistic entrepreneurs out of management positions, Wood advocated a heavy entertainment tax which would cripple itinerant starring and insure monopolistic control by one manager of all theatrical activity in a single locality. "No one except a manager can conceive the advantage of a monopoly in theatrical concerns," the unreformed mercantilist stated without irony.[33] Wood, in other words, envisioned the theatre as a kind of asylum from history where benevolent managers might train potentially wayward youths in the traditional lessons of deference and good character. This could be accomplished, however, only if the local stock company were removed from the "exhilaration" and the chance for instantaneous (but characterless) success embodied in the villainous star network.

True to its evil essence, the pattern of hiring stars was beginning to self-destruct, believed Wood. "When the manager is thus ruined," he asserted, "the stars must follow him and the very star system itself is broken up." Consequently, Wood concluded, "we are likely to find ourselves in a position where we can again at least see the place from which we departed and by great efforts and by retracing our steps get ourselves safely brought up to it again." Entranced with the prospect of a return to theatrical mercantilism, Wood would even make room in his paternalistic vision for some of the great stars like Cooper and Forrest who, because of their dependability, said Wood, are in effect permanent "stock actors attached to several companies." Accorded "their proper and exceptional place," such stars "will move in proper regard to the larger sphere of their traverse and not destroy the control and harmony of the system through which, in regulated reference to humbler bodies, they are expected to make their transit."[34] In effect, Wood wanted to have it both ways—popular luminaries and a powerful stock system—implicitly relying on traditional management to rein in the stars to their proper sphere and to prevent their success from giving birth to a host of minor luminaries. In its reliance on greater control, Wood's vision betrayed the "false love" of paternalism.

Even in 1855 at the writing of his *Personal Recollections*—twenty-five years after entrepreneurs of itinerant starring had wrested effective control of most of the theatrical business in the United States—Wood remained convinced that the new network would not continue. By that time, however, most local managers had made their peace with stars, national circuits of touring had evolved, and public clamor for the luminaries was louder than ever. In short, Wood remained too committed to the mercantilism of the past to envision innovative managerial strategies for the present and the future. Like other paternalistic businessmen, political leaders, and utopians during the nineteenth century, Wood had confused economic ties with familial ones, thus seeking refuge from historical change through fatherly control.

2. "Wert Thou Not Born in Fairy-land?"

Despite steam-driven competition from the stars, the northeastern patriciate maintained its traditional hegemony in local theatres into the mid 1830s. They did this, in part, by applauding melodramas that bolstered their own sagging convictions about the right of benevolent fathers to control the lives of those less fortunate than themselves. Fairy-tale melodramas, so called because they share many formal characteristics with folk and fairy stories, were especially popular with upper-class males. These plays worked rhetorically within the general conventions of French melodrama, a politically conservative genre shaped initially by Guilbert de Pixérécourt during the Napoleonic era. For local American elites, performances of fairy-tale melodramas in the 1820s and early 1830s were pep rallies for paternalism. In the anxious rhetoric of these plays may be seen a patriciate battling its own doubts from within and the incursions of egalitarian democracy and market capitalism from without. As stars lured more nonelite spectators into urban playhouses, however, patrician males gradually lost control over their theatres. By 1840, the elite was abandoning public intercourse in playhouses to enjoy the class-based rituals of grand opera. With their audiences in retreat and no longer wedded to the ideology of paternalism, fairy-tale melodramas gradually ceased to draw an audience.

Social-historical evidence suggests that upper-class males had a lot to worry about in the 1820s. As historian Gordon S. Wood remarks, the gentry of the Revolutionary era looked forward to the gradual expansion of a mercantilist economy, controlled by themselves, but "they hardly anticipated, let alone intentionally brought about, the scrambling, individualistic, acquisitive society that suddenly emerged in the early nineteenth century." Committed ideologically to hierarchical social and political relations, the patriciate was ill prepared for what Robert Wiebe terms the "revolution in choices" in the 1820s that animated the newcomers to economic power to reject their authority and push for greater freedom in politics and business. Lacking a nobility, a church, or an army, the props of hierarchical authority in Europe, the American gentry had few weapons with which to oppose what they believed to be their waning power and influence.[1]

Several of the early consequences of economic expansion—increased wealth, greater mobility, and problems of social cohesion, among them—created situations of agonizing ambiguity for many upper-class Americans in the 1820s. Although the urban elite often expressed pride in its accomplishments and the expectation that the future would reveal the moral worth of its success, many of these same merchants, preachers, and writers feared that the perceived solidity of the past was gone forever and that the future held moral decline or even chaos. How, they asked, could so much wealth not lead us to luxury and corruption? What would become of our sacred ties to the land if Americans continued to abandon the patrimony of their forebears to speculate on new property in the West? If everyone pursued his or her own selfish interests, how could the public good be preserved and the national republic of virtue remain untainted?

Crowed a Fourth of July orator in Boston in 1822: "We cannot open our eyes without beholding the most unequivocal monuments of the general success, which has crowned the industry and economy of our citizens." The twenties through the mid thirties were boom years economically for the northeastern United States. By 1840 per capita income was 35 percent higher in the Northeast than in the nation as a whole. Among the many reasons for the region's increase in wealth were the growth of agricultural productivity, the transfer of capital from trade to industry, the flexibility of the labor force, the relative cheapness of land and raw materials, and an increase, generally, in the scale of production in many businesses. In 1820 only about 15 percent of all Americans were employed in commerce, industry, or administration, or in one of the professions, a figure that had changed little since the mid eighteenth century. By 1840, over 36 percent of all Americans were so employed, and the figure was significantly higher in the Northeast. Economists see the 1820s as the critical take-off decade for American industrialization, a decade which saw the fastest rate of overall economic growth in the antebellum era. Stoking the fires of this economic expansion was an urban elite whose personal income and percentage of overall urban wealth increased dramatically in the 1820s and 1830s.[2]

Although the patriciate continued to dominate American overseas trade through their links with the English commercial system, they lost control of the burgeoning interior market in the 1820s. Traditionally, the eastern elite had shaped the economy of the West through speculation in large tracts of land, private banks, and state-chartered turnpikes—much-needed mercantilist practices that had effectively channeled credit into the interior but had restricted competition. Henry Clay's and John Quincy Adam's American System, a series of proposals for a stiff tariff, nationally subsidized canals and turnpikes, and high land prices, was designed, in part, to continue patrician control of western development. Following the 1819 depression, which punctured the western speculations of many eastern promoters, numerous smaller investors in several regional centers beyond the influence of the seaboard elite established their own commercial enterprises. They, too, sought protection from competition in state charters and corporations, but they were less successful than the old patriciate had been in restraining the growth of market capitalism in the West.[3]

The partial loss of control over economic expansion, coupled with the rapidity of economic growth itself in the 1820s, created unlooked-for and often unrecognized strains and conflicts among the patriciate. Wealth itself was a problem. While many antebellum Americans saw their increasing prosperity as a sign of God's favor, this transformation of the old Puritan idea wherein the elect might be known by the virtue of their economic behavior was highly suspect to others. Providence might provide an occasional justification for personal or national wealth but God's will was more frequently invoked to condemn prosperity as an invitation to luxury and avarice. Typically, poets and painters pictured the wrath of God as a fiery volcano bursting forth to bury a corrupt and idle civilization. "Conquest of Canaan," a popular poem by President Timothy Dwight of Yale College, imagined a Judgment Day of fire-spewing volcanoes burying a decadent society, for example.[4] The urban elite and their spokespersons feared that a righteous God could not love a wealthy nation.

The increasing mobility of American life also called forth melodramatic fears. As business productivity and its consequent specialization picked up in the Northeast, immigration from American farms and small towns, and from Europe, to centers of economic activity increased. A transportation revolution which tied cities more firmly to their surrounding countrysides through a network of roads, canals and, eventually, railroads, made it easier and more profitable to sell the family farm and move on to greater opportunity. The result was a rapid increase in urbanization beginning in the 1820s and continuing beyond the Civil War. Overall, the urban population of the United States increased from 7.2 percent in 1820 to 19.8 percent in 1860, with the cities of the Northeast increasing by almost twice that rate. In New York, for example—the fastest-growing city in the country—the population increased by more than half again as much during each decade from 1790 to 1860, rising from a mere 33,000 to over 800,000 by the Civil War.

For the urban elite of the 1820s, many of whom still remembered the simpler, slower-paced cities and towns of their childhood, the changes in city life were as much qualitative as quantitative. From their point of view, cities were becoming impersonal, immoral, and dangerous. The "unsocial indifference" of New Yorkers drew comment from one visitor as early as 1818. Only a year before that, the Reverend Ward Stafford warned that the city's poorer wards contained "a great mass of people beyond the restraints of religion," among whom "thousands . . . are grossly vicious."[5] In the mid 1820s, the elite witnessed the growth of local unions and workers' political parties in the urban Northeast. Demanding the right to settle their grievances without interference from the city leaders, many workers broke the remaining ties of paternalism, already seriously frayed since the Revolution. More than one elite speaker fused the notion of a rebellion of the working poor with the image of a volcanic God punishing a wayward nation.

Beyond occasional fears of an attack by the embittered masses lurked a more general malaise stemming from American mobility: the sense among the elite that America had lost its moral rootedness to the past. This nervousness frequently found expression through the idealization of a lost home. Many patricians probably agreed with Charles B. Haddock, nephew of Daniel Webster and professor at Dartmouth, who spoke to New York business leaders of the "love of home" as the truly distinguishing characteristic of American life in 1841. Recognizing that the "true lovers of home" often "fly from it," Haddock nonetheless insisted that the farther from home one journeys, the more one's "tenderest sensibilities cling around the spot of [one's] birth." "The heart wants visible memorials to fasten upon," he noted. "It requires a center to revolve about." Haddock spoke to a sympathetic audience: New Englanders who had left the land of their heritage to find success in New York City. Even Henry Clay, Whig proponent of the American System of economic development, could wax nostalgic about the anguish of early western migration, a migration his policies had helped to facilitate. The new westerner, he lamented, was "separated, forever, from the roof under which the companions of his childhood were sheltered, from the trees which have shaded him from summers' heats, the spring from whose gushing fountain he has drunk in his youth, the tombs that hold the precious relics of his venerated ancestors." Philip Hone, onetime mayor of New York, businessman, and inveterate theatregoer, summed up much of the frustration of his generation of the elite when he complained that everything was "flying": "Improvements, Politics, Reform, Religion—all fly. . . . Flying is dangerous."[6] Hone's complaint echoes Wood's fear of the "locomotiveness" of the age.

Burdened with these and other anxieties, elite urban males sought relief in melodramas imbued with the ideology of traditional paternalism. Although these play performances probably had less appeal for the "middling" classes in the pit and the workers in the gallery, they evidentally retained enough flexibility to charm most males in the playhouse. Like other successful theatrical productions, fairy-tale melodramas induced their willing spectators to project emotional significance onto certain characters and objects on the stage, identifications which helped to construct the subjectivity of their audience members. The symbolic codes of the fairy-tale formula probably exercised substantial constitutive influence over their patrician spectators.[7]

Although theatregoers enjoyed more than fairy-tale melodramas on northeastern stages in the twenties and thirties, most other successful genres reinforced the general values of paternalism. Shakespeare was the single most popular playwright among elite audiences of the period, James Fenimore Cooper terming him, facetiously, "the great author of America." Several of his most frequently performed plays, however, had to be smothered with a rich dollop of sentimental syrup to make them palatable to American tastes. Most of the earlier alterations of characterization designed to smooth away the foibles of Juliet and Hamlet, for instance, and to moralize the fate of Macbeth remained intact. Few of Shakespeare's plays were radically restructured, although the Cibber version of *Richard III* and Nahum Tate's bowdlerized *King Lear* continued on the boards. In Tate's *King Lear*, Edgar saves the old king and then marries Cordelia, who is still alive, while Lear and Gloucester, smiling patriarchs at the end of the show, look on. "The moral's now more complete," wrote William Wood, since Lear and Cordelia "survived their enemies and virtue is crowned with happiness."[8]

Paternalistic values in eighteenth-century English and German comedies also won American elite applause in the 1820s and 1830s. Although such bawdy Restoration pieces as *The Country Wife* were acceptable only in sentimental versions, a few early plays—among them, *The Beaux' Stratagem* by Farquhar and especially *The Wonder*, by Centlivre—continued to be performed. The most popular of the eighteenth-century comedies was Sheridan's *School for Scandal*, a reliable old battleship continually pressed into service to launch a new theatre or to plow the way at the opening of a theatrical season. Although Sheridan's witty masterpiece satirizes sentiment when used as a mask for villainy, the play firmly embraces sentimental paternalism in the end. August von Kotzebue's weepy comedies, especially *The Stranger* and *Lovers' Vows*, continued successful with American audiences long after William Dunlap adapted them for production at the Park Theatre at the turn of the century. Generally relying on circumstances rather than villainous intrigue to motivate their plots, Kotzebue's plays typically center on the pitiable situation of a divided family. Their concentration on the pathos of ordinary people, their celebration of family feeling over rationality, and their elevation of benevolent paternalism place these comedies close to the dramatic world of Pixérécourt's more popular melodramatic formula.

The *Wandering Boys* by Mordecai Noah and *Thérèse, the Orphan of Geneva* and *Clari, the Maid of Milan*, both by John Howard Payne, are representative of American fairy-tale melodramas popular with elite auditors in the 1820–35 period. Noah adapted *The Wandering Boys* from *The White Pilgrim* by Pixérécourt for an actress in Charleston in 1812. Subsequently, the play was altered and improved before its London premiere; it reemerged in 1815 at the Park Theatre, where it enjoyed a considerable initial run. Northeastern theatres produced the melodrama frequently in the 1820s, in part because it required the actresses performing the two boys of the title to don breeches to show off their legs. Following some modest successes of his French adaptations on the London stage, the American-born Payne scored his first big hit in 1821 with *Thérèse*, an Anglicized version of a melodrama by Victor Ducange. After a long run in London, the play enjoyed wide popularity in the United States, attaining over sixty performances in New York theatres before 1840, an impressive number in those days of large dramatic repertories. Payne's *Clari*, adapted from a French ballet-pantomime, opened in America in 1823 and also became a sentimental favorite among elite audiences. Much of its success was due to the recurring melody of "Home, Sweet Home," a song set to music by English composer Henry Bishop and sung in parlors throughout nineteenth-century America.[9]

These melodramas were among the many ballets, English plays, and pantomime spectacles dramatizing the extreme conflicts and magical resolutions of fairyland in the 1820s and 1830s on northeastern stages. *Cinderella*, popular both as a ballet-pantomime and as an English opera, won elite applause in several productions in Boston, New York, and Philadelphia. Other stories out of the Brothers Grimm or Perrault collections, including "Little Red Riding Hood," "Sleeping Beauty," and "Bluebeard," found their way onto elite stages. English plays with fairy-tale-like actions, such as *The Mountaineers* by Colman and *The Magpie or the Maid* and *Zembuca* by Pocock, also flourished. Added to these attractions were the continuing, though waning popularity of several adaptations of Pixérécourt's early works. Despite steep costs in scenery, costumes, and special effects, fairy-tale spectaculars such as *Aladdin, Cherry and Fair Star,* and *The Forty Thieves*—the latter done in Philadelphia with forty horses in 1826—continued to be mounted. Fairy-tale productions in a variety of dramatic and theatrical formats were a primary genre of elite entertainment in the twenties and early thirties, accounting for perhaps a quarter of all performances in the Northeast.

One reason for this popularity was the increasing success of fairy tales among American readers. Long available in chapbooks and dreambooks for children, fairy-tale stories began to gain a grown-up American audience after 1800. Their popularity among children of all ages increased after 1823 with the first translation of some of the Brothers Grimm stories into English. While their literary influence may be seen in the works of Irving, Poe, Hawthorne and others, the fairy tale's impact on elite tastes in theatrical production was immediate and wide-ranging. Patrician theatregoers began to expect more lavishly mounted productions replete with choreographed fairy-dances, exotic scenic transformations, and miraculous lighting effects with the new gas technology. The 1825 production of *Cherry and Fair Star*, a "grand Asiatic melodramatic romance," for instance, featured a blooming aloe tree, a "dragon spitting fire," a "burning forest," and a "waterfall in motion" (which burned up on opening night).[10] The financial burden on the ordinary stock company in producing such spectacles was one of the causes of bankruptcy among several theatres in the late 1820s.

John Howard Payne recognized that the kinds of plays he wrote had as much or more to do with audience desires than with his own literary abilities. In a preface to the London edition of *Thérèse*—a preface repeated in later American editions—Payne stated:

One word to my friends the critics and I have done. They have honored me with more attention than I ever coveted, but I wish them to understand that this, like former publications of mine, is a work planned for stage-effects exclusively, and printed for managers and actors only. It is so necessary in the production of the modern drama to consult the peculiarities of leading performers, and not to offend the restive spirit by means of situations almost pantomimic and too impatient to pause for poetical beauty, that it seems almost hopeless to look to the stage of the present day for a permanent literary distinction. An actable play seems to derive its value from what is done, more than from what is said, but the great power of a literary work consists in what is said, and the manner of saying it. He, therefore, who best knows the stage can best tell why, in the present temper of the audience, good poets should often make bad dramatists.[11]

Payne's defense of his playwriting, while not entirely credible, covers Noah's dramatic efforts as well. Like virtually all other melodramatists of the period, including their European role models, these American playwrights looked to "stage-effects," "pantomimic" situations, acting "peculiarities," and strong plot lines to keep audiences on the edges of their seats or benches and unmindful of the shortcomings of their contrivances.

Soon after the opening of *Thérèse, the Orphan of Geneva*, the villain, Carwin, informs a rich countess that her ward, Thérèse, is wanted in Geneva for forgery and fraud. The countess, fearing that the planned marriage of her son to Thérèse will now create a scandal, calls off the wedding and banishes the innocent victim from her home. Thérèse finds temporary refuge in a peasant cottage where Carwin mistakes the countess for the orphan and stabs the lady to death. Finally, a kindly father figure, the pastor Fontaine, solves the mystery of the murder by shocking the villain into a confession. As a result, the heroine's true background as a rich heiress is revealed, Thérèse embraces her fiancé, and the lovers, joined by Fontaine, pose for the final tableau. "Heaven has heard our prayers," asserts the pastor (III,1).

Payne's *Clari, the Maid of Milan* also demonstrates the union of heavenly and fatherly justice. In act 1, performers at Duke Vivaldi's palace present a play which dramatizes the heroine's situation in the larger action of the melodrama: a peasant girl carried off against her wishes by a nobleman. When the player-father curses his daughter for losing her virtue, Clari rushes on stage and protests the player-daughter's, and her own, innocence. In the next act, she escapes from the duke's castle and returns home to face the same charge from her own father. But the duke, no longer bent on seducing Clari, arrives at their "home, sweet home" to assure Rolamo, the heroine's stern father, that his daughter's virtue is intact and to plead for her hand in marriage. Payne, following the plot of a French ballet, has altered Pixérécourt's formula somewhat by allowing the villain to reform. Even more so than in *Thérèse*, the action of *Clari* centers on the heroine's return to the bosom of her home, her father, and her God.

A similar hierarchy of affection and control structures *The Wandering Boys*. Entering in the midst of a village festival, Paul and Justin win the sympathies of the kindly villagers and are led away to the baroness's castle. There, a mysterious old porter rescues them from prison after the baroness's evil steward locks them up. The audience soon learns that the old porter is none other than the Count de Croisy, who has altered his looks and feigns muteness while awaiting his chance to regain the castle, which is rightfully his. The wandering boys, of course, are the true count's grandsons. After their innocence and trust cause the baroness to suffer the pangs of a guilty conscience, the count foils the further designs of the wicked steward. By play's end, the reunited family poses with happy peasants and villagers for the final tableau, an organic hierarchy of loving relationships centered on paternal affection.

Each of these three American plays may be identified rather easily with the general action of a particular fairy tale. *Thérèse* is close to "Snow White": a stepmother (the countess) drives her young ward (Thérèse) from her palace; the girl goes to live with dwarfs (the peasants who give her shelter), but is eventually stricken with helpless sleep (Thérèse's madness); finally, she is awakened and marries a prince (the countess's son). The parallels between *The Wandering Boys* and "Hansel and Gretel" are even more striking. The melodrama features a kindly father, two curious and outgoing babes-in-the-woods, and a wicked stepmother-witch who puts the children in jail. *Clari*, of course, is a variation of "Beauty and the Beast" with the threatening monstrosity of the duke magically changed into tractable concern and affection.

Historian Jack Zipes points out the potential for emancipation evident in many folk and fairy tales:

Insofar as they have tended to project other and better worlds, they have often been considered subversive, or, to put it more positively, they have often provided the critical measure of how far we are from taking history into our own hands and creating more just societies. Folk and fairy tales have always spread word through their fantastic images about the feasibility of utopian alternatives, and this is exactly why the dominant social classes have been vexed by them.

German peasants enduring the wars and famines of late feudalism, for instance, could take hope from the story of "Hansel and Gretel," which depicted the victory of abandoned children over a symbol of oppressive greed; the children not only kill the witch in the original tale, but also return home to their father with her hoard of jewels to save him from starvation. Despite their valorizing of peasant resistance, however, folk tales suggested that the social relations of feudalism were universal. Queens, peasants, princesses, soldiers, and other precapitalist characters people "Snow White," for example, and the resolution of the conflicts in the story leaves its patriarchal, absolutist world intact. Indeed, the tellers of folk tales used impenetrable metals and imperishable jewels to symbolize the masters of feudal society. The *Volk* might dream of becoming knights or princesses themselves, but their stories did not envision overturning the feudal order for a more progressive future.[12]

After the mid sixteenth century, writers and publishers appropriated the oral performances of folk tales and sold them as printed texts, adapting the stories to suit the ideological preferences of their mostly aristocratic readers. An eighteenth-century version of "Beauty and the Beast" by Madame Le Prince de Beaumont, for example, launches the story as a didactic attack against an upstart bourgeoisie. As Beaumont tells it, the beast is transformed into a prince and marries the loving daughter of the merchant because she, unlike her father and sisters, saw the noble nature of the aristocratic beast under his ugly exterior. Consequently, the daughter gets to live in a palace while the rest of her crass and arrogant family are turned into statues, perpetual models of bourgeois foolishness and pride. Other writers of "fairy tales"—a late seventeenth-century term signaling the transformation of the folk originals—also reversed the antiaristocratic bias of their precursors. Not all fairy tales attacked the bourgeoisie, but most upheld aristocratic privilege and power. Although later romantics would invest some of the old stories with more liberating visions, nearly all fairy tales in the early nineteenth century constructed traditional ideologies for their readers.[13]

The fairy-tale melodramas of Pixérècourt, like the later spin-offs of his formula by Payne and Noah, mostly perpetuated the reactionary ideology of their literary antecedents. Together with several novels, musical compositions, and other works of both popular and elite culture, Pixérécourt's plays helped to constitute what historian Louis Bergeron terms "the anti-rationalist reaction" in Napoleonic France. The antirationalists blamed the excesses of the 1790s on the Enlightenment values of empiricism and materialism. "It is to the vanity of knowledge that we owe almost all our misfortunes," claimed François René Châteaubriand, the leading illuminist of the movement. In his widely-read *Genius of Christianity*, Châteaubriand promoted emotional mysticism to salve current distress, a balm touted by other French writers in the first decades of the nineteenth century. Joseph Fievée, for instance, exalted the lost morality of the *ancien régime*, while Mme. Marie Cottin praised the nobility and holiness of medieval royal love in her novel *Mathilde*. Most antirationalists followed Châteaubriand in praising Napoleon as a "man of Providence who has saved us from the abyss." Pixérécourt, too, preached the virtues of traditional mysticism and authority. Recalling the influence of his melodramas on French audiences before the widespread reestablishment of Catholicism, one critic noted, "I have seen them, in the absence of religious worship, take the place of the silent pulpit."[14]

Like the fairy tales they resembled, the melodramas of Pixérécourt and his American imitators turned the potentially liberating rhetoric of the folk-tale tradition into an apology for patriarchal conservatism. Thérèse, Clari, and the wandering boys struggle for freedom against villains, but in all three plays the villains embody forces which threaten a presumably just feudal society. In *Thérèse*, for example, the villain Carwin is a lawyer who cloaks his greed for Thérèse's inheritance (he alone knows she is an heiress) in the modern, rationalized rhetoric of the law. Opposing villainous conspiracy at the climax of these melodramas is the assembled force of the feudal order. Kindly villagers, concerned peasants, and an army led by the Count de Croissy capture the villainous steward Roland at the high point of *The Wandering Boys*, for instance. Yet it is finally fatherly concern, not noble rank, which claims the moral center in these plays; stern but compassionate patriarchs of middling status are the true heroes. In *Thérèse*, Payne used Father Fontaine, a village priest, to wrap the reality of feudal power in the mantle of providential design and paternal benevolence. By blessing the union of the young count and the "orphan of Geneva," Fontaine legitimizes the maintenance of the social status quo. Like those who transformed folk into fairy tales, Payne and Noah sentimentalized the feudal order, inducing nostalgia for a never-never land of patriarchal justice and stability.

Beyond their plot structure and character types, these fairy-tale plays muster all the rhetorical force of "stage effects" and "pantomimic situations" typical of early nineteenth-century melodrama to justify conservative paternalism. Within the conventions of Pixérécourt's melodrama, what the audience sees is what there is; appearances are revealing, not deceiving. Stage pictures, pantomimed action, and final tableaux presented the core of melodramatic truth to the audience. The pantomime at the end of *Clari*, for instance, left no doubt about the moral hierarchy of the play: "Rolamo takes [Clari's] hand and unites it to the Duke's. They both kneel. Rolamo extends his hands over them. His eyes turn upward and streaming with tears and, with a choked voice, [he] exclaims, 'Heaven bless ye'" (III,2). Even when paternal virtue was disguised, as in *The Wandering Boys*, the audience was never in doubt about its innate morality. Noah borrowed from Pixérécourt the convention of mute goodness to signal the beneficence of the Count de Croissy.

In *Thérèse*, Father Fontaine stages a ghostly pantomime to reveal Carwin's guilt to the magistrate and the assembled villagers. Playing upon Carwin's conscience, the pastor induces the villain to approach the body of the person he believes he has killed. Payne's stage directions tell the rest:

(When [Carwin] is near the middle door [of the farm house], it opens, as if spontaneously, and Thérèse appears—in one hand holding the knife, and pointing to it with the other.—She comes slowly forward.—Carwin recedes before her, in agony and consternation.)

Lash me not, furies!—Lash me not to madness!—Hold! hold! Terrible spectre, hence!—Spare, spare your murderer!—(kneels)—The world shall know your innocence—my guilt.—Here, at your feet, I cast the damning proofs.—Let them appease you—but save! oh, save—save me from vengeance!—Shield me from despair! (Falls senseless. When he throws down the papers, they are instantly caught up by the count and taken to the magistrate, who runs over them, and hands them to Fontaine. All having read, the count rushes to Thérèse, who, being overcome by the madness of Carwin and her own situation, falls into her lover's arms. Fontaine exultingly springs forward, displaying the papers. All the characters advance at the same time before the body of Carwin.)

Fon[taine]. Heaven has heard our prayers!—Triumph, my daughter!—Shout all for rescued innocence!—Shout for Thérèse, the Countess of Belmour! (III,1)

In this climactic scene, pantomimic action damns villainy and reveals the immutable bond between paternalism and Providence.

The gospel according to fairy-tale melodrama, a faith anchored in the bedrock of conservative paternalism, is popular neoplatonism. Neoplatonism began in the third century B.C. in the philosophy of Plotinus and flourished six centuries later during the decline of the Roman Empire. Denounced as heresy by the Catholic church, it continued in underground sects of medieval and Reformation Christianity, influenced the popular traditions of alchemy and folk tales, and emerged in romantic poetry and philosophy, including the works of Schiller and Emerson. Central to neoplatonic belief, from Plotinus onward, is the notion that cosmic reality is circular; that all things emanate from a primal unity, achieve separation and differentiation, and then reconverge into "the One," their initial point of departure. "To Real Being we go back, all that we have and are; to that we return as from that we came," states Plotinus. At one point, the philosopher imagines the circular journey as a quest for a lost home in which a wandering daughter, temporarily swayed by mortal desire, leaves her father. "But one day coming to hate her shame she puts away the evil of the earth, once more seeks the father, and finds her peace," Plotinus concludes.[15]

Neoplatonic circularity shapes the action of fairy-tale melodrama, linking its sequence of events to its ideological point of view, its form to its rhetoric. *Thérèse* ends essentially where it begins: Father Fontaine presiding over the marriage of Thérèse and the count in the midst of a beautiful country scene, with a happy hierarchy of servants and peasants to welcome them home. A similar return is effected metaphorically in *The Wandering Boys*. Paul and Justin have not been home since their mother's death, but they recall it vividly. Justin sings to the assembled villagers early in the play:

> Our cot was shelter'd in a wood
> And near a lake's green margin stood;
> A mountain bleak behind us frown'd
> Whose top the snow in summer crown'd;
> But pastures rich and warm to boot,
> Lay smiling at the mountain's foot:
> There first we frolick'd hand in hand
> Two infant boys from Switzerland. (I,1)

By the end of the melodrama, the boys have regained their happy home of pastoral, precapitalistic bliss. Reunited with their grandfather, the Count de Croissy, they pose for the final tableau before a picturesque "olive field terminated by a river" (II,3), according to the stage directions.

Reconstituting the paternalistic family circle is also the central action of *Clari*. As in *The Wandering Boys*, the oneness of family love has already been sundered, but Payne, following the French ballet original, represents its initial happiness by staging his melodrama within a melodrama. While Clari and the duke look on, the players depict a father-daughter scene of paternalistic reciprocity in front of a rural village backdrop. The player-daughter gives her player-father a bouquet of roses because, she says, "You give me, in exchange, those sweet smiles of affection which are, to me, of more value than anything else in the world." To which the father replies, "Darling child! The look of affection will always reward innocence" (I,3). Later, when the player-father damns his daughter, Clari "rushes on the stage and falls at [the player-father's] feet, shouting, 'Hold, curse her not. She is not lost—she is innocent'" (I,3). Next, as in the mousetrap scene in *Hamlet* (which Payne's audience knew well), the scene ends in consternation and the character who destroyed the players' illusion flees in terror. The players' melodrama and Clari's response, of course, presage in microcosm the action of the entire show. Payne delays the resolution of the father-daughter conflict until the final scene, but the audience already knows how it must end and looks forward to the fatherly embrace welcoming the innocent back to the nest. Indeed, by play's end, all uncorrupted emanations from the One have returned to the primal unity of the One: Rolamo thanks Providence for restoring his family.

Popular neoplatonism also imbues the conception of nature apparent in these plays. Nature in neoplatonic cosmology, as in that of the Stoics, is explicitly linked to a person's deeds through cosmic sympathy. Since the universe is essentially a single moral organism in Plotinus' concep-tion, a human activity such as a heroine's prayer or a villain's revenge will lead to a sympathetic reaction in another part of the cosmic body, as when thunder and lightning "object" to Carwin's murder of the countess in *Thérèse*. Cosmic sympathy also explains why a character's appearance mirrors his or her villainy, benevolence, or innocence; na-ture cooperates with the purposes of worldly and transcendental jus-tice. An important consequence of nature's compact with morality in these plays is the freedom it allowed their producers (and spectators) to apply natural metaphors to social constructions. Early in *The Wan-dering Boys*, the count, still disguised as a castle porter, remembers nostalgically when "once the lisping village babes flock'd playfully about this castle's lord [i.e., himself], and clung to him like tendrils round the oak, gracing their support and shelter" (I,1). Social groups exercising domination often claim that their authority is "natural"; melodramatic neoplatonism helped American paternalists to legiti-mate this assertion.

It also helped to persuade them and perhaps others in the audience that their authority could banish evil from the world. Neoplatonism and these fairy-tale melodramas dispense with any notion of original sin. Since emanations from the One are the source of all matter, including human beings, people are not doomed to sinfulness.[16] The good characters in fairy-tale melodramas—fathers, daughters, peas-ants, and most servants—are transcendentally good. All, like Clari, are innocent, not only of worldly pollution, but of transcendental stain. Minor characters may be less perfect than major ones—the bickerings of peasants and servants often give rise to comic relief in these plays—but even these humble folk are perfectible, as is evident by their compassionate assistance of the heroine and their inclusion in the final tableau. The tableau, in effect, reveals the neoplatonic moment when materiality rejoins the One, when the multiplicity of intentions and emotions on stage melts into a single image fusing mundane relationships with spiritual grace. The final tableau projects a paternalistic utopia.

Villains, of course, are excluded from the transcendental hierarchy of the final picture. According to the followers of neoplatonism, the tarnish of evil is simply polished off when the One reclaims its own, much as alchemists believed unnecessary substances would fall away in the transformation of base metals into their primordial perfection as gold. Evil has no essential existence in neoplatonic thinking. Rather, it is the simple absence of good in ephemeral matter, a polar separation from the One resulting when people's souls "become partial and self-centered; in a weary desire of standing apart they find their way, each to a place of its very own," states Plotinus. Hence, evil is "isolated, weakened, full of care, intent upon the fragment, severed from the whole" (IV.viii.4).

Melodramatic villainy is close indeed to neoplatonic evil. Payne's and Noah's "monsters," their (and Pixérécourt's) favorite epithet for these evildoers, are mired in materialism: Carwin in greed, Roland in lust for power, and the duke, before his act 3 conversion, in sensuous luxury. Evil stands apart from the happy hierarchy of virtuous society in fairy-tale plays; villains are melodrama's individualists, having severed their ties to family, village, lord, and God to seek their own self-interest. Seemingly omnipotent at the start of the play, villainy is gradually burned away in the transforming alchemy of the action until it disappears from the stage. "Do you forget that you are in my power?" sneers Carwin to Thérèse in act 1, "that one word of mine can yield you to the executioner? that without me you are a being without a name, an outcast, a sentenced felon?" (I,1). By the end of act 3, of course, Thérèse and Father Fontaine have wrung from Carwin a terrified confession and they step downstage of his prostrate body, obscuring it from the audience, to celebrate their utopian tableau. Roland, too, is out of the picture for the finale of The Wandering Boys. The duke remains in Clari, but that is only because he has repented the error of his ways, a reformation prophesied by the heroine. In the neoplatonic world of fairy-tale melodrama, a villain's disgust with the "blandishments of pleasure" (II,1) and his conversion to heroism were altogether believable.

Equally believable were the declarations of truth gushing from the hearts of the heroines. Unlike modern realistic plays which entice their viewers with the dynamics of repression, fairy-tale melodramas center on characters who seek to tell all, thus involving the audience in their innocence and vulnerability. Even at times when the most naïve might hold their tongues, heroines reveal their thoughts and desires, trusting in the ultimate goodness of their audience onstage and off. In *The Wandering Boys*, Paul and Justin praise the baroness, not knowing that she and Roland plan their murder to preserve her wealth:

Paul: And to be sure, you can have nothing to make you
           uneasy because you are so rich.
Bar[oness]: Do riches always give ease to the mind?
Paul: Yes, rich folks must always be happy for they can make
           everybody else so.
Justin: And if we were rich, we would try to be as good as you,
           ma'am, and do no harm to anybody. (II,1)

Innocent trust seeks reciprocity in these melodramas. Like the overflowing goodness of the One, trust emanates from the hearts of the pure, causing the souls of even the blackest villain to throb with remorse and guilt. In the above example, Paul and Justin's declaration partly immobilizes the baroness, allowing the count to help the boys escape from her castle later in the scene. Insuppressible emanation also leads heroines to directly confide their hopes and fears to the audience. Alone on stage and facing the threshold of her father's farmhouse, Clari tells the spectators: "I seem to tread upon the earth like a criminal, yet still must I steal upon the hallowed spot. Heart be firm" (III,2). This direct address was intended to evoke sympathy and protectiveness from the fathers in the playhouse.

For the most part, performances of fairy-tale melodramas succeeded in inducing a paternalistic response. *Clari* rarely failed to move elite male audiences to tears. When the play was first presented at the Chestnut Street Theatre in Philadelphia in 1824, a reviewer noted that Mr. Duff, "as the distressed and agonized father of Clari . . . portrayed the parental affliction with a pathos that commanded tears to flow in all parts of the house." The actress performing Clari overwhelmed one reviewer of the Park Theatre production in New York:

> Miss Johnson in *Clari* was inimitable. The deep feeling of her act-ing—the struggling of a powerful memory in her bosom at first—the song, such as we might suppose an imprisoned bird would warble for the blue sky—the clear sunshine—and the still, beautiful forests it was no more to see—the pale, startling astonishment at the Duke's perfidy—the overflowing of her bosom at the sight of her village—and her emotion, deep and still, as she listened to the echoing music that so sadly welcomed her home—we have *never* seen equalled. It was the truest, tenderest acting we have ever beheld.

Likewise, the same reviewer termed "Home, Sweet Home" "the most beautiful and tender music we have ever heard."[17]

Clara Fisher was the most popular American performer of heroines in these fairy-tale melodramas in the late 1820s. Some of the reasons for her success shed significant light on the father-child relationship in the plays she made famous. Born in England, Fisher made her debut at the age of six and a half, performing Richard in the final act of *Richard III* in a "Lilliputian" version (i.e., with a cast of children) of Shakes-peare's play. Emigrating to the United States in 1827, she gained star-dom quickly through such roles as Clari, Thérèse, Ophelia in *Hamlet*, Lady Teazle in *The School for Scandal*, and Little Pickle, an energetic, gaminlike role in *The Spoiled Child*. Theatre historian George C. D. Odell reported that "excitement was high" in 1829 when it was an-nounced that Clara Fisher was to appear in New York with her sister Amelia as Paul and Justin in *The Wandering Boys*. In a "Theatrical Portrait" of Fisher published in the *New-York Mirror* in 1829, the ob-servant critic William Cox summed up the actor's appeal:

> In form and feature, Clara Fisher is neither dignified nor beautiful, but she is irresistibly fascinating. . . . If we were asked in what single particular Clara Fisher was superior to any other actress, we should answer in the perfect grace and freedom of her motions. . . . She is one of nature's actresses. Perhaps no one ever so completely possessed the faculty of mobility or entered with more keen enjoy-ment into the spirit of the part represented. Her whole soul appears

to be in everything she does, and we believe it is not only so in seeming, but in reality.[18]

Here was an actor indeed who could touch the innermost feelings of elite male playgoers, evoking warm-hearted, paternal concern with her spirited innocence and apparently natural pathos.

Clara Fisher's effect on the theatre and society of her day was immediate and wide-ranging. Theatre managers and stage mothers, hoping to duplicate Fisher's success, placed their protégés and daughters on stage in hastily arranged debuts as Clari, Thérèse, or Little Pickle. A few of these fledglings even gained modest success. One of them, Miss Rock, "won distinction" in Philadelphia in 1828 in performances "in those *protean* characters such as Clara Fisher shone in," according to a reviewer. A play entitled *Home, Sweet Home*, an obvious spin-off of *Clari* and involving, said one reviewer, "a quantity of love, gratitude, [and] thankfulness with a merry finale," was written as a vehicle for Clara Fisher's 1829 tour of American theatres. In the early thirties, another playwright borrowed the plot of *Thérèse* for his *The Murderers of Grenoble* at the Bowery Theatre. Clara Fisher herself, as she later recalled in her *Autobiography*, was regularly invited into the homes of elite theatregoers after performances in all the cities of the Northeast. Enthusiastic admirers appropriated her fame to give distinction to a curious range of objects. One actor reported in his memoirs, "Clara Fisher was the name given to everything it could possibly be applied to: ships, steamboats, racehorses, mint-juleps and negro [*sic*] babies."[19]

While it is never easy to determine the several reasons that bring fame to any actor at any time, it seems likely that, apart from her considerable talents as an actor, Clara Fisher helped her male admirers to fantasize a father-child relationship that was pleasing and necessary for them. It was as a child, after all, that Clara Fisher first won applause, and she continued in childlike roles long after reaching maturity. Significantly, her popularity plummeted after she married in 1834. Further, she tended to play daughters who appeared both sweet and spunky, enlivening those character attributes through the grace and energy of her performance. Above all, commentators on her acting singled out her vulnerability on the stage, a characteristic that elite fathers in need of bestowing paternal protection and affection must

Portrait of Clara Fisher, *oil on canvas, 1828, by Henry Inman (Indianapolis Museum of Art, gift of Mrs. John E. Fehsenfeld, Indianapolis). The locket and miniature around Fisher's neck and arm, like the picturesque scenery behind her, signal her sentimental affections.*

have cherished. In short, the accepted definition of Clara Fisher as virtuous, vulnerable, and obedient allowed the fathers in her audience to define themselves as moral, benevolent, and commanding. They could easily imagine themselves playing Rolamo to her Clari.

Yet there was probably more than paternal sympathy that attracted elite males to the spritely young females who played Clari, Thérèse, and the wandering boys on northeastern stages in the 1820s and early 1830s. In 1829, one spectator with poetic ambitions wrote the following lines to Clara Fisher and got them published in the *New-York Mirror*:

> Wert thou not born in fairy-land,
> Young spirit of delight?
> Or hast thou not at thy command
> Some spell of power and might?
>
> .   .   .   .
>
> The forms which haunt our dreams in youth
> Can never come again
> Too beautiful and bright for truth,
> We seek them still in vain.
> So like thou art to these that we,
> When thou dost greet our view,
> Forget life's dark reality,
> And deem its day-dreams true. [20]

Induced to imagine "the forms which haunt our dreams in youth," this patrician, probably an older man, seems to have been sexually stimulated by Fisher's performance. This is not to say that Fisher's acting was openly lascivious. Nonetheless, the image of a helpless girl on her knees before a strong patriarch must surely have excited the fantasies of many males in the audience; there is little paternalism involving older males and mature young females that is not tinged with sexuality. Significantly, no plays featuring the paternal protection of young men gained success with the patriciate during this period. Besides, the theatres of the time provided numerous opportunities for males to gaze on women as sexual objects (with breeches roles the most obvious example) as well as direct inducements for male sexual adventures with prostitutes.

Audience members aroused by the images portrayed by Clara Fisher and others playing these roles could displace and consciously disavow their attraction by scapegoating the villain. It may be no accident that two out of the three villains in these popular melodramas, Carwin and Duke Vivaldi, are sexually aggressive males. (And the third, Roland, has no young women to persecute and seduce.) To gain Thérèse's inheritance, Carwin demands, "Your hand, your hand—or fearless endless vengeance" (II,1). When she refuses, the villain seizes a knife and threatens to "plunge this into your heart" (II,1). Vivaldi and Carwin may embody the sexuality fantasized by males in the audience, but this desire must remain covert if male spectators are to celebrate the triumph of paternalism by the final tableau. The patriciate, in other words, did not want to admit that their benevolence was entangled in sexual desire. Consequently, they applauded plays that allowed them to heap their fantasized sexual sins on the backs of villains who had to be driven off the stage and out of consciousness before their paternalistic utopia could emerge. To legitimate patrician ideology, fairy-tale melodrama first aroused, then expunged, male sexuality.

The rhetoric of Pixérécourt's early melodramas worked in much the same way. Also situating his Parisian audiences as kindly fathers who were invited to sympathize with victimized females and to scapegoat villainous males, Pixérécourt wrote plays celebrating the virtues of patriarchy. Despite a general similarity in form and effect, however, key differences between Pixérécourt's plays and those of his later imitators throw into sharp relief the major tensions of elite male culture in the 1820s and 1830s. More didactic and strident, less ambiguous and encompassing than their original models, the American fairy-tale melodramas reveal a nervous patriciate manning the battlements of paternalism.

Coelina, or the Child of Mystery, The Man with Three Faces, and *The Dog of Montargis*, written by Pixérécourt in 1800, 1801, and 1814, respectively, are generally representative of his formula, displaying minor variations within consistent conventions. *Coelina*, accepted by most theatre historians as the first true nineteenth-century melodrama, was also the first French melodrama to be translated into English. This story of a young girl's quest to wed her beau and to save her unknown father from villainous persecution was drawn from a popular novel of the period by Ducray-Duminil. Pixérécourt based *The Man with Three Faces* on the German drama *Abelino* (1793) by Johann Zschokke, reworking this romantic costume piece—replete with conspirators, outlaws, and disguises—into conformity with his own more traditional notions of morality. Pixérécourt termed *The Dog of Montargis* a *mélodrame historique* since his source for the story was popular history. It is actually closer to a conventional thriller, however, involving a dog who "identifies" his dead master's murderer. These three plays, popular throughout the western world, continued to flourish on American stages into the 1820s in adaptations of the French originals: *A Tale of Mystery (Coelina)*, *Abaellino (Man with Three Faces)*, and *The Forest of Bondy (Dog of Montargis)*.[21]

Overall, *Clari*, *Thérèse*, and *The Wandering Boys* are less imbued with religious mysticism than their French predecessors. In *Coelina* and *Montargis*, Pixérécourt draws from the tradition of French pantomime to depict mute characters who, partly because of their disability, intuit and enact the will of heaven. These silent saints, both mature men, are mundane embodiments of the One. By emanating goodness themselves and activating it in others, they speed the return of the neoplatonic utopia. It is less these males and other worthy patriarchs who bring the conflicts of the melodramas to a happy conclusion, however, than Providence itself. Pixérécourt's patriarchal God reunites Coelina with her father, restores Venice to just rule in *The Man with Three Faces*, and even empowers the dog of Montargis to bark at the villain. Throughout these plays, good characters spontaneously drop to their knees and thank heaven for its benefactions. In contrast, the American melodramas restrict this gesture to daughters bowed before fathers. If the God of Pixérécourt's melodramatic universe is more energetic in righting human affairs than traditional notions of the Christian deity would generally allow, villainous conspiracy and the weakness of mortals have simply given him more work to do.

With God the Father more intrusive, flesh-and-blood fathers become less heroic in Pixérécourt's dramatic world. The bumbling patriarch in *Coelina* lets the villain into his house and cannot protect his ward from his murderous advances. The senators of Venice seem powerless to prevent a coup d'etat until Abelino and Providence save them. And in *Montargis*, a district judge almost convicts the innocent mute of murder before a female innkeeper corrects his shortsighted judgment. In the later American melodramas, however, the father is no longer a misguided dupe or a sainted victim; he has become the primary savior and protector of the heroine. Where Pixérécourt depicts a variety of fatherly types with a range of attributes and intentions, Payne and Noah narrow the character's definition to beneficent protector or patriarchal judge. The Count de Croissy embodies the former ("Come, come my children, to my arms![11] [III,3]) and Rolamo is the latter ("Virtue can hold no intercourse with vice, though vice, with double baseness, kneels, affecting reverence for virtue" [III,2]). Father Fontaine plays both roles at different times in *Thérèse*, but escapes the moral straitjacket of neither. Pixérécourt's fathers, on the other hand, seek help as well as provide protection, apologize as well as judge, and laugh as well as cry. The American patriciate, it seems, could not allow their role models the same variability.

Another characteristic separating the early and later plays is an American concern over money. In *Clari*, Rolamo and his family live in virtuous poverty, the moral-economic status of Thérèse and the wandering boys and their protectors at the start of their plays too. "In my earliest infancy, I was taken by the Marchioness de Ligny, who loved me like a mother," explains Thérèse.

> The Marchioness died—Her will was opened. . . .
> How great was my astonishment and her family's
> indignation on finding that I was left sole heiress
> of her wealth, with authority to bear the title
> of her principal estate. Oh, fatal benefactions!
> Her family, noble, rich, powerful, resolved upon
>   my ruin. (I,1)

Even heroines like Clari who escape the fatal benefaction of a wealthy inheritance yearn for the simple joys of poverty amidst the dazzle of riches. The first two verses of "Home, Sweet Home," sung three times during the play, sum up the contrast found in these plays between virtuous simplicity and villainous wealth:

> 'Mid pleasures and palaces though we may roam
> Be it ever so humble, there's no place like home,
> A charm from the sky seems to hallow us there
> Which, seek through the world, is ne'er met with elsewhere.
>   Home, sweet home!
>   There's no place like home.
> An exile from home, splendor dazzles in vain!

Oh, give me my lowly thatched cottage again!
The birds singing gaily that come at my call,—
Give me them, with the peace of mind dearer than all!
Home, sweet home! . . . (I,1)

For those unfortunate enough to be born wealthy, these plays have a
simple answer: give your money away to the lowly, the virtuous, and
the needy. The duke in *Clari* essentially takes this advice when he de-
cides to marry the heroine, joining the wealth of his family to the
poverty of hers. Injunctions favoring the beneficence of the wealthy
abound in these plays. *The Wandering Boys* features two generous
patriarchs, the disguised count and Hubert, the peasant spokesman of
the village. When the villainous steward accuses the boys of having
stolen the money given them by the baroness, Hubert tells him bluntly:
"Let it never be said in any civilized country that the dispensations of
the affluent to orphan poverty are so rare as to throw a suspicion of
theft on the receivers" (II,3).

All three plays end with inherited wealth providing for the needs of
virtuous victims. In *Clari*, Rolamo blesses the betrothal of his daughter
to the rich duke. The question of who will inherit the money is a central
device of suspense in *Thérèse* and *The Wandering Boys*, settled in
favor of the orphan of Geneva through legal papers and of Paul and
Justin through a mysterious box containing their mother's picture and
a letter explaining their true identities. Inherited wealth, apparently, is
moral as long as it is used for virtuous ends. Significantly, men on the
economic make like Carwin and Roland are damned immediately as
villains.

Why this rhetorical stress on the virtue of poverty and the importance of inherited wealth for philanthropic purposes? Partly, this emphasis shows the neoplatonic legacy of Pixérécourt. *Coelina, The Man
with Three Faces*, and *The Dog of Montargis* treat philanthropy as an
emanation of virtue, a generous outflow of paternalistic goodwill and
concern for those in need. But Pixérécourt was hardly as insistent
about the morality of philanthropy as are Payne and Noah. And acts of
philanthropy occur far less frequently in the French than in the American dramas. Only one of Pixérécourt's plays, *Coelina*, centers on inherited wealth, but this melodrama makes no moral point about the virtue
of poverty. In *The Dog of Montargis*, the innocent victim gains no in-

heritance at all; he is simply restored to his lowly life as a porter at a country inn. *The Man with Three Faces* takes the wealth of all of its major characters for granted. In short, money is not a major moral problem in the dramatic world of Pixérécourt.

The American plays' fixation on money matters may be related to their audience's need to legitimate the traditional authority of melodramatic fathers in a fictitious world more secular and more capitalistic than that in Pixérécourt's early plays. As money becomes a subject of more frequent discussion in these American melodramas, mention of Providence and the controlling hand of God decreases. In effect, God the Father is reduced simply to father, his attributes narrowed from divine love and power to mundane comfort and command. Likewise, his heaven-home of the final tableau is becoming plain old home, sweet home, a pleasant place for fathers and daughters to repose in utopia but no longer the locus of eternal fulfillment. With the traditional children-fathers-Father pyramid somewhat truncated, fathers have to gather more legitimacy to themselves to merit their new position; this partly explains the shift from Pixérécourt's Dufour, the confused and easily duped father in *Coelina*, to Rolamo in *Clari*. But father can't seem to be Our Father if the taint of ill-gotten gains attaches to his image. Better to keep him poor, like Father Fontaine and Rolamo, or attach him to traditional wealth as in *The Wandering Boys*, where the sources of the count's income can be conveniently forgotten. Better still to push philanthropy, so that fathers in general can appear to be imitating the selfless emanations of the Almighty. Consequently, the cant in these plays about virtuous poverty and benevolent paternalism is essentially an unknowing evasion to cover the nervous hegemony of the fathers. Payne and Noah are saying, in effect, that these fathers deserve all the power they have because they are good, not because they are rich.

Lost in this transfer of power from Father to the fathers, however, is much of the encompassing mystery of Pixérécourt's more neoplatonic (and more Catholic) vision. To chalk up happy endings to Providence is to mystify the ways of the world. A more distant, more Protestant deity puts the fathers center stage in the plots of the American plays. They may have more power, but they also have less room in which to make mistakes because the playwrights have given them a weightier image to maintain. The very workings of power in society are consequently less mysterious, more naked, than in the persuasion induced by Pixérécourt. Little wonder that the American plays are more didactic, less confident than their French predecessors. This shift in melodramatic ideology from the early 1800s to the 1820s was occurring in France as well as in the United States, of course. Payne and Noah based their melodramas on French originals that had already retreated somewhat from Pixérécourt's initial embrace of a neoplatonic Catholicism and late feudalism.

Clearly, the patriciate applauded and wept over the plays of Payne and Noah because they projected their own paternalistic desires and anxieties onto the fairy-tale stage. But apart from general elite concerns in political and business matters, the popularity of these plays suggests that much of their nervousness centered on their families. What was happening in elite families during this period, specifically in father-daughter relationships, to provoke such a melodramatic response at the playhouse?

Impressionistic evidence of these relationships, while often perfunctory and vague, indicates more tension among fathers and daughters than had probably been the norm before. Upper-class, unmarried American females struck many foreign observers as stubborn, independent, and cold. A German visitor in the 1820s, for instance, saw young women "in convulsive anger at their parents," and other Europeans, too, reported significant father-daughter strain. Partly because they had much more freedom than in colonial times but were still expected to maintain high standards of morality and propriety, elite females typically married early as a means of escaping the pressure of their father's household. For several Europeans, the calculating coolness of unmarried American women suggested that family affection among the elite was disintegrating. According to Frederick Marryat:

> Beyond the period of infancy, there is no endearment between the parents and children; none of that sweet spirit of affection between brothers and sisters; none of those links which unite one family, of that mutual confidence, that rejoicing in each other's success, that refuge, when they are depressed or afflicted, in the bosoms of those who love us.

Other Europeans pointed to the loving care often given to American children by their parents—care that was usually too permissive by their standards—but few mentioned permissive love from parents to children during their young adult years. Instead, the most frequently used word to describe the relationship between father and adolescent son or daughter was "freedom." In some instances, parents were seen to be pushing their children to grow up, to leave the house, and to assume adult responsibilities.[22]

This change in parent-child relations occurred because a more democratic family was creating new role models and different norms of authority and obedience. During early colonial times, the patriarchal extended family had been the social and economic backbone of American life. In the mid eighteenth century, the family began to change, slowly at first, then more rapidly with the ongoing isolation of the nuclear family and the softening of patriarchy into paternalism. After 1800, a more democratic family structure left fathers with less of a voice in the career and marital choices of their offspring. Patrician fathers were no longer the patriarchs of old but became, as one historian concludes, "more oriented to shaping the behavior of [their] children in order to make them conform to norms of behavior" determined beyond the family circle. By 1820, most fathers in the mercantile elite had lost the power of familial command; instead, they exercised mostly sentimental influence and paternal guidance.[23] Not surprisingly, some elite fathers believed that villainous ideas had invaded their happy home to corrupt their sons and daughters to rebellion. Most others, apparently, accepted the new situation but hoped that emerging ideas of family government might restore what they perceived as a lost home, sweet home, of familial bliss.

Much of the child guidance literature which began to proliferate in the mid 1820s centered on the problem of waning parental, primarily fatherly, authority. Anxious merchant-class parents learned they were not alone; "disorder," "disobedience," and even "licentiousness" were rife among the adolescents (a term not yet in use) of their friends and neighbors. One typical statement confessed "that an irreverent, unruly spirit has come to be prevalent, an outrageous evil among the young people of our land. . . . Some of the good old people make facetious complaint on this. . . . 'There is as much family government now as there used to be in our young days,' they say, 'only it has changed hands.' " Elite parents and their advocates complained that their young people were being given too much money and fine clothing, that they spurned the society of their elders for the company of their own generation, and that they used love as an excuse to marry young men or women their parents had hardly even met. One writer blamed the parents themselves for abandoning the "old-fashioned, fundamental, patriarchal, God-given idea of the household" in the scramble for wealth—a notion containing a significant germ of truth.[24]

Most child guidance writers, however, backed away from a vigorous endorsement of traditional methods of child rearing in favor of "moral influence," a technique which sought to balance external parental authority with internalized restraints. As social historian Steven Mintz states:

> The main aim of this literature was to find ways to instill self-discipline within children without physical coercion, by invisibly instilling habits of deference and respect. The emphasis in the childrearing literature on moral influence as the basis of authority was one expression of a much wider concern with establishing modes of social control that would not be regarded as authoritarian and illegitimate. Because moral influence supposedly derived its efficacy from children's recognition of its legitimacy, this childrearing technique could be upheld as intrinsically non-coercive. Yet the purpose was to make parental restraint as invisible as possible, and in this sense the concept of influence shares characteristics with modern behaviorism, in particular, a blindness to the dangers of psychological coercion when used for moral ends.

Child guidance writer Heman Humphrey, for example, stressed that the child's need for parental affection was the most legitimate source of parental control. "There is no constraint like that of love," he admonished.[25]

There is a striking affinity between this reliance on binding a child to habits of obedience and respect through the manipulation of his or her own heartstrings and the rhetoric of fairy-tale melodrama. Payne's and Noah's plays pictured father figures as saviors and heroes to their children. Rather than coercing their errant charges into obedience, the Rolamos and Counts reassert their control over their Claris and wandering boys by inducing guilt and playing upon their affections. Humphrey, in fact, recommends the precise strategy used by Rolamo to shame Clari into deferential submission. "Whatever the privation or other token of your displeasure may be," he advises, "the delinquent must, if possible, be made to feel that he has brought it upon himself by 'hating instruction and despising reproof.' " Humphrey further admonishes the father to exclude the child from his presence with some such remark as, "Much as I love you, I cannot bear to see you till you are sorry for what you have done and will promise amendment."[26] Rolamo, arguably, is harder on Clari than is Humphrey's exemplary father on his son, but the technique of moral influence is the same in both instances.

For many elite fathers, reestablishing their authority in the family provided the first line of defense against the tides of capitalistic and democratic change. Few Americans in the 1820s and 1830s drew firm distinctions between the domestic and the social realms, a separation which would later come to dominate business-class American belief about the function of home life. From the point of view of the male upper class, family government ought to reflect a hierarchical government for society in which wise fathers exercised moral influence and, at times, direct control over other less fortunate or more childish citizens. The domestic microcosm should embody the social macrocosm. How else to reform republican morals and instill new respect for the fading virtues of 1776? Paternal family government, then, was a necessary first step in getting the younger generation to commit itself to character over wealth, self-discipline over loss of control, and home virtues over the temptations of competitive wandering. No wonder that by 1835 one child guidance writer complained about "the current of popular treatises on the subject that almost daily issues from the press." At stake for many anxious parents was nothing less than the redemption of the republic.[27]

When they stepped beyond the family circle into society, many Americans took traditional images of family government with them. Scenarios of father-heroes and their agents saving victims of villainy are embedded in the actions and the rhetoric of the voluntary moral-control societies of the 1820s and 1830s, for example. In these groups, young men under the direction of city leaders sought to rescue the helpless from such urban vices as gambling, profanity, and prostitution. Many American utopians, as well, urged the centrality of paternal authority and the need to restrict individual freedom in order to regain the security of a traditional family writ large in a utopian community. An advertisement for one utopian community, for instance, rested its entire appeal on the value of home and family: "Home money, home employment, home protection, home franchise, home virtue, home worship, home ideals, home people and home day." Though partly a product of the unbounded expectation that human will could shape human society to perfection, the utopian movement, most popular in the United States from 1820 to 1850, may also be seen as a response to fears of familial and social democracy.[28]

The paternalistic persuasion of the elite is most evident, perhaps, in the asylum movement of the first half of the century. As in their theatregoing, elite advocates of asylums rarely admitted to themselves or others that control per se was their goal. Historian David Rothman makes it clear that their conscious purposes were idealistic, even utopian: to protect the homeless, to reform and rehabilitate the criminal, the insane, the juvenile delinquent, even to provide a Christian model of family government that would cause parents throughout America to look to asylums for the proper methods of raising children. Against the villainous traps posed by urban life, patrician advocates built and managed institutions which they expected would provide spatial salvation to the problems posed by temporal change. Believing in the natural innocence of the orphans and lunatics, even of many of the criminals, under their charge, the superintendents of these asylums used the techniques of moral influence to wean their "children" away from wickedness. "What is needed for the children whom the law entrusts to us," asserted the superintendent of the New York Juvenile Asylum, "is the government of a well-ordered Christian household."[29]

Rothman concludes that the orphanages, asylums, and penitentiaries of the early national and Jacksonian periods relied on the new techniques of behavioral manipulation to teach their charges "the precepts of traditional social theory":

By these standards, men were to take their rank in the hierarchy, know their place in society, and not compete to change positions. Children were to be content with their station, taking their father's position for their own. Politics and learning were to be the province of trained men, and ordinary citizens were to leave such matters to them. Family government was to instill order and discipline, and the community to support and reinforce its dictums.[30]

In nominating heroic fathers to save the innocent victims of calculating villainy by returning them, via moral influence, to an antidemocratic, premarket economic order, elite asylum advocates revealed an unknowing commitment to the rhetoric of fairy-tale melodramas. Both centered on the controlling false love of paternalism. Michel Foucault calls such parallel discourses occurring in different social situations "similitudes." Because similitudes rely on much the same rhetorical force and generate congruent meanings, they lend significance and believability to human actions within their range of domains.[31] Fairy-tale plays, then, helped to sustain the asylum movement during the 1820s and 1830s. The performance of these melodramas legitimated the dependence on paternal authority fostered by asylums. In neither the plays nor the institutions were the "children" allowed to grow up.

While asylum paternalism lasted into the 1850s, the melodramatic formation centered on elite audiences, mercantilist production, and fairy-tale plays, already in decline, fell apart after 1835. The ascent of the stars brought many newcomers into urban playhouses, theatregoers less comfortable with the norms of paternalism which had traditionally structured relations between the elite and other groups in public theatres. Further, audiences cheering specifically American stars, who proliferated in the early thirties, tended to be Jacksonian in their social relations, eager to assert the power of the people over the aristocracy. The result was a gradual decline in elite attendance at the Park, Chestnut, and Tremont theatres during the 1830s. As early as 1830, a Tremont Theatre Investigating Committee complained of the "mass of vulgarity" attending their theatre and worried that the Tremont might soon cease to be fashionable. A British visitor in 1837 noted the decrease in gentry at the Park and added, "It was only on occasions when some great attraction or some new or distinguished performer is presented that an [upper-class] audience can be collected." By the early forties, one fashionable lady complained that, though she would have preferred going to an exclusive opera house instead of the Park Theatre, "we of ourselves are not sufficiently numerous to support an opera so we have been forced to admit the people."[32] Elite hegemony in theatres in the 1820s had depended upon attendance from "the people"; without them, much of the public show of benevolence and control would have been meaningless. By 1840, the patriciate had withdrawn from such overt manipulation at the play-house, seeking out theatrical entertainment more for private enjoy-ment and class-based friendship than for public purposes.

Their new entertainment of choice was grand opera. Upper-class Bostonians and Philadelphians continued to patronize the old theatres when the managers brought in opera companies. New Yorkers turned even further away from the practice of public playgoing by building socially restrictive opera houses. By 1850, the northeastern patriciate had established the rituals of elite operagoing, including codes of behavior, dress, and language, as necessary hurdles for membership in the upper class. Attendance at Italian opera helped the patriciate to solidify its ranks by minimizing the differences among subgroups through the elaboration and celebration of common practices and dis-courses. Like the elite magazines, private schools, and clubs that pro-liferated in the Northeast in the 1830s and 1840s, the opera socialized upper-class patricians in a class consciousness increasingly useful in perpetuating their power.[33]

Underlying the shift from public playgoing to class-based operagoing were new historical pressures motivating the elite to shape a more flex-ible hegemony. Directly exercising control over other classes—the tra-ditional means of maintaining elite domination—was no longer as effi-cient as it had been when New York, Boston, and Philadelphia had been "walking cities." With real power passing from those in public view into the hands of men and women sitting behind closed doors, public rituals involving all classes were becoming less necessary. The rise of political parties as legitimate power brokers in the late 1830s and 1840s encouraged the elite to master more private means of public influence. In the business world the rise of the corporation meant the gradual demise of the publicly known merchant, who was replaced by a controlling board of directors. Anonymous boards, committees, and supervisors were even taking over philanthropic giving and urban so-cial services, a traditional area of high visibility for the elite. Although the antiaristocratic rhetoric of Jacksonian times convinced many in the upper class to retreat from leadership roles in politics and philan-thropy, their success in carving out for themselves private roles that preserved much of their power more than made up for their loss of public esteem.[34]

Lacking their former institutional and ideological support, performances of fairy-tale melodramas declined after 1835. Presumably the city elders who had wept over the reconciliation of Clari and Rolamo looked elsewhere to ease their burdens of anxiety and guilt. Operagoing provided some relief, since the three most popular operas in the 1830s and 1840s—Rossini's *Cinderella*, Bellini's *The Sleepwalker*, and Auber's *Masaniello*—continued to dramatize father-child relations through conflicts and resolutions redolent of fairy-tale paternalism. With the rise of a new generation of the elite less tied to the concerns of the past, the rhetoric of overt paternalistic control in plays, operas, and spectaculars gradually faded. Some fairy-tale melodramas continued on the boards, especially at the new museum theatres in the late 1840s, but mostly in shortened versions as afterpieces. Edwin Forrest was fond of performing the villain's role in *Thérèse*, for instance, but he and his Jacksonian audience probably turned the cutdown melodrama to very different purposes than Clara Fisher and her spectators had done. The pantomime-ballets of the Ravels kept alive some of the fairy-tale experiences of such spectaculars as *Cherry and Fair Star*, but this tradition, too, gradually changed, finally to be transformed into the knockabout pantos of G. L. Fox's *Humpty Dumpty* for New York audiences.

As did other theatrical formations, paternalistic melodrama of the 1820s and early 1830s folded its tent because the theatre artists found better work elsewhere and the audiences drifted away. Behind these numerous individual choices was the gradual shift in American society away from paternalistic and toward more charismatic social relations. But if the Age of Jackson meant the rejection of paternalism for charisma, it also meant the triumph of market capitalism over the remains of mercantilism and the emergence of a residual republican culture in the theatre.

PART II

Theatre of Yeoman Independence

for Jacksonians, 1830–1855

Ⅰn searching for a name for much of the American rural economy of the nineteenth century, an economy of petty producers who participated in but kept their distance from commercial markets, the historian Alan Kulikoff adopts the term "yeoman society."[1] These yeomen sought to sustain their economic and political independence in a world increasingly shaped by capitalist expansion. Kulikoff notes that their urban counterparts in the Northeast—many of them workers—were committed to the beliefs and practices of Jeffersonian republicanism and their later extension in Jacksonian democracy. Earlier than most farmers, however, urban workers and small tradespersons experienced the wrenching dislocations of the transition to liberal capitalism, as entrepreneurs took over the means of production and dominated marketplace exchange after 1820. In response to capitalist incursions, urban "yeomen" drew strength from their traditional culture, which emphasized community solidarity, family honor, and manly independence. Yet this residual culture was seriously flawed; based upon the antithetical ideologies of republicanism and liberalism, traditional yeoman culture gradually caved in under the weight of its own contradictions and the pressures of capitalist transformation.

Yeoman culture drew many of its values from the legacy of eighteenth-century republicanism. Itself a derivative of Renaissance political thinking, the republican tradition emphasized the need to subordinate self-interest to preserve the public good. Hence, as historian Joyce Appleby asserts, "the classical republican paradigm provided no role for the capitalist as citizen." According to this tradition, the virtuous republican must be socially and economically independent, capable of sustaining himself and his family without relying on the beneficence or employment offered by another. Eighteenth-century Americans who fought the Revolutionary War and established the Constitution added the notion of political equality to republicanism; all citizens must be equal at elections and before the law. This addition created tensions between republicanism and paternalism, hitherto generally congruent in practice and belief. Republicanism had both restraining and liberating effects on the social and political behavior of Revolutionary-era Americans. Since most believed that women were and ought to remain dependent upon their fathers, brothers, and husbands, mature women, lacking independence, could not become citizens. On the other hand, some urban artisans argued successfully that their independence and political equality made their labor a form of personal property which should not be degraded to the "slavery" of working for a wage.[2]

Most eighteenth-century male republicans fused these notions of citizenship, independence, and equality with a firm sense of their personal honor. "To the extent that a search for honor involves a concern for personal autonomy and a distrust of power," notes political historian Kenneth Greenberg, "it is compatible with the republican tradition." As social historian Bertram Wyatt-Brown concludes, the culture of male honor involved several strands of belief and behavior deriving from the feudal past. Chief among these was the notion that honor was socially attributed, not individually possessed; only a man's peers could judge a man honorable or dishonorable. This assumption, notes sociologist Peter Berger, distinguished honor from dignity. Dignity, the "belief that personal worth inheres equally with each individual," "frees the evangelical to confront God alone, the capitalist to make contracts without customary encumbrances, and the reformer to uplift the lowly. Naked and alone, man has dignity; extolled by peers and covered with ribbons, he has honor."[3] Most male Americans who cheered Jacksonian stars in the theatre looked to their fellows, not to themselves, to affirm their worth as honorable republicans.

Nineteenth-century liberals, on the other hand, turned more to their consciences than to their compatriots to reinforce a sense of their inherent worth. Building on this new type of self-confidence, earlier liberals like Benjamin Franklin and Adam Smith advocated contractual social and economic relations. This differed radically from what E. P. Thompson terms a moral-economic concept of justice, a community-based "consensus as to what were legitimate and what were illegitimate practices in marketing, milling, baking, etc. [The moral-economic sense of justice] was grounded upon a consistent traditional view of social norms and obligations, of the proper economic functions of several parties within the community." Also upsetting traditional republican notions of citizenship and the public good, liberals championed economic competition to achieve moral and economic, but rarely civic progress. Their notion of political equality derived from the philosophy of John Locke, which envisioned rights as natural and individual rather than following from the construction of republican government. Despite these fundamental differences, liberalism and republicanism effected an uncomfortable synthesis in the conflicted image of the Jeffersonian yeoman farmer. Although a virtuous citizen and an independent producer, the yeoman of the Jeffersonian myth believed in his natural right to pursue individual economic success.[4]

Justified by the increasingly dominant ideology of liberalism, American capitalists transformed their society in the first three decades of the nineteenth century. Household economies gave way to regional markets, a business revolution involving widespread incorporation altered the nature and the scale of commerce, capital accumulation led to increased concentrations of wealth, and sharp divisions between capital and labor emerged in traditional modes of artisan production. By 1830, the economics of liberal capitalism, based on acquisitive individualism and competitive market relations, had triumphed in most sectors of American society, even in the field of urban entertainment. The Jacksonian model of the yeoman farmer further collapsed the distance between liberalism and republicanism. Still an independent and honorable producer, this yeoman had virtually erased the difference between his own self-made success and the good of the commonwealth. Under the ambiguous and shifting surface of the myth, however, the antinomies of liberalism and republicanism remained.[5]

Productions of heroic melodramas starring Edwin Forrest and apocalyptic melodramas popular with working-class spectators helped to sustain the residual Jacksonian culture of many urbanites. Forrest's yeoman heroes fought tyrants, rescued helpless women, and sought to return "the people" to Arcadian utopias of precapitalist independence and morality. Apocalyptic plays, part of a subformation within yeoman melodramatic culture, also celebrated these heroics, with particular emphasis on masculine honor and suicidal revenge. Performances of these plays induced hero worship in their mostly Jacksonian spectators, a desire for charismatic authority given institutional form in the new conventions of the star network. The yeoman ideology of manly honor, republican independence, and hero worship circulated in other social arenas beyond the theatre, including the public image of President Jackson, the campaign practices of the Democratic party, and the Astor Place theatre riot.

This melodramatic formation, especially its piggybacking of stars onto traditional stock production, drew legitimacy from both liberalism and republicanism between 1830 and 1855. In effect, Jacksonian yeoman theatre provided an arena of conflict for highlighting and partly resolving the ideological differences between the two positions so that the culture of liberal capitalism, a nexus of beliefs and behavior centered on male individualism, female domesticity, and social respectability, could emerge as fully hegemonic in the mid 1850s. As before, Americans worked through their political anxieties and desires at the melodramatic theatre, not by listening to speeches on political philosophy but by applauding heroes, scapegoating villains, and weeping for victims. The theatre of yeoman independence facilitated the transition from paternalistic to bourgeois forms of cultural authority.

3. "The People's Verdict"

When Edwin Forrest stepped on the stage of the Broadway Theatre on February 9, 1852, as Damon in *Damon and Pythias*, 4,500 spectators greeted him with a standing ovation and a huge banner on which was printed, "THIS IS THE PEOPLE'S VERDICT." The words on the banner referred to Forrest's recent and widely publicized divorce case, in which a New York jury had found him guilty of adultery and ordered him to pay three thousand dollars per year in alimony. Forrest understood the applause and the banner as complete vindication. In a curtain speech after the show, he thundered:

> Why is this vast assemblage here tonight, composed as it is of the intelligent, the high-minded, the right-minded, and last, though not least, the beautiful of the Empire City? . . . It is because you have come to express your irrepressible sympathy for one whom you know to be a deeply-injured man. Nay, more, you are here with a higher and holier purpose—to vindicate the principle of even-handed justice. I do not propose to examine the proceedings of the late unhappy trial. . . . I submit my cause to you; my cause, did I say? No, not my cause alone, but yours, the cause of every man in the community, the cause of every human being, the cause of every honest wife, the cause of every virtuous woman, the cause of every-one who cherishes a home and the pure spirit which should abide there. Ladies and gentlemen, I submit my cause to a tribunal uncorrupt and incorruptible; I submit it to the sober second thought of the people!

The crowd roared its support and approval.[1]

This ritual of vindication rested upon the social dynamics of hero worship for theatrical superstars; it involved some of the most important constructions of gender and class within the yeoman melodramatic formation. In 1852, Edwin Forrest was the premier star of the American stage. Packed houses and standing ovations were the rule for Forrest's charismatic performances, especially between 1835 and 1855 when the star was at the height of his powers. One theatre manager wrote in amazement of Forrest's effect on his spectators: "Witness the furor of audiences subjected to his control, the simultaneous shouts of applause which follow his great efforts, see the almost wild enthusiasm he kindles in the breasts of his auditors, and who will deny that Mr. Forrest has got the heart, nay 'the very heart of hearts,' of the masses." Forrest's charisma affected the public offstage as well as on. Actor Lawrence Barrett remembered when "the presence of Forrest upon Broadway attracted marked attention from friend and foe and led to a free exchange of opinions upon his appearance, expressions of admiration or condemnation being as vigorously offered as if in the theatre itself." Forrest's larger-than-life public image led people to name objects of power and danger after him: steamboats, racehorses, fire engines, and locomotives. As one commentator noted after his death in 1872, Forrest was "the object of a hero worship which is now impossible."[2]

Forrest had married Catherine Norton Sinclair in 1837: she was nineteen, he was thirty-one; she was English, he was American; she and her family had pretensions to bourgeois gentility, he gloried in the rough democracy of his working-class acquaintances. After a few years of initial happiness, their social lives moved apart. Sinclair (who resumed her family surname after the divorce) made friends with several in the social elite. Forrest lived much as he had before marriage, carousing with his friends from Tammany Hall, whoring with prostitutes and actresses, and earnestly pursuing his career as a star. The rupture came in 1849 when Forrest discovered a love letter addressed to his wife from a minor actor and assumed that they had shared the "bliss" spoken of in the letter. Sinclair denied Forrest's accusation and even signed a vow, written by the suspicious star, that she had "never been unfaithful to the marriage bed." But in Forrest's eyes, his wife's possible infidelity was more a matter of public honor than private trust. Following their separation, Forrest wrote that he was driven to address her "by reports and rumors that reach me from every side." Commanding her to keep her mouth shut about their troubles, he concluded, "I am content that the past shall remain in silence, but I do not intend, nor will I permit, that either you or anyone connected with you shall ascribe our separation to my misconduct."[3] Nothing Sinclair said in their subsequent exchange of notes convinced the star that she and others would not continue to impugn his honor. Forrest's lawyers initiated divorce proceedings in 1850.

If marriage was a matter of public reputation for Forrest, Sinclair, influenced by the rising chorus of bourgeois discourse on domesticity, saw the social institution very differently. In an 1848 letter to a mutual male friend of hers and Forrest's, Sinclair reminded him that most people now understand "that for man to attain the high position for which he is by nature fitted, woman must keep pace with him." Further, "woman has as high a mission to perform in this world as man has." Chiding her friend for believing that wives ought to be dependent on their husbands, Sinclair asked, "What! Do you value the love of a woman who only clings to you because she cannot do without your support?" Sinclair's letter recapitulates several of the major themes of business-class domesticity: separate spheres of influence for men and women, marriage as a private relationship involving mutual respect and affection, and a wife's duty to civilize her husband and family. Sinclair even admitted that her civilizing function might involve "pride in self-sacrifice," if the husband should "indulge his fancies" for other women.[4] From Forrest's republican point of view, women were inferior to and hence dependent upon men; in his curtain speech at the Broadway Theatre women were "the beautiful," but could not be "high-minded" or "right-minded" citizens. In Sinclair's liberal, bourgeois thinking, men and women were natural equals and should work together for moral progress.

Forrest's and Sinclair's misunderstandings of each other's notions of gender were compounded by their differences in class. Sinclair's journalist friend Nathaniel Parker Willis wrote in his *Home Journal* that her social circle was "of a different class" than the star's: "She is a person of the highest intellectual culture, and her friends were authors, clergymen, professors, and artists, before whom the class of stories could not be ventured upon, in the telling of which constitutes, as we understand, Mr. Forrest's conversational powers." Consequently, Willis continued, Forrest sulked in his study or "was uncomfortably dumb" when his wife's friends came to call. Willis's depiction of the class divide running through the Forrests' marriage, though colored by his devotion to Sinclair, was generally corroborated by witnesses at the divorce trial. Forrest resented his wife's inclusion in social gatherings centering on a class above his own, especially when these parties occurred in his own home. At the trial, his lawyers attempted to prove that "a literary coterie, by the fiat of whom every man must fall, and at the head of which was Mr. N. P. Willis, were in the habit of visiting Mr. Forrest's house during his absence, and that by them his wife was taught to look down upon the simplicity of her husband's character."[5]

Such was Forrest's republican simplicity that he took Willis's interest in his wife and his journalistic accusations of his own boorishness as an affront to his honor. In the summer of 1851, Forrest accosted Willis on a New York street, "took away his cane [according to a witness], placed his foot on his neck, and laid upon his person with the cane." While beating him, Forrest warned off passersby by shouting, "Gentlemen, this is the seducer of my wife; do not interfere." The next day in a "card" published in the New York *Herald*, Willis asserted that Forrest had attacked him from behind. Forrest denied the accusation in a following card, but the matter was never resolved. Nonetheless, Willis sued Forrest for assault and was eventually awarded $2,500 in damages.

As in the caning that Preston Brooks inflicted on Charles Sumner in the United States Senate in 1856, Forrest, a traditional Democrat, interpreted Willis's actions as an unmanly affront to his public reputation and answered according to the code of honor.[6] Forrest might have sued the journalist for defamation of character, but matters of honor, following the traditional code, were best settled outside among witnesses in man-to-man physical combat, not inside a courtroom with the antagonists hiding behind their lawyers. Forrest probably did not believe that Willis had literally seduced his wife, but he did know that the journalist was one of the agents who had encouraged Sinclair to question his patriarchal authority, almost as bad a blow as seduction to the honor of his household.

The divorce trial began in September 1851. Forrest's lawyers called house servants to testify to the "scenes of wassail" Sinclair had enjoyed in Forrest's house in the master's absence and tried to convince the all-male jury that Sinclair had been unfaithful to her husband. Sinclair's lawyers, who had countersued Forrest, easily discredited most of the defendant's witnesses and allegations. They then produced compelling evidence that Forrest was a regular patron of a local house of assignation and that he had committed adultery with Josephine Clifton when the two actors toured together in the early 1840s. On January 26, 1852, "thousands and thousands of the anxious public" waited outside the courthouse for the verdict. Sinclair beat Forrest on every count.[7]

Stung by defeat, Forrest sought vindication from his fans in the playhouse. He performed his starring roles at the Broadway Theatre from mid February to the end of April for sixty-nine performances to an estimated eighty thousand spectators, an "engagement unparalleled in the history of the stage," according to one reporter.[8] Here too, honor was at stake. By breaking the record for the longest star engagement, Forrest demonstrated his honor through courageous action. Further, the accolades of his fans told the world that he was still an honorable man; "the people's verdict" could overwhelm the minority judgments of lawyers and judges in the public court of honor. But why did so many New Yorkers ignore Forrest's guilt and hail a convicted adulterer as their hero? The answer to that question requires an understanding of star entertainment and the charismatic public image of Edwin Forrest.

The popularity of itinerant starring rested on hero worship, a historically unique tie between actors and audiences. In earlier times, actors enmeshed in relations of patronage might gain great prestige with their audiences—Louis XIV had praised Molière, for example—but such artists were not stars because of their subordinate role in theatrical production. Betterton, Garrick, and other premier performers of the eighteenth-century stage were transitional figures in the shift from prominent actors in stock companies to independent charismatic stars. With the emergence of market labor relations in the American theatre in the early nineteenth century, actors became stars by cutting loose from the restraints of stock company production and taking charge of their own careers. At the same time, audiences were turning to great men and women to give order to their lives. As the social philosopher Thomas Carlyle explained,

> That man, in some sense or other, worships Heroes; that we all of us reverence and must ever reverence Great Men: this is, to me, the living rock amid all rushings-down whatsoever, the one fixed point in modern revolutionary history, otherwise as if bottomless and shoreless.[9]

The confluence of a popular desire for hero worship and the possibilities of new productive relations in the theatre elevated some actors to star status, an attributed social role based more on the relationship between the star and his fans than on qualities intrinsic to the actor. Theatrical stardom had the same economic base and psychosocial dynamics as charismatic political leadership, which also flourished in the nineteenth century. Audiences had respected Betterton and Horace Walpole; they worshipped Forrest and Andrew Jackson.

The emergence of virtuosity in the American theatre paralleled similar developments elsewhere in the arts. The violinist Paganini was one of the first and most electric of western star performers. Following his death in 1840, Franz Liszt wrote that "the world wonderingly looked upon him as a super-being." In the French theatre, Frédérick Lemâitre thrilled audiences with his power and élan. On the English stage, Edmund Kean "suggested something portentous, preternatural, supernal, that blinded and stunned the beholders, appalled the imagination and chilled the blood" for one American reviewer. The historian of romanticism Morse Peckham concludes that the virtuoso-star symbolized "the uniqueness of the self as the source of value by transforming his role into a source of unimagined splendor, order, power, and beauty" for his audience. Hero worship in the arts reversed the traditional patron-artisan relationship: From their followers' point of view, stars had exceptional, heroic powers that commanded their deepest devotion. Max Weber explored the depredations of such charisma on traditional social ties. Bonded to a hero, the follower became less a member of a specific class, church, and ethnic group, and more an isolated individual. As sociologist Bryan Turner notes, the process of individuation at work in charismatic relations, "by making people different and separate . . . , makes them more subject to control." [10]

Forrest was one of several American stars whose charismatic appeal transformed the nature of antebellum audience response. Junius Brutus Booth, the father of Edwin and John Wilkes, won public acclaim for his fiery vehemence as Richard III, Macbeth, and Othello. Of equal power was Charlotte Cushman. Her Meg Merriles, for instance, "half woman, half demon," terrified and thrilled audiences with her "savage animal reality of passion" and her "weird fascination with crime, redeemed by fitful flashes of womanly feeling." Several comic actors also achieved star status, among them James W. Wallack, who, said one observer, "filled the scene with pictorial vitality and dazzled the observer by the opulence of his enjoyment." Like the other theatrical stars of their era, Booth, Cushman, and Wallack delivered aesthetic shock treatment to their viewers. Their spectators, in gratitude, termed their performances "sublime," the ultimate accolade for the high-voltage star. [11]

Three new conventions institutionalized stargazing in the American theatre: the curtain speech, the floral tribute, and the play contest. Kean initiated curtain speeches in the United States during his tours in the 1820s. Before then, the manager had been the only person from the company to appear before the audience with any regularity at the end of the show, usually to seek the approbation of the house. By the 1830s several stars, Forrest included, had followed Kean's lead and audiences began to look forward to this chance to "meet" the star "out of character." George "Yankee" Hill told dialect stories and Fanny Ellsler, an English singer, thrilled Americans with "a thousand thanks—my heart is too full to say more." So much a part of the star performance had the curtain speech become that George Vandenhoff apologized for his short talk to a Boston audience in 1857, explaining that if they knew "the immense physical exertion required to act Macbeth they would not expect the actor to make much of a speech after acting the part." [12]

The floral tribute, given to male as well as female stars, also gained popularity in the 1830s. An 1837 newspaper report in New York complained of "gallant young gentlemen who are wont, under the influence of admiration and late dinners, to shower upon the object of their enthusiasm whole boxes of artificial roses and daffy-down-dillies." Sometimes money and jewelry accompanied the flowers given to women stars. By the 1850s, several critics were satirizing these practices. One wag in Washington, D.C., reported the acceptance speech of a floral wreath by the star performer in *Mazeppa* which was, of course, a horse. Noting that she was surprised to be "trotted out like this," she promised to wear "this gratifying mark of your esteem around my neck like a halter." [13]

The curtain speech and the floral tribute were primarily rites of hero worship bonding audiences to stars. Critics of the new conventions, however, generally missed their significance. "What has the audience to do with the actor except to witness, to approve, or to condemn his performance," noted an irate editor. "As things are now," he continued, the star "is compelled to drop the character he is portraying and come, in his private person, before his audience and be be-cheered and be-bouquetted ad nauseam." From a traditional point of view, the editor was right to complain. But the luminary's appearance at the end of the show in his or her "private person" underlined the individuation of both star and stargazer at work in this new relationship. Carlyle praised sincerity as the main attribute of the hero. Heroes were not to wear masks, not to engage in character playing before their publics, but to appear simply and magnificently as their individually unique selves. Curtain speeches and floral tributes partly satisfied audience hunger to see the stars as they "really are." [14]

The dynamics of such "sincerity" and individuation also led stars in quest of new plays. Traditional playwrights had written for stock companies, rarely for individual actors. The early stars used the heroes of Shakespeare and a few other playwrights to build their careers, but several sought to perform roles closer to their public personas. Urged on by a rapturous public, the stars were also eager to limit the number and kind of roles they performed, specializing their vehicles much more than leading actors in stock companies had usually been able to do. Soon after Macready started the practice in England, Forrest held the first play contest in America in 1828. This initial competition netted him *Metamora, or The Last of the Wampanoags*, by John Augustus Stone, the most popular play of his career. Eight more contests brought two more successful vehicles, *The Gladiator*, by Robert Montgomery Bird, and *Jack Cade*, by Robert T. Conrad. By 1855, over a million Americans had seen Forrest in one or more of these heroic melodramas. Despite his phenomenal success in these vehicles, Forrest paid his playwrights nothing beyond the initial prize money and third-night benefit, little more than the traditional remuneration for new plays. The elevation of stars within the stock system continued the subjugation of playwrights in the productive relations of the theatre.

Other stars hoping to duplicate Forrest's success held dramatic contests or commissioned American authors to write for them (and typically paid them even less than Forrest did). Wallack's and Booth's contests brought them *Tortesa, the Usurer* and *Sertorius*, respectively, both profitable additions to their repertoires. Minor stars William Pelby and Josephine Clifton also paid for prize plays. Next to Forrest, James E. Murdock performed in the most new heroic dramas by American authors: he produced *Conrad, King of Naples*; *Velasco*; *Witchcraft, or The Martyrs of Salem*; and *Desoto*. These star vehicles were "a sort of mono-drama, or play with one absorbing character," as one critic complained. Play contests and commissions declined in the 1840s and nearly ceased in the 1850s. One critic mocked the purported interest of the stage Yankee Dan Marble in fostering "native genius" through an 1851 play contest as "mere lather and prunella." For most of the Jacksonian period, however, and especially during the 1830s, stars won public applause by sponsoring and performing new American plays.[15]

Audience desire for sincere individuality in their stars led them to confuse the personality of the actor with the type of role he or she usually performed, a confusion that continues to this day. Not only newspaper reports, but the stars themselves fostered this confusion. Recounting her 1845 debut in her autobiography, star actress and occasional playwright Anna Cora Mowatt Ritchie focused on details which intentionally blurred the distinction between her fright as a performer and the plight of the character she was portraying:

In the fifth act, Pauline's emotions are all of calm and abject grief—the faint, hopeless strugglings of a broken heart. My very weakness aided the personation. The pallor of excessive fatigue, the worn-out look, tottering walk, and feeble voice suited Pauline's despair. The audience attributed to an actor's consummate skill that which was merely a painful, accidental reality.[16]

Here indeed was total sincerity; if Mowatt is to be believed, she wasn't acting at all. The opposite side of this coin, especially for women stars of ingénue roles, was the increased difficulty they encountered when their public reputation contradicted the innocence of the character type they played. When manager Thomas Hamblin's star protégé Miss Missouri died in mysterious and probably immoral circumstances in 1838, newspaper writers dug as deeply into the dirt of the scandal as contemporary mores would allow. The nineteenth-century star network has many legacies. The public desire to watch actors playing "themselves" continues to be one of the most stultifying.

Minor actors supporting the stars were never expected to mesh their various stage roles with their personalities; indeed, they weren't expected to be very good in any role. As one manager noted of starring engagements, "The minor parts are filled in such a manner that all gratification derived from the talents of a superior actor is marred by the miserable bungling and worse grammar of those who are deemed of too little importance to attract the notice of even a paid critic." Ample evidence supports this contention. When *The Gladiator* premiered in 1831, the worried playwright of Forrest's vehicle reported that most of the secondary performers "were horribly imperfect" in their lines. Although few critics of the performance even mentioned the stock actors, one went out of his way to compliment the manager for "having taken great care" to cast the most incompetent actors as characters who are killed so that their "timeless deaths do not draw to an unnecessary extent upon the sympathies of the audience." Starring constructed the unique individuality of the itinerant "genius" in part by contrasting him or her to the bumbling anonymity of the actor's support.[17]

The journal of Harry Watkins, a minor actor in the late 1840s and 1850s, provides revealing insight into the daily lives of stock actors hired to support the stars. A former soldier, young Harry took up acting in 1845 with no more training than occasional performances with his regiment. Watkins soon discovered that he had to travel continually to find work, since few of the smaller companies hired for an entire season. Several of his journal entries recount the perfidy of managers: they paid him irregularly, gave the best supporting roles to older actors, and broke their contracts with him whenever they pleased. Especially galling to Watkins was the treatment accorded the stars and their disdain for their fellow actors. On October 10, 1848, Watkins wrote:

Forrest in *Othello*. They treat Forrest as if he were a God. . . . Thorne [the manager] fawns on him like a spaniel. During last night's performance of *Damon and Pythias*, I waited for Forrest to meet me (Lucullus) at the change of scene, but he did not come. I then went on stage and spoke a speech, *ad lib*—after a while he came rushing on, mad enough. When the scene was over he called me into his dressing room and told me that I had no business to go on—that it made it palpable to the audience that something was wrong behind the scenes. And that's what I got for trying to save the situation for a great actor! He kills every part in the piece but his own.

Despite these and other setbacks, Watkins eventually achieved modest success as a manager and occasional playwright. His experiences as a stock actor in the late 1840s probably typified those of others hired to support the stars.[18]

No actor in the star network was as ill used and as poorly paid as the supernumerary. Given the desire of heroic stars to be seen addressing a stage full of citizens, commanding a large army, or causing an entire city to tremble, the number of supers employed by managers increased with the popularity of stars. Usually hired for the run of a star's appearance and paid only a dollar a day, supers rarely worked for an entire season. Most had little or no rehearsal time, poor costumes, cramped, unheated dressing rooms, and no respect from managers, stock actors, or star-crazed audiences. When their ragged, uncertain appearance on stage sometimes produced "long horse-laughs in the most serious and affecting scenes," reviewers invariably blamed the supers themselves for their unwitting errors. "With what a noble tranquility they pass through a revolution or an earthquake; and how some of the ladies hold up their dresses from the dust, while flying from the eruption of Mt. Vesuvius," cracked one critic. Harried, mocked, underpaid, and often unemployed, the supers were the unskilled laborers of a stock system warped by the aggrandizement of the stars.[19]

The stars' use of stock companies turned theatre troupes into "distributive intermediaries" of the stars' talents. As Raymond Williams explains, this type of productive relationship occurs when an artisan or group of artisans sells its commodity, in this case theatrical entertainment, not directly to the public "but to a distributive intermediary, who then becomes, in a majority of cases, his factual if often occasional employer." Although stars did not hire stock companies and rent theatres, they exerted substantial control over these means of production and used them to facilitate their profit taking. The stars pushed stock actors into minor roles, subjugated playwrights to their needs, and grabbed as much money and fame as they could wrest from weakened managers. Forrest, for example, usually demanded and received a clear half of the receipts of the night, leaving the manager to pay salaries and expenses as best he or she could. Late nineteenth-century actor Otis Skinner recalled that "caste distinctions were observed" whenever a star rehearsed with a stock company.[20]

Skinner's observation, which echoed Watkins' view from below, exaggerated the situation somewhat. The real distinction between stars and the utility people in the stock company was based not on inherited caste but on socioeconomic class; the star network turned stars into protocapitalists and stock actors into workers. Indeed, like their counterparts among shoemakers and carpenters who elevated themselves from craftworkers to capitalists in the mid nineteenth century, most stars thrust themselves into the new business class by climbing up the backs of their peers. In the process, they flattened the traditional hierarchy of productive relations in stock companies by turning actors and even playwrights into hands necessary only for support. When a stock company hired a star, it also bypassed elite control through patronage and flung the business of the theatre squarely into the marketplace. Stars charged what the market would bear for their services.

The new network of star engagements benefited other protocapitalists besides the stars themselves. A few company managers, most of whom continued to work for the shareholder owners of their troupes, created minor stars. These stars remained contractually committed to their managers and earned their distributive intermediaries handsome profits through their appearances at their own and others' theatres.

After Forrest made his first big splash at the Bowery Theatre in 1826, manager Charles Gilfert, for instance, hired out the young star to other managers for two years. Gilfert demanded four hundred dollars per performance and paid Forrest only forty of it, pocketing the difference. Gilfert's successor at the Bowery, Thomas Hamblin, launched three in-génues as stars in the 1830s, hoping to cash in on their success. During the 1840s, after Hamblin had purchased control of the Bowery company, he controlled the touring of John R. Scott, a minor star popular with working-class audiences.

Ethelbert A. Marshall went further than other managers in exploiting the public's hunger for stars. A contemporary described Marshall as a "quiet" man with "energetic business habits, tact, bland and amiable manners, and social and sagacious perceptions." Marshall, who was never an actor, became the first capitalist to dominate the American theatre. Understanding better than his contemporaries the economic implications of the new network, Marshall not only monopolized the tours of his stars but displayed their talents in enormous theatres so as to capitalize fully on their drawing power. Further, he was the first to move to mostly all-star seasons at his main theatre by featuring a succession of stars and employing a skeletal stock company which mounted very few productions of its own.[21]

Marshall began building his empire in 1840 when, with William Dinneford, he took over the management of the Walnut Street Theatre in Philadelphia. Dinneford withdrew from the struggling company the next year, but Marshall hung on, gradually pulling his theatre through the worst months of the depression in the early 1840s. In the middle of the decade, Marshall turned more exclusively to star entertainment, featuring Forrest, Booth, Wallack, Cushman, and others at the Walnut. Since he also controlled the Holiday Street Playhouse in Baltimore and the Washington City Theatre in the District of Columbia by this time, Marshall could offer American stars long engagements and convenient steppingstones on their journeys to theatres in the South—advantages no other manager could match. In 1848 Marshall made the most daring move of his career when he took over the joint management of the failing Broadway Theatre in New York. Built to accommodate 4,500 spectators but hobbled by a stock-only approach to production, the Broadway floundered during the first months of its existence. During the 1848–49 season, Marshall bought out his partner and invested in costly spectacles and stars to attract the public. His gamble paid off, aided by the timely burning of the Park Theatre in December of 1848. By 1850, with control of the largest playhouse in America, European agents contracting operatic and legitimate stars for American tours, and the management of tributary theatres in Philadelphia, Baltimore, and Washington, D.C., E. A. Marshall had established himself as the star-maker of the American stage.[22]

Marshall consolidated and extended his empire in the early 1850s but could not prevent its demise in the last years of the decade. He formed an alliance with theatre owners in Cincinnati, Louisville, Saint Louis, and New Orleans, in which he agreed to tour his stars to their theatres provided that they, in return, gave him a cut of the profits and refused to engage foreign stars not under his management. And Marshall took out advertisements in London newspapers to insure that foreign stars understood the terms of his monopolistic control. The first cracks in his system appeared in the mid 1850s when the Broadway Theatre, the cornerstone of his empire, began to lose business-class patronage because of its location too far downtown and its proximity to Barnum's American Museum theatre. These factors and others, plus the panic of 1857, caused Marshall to sell the Broadway in 1858. He left New York and managed the Philadelphia Academy of Music for several more years before his death in 1881.

Unlike later merchandisers of theatrical entertainment, however, Marshall exerted incomplete control over his product. American stars, especially the big names, could arrange to work outside of Marshall's circuit or bargain with him for favorable terms. Cushman, for instance, who had managed the Walnut Street Theatre for Marshall in the early forties, often struck deals with her former boss. Their correspondence suggests that he needed the American stars more than they needed him. For Marshall not to have accommodated some of their demands would have induced Cushman, Wallack, Forrest, and the rest to arrange their tours with other managers and, in the long run, would have undermined Marshall's control of the foreign star market. Then too, the American stars probably appreciated Marshall's booking system since it made their tours much easier to plan. Economically, itinerant starring was a part of the wide-open market capitalism of the antebellum era, too fluid to be controlled, much less monopolized, for long.[23]

Forrest was the most popular American star of the Jacksonian stage.

To his contemporaries, Forrest seemed built for stardom: "His figure was symmetrically proportioned and suggestive not only of perfect health and herculean strength, but of a certain kind of grandeur." Perhaps Forrest's greatest attribute was his voice. In an 1872 obituary, one reviewer remarked:

> No living man, perhaps, could vie with Forrest in the richness and spleddor [sic] of his tones. His voice was the voice of Magog: full, mellow, pervading, tender, round. His softest tones filled and penetrated the largest theatre, while when roused to the fullest dramatic frenzy, its [sic] loudest were as the blasts of a trumpet and, aided by the magnificent stature of the man, gave to his feigned passion the grandeur of giants.

Like Kean, with whom he had acted early in his career, Forrest shocked his auditors by jumping from conversational tones to energetic bursts of passion. Forrest's style, however, was more athletic than that of the English star. During Forrest's first London tour in 1836, one typical English reviewer found his acting more "powerful" but less "spiritual" than Kean's. Overall, the critic remarked on Forrest's "simplicity, sincerity, and energy" as the dominant characteristics of his style.[24]

Forrest, ever sensitive to his public reputation, lapped up the hero worship lavished on him by American audiences. Even his paid biographer, William R. Alger, admitted that "nothing else could have given him so much pleasure or have been so stimulating to his ambition as this idolatry from the masses." Coming to believe that hero worship was his just due, Forrest grew incapable of self-criticism. Although he had worked assiduously early in his career to control and shape his power, Forrest took fewer chances as a performer after 1840. In his personal life, too, Forrest fed on his own glory, gaining a self-righteous sincerity and defensiveness that lashed out at his wife, his critics, and other enemies he believed to be conspiring against him. He knew he had faults, he told Alger, "but I would not change the honest vices of my blood for the nefarious hypocrisies and assumed virtues of my malignant detractors."[25]

Forrest capitalized on all the possibilities for hero worship emerging with the new star network, conventions which he, as much as anyone, helped to shape in the United States. Casting himself as the munificent benefactor of struggling young authors, Forrest pumped his play contests for all the publicity he could get. In fact, all the playwrights who won awards had written plays before. He transformed the curtain speech from a simple thank-you into a full-blown oration. When the Forrest Life Guards, in full-dress uniforms, came to watch his *Corio-lanus*, Forrest lectured them after the show for twenty minutes on the virtues of self-help. At the same time, Forrest continued some of the traditional conventions of stock-company theatre, such as underpaying playwrights and taking benefit performances, usually one at the close of each two-week engagement. Benefits, of course, made no sense for stars who could gross $33,000 in one season, as Forrest did in 1837.

Relying mostly on the representation Forrest projected of himself, American hero-worshippers of the star constructed a public image of Forrest strikingly at odds with the historical man. Believing that For-rest sincerely played himself in his heroic roles, his admiring public painted him as a self-made success, a child of nature, an iron man of Napoleonic power, and an artifact of God's handiwork. This image is important for three reasons. First, since the public's impression of the star preceded and fused with the appearance of the actor on stage— especially after 1840, when Forrest's public image was set—his image conditioned audience response to his performances. Second, Jackso-nian Americans saw in Forrest the main attributes of heroism they also perceived in Andrew Jackson. Finally, beneath this general construc-tion of the hero shared by the president and the actor lay the antago-nistic ideologies of republicanism and liberalism; Forrest's public im-age was a deeply conflicted representation.

Early in Forrest's career, the *New-York Mirror* marveled that the young star "had ascended so far in so short a period." For this reporter, Forrest's self-made success was the reason for his popularity: "Disdain-ing to copy even the most celebrated and perfect models, the incessant flashes of excellence which enlighten his path all emanate from the fire of genius within. His beauties are all his own. He never borrows, but trades upon his own capital, which is daily increasing in almost geo-metrical progression." This assertion is revealing nonsense. Like other actors, Forrest drew on personal capital that was uniquely his own, but he modeled his style primarily on Kean's. The majestic formality of Thomas A. Cooper, a transplanted Englishman, was also an early influ-ence. Few of his fans, however, were willing to admit that their Ameri-can-born hero may have picked up some tips from English-born stars.

For many Jacksonians, Englishmen were either villainous aristocrats or effete fops. In contrast, Forrest was often pictured as a powerful man of the people unafraid to get his hands dirty: "It is no painted shadow you see in Mr. Forrest, no piece of costume . . . , but a man, there to do his four hours of work brawnily [sic], it may be, and sturdily, and with great outlay of muscular power, but there's a big heart thrown in." The myth of Forrest as a symbol of America drawing strength from inner resolve and owing his success to no one but himself flooded the obituary pages after his death in 1872.[26]

Frequently this image mixed with the belief that the actor drew his uniqueness and virtue directly from the American soil:

> One thing must be said of Edwin Forrest, now that he lies cold in the tomb—he never courted popularity; he never flattered power. Importuned a thousand times to enter society, he rather avoided it. . . . His genius developed itself irresistibly, even as a spire of corn will shoot up despite encumbering stones.[27]

Here is Forrest as a natural man, a "spire of corn" spurning the unnatural power and pomp of society. Never mind that the society of Willis and finally Sinclair rejected rather than importuned him, or that Forrest did all he could to court the popularity of male Jacksonians.

That Forrest was a self-made American with agrarian roots was important to his fans, but it was not enough to inspire their hero worship. What attracted many of them to the star was Forrest's Napoleonic aura. One reviewer, for instance, prefaced his comments on the superstar with a paragraph on the "genius" of Napoleon. He noted that "the naturally energetic man possesses the prerogative of breaking from the trammels of common regulation and of creating new laws for others to obey, new models for others to copy. With these sentiments [in mind]," he continued, "we sit down to devote a few lines to Forrest." The reviewer then complimented the star on his power to excite, his "range of parts," the sincerity of his emotions, and his "majesty and grace." Forrest's image as the Napoleon of his profession affected at least one of his playwrights, Robert Montgomery Bird. Next to a speech in a draft of *The Gladiator* describing Spartacus' rapid climb to power on the "regal necks" of his adversaries, Bird penned the note, "Improve this idea, alluding to Bonaparte." Given the historical frame of the play's action, the idea was impractical, and Bird never made the change. But his notation points up the ease with which Jacksonian imaginations associated the popularity and heroic qualities of Forrest with the success and charisma of the French emperor.[28]

An idealized image of Napoleon fascinated many Jacksonian Americans. Plays, books, and pictures celebrating Napoleon's military campaigns and imperial rule enjoyed widespread popularity. Emerson praised the French emperor as a representative modern man for his will power and creativity. Forrest himself admired Bonaparte and prominently displayed his portrait in his study. He once trumpeted: "Wherever [Napoleon] passed he has left traces of his greatness stamped in indelible characters. A thousand imperishable monuments attest the magnificence of his genius."[29] Like many Jacksonians, Forrest overlooked Napoleon's despotic regime and his drive for European domination to celebrate the emperor as the champion of the French people against the aristocracy of Europe. Indeed, Forrest partly modeled himself on the Corsican upstart; donning the imperial wreath of American greatness, Forrest eagerly confronted the fame of European stars.

Specifically, Forrest challenged the English star William Charles Macready, a ready-made symbol of European aristocracy for ardent Jacksonians. Forrest's actions between 1845, when he hissed Macready in Edinburgh, and 1849, when his fans fomented the Astor Place riot to chase Macready off the American stage, were petty and vindictive, hardly in accord with his public image of Napoleonic majesty and power. Forrest justified his ill-mannered act in Edinburgh by claiming that Macready and his minions were conspiring, out of jealousy, to prevent the success of his second English tour—a charge that was never proven and was probably false. Apparently Forrest took no part in the plans to disrupt Macready's opening performance at the Astor Place Opera House, but he certainly encouraged them. The leaders of the mob, "Captain" Isaiah Rynders and E. Z. C. Judson (better known as Ned Buntline, the dime novelist), were Tammany Democrats, and Forrest had long been on friendly terms with Tammany Hall. (Three years later, after Forrest's divorce, Rynders arranged for the unfurling of the "people's verdict" banner to greet the star at the Broadway Theatre.) The ensuing riot, which turned bloody when the militia fired into the crowd, led to twenty-two deaths; but the mob had chased the aristocrat from the stage and vindicated Forrest's honor. Through it all, Forrest's

Edwin Forrest as Metamora, engraving by Rawdon Wright from a painting by Frederick S. Agate (Harvard Theatre Collection). Set against rugged mountains and jagged beams of sunlight, the image emphasizes Forrest's sublime and Napoleonic qualities.

admiring fans ignored his petulance and paranoia, and pictured their hero as a man of Napoleonic forbearance and resolve.

The values of masculine honor played a significant role in the public image of Forrest as a Napoleon of will power. Noting the personal qualities that Forrest brought to his roles, the Reverend William Alger, the star's friend as well as his official biographer, concluded:

> This imperial self-reliance and instinctive honesty, this unperverted and unterrified personality poised in the grandest natural virtues of humanity is the key note and common chord to the whole range of his conceptions. Fearless faithful manhood penetrates them all as the great elevating principle which makes the harmonies of one essential ideal.[30]

Indeed, it was just such an imperial construction of masculinity, neither honest nor unperverted, however, that led Forrest to divorce his wife and his fans to applaud him for it. No doubt Forrest's honorable manhood was a distinguishing feature of his major roles, penetrating, as the oblivious reverend would have it, the hearts and minds of his audiences. Some of his fans took their hero worship a step further and merged Forrest's Napoleonic will power with God's design. Objecting to those who termed Forrest's style melodramatic, actor-author Gabriel Harrison asked,

> Is Niagara unnatural and full of trick because it is mighty and thunders so in its fall? . . . Whenever I saw [Forrest] act I used to feel with exultation how perfectly grand God had made him. How grand a form, how grand a mind, how grand a heart, how grand a voice, how grand a flood of passion, sweeping all those to their mark in perfect unison.

Napoleon too had seemed to sweep all Europeans to their mark in perfect unison. Harrison's comment provides a fitting summation of Forrest's charismatic power over his fans. In it, the superstar is a natural force so compelling and so sublime that audiences are mesmerized by its might.[31]

In general, the image of heroism perceived by Forrest's fans was the same image seen in Andrew Jackson by worshipful Democrats. Historian John William Ward discerns three major strands in Jackson's public image: Jackson as yeoman farmer, as agent of God's will, and as

Napoleonic man of iron. Like American notions of Forrest, considerable distance separated the myth of the hero from the truth of the man. Many Americans pictured the slave-owning planter of Tennessee as an ideal tiller of the soil who steered a middle, moral course between the decadence of Europe and the savagery of the frontier. Further, as an instrument of God, Andrew Jackson could do no wrong on the stage of history, though his personal life might be blemished by minor sins. Finally, many Democrats believed Jackson was a Napoleonic man of destiny who had forged his success through sheer will power and honorable bravery by defeating the British at New Orleans, routing the American Indians in Florida, and crushing the foes of democracy in the 1828 election. Ward notes that Jackson's public profile fit the era's general image of heroism: "The symbolic Andrew Jackson is the creation of his time. Through the age's leading figure were projected the age's leading ideas. Of Andrew Jackson, the people made a mirror of themselves." So did they too of Edwin Forrest.[32]

If Jacksonian Americans used the Jackson-Forrest mirror to reflect back a heroic image of themselves, it was an image shimmering with ideological divisions and contradictions. Forrest as self-made yeoman American, for instance, drew almost equally on the antagonistic traditions of republican and liberal ideology. On the one hand, this imagined hero, by maintaining his roots in the soil of an Arcadian past, preserved his republican simplicity, virtue, and independence. This is the Forrest who does his work "brawnily" and spurns the entrapments of luxury and decadence in "society." On the other hand, the young actor had "capitalized" on the "fire of genius within" to vault above his humble beginnings and achieve international renown. But why would a virtuous republican want to become a protocapitalist star? And what was the cost to Forrest's republican citizenship of his liberal-minded striving? Surely one of the costs was the star's narcissism, manifested by his compulsive weightlifting and preening self-glorification. These questions are left unanswered, however, in the rush of journalists and others to marry his republican virtue to his liberal success.

A more serious contradiction is evident in the rift between Forrest as a battler for republican honor and as a Napoleon of liberal power. To his ardent fans, Forrest, like Napoleon and Jackson, vindicated male republican honor through his triumphs over the aristocrats at Astor Place and his postdivorce engagement at the Broadway Theatre. But the relation of the code of honor to classical republicanism had always been ambiguous. Honorable republicans might fight against tyranny for their independence, but men also demonstrated their claim to an honorable reputation by dominating others. As the political philosopher Thomas Hobbes reminded seventeenth-century Englishmen, "To obey is to honor; because no man obeys them, whom they think have no power to help or hurt them." In Kenneth Greenberg's gloss of this Hobbesian insight, "those who seek honor must also seek power over others but must simultaneously be ever watchful that others do not attain power over them."[33] Forrest as the Napoleon of his profession both tweaked the noses of the urban elite and "created new laws for others to obey." What, then, was to insure that this embodiment of Niagara would not trample the republican rights of other Americans in his desire to maintain his honor? This contradiction gets at the central problem of charismatic stardom and Jacksonian democracy: could Americans in the 1830s and 1840s separate the worship of heroes from the practice of democracy, or did the one necessarily compromise the other? Answering this question requires a closer look at Forrest's audience, his plays, and his performances.

4. "Freedom! Revenge or Death!"

Much of Edwin Forrest's public persona as a Napoleonic hero was shaped by the roles he performed in his three most popular prize plays: *Metamora* (1829) by John Augustus Stone, *The Gladiator* (1831) by Robert Montgomery Bird, and *Jack Cade* (1835) by Robert T. Conrad. Although similar to romantic tragedies, these vehicles manifest a structural reliance on villainy and Providence that aligns them with the conventions of melodrama. Ostensibly concerned to assert the equality of all men, these heroic melodramas actually empower a charismatic hero and reduce the people to the status of victims. This contradiction between egalitarianism and charismatic authority also fractured the Jacksonians' commitment to democracy.

Having established his public persona as the Andrew Jackson of his profession by the mid 1830s, Forrest acted his popular vehicles before predominately Democratic audiences. By that time, most elite Whigs had stopped attending Forrest's performances. James E. Murdoch, another performer of heroic roles, reported that "many of the culti-vated frequenters of the theatre in Boston were prejudiced against Mr. Forrest for what they considered an offensively independent bearing which at times amounted to arrogance." On hearing that Forrest might be nominated for office by the Democrats, patrician New Yorker Philip Hone remarked in his diary that Forrest had "no claim that I ever heard of to the honor of representing the people of New York in Con-gress, but that of exciting, by dint of loud words and furious stamps, the pit of the Bowery Theatre to raise their shirt sleeves high in the air and shout 'Hurrah for Forrest.'" Forrest's flirtation with the Democratic nomination for Congress in 1838—a position he finally declined—probably pulled other upper-class Whigs out of his audience as well. By the time of the Astor Place riot in 1849, one actor stated bluntly, "The people loved Forrest and followed him, while those who claimed to be in the elite admired and applauded Macready."[1]

The elite aside, a demographic profile of Forrest's audience in the Northeast would include nearly all other social and economic groups of theatregoers. Writing in 1863, an editor of *Harper's* magazine ex-pressed astonishment at meeting a New Yorker who had not watched the superstar on stage: "If he had said he had never seen Trinity Church, or the Astor House, or the Hospital, it would have been strange; but to aver that he had never seen Forrest was to tax credi-bility." As Artemus Ward put it succinctly in 1860, "Ed draws like a six-ox team."[2]

By the mid 1830s Forrest was already attracting significant numbers of working-class fans in New York. He played as often at the Bowery as at the Park; and even when performing at the higher-priced Park The-atre, Forrest drew workers there to watch him, as is evident from elite comments on their loss of control to "the people" at that theatre and elsewhere. Walt Whitman, theatre critic in the forties for the *Brooklyn Eagle*, captured the rowdy working-class fraternalism of the Bowery Theatre in the late 1830s in his recollection of a typical stage entrance by Forrest: "The whole crowded auditorium and what seeth'd in it and flash'd from its faces and eyes (to me as much a part of the show as any) [burst] forth in one of those long-kept-up tempests of hand clapping—no dainty kid-glove business, but electric force and muscle from perhaps two thousand full-sinew'd men." By the end of the decade, several in the elite were cursing the Bowery as a sinkhole of working-class degradation, but Hamblin pocketed much more than the wages of sin from his animal shows, historical melodramas, and American stars.[3]

Before E. A. Marshall took over the Walnut Street Theatre in 1840, Francis Wemyss leased the building in 1834 and established his company as the Philadelphia counterpart of the Bowery, including frequent appearances by Forrest. Wemyss's first order of business was to refurbish the interior of his theatre:

> Each tier of boxes was decorated with paintings representing some celebrated battle in the history of the United States. Around the dress circle were placed medallions of the heads of the presidents. Around the second tier, the heads of celebrated generals; and around the third, the heads of naval heroes. Between each medallion and its corresponding painting was a large burnished gold star, the whole forming on a pink background.

Here was a playhouse interior well suited to the patriotic heroics of Forrest's efforts! Recognizing Hamblin as the master of working-class entertainment, Wemyss formed an alliance with the irascible New Yorker which profited them both. The Philadelphia manager rented scripts, scenery, and costumes from Hamblin, once borrowing all the movable items of the Bowery's production of *Napoleon* for a "clear half of the receipts."[4]

During the 1840s, Forrest abandoned the Chestnut to play exclusively at the Walnut, by then under Marshall's leadership. Although Marshall may have attracted a slightly more upscale clientele to his Philadelphia theatre than had Wemyss, the Walnut continued to present many working-class melodramas, give benefits for working-class fire companies, and feature American stars like Booth, Murdoch, and Forrest. Marshall strove to attract much the same audience to his Broadway Theatre in New York. According to one nineteenth-century theatre historian, the Broadway Theatre would accommodate 4,500 persons, having seats for 4,000. There was an immense pit to which only men and boys were admitted. The price of admission [to the pit] was twenty-five cents and the seats were plain benches without backs, and on crowded nights the jam used to be terrific. The first and second galleries were called the dress and family circles. Three rows of benches were set apart in the latter for the accommodation of colored persons.

This and other evidence suggests a broadly based audience, probably dominated by white male workers but including some business-class fans and even some free African-Americans. This was the audience that cheered Forrest during his record-breaking engagement at the Broadway Theatre in 1852.[5]

Since theatregoing remained a predominately male activity at the Bowery, Walnut, and Broadway theatres in the two decades preceding 1855, Forrest's urban hero-worshippers must have been mostly men and boys—a conclusion that also fits with the welcome given the star after his divorce and with his public image. To judge from the prices and architecture of these theatres, the composition of Forrest's supporters at the Astor Place riot in 1849, and the fact that roughly 65 percent of the urban populations of Philadelphia and New York in 1850 were working-class, most of Forrest's fans in the 1840s were male workers.[6]

But not all workers went to the theatre. Some preferred union meetings or evangelical gatherings to the drinking and rowdiness of playgoing. Others could ill afford frequent theatrical visits. Labor historian Sean Wilentz estimates that the average yearly income of a skilled worker in 1850 in New York City was a mere three hundred dollars. At the same time, the minimal living costs for an average-sized family were over five hundred dollars.[7] On the other hand, urban working-class families often included working wives and older children, although their wages were generally far below an adult male's. Thus a married working-class couple might get to the playhouse occasionally. Further, young, unmarried workers, even some unskilled ones, probably had enough money to go to the theatre more often. Contemporary accounts, condescending and vague though they are, give the impression that young men made up the bulk of the audience. In his report on the Bowery audience of the late 1840s, journalist George Foster noted the presence of "the shop-woman," "the map-colorer," and "the straw-braider" (three female occupations), in addition to several male types, including the "butcher-boy, the mechanic with his boisterous family, [and] the b'hoy in red flannel shirt-sleeves and cone-shaped trousers." Social historian Christine Stansell concludes that working-class society on the Bowery was primarily a "youth culture."[8]

Forrest's working-class fans were predominately traditionalists in orientation. Historians Paul Faler and Alan Dawley define three types of response among workers to the incursions of capitalism after 1820. Some mechanics, the "radicals," formed political parties and labor unions to demand better pay, the ten-hour day, free public education, and an end to the monopoly power of the rich. By the late 1830s, radical action had forced modest gains in public education, working conditions, wages, and hours of employment for skilled journeymen. With few exceptions, the panic of 1837 and the following six years of depression obliterated these achievements, which were not won again until the 1850s. Other workers, the "revivalists," looked to religion, temperance, hard work, and deference to their employers as the path of success. These workers, a small minority in the 1830s which increased rapidly during the depression, tended to model themselves on the emergent business class. The obligations of industry, frugality, and temperance meant no theatregoing for the revivalists. Radicals, on the other hand, might occasionally venture from their union meetings and Tom Paine clubs to take in a show.[9]

The traditionalists, the third and most numerous group of urban workers from the 1830s through the early 1850s, constituted the overwhelming majority of workers who enjoyed Forrest at the Bowery, Walnut, and Broadway theatres. Because traditionalists tended to be skilled or semiskilled workers laboring at home, out of doors, or in small neighborhood shops, most were able to continue some of the work habits of preindustrial times: beginning work when it suited them, taking frequent breaks for horseplay and alcoholic refreshment, and, in general, working at their own pace regardless of the clock or the customers. Traditionalists sought their social life in the volunteer fire companies, taverns, and street corners of their neighborhoods; they shunned the debating societies of the radicals and the churches and temperance halls of the revivalists. In addition to theatregoing, traditionalists enjoyed contests of working-class honor such as cockfights, horse races, and boxing matches. For the most part, traditionalists sought self-esteem through honorable camaraderie, not self-denial, and success through the assertion of traditional artisan rights, not self-improvement.

These kinds of workers tended to vote for Jacksonian Democrats; indeed, most Jacksonians, working-class or not, shared a traditionalist orientation toward work, society, government, and enjoyment. Drawing on David Riesman's notions of "social character," historian Lawrence Kohl explains that white male Americans during the age of Jackson ranged along a continuum "from strongly tradition-directed to strongly inner-directed. Those toward the tradition-directed end of the continuum were more likely to join the Democratic ranks, while those more inner-directed were likely to be found among the Whigs." Kohl continues:

> The Democratic party appealed chiefly to those still living in the
> web of traditional social relationships. There was a security in such
> ties that was difficult to relinquish, though a new social order de
> manded that they abandon this personal world. Because their char
> acter structure was not well suited to modernity, modern institutions
> and modern social relations seemed constricting and degrading,
> rather than liberating and beneficial. They condemned the cold and
> heartless nature of Whiggish institutions and denounced those who
> would speed their development. Their accommodation to an imper
> sonal world was reluctant and grudging.

Specifically, Jacksonians objected to the impersonality of banks, large businesses, and the federal government; they tended to believe that insiders in these institutions with more power and wealth than they themselves had sought to control and oppress them. Consequently, drawing on both republican and liberal traditions, they urged the abolition of all legal monopolies and special privileges to reestablish what they took to be the natural equality of all white men. Their heroes, like Jackson, combined traditional honor and Napoleonic authority; Jackson himself, they believed, fought aristocratic power to restore republican independence and liberal equality.[10]

This is not to say that all of Forrest's fans voted for Jackson and the Democratic-Republicans, the party's full name. Although working-class districts in New York usually voted Democratic, those in Philadelphia and Boston were more evenly split between the two major parties. Also, many workers in northeastern cities in the 1840s voted for Know-Nothing candidates, antiforeign nativists who drew heavily on traditionalist values. Besides, some of Forrest's admirers were neither working-class nor male. But it is to assert that tradition-directed citizens—those men who judged their self-esteem on the basis of honor rather than dignity and felt more comfortable with republican rather than liberal values—constituted Forrest's core audience. Since, as Kohl asserts, these men were more likely to be Jacksonians than Whigs, Democrats were probably in the majority among his spectators in the theatres of the Northeast. Impressed by his muscular style, cheered by his self-made success, and awed by his Napoleonic force, such men applauded Forrest's triumphs onstage as well as off.

Forrest's success among Jacksonian Democrats with several of his prize plays led to the writing and production of similar romantic dramas. These included more dramas by Stone and Bird and romantic plays on Roman and Native American subjects by Richard Penn Smith, David Paul Brown, and George Miles written for Junius Brutus Booth, James E. Murdoch, and other stars.[11] Not all of these heroic melodramas followed the formula of *Metamora*, *The Gladiator*, and *Jack Cade*, of course, but these vehicles, especially the first two, established a model that was widely influential, if not slavishly copied. Like Forrest's plays, these romantic vehicles were set in exotic lands or historical periods, written in pseudo-Shakespearean verse, and overflowing with liberal and republican sentiments. Most also worked within what the literary historian Michael D. Bell terms "the conservative theory of romance," which attempts to synthesize historical facts with the writer's romantic imagination. Like Walter Scott and other conservative romancers, these playwrights attributed "the 'romantic' or 'poetic' qualities of the subjective imagination" to the reality of the historical events about which they were writing.[12] Conrad's *Jack Cade*, in other words, implicitly insists that the true story of this medieval peasant is also, luckily, brimful of heroic action, romantic characters, and poetic speech. The conventions of the historical romance granted the author the right to tidy up and even embellish the historical record, but rested their credibility on the factual outline of the story. The historical Cade, of course, did lead a peasant rebellion, just as Spartacus headed a

Roman slave insurrection, a Wampanoag chief resisted the Puritans, and the various other Romans, explorers, and indigenous peoples of these plays more or less accomplished what their playwrights claimed for them.

The success on the English stage of earlier dramas of conservative romance influenced the content of many of these plays, including Forrest's most popular melodramas. Three of these in particular—*Virginius* (1820) by Sheridan Knowles, *Brutus, or The Fall of Tarquin* (1818) by John Howard Payne, and *Pizarro in Peru* (1799), adapted by Richard Brinsley Sheridan from Kotzebue's original—helped to shape the plots and characters of *Metamora, The Gladiator*, and *Jack Cade*.[13] Knowles and Payne wrote their plays specifically for Kean, although it was Macready who popularized *Virginius* in the mid 1820s. British and American stars were performing these pieces when Forrest was perfecting his craft and rising in the ranks. Forrest, in fact, played roles in all three shows early and throughout his long career, though neither as often nor to as many people as his popular prize plays.

Virginius, Brutus, and *Pizarro*, like Forrest's successful vehicles, mix together family affection, rape, pitched battles, and madness to center on male heroes who are at odds with the present political order and who sacrifice their own happiness to attack villains oppressing their loved ones. Several contemporary critics noted that Stone borrowed the ending of *Metamora*, in which the American Indian chief stabs his wife to save her from the conquering white men, from *Virginius*. In Knowles's play, a sorrowing father stabs and kills his daughter to save her honor. *Metamora* is closer overall, however, to *Pizarro in Peru*. Like Kotzebue's Incan hero Rolla, Metamora stands above and between the decadent pleasures of the Europeans and the squabbling and savagery of his own followers. A virtuous norm between two immoral extremes, Metamora argues for peace with the Puritans and restrains his people from murder and torture. The plots of both plays show striking similarities as well. Both feature a Native American victory against the European invaders early in the action, and both involve the hero's rescue of a helpless victim from the enemy camp—an Incan child in *Pizarro* and the chief's wife Nahmeokee in *Metamora*. Finally, both end in the death of the hero (following, incidentally, a chase over a natural bridge) and the mourning of his passing by both Europeans and indigenous Americans. Stone, who had seen Forrest perform Rolla in *Pizarro* early in his career, had no compunctions about borrowing plot incidents from a play he knew had worked well for the star.

The differences between the earlier plays and Forrest's vehicles, however, point up the distance heroic melodrama traveled from sentimental and romantic tragedy. Despite their use of some of the character types and situations from *Virginius* and *Brutus*, Stone, Bird, and Conrad reduce the traditionally virtuous social order apparent in these two plays to the prerogatives of villains. In the three heroic melodramas, aristocrats use their power to oppress innocent people—seducing maidens, striking down mothers, and robbing the virtuous of the fruits of their labor. Jack Cade, for instance, tells his medieval English serf followers: "We bleed / To back their quarrels; coin our sweat and blood / To feed their wassail and maintain their pomp" (II,3). Cade's chief antagonist is the brutal Lord Say, who killed Cade's father and burned their home. In *Metamora*, set in seventeenth-century New England, Lord Fitzarnold and his Puritan cohorts both overtax the settlers and steal American Indian land. Spartacus in *The Gladiator* taunts his Roman captor with the immoral basis of the imperial city: "Look ye Roman: there is not a place upon these hills that cost not the lives of a thousand innocent men; there is no deed of greatness ye can boast, but it was achieved upon the ruin of a nation; there is no joy ye can feel, but its ingredients are blood and tears" (I,1).

Virginius and *Brutus* feature villains who have seized power too, but Payne and Knowles make it clear that Roman rule prior to tyrannical usurpation was just and benevolent. Indeed, several secondary characters in both plays remember the political past and plot with the hero to reestablish the old order. In Forrest's plays, on the other hand, traditional justice is tyrannical; greed, cruelty, and injustice are built into the traditional order and nothing but its complete overthrow will make any difference. Where the plays of Payne and Knowles feature a group of good patricians planning to overthrow a group of bad ones, Forrest's vehicles pit the people against all forms of patrician power; instead of leading a palace coup, Forrest's hero attempts to destroy the old order, root and branch. In *Virginius* and *Brutus*, the rebellions succeed in returning traditionally legitimate power to the virtuous of the ruling class. Although the revolutions against this class fail in *Jack Cade, Me-*

tamora, and *The Gladiator,* and all three heroes die, both sides join together at the end to celebrate the honor and glory of the people's martyred hero.

In the place of traditional political authority, Forrest's vehicles present a utopian vision of an Arcadian past. Before being dragged off to Roman slavery, Spartacus lived in Thrace "among the hills piping to his father's flocks" (I,1). Images of Thracian pastoral bliss motivate his slave revolt against Rome. Similarly, Jack Cade strives to return medieval England to a state of nature, a utopian realm he enjoyed in Italy where, states Cade, "the tiller is a prince [and] / No ruffian lords break Spring's fair promises" (I,4). Metamora, though not a shepherd or a farmer, also seeks to regain the land of his fathers. "Our lands! Our nation's freedom! Or the grave!" (V,3), he shouts in a battle cry that echoes the hero's demands in the other two plays. This dream of a utopian state of nature, though reliant mostly on a Lockean conception of natural equality, is also republican in its depiction of a virtuous citizenry living independently off the land. Yet republican government is hardly necessary in these plays since the bounty of nature renders any political order nearly superfluous. This desire for primitive, ungoverned equality plays no role at all in *Brutus* and *Virginius.*

More differences are apparent in these plays' conception of the hero. In *Pizarro in Peru,* Rolla is divided against himself, seeking both romantic love with an Incan woman and the victory of the Incas over the Spaniards—desires which the plot manages to set at odds with each other. Likewise, Brutus and Virginius struggle against internal conflicts involving their love of family and their duty to Rome. Forrest's heroes, on the other hand, are completely heart-whole. Suffering from no inner doubts or guilty consciences, these heroes can direct all their attention to the external problem of combating villainy. Metamora defies Puritan resolve and Indian duplicity. Spartacus faces the military might of Rome and jealous rebellion from his own brother. Neither hero, despite occasional moments of despair, doubts the righteousness of his cause or even questions his strategy to win his people's freedom. In the midst of similar troubles, Jack Cade glories in adversity:

> The wren is happy on its humble spray,
> But the fierce eagle revels in the storm.

Terror and tempest darken in his path;
He gambols 'mid the thunder; mocks the bolt
That flashes by his red unshrinking eye,
And, sternly joyful, screams amid the din:
Then shakes the torment from his vigorous wing,
And soars above the storm, and looks and laughs
Down on its struggling terrors. Safety still
Rewards ignoble ease; Be mine the storm. (II,1)

Metamora, Spartacus, and Cade are yeomen men of iron with no chink in their armor.

Having strapped on their shields and bucklers for the war with aristocratic villainy, Forrest's heroes lose most of the vulnerability and gentleness of Virginius, Brutus, and Rolla. At stake here are different conceptions of heroic innocence. For Rolla especially, natural innocence is a key to understanding experience—an open state of mind which facilitates the search for purity and truth. Cade, Metamora, and Spartacus, on the other hand, wear their innocence as a badge to justify their vengeful fight for freedom. Rather than emphasizing the natural ties that men of different cultures have in common, as does Rolla when he voluntarily surrenders to Pizarro, Forrest's superheroes seek to heighten their differences, drawing uncompromisingly moral lines between Roman and barbarian, white man and Indian, aristocrat and peasant. Unlike the Peruvian hero, Cade, Metamora, and Spartacus do not use their innocence to gain enlightenment because they have nothing more to learn. Metamora is already "the grandest model of a mighty man" (I,1) at the start of the play. Like Cade and Spartacus, he is poised for action, not perception. The innocence of Forrest's heroes simply emboldens their Napoleonic will.

Further, Spartacus, Cade, and Metamora are not only generous fathers and exceptional fighters like the heroes of *Virginius* and *Brutus*; Forrest's characters, following the Jacksonian definition of heroism, are also Natural Men and God's Chosen Instrument on earth. Nature speaks directly to Metamora: "The high hills sent back the echo, and rock, and ocean, earth, and air opened their giant throats and cried with me, 'Red man, arouse! Freedom! Revenge or death!'" (III,1). Nature also voices God's commandment to Cade:

The storm broke as heaven's high masonry were crumbling
And the wide vault, in one unpassing peal,
Throbbed with the angry pulse of Deity.

.   .   .   .

I heard the genius of my country shriek
Amid the ruins, calling on her son,
On me. (I,4)

Spartacus, too, is called by God through nature to lead his people,
Moses-like, to the promised land of Thrace.

Unlike the protagonists of romantic tragedy, Forrest's heroes are
charismatic leaders, called by God to deliver their people from villainy.
Cade's presence in England answers the prayers of Father Lacy, "the
peasant's priest," for divine rescue from aristocratic bondage. Even a
pagan Indian chief may be the instrument of the Almighty. Metamora's
worship, "though untaught and rude, flows from the heart and Heaven
alone must judge of it" (I,1). Heaven's judgment is soon known. An innocent white maiden sobbing on the grave of her parents calls on God
to save her from Lord Fitzarnold's rapacious intentions, and Metamora's voice from within the tomb responds, "Hold! Touch her not!" (V,1).
Then Metamora, who had escaped from the Puritan jail through a secret passage ending in the monument, bursts through its doors, rescues
the girl, and slays the villain. The hero's Christ-like emergence from
the tomb cements his divine connections. The God of Metamora, Spartacus, and Cade is the Christian God of judgment.

If the Almighty is backing the hero's quest for his people's freedom,
however, why does this quest end in failure and the death of the hero?
Metamora's defense of his people leads to the slaughter of his tribe, his
wife and child, and himself. The Romans kill Spartacus and most of his
followers and crucify the rest. Although Cade dies, he does win a charter of freedom for the peasants. Jacksonian audiences knew, however,
that the promise of this charter—roughly captured in Cade's statement, "There are no poor where freedom is; / For Nature's wealth is
affluence for all" (I,4)—was never realized historically. These deaths
and failures, however, are part of God's plan too. Forrest's spectators
understood these melodramas as negative history lessons, examples
for the audience of what *not* to do when a charismatic redeemer tries
to lead you to freedom. As such, they partly recapitulated the lesson

believed by nearly all nineteenth-century Americans as fundamental to the history of humanity: the lesson of Christ's crucifixion.

Audiences understood Cade, Metamora, and Spartacus as symbols not only of Moses but also of Christ, mostly a militant Christ upsetting the tables of the moneychangers and prophesying doom for the sinners who disobey their Father's just commands. But each of these heroes is also given moments of meekness and mildness. Metamora, Cade, and Spartacus emanate love toward their wives and children, even toward victims who are nominally their enemies but innocent of any specific wrongdoing toward the people. Spartacus, for instance, treats a captured Roman woman with gentlemanly concern. In *Jack Cade*, the hero swings somewhat awkwardly between righteous wrath and base humility. In hiding with his family after the initial failure of his uprising, Cade stops Lord Say on the road and demands gold so that he might feed his starving child. When the nobleman refuses, Cade threatens to kill him, but cannot bring himself to commit a robbery and finally kneels to beg for bread. Republican Cade has just led a revolution, but liberal Cade refuses to compromise the sanctity of private property. Significantly, each of these melodramas features a Judas figure from the people who sells out to the enemy, causing the hero's death. In none of these plays are the people worthy of the hero's trust, goodness, or sacrifice. Hence the dramatic action of these heroic melodramas represents the promise, not the failure, of a partly secularized providential design: God has intervened in the history of his people by sending his Son to point the way toward future freedom and to die a martyr fighting for his cause.

Brutus and *Virginius*, on the other hand, are tragedies set in a completely secularized dramatic world. Both focus on a father's painful decision to kill his son or daughter in order to uphold Roman law. This conflict between fatherly affection and public duty is bereft of transcendental dimension; Payne's and Knowles's Roman characters don't even appeal for guidance to a Christian God. By inducing audiences to identify with the difficulties of fatherhood, these romantic tragedies legitimized much the same sort of paternalism as did fairy-tale melodramas. Forrest's vehicles, by inviting their Jacksonian spectators to applaud the heroic defense of the people against aristocratic oppression, reject paternalistic control. If tragedy, by definition, requires that the protagonist helps to cause his or her own fate, the role of villainy and the unseen hand of the Almighty in shaping the martyrdom of Forrest's yeoman Christs mandate a nontragic form for *Metamora, Jack Cade*, and *The Gladiator*. In effect, Jacksonianism shifted Forrest's vehicles out of the world of romantic tragedy and into the form of heroic melodrama.

The formula of these heroic melodramas follows a four-step progression. Each play begins by positing the possibility of a natural Arcadia of egalitarian freedom and introducing a hero in quest of this utopia for himself, his family, and his people. The first phase of the formula ends when the aristocratic rulers forcibly prevent the people from returning to the home they seek. In the second phase, the hero uses his charismatic, God-given power to mount a successful revolution against the oppressors. Next, the people desert and betray their Christ-like leader, and the aristocrats counterattack the hero's warriors. This leads to the fourth and last phase, in which the hero, bereft of allies, friends, and even wife and child, flings himself on the villains and dies a martyr for the republican freedom and liberal equality of his people. *Jack Cade, The Gladiator*, and *Metamora* devote more or less time and dramatic intensity to each stage and weave different subplots in and out of them, but follow this four-phase outline in their overall action.

Undergirding this dramatic formula was much the same mix of republicanism and liberalism evident in the yeoman ideal of Jacksonian ideology. According to a typical New York Democrat, the Jacksonians stood for "a perfect equality among mankind of legal, social, civic, and political privileges." Like Forrest's Spartacus, tradition-directed Democrats idealized the independence of yeoman farmers and denounced any law that would "necessarily subject one man to the power or influence of another." They worried that cities and commercial expansion threatened "all true independence and elevation of character." Some Democrats claimed that the new factories resulted in a labor force that was "bound hand and foot by a system of petty despotism as galling as ever oppressed the subjects of a tyranny in the old world." To regain the traditional independence and equality of the yeoman farmer, Jacksonian politicians opposed the monopoly power of the rich, in true republican fashion, but, like good liberals, never questioned the private ownership of property.[14]

The Democratic desire for a yeoman republic led Jacksonians, in a seeming contradiction, to advocate both limited government and a strong executive. Fearing that an active legislature would "compromise the principle of equality with that of property," Democrats voted against laws establishing corporations to build internal improvements like roads and canals. Since judicial discretion and legislative action had traditionally favored the propertied class, Jacksonians sought to curb their power by strengthening the presidency. In Democratic thinking as in Forrest's plays, governmental power is typically the means of oppression, not the way to republican virtue and liberal prosperity. Ironically from a modern point of view, tradition-directed Jacksonians looked to charismatic leadership to restrain governmental power. The Democratic theorist George Bancroft said of Andrew Jackson: "By intuitive conception, he shared and possessed the creative ideas of his country and his time; he enforced them with an immovable will; he executed them with an electric power that attracted and swayed the American people." Bancroft might as well have been speaking of Forrest's yeoman heroes and the peasants, American Indians, and former slaves in his plays.[15]

On the other hand, the traditional representatives of the folk in Bird's, Conrad's, and Stone's dramas lack the virtue of the Jacksonian people. Democratic leaders beating the drums for Manifest Destiny looked to hardy and industrious yeoman farmers to insure the continuation of agrarian egalitarianism. While heroic melodrama likewise praises the people in general, most members of the folk are unworthy of the hero's efforts on their behalf. Before Jack Cade's arrival in England, the peasants were confused and cowardly when facing aristocratic oppression. The superhero puts iron in their backbones when they fight the nobles, but they remain perplexed and divided when he is not among them. Later, the peasants refuse to give him shelter, fearing their help might endanger themselves. "Those citizens own no God / But Mammon" (III,1), comments one sympathetic character. In *Metamora*, a secondary hero dismisses the Puritan settlers as a "senseless crowd" (IV,1) for their hatred of Native Americans. The Wampanoags are no better than their adversaries; Metamora must intervene to save a helpless white man from his bloodthirsty tribe. Without Metamora and Cade to guide and protect them, these people would continue to wallow in unrepublican greed and illiberal savagery.

The Gladiator provides the best example of the fickle, childlike nature of the people. Early in the play Forrest's Jacksonian audience learned that Roman citizens

> Are something bauble-brained; and like to children,
> Pass qualmish by their needful medicines
> To snatch at sugary playthings. What do they
> In their elections? Faith, I have observed
> They ask not if their candidate has honor
> Or honesty, or proper qualities;
> But with an eager grin, "What is his wealth?"
> If thus and thus, "Then he can give us shows
> And feasts; and therefore is the proper man." (II,1)

Once freed by Spartacus, the former slaves are no different. A group of Germans foolishly leaves Spartacus's army to find their own way to their homeland and are cut down by the Romans. Pharasius, Spartacus's younger brother, leads fifty thousand of the hero's army in a vain attack on Rome itself, hoping to win pillage for his troops and glory for himself. When this fails, Pharasius betrays his brother, leaving Spartacus hopelessly outmatched in his suicidal attack on the Romans. In all three plays, the people themselves are implicated in the hero's death; they do not deserve his martyrdom.

Clearly, Forrest's yeoman heroes have honor, but the people he attempts to save do not. Gender relations in all three plays cast women as home-centered dependents, often the hapless victims of villainy. Typically, the central woman character is the wife of the yeoman hero who, lacking resourcefulness and heroism herself, must await rescue by her husband. The presence of Nahmeokee and her babe-in-arms in *Metamora*, for example, allowed Forrest to demonstrate fatherly affection and honorable pride toward his family, righteous rage and self-sacrifice when the Puritans capture them and he gives himself up to free her and his child, and piteous despair when they are killed at the end of the drama. "My wife, my queen, my Nahmeokee!" are Metamora's last words (V,5). These gender relations were imbued with the inequality that separated honorable, republican men from weak, dependent women. (Perhaps performing his yeoman heroes led Forrest to expect that all wives would happily cede center stage to their husbands. But Sinclair was no Nahmeokee.)

As extensions of the hero's honor, Forrest's dramatic wives and children were at least virtuous, which was more than most of the hero's supporters among the people could have claimed. This contradiction in the plays between the people in general, as the repository of virtue, and specific people as fickle cowards or even betrayers, occurred on a more covert level in Jacksonianism as well. As Lawrence Kohl points out, Democratic rhetoric generally sought to reassure and even flatter its tradition-directed voters. Concerned about their reputations and their lack of equality, tradition-directed Democrats needed to be told that they were honest, incorruptible, and the equal of any man. Other Jacksonian assertions, however, contradicted this generally sunny estimation of human nature. In a natural economy, argued the Democratic theorist George Camp, the virtuous will prosper by their "industry and frugality; while the largest accumulations will pass rapidly from the prodigal and licentious and reduce them and their posterity to a condition of want and dependence." The Calvinistic assumption underlying this widely shared Democratic belief is clear: if people were poor in Arcadia, they deserved to be, and the government should do nothing to save them from the consequences of their own corruption. As historian Rush Welter notes, the Jacksonian view of the just society "involved a deeply pessimistic view of human nature, in that they assumed that all men would do evil if they were given the political opportunity to do so. Hence they would diminish men's power to affect the lives of others through politics, while at the same time insisting that everyone confront his own destiny unaided." This Calvinistically tainted pessimism colors the conception of the peasants, settlers, American Indians, and former slaves in Forrest's plays.[16]

But if the people are inevitably greedy, cowardly, and "baublebrained," what are the chances for democracy? Significantly, antidemocratic hero worship also pervaded the typical romantic novels of the antebellum South, the region most attracted to Jacksonianism. The plots of narratives such as *The Valley of Shenandoah* by George Tucker, *Cavaliers of Virginia* by William Caruthers, and several of the novels of William Gilmore Simms feature conflicts between charismatic heroes and characters representing more-democratic possibilities. As critic Michael Kreyling notes, these southern heroes were typically the chosen of their people:

Heroism is self-evident; it is not subject to appeal. To deny heroism is to deny the absolutely ordained, an act of heresy or even blasphemy against the transcendent ideals of the people for whom the hero acts. Embedded in the figure of the hero, then, is the assumption of primacy in human society, or of singleness in history—the chosen society is so ordained that heroic figures (always male) by their very presence among a people bring that people to a new degree of self-conscious unity.

Likewise, the martyrdom of Forrest's heroes causes even the soldiers of the aristocrats to join with the people in worshiping the fallen superman for the final tableau. In such circumstances, discussing individual rights or taking a vote is blasphemy.[17]

A similar problem shadows the expectation of utopia in these plays. As in fairy-tale melodramas, God and the hero move the good characters of heroic melodrama toward a utopian conclusion. Fairy-tale plays gratify their audience's need for immediate wish fulfillment by providing a timeless home-sweet-home by the end of the show. Heroic melodramas, however, offer the reassurance of providential design but do not lead the chosen people to the promised land. How and when, then, is this liberal-republican utopia to be reached? Is it to occur within history or beyond it in some neoplatonic oneness of transcendental reconciliation? Will history stop when utopia is reached or will the Almighty's promise of political deliverance continue to recede into the future? At issue here, fundamentally, is the ability of Bird, Conrad, and Stone to fuse the neoplatonic, Greek notion of an ahistorical, abstract deity with the Judeo-Christian conception of a historical, personal God. The nature of providential design has important implications for the possibilities of democracy held out in these plays.

As usually happens in forms of popular entertainment, Forrest's playwrights fudge rather than fuse the dichotomy by incorporating a bit of both notions and ignoring inherent contradictions. Utopia is nigh at the end of *Jack Cade*, but the superstar who returned the peasants to this blissful oneness with God's nature is no longer alive, hardly a just ending to his and their travail. *Metamora*'s conclusion swings the other way, dooming him and his "race" and prophesying an eventual apocalypse for the conquering whites:

My curses on you, white man! May the Great
Spirit curse you when he speaks in his war voice
From the clouds! Murderers! The last of the
Wampanoags' curse be on you! May your graves and
The graves of your children be in the path the
Red Man shall trace! And may the wolf and
Panther howl o'er your fleshless bones, fit
Banquet for the destroyers. (V,5)

Here is no neoplatonic return to oneness, but a vengeful jeremiad looking to history for ultimate vindication. *The Gladiator* squats between
Jack Cade and *Metamora*; its ending attempts to project both a neoplatonic and a Christian victory for its hero. "There are green valleys
in our mountains yet. / Set forth the sails. We'll be in Thrace anon"
(V,7), says Spartacus with his dying breath. The Thracian Arcadia has
now become a Christian heaven, a convenient metaphor which allows
the hero to gain a kind of neoplatonic utopia and the hope of a Christian heaven at the same time. Poetic conceptions, of course, need not
fit neatly into philosophic categories, but Forrest's playwrights are more
evasive than purposefully ambiguous about the antinomies involved.

The inability of these melodramas to inscribe either history or utopia
or to synthesize these polarities pervades their structure and ideology.
On the one hand, these are historical, Christian dramas which focus on
a redeemer-hero whose strong personality shapes history and whose
martyrdom guarantees the eventual republican salvation of the people.
On the other hand, these are ahistorical, neoplatonic plays that depict
an elemental and perfect hero, who embodies the impersonal force of
a divinely imbued nature and strives to return his people to an abstract, liberal utopia beyond the vagaries of history. Likewise, the
Christian-historic and neoplatonic-utopian ideologies of these plays offer different solutions to the problem of evil. The long-range, historical
option promises divine vengeance against aristocrats in the future
while the short-range, utopian desire wipes out conspiring villainy at a
stroke. Either God or the superhero will take care of the Fitzarnolds,
Crassuses, and Says of the world. In neither scenario, however, do the
people play a role in securing either republican or liberal freedom for
themselves.

This ambiguity about history and utopia, plus its antidemocratic implications, was present in Democratic thinking as well. It pervades a key 1837 article on Jacksonian ideology by John L. O'Sullivan in *The Democratic Review*:

The [Democratic] Administration occupies a position of defense; the Opposition of attack. The former is by far the more arduous task. The lines of fortification to be maintained against the never-relaxing onsets from every direction are so extensive and exposed that a perpetual vigilance and devotion to duty barely suffice to keep the enemy at bay. The attacking cause, ardent, restless, ingenious, is far more attractive to the imagination of youth than that of the defense. It is, moreover, difficult if not impossible to preserve a perfect purity from abuse and corruption throughout all the countless ramifications of the action of such an executive system as ours, however stern may be the integrity and high the patriotism of the presiding spirit [i.e., President Van Buren] which, from its head, animates the whole.

Although the government of the United States was already a "perfect purity" for O'Sullivan and most other tradition-directed Democrats, somehow the villainous ingenuity of the "attacking cause" kept genuine utopia just out of reach. In O'Sullivan's phrasing, Democratic history was moving both forward and backward at once: forward toward more battles with the Whigs and backward to the purity of its origins. With a new charismatic leader in the presidency who "animates the whole," however, all the people had to do was mount the barricades. Like "the people" in Forrest's melodramas, Democratic voters were little more than supernumeraries in the eyes of their political leaders.[18]

Sullivan's military metaphors were no accident. Democrats thought of their strategies to win votes as military campaigns and frequently dramatized their military might through tightly drilled parades designed to separate and control the party rank and file. As political historian Jean Baker notes,

Democratic parades were invariably organized like a nineteenth-century army. . . . Led by a commander in chief, chosen by the parade's self-appointed organizers, the host was arranged in divisions and subdivided into company units of one hundred, officered by a captain, who as president of a Democratic society usually carried his unit's banner. Dressed in caps and capes resembling army uniforms, paraders met in the early evening and were handed the torches and transparencies they would carry during the march. Each division began on a parallel street, for the intent was to arrive simultaneously at the speakers' stand, thus creating among participants the sense of a huge mass of individuals being merged into the single element of the Democracy.

No doubt nineteenth-century stage managers envied the parade organizers' control over their supernumeraries. Nonetheless, the effect aimed at in heroic melodrama was much the same as at the climax of a Democratic march through the streets: a male chorus of cheers punctuating the oratory of a charismatic speaker who promised victory over aristocratic villainy. Baker borrows from Kenneth Burke to term such rituals part of the "secular prayer" of Democratic elections. The similitudes of torchlight parades and Forrest's melodramas circulated many of the same meanings for their participants.[19]

What was it about these events, both on the stage and in the streets, that induced such awe? A closer look at the rhetoric of Forrest's plays and his performance style—specifically their remote formality and their hortatory appeal—is necessary to understand why many Americans in the audience embraced both democratic egalitarianism and the antidemocratic hero worship of charismatic authority.

The persuasive power of heroic melodrama owes much to the generalized rhetoric of patriotism pervasive in the United States during the Jacksonian years. Historian of rhetoric Howard Martin notes the prevalence of generic rather than specific terms in Fourth of July orations, for instance. Likewise, rhetorician Richard Weaver comments on the ease with which most antebellum orators used such words as "freedom" and "morality" without bothering to define them. The typical orator, he states, "seems to be speaking *in vacuo*," his oration echoing "over broad areas" and calling up "generalized associations." The hero's rhetoric in Forrest's plays is no more specific; his definition of "freedom," for example, is vaguely Lockean and republican with nothing like the mention of a bill of rights to clarify the issue. Further, Martin notes an oratorical preference of allusion and epithet in the place of precise names: "Columbia Fair," for instance, instead of the United

States. Among Forrest's playwrights, Conrad and Stone carry these tropes to near-ridiculous extremes. Metamora is no mere indigenous chief, but "the noble sachem of a valiant race." Finally, Martin remarks on the prevalence in antebellum rhetoric of imagery drawn from three main sources: classical history and mythology, the Bible, and nature—all three, of course, primary sources of metaphor in Forrest's three prize dramas.[20]

In patriotic speeches and performances of heroic melodramas, orators and actors built their axiomatic and image-laden language into formalized arrangements of aural and visual signs. Antebellum orators strove for a cadenced flow of sound, punctuated occasionally by broad gestures and building majestically toward a climactic conclusion. One historian notes that the rhythmic arrangement of sonority and gesture was considered more important by speakers and auditors than the content of the speech: "People then, if not now, took straightforward satisfaction from hearing an exhibition of language mastery, matters of substance probably being of secondary consideration."[21] Audiences looked to actors, too, for an exhibition of language mastery. By emphasizing the pattern and climactic arrangement of the verse in his plays, Forrest conformed to the conventions of oratory in Jacksonian America.

Beyond the formality of the language itself, Forrest and other antebellum actors worked within a highly conventional system of poses and gestures which physicalized states of emotion for the audience. According to one acting manual, for instance, "rage or anger expresses itself with rapidity, interruption, rant, harshness, and trepidation. The neck is stretched out, the head forward, often nodding and shaken in a menacing manner against the object of the passion." "Courage," it stated, "opens up the countenance and gives the whole form an erect and graceful air." Broader movement on the romantic stage was also presentational and formulaic. Forrest's heroes strode with chest out and head held high while the villains in his vehicles skulked with "alternate brandishings of [their] legs, each of which manoevores [sic] constitutes in itself a separate and distinct gymnastic exploit," noted one commentator. Overall, melodramatic movement was highly patterned and pantomimically expressive. As one theatre historian concludes, the conventions of acting in Forrest's time presented to the audience "an immediately translatable and unified 'ritualized' physical expression of emotion."[22]

Complementing and adding grandeur to the formal pattern of language, gesture, and movement in the theatre was the remoteness of the stage from much of the audience. New and renovated theatres added room for more spectators. While 1820s theatres generally accommodated around 2,000 spectators, the Bowery held over 3,000 (4,000 after its 1845 renovation), and 4,500 could be stuffed into the Broadway. Midcentury patriotic speeches, too, were best delivered and heard by thousands of spectators. The physical remoteness of the actor-orator from his audience no doubt reinforced the remoteness of the rhetorical images and stage pictures from the spectators' notion of everyday reality. Such aesthetic distance, as Weaver points out, keeps in check "a kind of officious detail which would only lower the general effect." In a seeming paradox, the formality and remoteness of antebellum oratory and star acting led to some of the most emotion-packed speaking and performing ever witnessed in America.[23]

Antebellum orators worked carefully for maximum emotional affect by building moments of expected applause into the rhythm of their speeches. Similarly, playwrights filled their melodramatic star vehicles with "clap traps," electric moments meant to encourage audience applause. In theatrical performance, as at a Fourth of July speech, the audience expected the performer to energize those moments or, in stage parlance, to "make a point." Following his point, it was conventional for the actor to turn full front to the house or to rush to the side of the stage and acknowledge audience applause with a bow. Among mediocre actors and orators, such a performance style amounted to little more than manipulation. Better performers manipulated their audience too, of course, but gave them a large helping of sincerely felt emotion in return. As an 1827 acting manual used in America makes clear, formal gestures and poses, though helpful in inducing genuine emotion, were no substitute for the real thing: "If the actor cannot feel what he utters, it would be useless to attempt to make him run the gauntlet through a set of emotions by rule." As Carlyle understood, audiences needed to sense sincerity in their star actors and orators before worshipping them as heroes.[24]

Within these conventions, Forrest's sincerity was more the product of his straining muscles and thunderous voice than the result of his probing and embodying his own and his characters' vulnerabilities. In a review of the superstar's *Virginius*, an 1841 critic praised his moments of "revenge, hate, scorn, and indignation." Regarding those emotions that "belong to the 'melting mood,'" however, the critic added charitably that such feelings "lie farther beyond the circle of his genius and resources." Forrest's apparent fear of exposing his softer side probably accounted for the woodenness of his Macbeth and the general failure of his Hamlet, both of which roles require the actor to explore his own "womanish" fears. Forrest also liked to display the physical exertion sustaining his performance. "[Mr. Forrest] seems, at times, ambitious to secure the groundlings by a sudden entrance, impressive invocations to heaven, certain menacing falls of the brow, and numerous seizures of a sort of histrionic asthma or shortness of breath," wrote one critic. "He always labors as if his powers were taxed," wrote another.[25] Watching Forrest as Cade, Metamora, or Spartacus, then, involved the audience in a kind of double martyrdom: the death of the character and the suffering of the star, who appeared to drive himself to physical exhaustion to please his public. For both of these reasons, Forrest's agonized death scenes were often the high point of the show.

Among good actors today, "showing the work" is derided as a cheap means of gaining sympathy because the tactic calls attention to the actor and not to the role. As the above comments indicate, some nineteenth-century critics also objected to the strategem, although it was more frequently employed; audiences expected star performers to draw attention to themselves, and laboring "as if [one's] powers were taxed" was one way of doing it. Performance theorist Bert O. States notes that the self-expressive mode of acting, where "the actor seems to be performing on his own behalf," saying, "in effect, 'See what I can do,'" was common among nineteenth-century stars. Typically, they alternated this emphasis on their virtuosity with the other two "pronomial modes" of performance, the collaborative and the representational, says States.[26] Forrest's reputation for sincerity and the near identity between his own public image and the image of the protagonists in his heroic melodramas, however, allowed him to collapse the distinction between his self-expressive and his representational modes in performance. Thus when Forrest as Spartacus in *The Gladiator*

Edwin Forrest as Spartacus (Billy Rose Theatre Collection, New York Public Library for the Performing Arts, Astor, Lenox, and Tilden Foundations). Urging the gladiators to revolt, Forrest-Spartacus meets the viewer's gaze directly in this print. For most of his career, Forrest played the scene barechested to show off his well-muscled body.

shouted, "Freedom for bondmen! Freedom and revenge!" (II,3) he was speaking not only to the enslaved gladiators on stage, but directly to the audience as well. From the spectators' point of view, both character and star were urging them to support an issue dear to the heart of fervent Jacksonians: the people's assault on aristocratic privilege. In this and other instances, Forrest gained ideological power by merging his virtuosity with his mimetic talents to appeal directly for Jacksonian principles.

A direct appeal by a speaker to request audience support on a matter of general principle and urgent concern is the distinguishing characteristic of the hortatory style of address. Political scientist Murray Edelman's discussion of the political implications of the hortatory style is revealing in this regard. The hortatory style usually suggests an active role for the listeners in righting perceived wrongs, but actually renders them passive and dependent on their leaders. As Edelman concludes:

> The emotional fervor covert or overt in political argument and in reactions to it conveys a sense of the reality of the battle, the importance of the stakes, the gripping quality of the great drama of the state. Through participation in it emotionally, it becomes a medium of self-expression, a rite which helps the individual to reflect in action his own interest in, and relationship to what Lasswell has called a symbol of the whole. . . . [Consequently], hortatory rhetoric reinforces the tendency toward a quiescent response toward political acts and events.

Edelman's conclusion mirrors George Orwell's ascerbic remark that the "reduced state of consciousness" generated by most political oratory is wholly "favorable to political conformity."[27] Forrest's audiences participated emotionally in a generalized patriotic ritual when they heard the superstar in *Metamora, Jack Cade*, and *The Gladiator*. Like the hortatory public rhetoric of many other male Jacksonians, Forrest's performances evoked a republican past, affirmed broad principles for the present and future, and endorsed heroic action by a political hero. But besides marching to the polls occasionally to cast their ballots, spectators at his plays were invited to take no more political action than the supernumeraries on stage.

The generalized, hortatory style of the rhetoric in Forrest's heroic melodramas also steered clear of specific social problems. Nonetheless, some theatre historians have quoted approvingly a few contemporaries who believed that these plays, *The Gladiator* in particular, spoke out strongly on antebellum social issues. Walt Whitman wrote that Bird's melodrama was "as full of 'abolitionism' as an egg is of meat." And Bird himself prophesied that if "*The Gladiator* were produced in a slave state, the managers, players, and perhaps myself in the bargain would be rewarded with the Penitentiary."[28] Whitman and Bird were wrong. The South, more strongly Democratic than the northern states, applauded *The Gladiator* whenever Forrest toured the region. Like other Jacksonians, southerners understood the rhetoric of slavery and freedom as referring to the traditional rights of white people; few of them supposed that a drama centering on a white slave revolt was meant to apply to Nat Turner or the threats of William Lloyd Garrison. While their response was linked to the racism that pervaded the country, it was also grounded in the expectations established by the rhetoric of heroic melodrama itself.

The only reported incident in which the audience linked the subject matter of one of these plays to a pressing social issue occurred in Augusta, Georgia, in 1831 when Forrest's performance of *Metamora* led to a near riot in the theatre. A gold-hungry audience identified the American Indians in the play with the Cherokees of the area, on whose treaty-given land the gold strike had occurred. Forrest had performed the melodrama at exactly the wrong moment: the settlers were enraged at the government's protection of Native American rights—only *[contingency]* a temporary guarantee, as it turned out—and could talk of little else when Forrest stepped on stage in Metamora's costume. The exceptional circumstances of this situation, however, probably prove the rule; no other record of spectators' linking *Metamora* or the other two plays with a current social or political issue survives. The rhetoric of Forrest's heroic melodramas encouraged generalized hero worship, not attention to specific political concerns of the day.[29]

The remote formality of antebellum acting conventions, the "sincerity" of Forrest's fusion of the self-expressive and the representational modes of performance, and the hortatory rhetoric of his vehicles led tradition-directed audiences toward authoritarian hero worship, not democratic empowerment. Like other charismatic leaders in revolutionary times, both Forrest and the heroes he played called to their disciples to turn against the villains who oppressed them and to follow his commandments. As in other organizations dominated by a charismatic leader, the Indian tribe and the ragged army of former slaves or freed bondservants had no clear hierarchical order; like pittites roaring for Forrest in the theatre, these men temporarily repudiated their involvement in everyday affairs to follow the call of Forrest-Metamora, -Cade, or -Spartacus. The superstar-superhero promised a new Jacksonian dispensation, a revolutionary overturning of the status quo in the expectation that someday, somehow, the last shall be first. The very ambiguity about how and when this final judgment might be rendered gave added authority to Forrest-Cade and his fellow Jacksonian charismatics. In the meantime, the superstar's performances convinced his tradition-directed followers in the audience that they should tender their enthusiasm and obedience to his charismatic command. In exchange, he would give them himself, an image of authority both personal and abstract, comforting and sublime. To tradition-directed Democrats laboring under a sense of their own sinfulness, following Forrest to revenge and glory was a more appealing prospect than fighting for their own liberal power or republican freedom.

5. "The Earthquake! The Earthquake!"

Tradition-directed workers enjoyed Forrest's heroic plays, but they cheered just as loudly for apocalyptic melodramas, especially between 1835 and 1850. Similar to the star's vehicles in their general affirmation of the yeoman ideal, these spectacles called forth a distinctive response through their depiction of working-class solidarity and a millennial end to villainy. Apocalyptic melodrama centered on Bowery honor, a variant of traditional honor which emphasized combative action, male bonding rituals, and the subjection of women to its masculinist code. Bowery honor also circulated in working-class urban riots, which included mob actions at playhouses. By the mid 1840s, this tradition-directed culture was veering away from the nexus of republicanism and liberalism that constituted the ideology of Jacksonianism toward belief and behavior that the dominant culture branded as deviant.

As manager of the Bowery Theatre, Thomas S. Hamblin produced more apocalyptic melodrama than any other manager in the Northeast. Taking over the Bowery company in 1830, Hamblin departed from managerial precedent by ignoring the tastes of the elite and choosing plays and actors to appeal to tradition-directed workers in New York City. This led him to several managerial firsts: a stock company built for blood-and-guts melodrama, not genteel comedy; occasional long runs, instead of the traditional daily change of bills; and a focus on American talent, including Edwin Forrest and Hamblin's in-house star, John R. Scott. Also, unlike most other managers of the 1830s, Hamblin owned the acting company and theatre that he ran. As a capitalist rather than an artisan in the employ of others, Hamblin profited from the demand for stars by renting out minor luminaries (including, for a while, Junius Brutus Booth) and introducing several ingénues to the New York stage. Although the Bowery burned down three times between 1835 and 1850, twice leaving Hamblin with a total loss, the intrepid manager had little trouble financing the construction of new theatres and rebuilding his extensive stocks of costumes, scenery, and props. In the words of one newspaper reporter, Hamblin was "a sort of stir-em-up-with-a-long-pole, go-ahead man." By the time of his death in 1853, he had amassed a fortune.[1]

Hamblin's success led to competition for working-class patronage from other managers in New York. At different times in the mid 1830s, managers at the Franklin and National theatres tried Bowery-like bills to lure away Hamblin's playgoers, but with little lasting success. Hamblin's toughest competition came from the Chatham Theatre, which opened in 1839 near the Bowery in the initial expectation of attracting the elite of the city. A succession of managers soon fell into the practices of the Chatham's neighbor as both theatres struggled during the depression years of the early 1840s. Other theatres on the Lower East Side concentrated on comic and musical entertainment for working-class spectators. The managers at the Chambers Street and Olympic playhouses, for instance, used blackface acts, stage Yankees, and burlesques of Shakespeare, programs seen at the Bowery and Chatham as well. As theatre historian Mary C. Henderson concludes, "During the third and fourth decades of the nineteenth century, the Bowery [district] began to develop an independent theatrical life of its own. The theatres built along it appealed mainly to the residents of the area and never constituted a strong threat to the fashionable theatres that were beginning to appear along Broadway at the same time."[2]

Because of New York's larger working-class population and its generally higher concentration of workers in certain areas of the city, working-class theatre flourished in Gotham more so than in other cities. While the Walnut Street Theatre in Philadelphia attracted many workers to its doors, it appears not to have been as exclusively working-class as the Bowery and Chatham, perhaps because Philadelphia workers were distributed more widely and evenly in the central part of the city than in New York. In Boston the North End, a working-class district similar to though smaller than New York's Bowery, provided a locus for leisure activity for workers. There, William Pelby patterned some of his techniques for running the National Theatre after Hamblin's successful strategies, including the latter's emphasis on spectacle and his hiring of an in-house melodramatist with a facile pen. Pelby kept his prices as low as Hamblin's to attract workers: 75¢ for a chair in a box, 50¢ for the third tier, and 37½¢ for the pit in 1838. He and his wife performed many of the chief roles in their melodramas which, as at the Chatham in New York, were sometimes mounted three to a night to draw in more spectators.

In part because of their size and success, critics attacked the theatres in the Bowery district in New York, but rarely criticized the Walnut and National theatres in Philadelphia and Boston. By the mid 1840s, newspapers and magazines cultivating a respectable readership were excoriating Bowery theatres that featured melodrama as staple fare. "The house was full, but what an audience!" sniffed *Brother Jonathan* in 1843 on a visit to Hamblin's theatre. "However, it was what we had been led to expect and induced us to make our visit as short as possible." Most contemporary critics treated the Chatham far worse; they generally agreed that its patronage was below that of the Bowery. "It has been useful as a kind of sewer for the drainage of other establishments," stated one writer. "There must be some place for a certain class of people to effervesce in their excitements of pleasure."[3]

For many business-class New Yorkers, working-class theatregoers were not only ill-mannered and immoral; they were also dangerous. In an 1847 article contrasting audiences at the new Astor Place Opera House with those at the Bowery Theatre, *The Spirit of the Times* underlined the surging, moblike quality of the pittites at the Bowery compared to the "cool, subdued tone" of the audience at the opera. The bar in Hamblin's theatre, for instance, featured Bowery regulars

> drinking, swearing, smoking, chewing tobacco, knocking each others' hats down over the eyes, and in a thousand such delicate and fantastic ways giving free vent to the coarsest and roughest species of mere animal spirits, stimulated and excited to a sort of good-natured madness with poisoned whisky colored with the blood of its victims to the complexion of lurid brandy. . . . The pit is a vast sea of upturned faces and red flannel shirts, extending its roaring and turbid waves close up to the footlights on either side, clipping in the orchestra and dashing furiously against the boxes—while a row of luckier and stronger-shouldered amateurs have pushed and trampled their way far in advance of the rest and actually stand with their chins resting on the lampboard [of the footlights] chanking peanuts and squirting tobacco juice.[4]

In the eyes of this journalist—and no doubt in those of many of his readers—workers enjoyed a small riot every time they went to a Bowery theatre.

As the above passage suggests, many respectable New Yorkers in the mid 1840s were classifying playgoing behavior at working-class theatres as deviant. Most sociologists now locate deviance in the eye of the beholder, not in the specific characteristics of the person or group so identified. By labeling a group or an individual as deviant, ruling groups help to define and legitimate their moral codes; proscribing the behavior of certain outsiders buttresses the "normal" social order. The journalist above, for instance, was enforcing societal norms: he enjoined his readers to rule drinking, swearing, roaring, knocking, pushing, trampling, chanking, and squirting out of bounds for theatregoers. From this perspective, the male youth culture of the Bowery was largely a deviant subculture by the mid 1840s. The Bowery b'hoys (and their g'hals) mocked genteel respectability through their dress, their sporting events and riots, and their behavior at the theatre.[5]

Following several scandals in the mid 1830s centering on Hamblin's sexual indiscretions, polite society also labeled him as a deviant. While still married to his first wife, Hamblin carried on a publicly known affair with Naomi Vincent, one of his young ingénue stars. Vincent died in childbirth after Hamblin's first wife divorced him. When it seemed that Hamblin was partly responsible for the death in 1838 of Miss Missouri, another apparently too-eager young star, several newspapers heaped calumny on the manager. *The Spirit of the Times,* for example, called Hamblin "selfish" and "reckless" (which he certainly had been) and concluded: "It cannot be that he has yet to learn that female reputation is forever blighted by the mildew of his society—that there is contamination, a most leprous and loathsome contamination in all association with him." Hamblin's second wife, melodramatist Louisa Medina, defended her husband against all charges. Elizabeth Blanchard, his first wife, took her revenge by hiring a hack writer to publish the truth in *A Concise History of the Life and Amours of Thomas S. Hamblin,* thus adding to the furor.[6]

Besides his womanizing, Hamblin committed other social crimes which helped the respectable to type him as deviant and dangerous. When the editor of the *New York Herald,* Gordon Bennett, questioned the propriety of Hamblin's taking a benefit at his theatre—Bennett acidly pointed out that Hamblin was rich enough—the theatre manager assaulted him in his office. In a later defense of his personal honor, he accosted William Dinneford, a rival theatre manager, who prosecuted him for assault and battery. Hamblin came from a working-class background in England and probably shared his masculinist ethos of sexual prowess and combative honor with many members of his Bowery audience. As often happens in cases of social deviance, the outsider thumbed his nose at respectable society and presented an even more flamboyant and immoral persona to the public. In Hamblin's case, working-class theatregoers, increasingly labeled as moral deviants themselves, celebrated the manager as one of their own and flocked to his theatre. (By the mid 1840s, however, the respectable press, perhaps impressed by Hamblin's financial success, no longer bothered to condemn him.)

Working-class theatre managers followed conventional practice by hiring their own playwrights and pirating melodramas from rival houses. Louisa Medina, Hamblin's most prolific playwright in the 1830s, turned out over thirty plays before her early death in 1838. Primarily an adapter of contemporary novels, Medina gained some renown in the press, a reputation partly paid for under the table by Hamblin. "She is partial to startling and terrible catastrophes," puffed the *New-York Mirror*. "Her knowledge of stage effect is very great and there is an impassioned ardour in her poetry, which enhances the thrilling interest of her pieces." Medina's adaptations also won her genuinely high praise from some contemporaries; actor Lester Wallack called her "one of the most brilliant women I ever met." The two most popular of Medina's adaptations were Bulwer-Lytton's *The Last Days of Pompeii* (1835) and Robert Montgomery Bird's novel *Nick of the Woods* (1838), both performed initially at the Bowery and frequently revived through the early 1850s. *Pompeii's* initial twenty-nine performances in 1835, in fact, constituted the longest run in the history of New York theatre at that time.[7]

Working-class playwright Joseph S. Jones wrote melodramas, stage-managed, and performed small roles for several managers in Boston, including William Pelby at the National Theatre. Acquiring a medical degree from Harvard in 1843 to increase his income, Jones had no illusions about the profitability of playwrighting before copyright protection. "It is often asked why there is no standard American drama," he wrote. "One of the best answers is, nobody will pay for it." Jones's *The Carpenter of Rouen* (1837), the most successful of his twenty or so plays, was popular with English as well as American urban workers. Knowing the republican sympathies of his audience, Jones wrote a publicity pamphlet on *Carpenter* which proclaimed: "In all countries where a wounded, insulted, injured and enslaved people are compelled to jeopardise [*sic*] life to secure their rights, leaders have been found among the artisans or mechanics, whose powerful minds, aided by a courage equal to their cause, have stayed, for a time, the Age of Tyranny."[8]

These three plays by Jones and Medina are representative of over a hundred scripts popular with working-class audiences in the 1835–50 period. Spin-offs, in many respects, of Forrest's heroic plays and their imitations, these melodramas also had unique features. Like Forrest's vehicles, some of these plays dramatized a republican revolution of the people against aristocratic oppression aided by providential design and heroic martyrdom. Unlike heroic melodrama, however, this popular

formula emphasized the importance of working-class solidarity to overcome villainy and rarely featured scenes of the people turning against
their hero. Heroism, in fact, is often split between two protagonists in
these plays—a representative of the oppressed group and a crazed
avenger—who must work together to overcome villainy. Although both
heroes more or less conform to the sturdy independence of the yeoman ideal, the primary dualisms held in ambiguous balance in Forrest's heroes—impersonal force/passion-driven man, inspired prophet/
doomed martyr—have been broken apart and reconstituted in different characters.

This split in heroism in apocalyptic melodrama translates into a split
in plot structure which divides the ambiguous, forced unity between
historical revenge and utopian desire evident in Forrest's plays. These
melodramas of catastrophe climax in a confrontation between the
avenger and the villain which results in an apocalyptic ending, a Last
Judgment of carnage and destruction that kills the oppressors and usually some good characters as well. Overall, these melodramas encompass less ideological ambiguity than Forrest's shows; they legitimate
millenarian hopes for the end of the world and a traditional notion of
male honor which centers on avenging group wrongs, regardless of the
consequences. Although generally more republican than liberal in orientation, these shows finally undercut the republican ideal of virtuous
citizenship. Because Forrest's vehicles had to appeal to a more diverse
audience, these apocalyptic plays promise to reveal aspects of working-
class belief and behavior only hinted at in the ideology of heroic
melodrama.

Playwrights working for Forrest fused the reality of history with the
romance of thrilling adventure and stirring rhetoric. Jones and Medina
also insisted on the historical reality of the events they dramatized, but
stretched the definition of the real further than the conventions of conservative romance allowed. Whereas Scott's historical novels had provided Forrest's vehicles with their claim to credibility, these two working-class melodramatists looked to the "symbolical" novels of Edward
Bulwer-Lytton as their model. Indeed, stage adaptations of his *Rienzi,
Paul Clifford, Ernest Maltravers,* and others of his books vied with
The Last Days of Pompeii for working-class applause in the United
States. Consciously antiempirical in approach, Bulwer-Lytton set out
"to employ Romance in the aid of History," as he put it, by setting a

mix of realistic and idealized characters against historical backdrops and shaping the patterns of their lives to reveal "symbolical meanings." In *Pompeii,* for instance, he used witches and a devilish wizard to depict a spiritual malevolence he believed actually existed in the historical Roman city—symbolical conventions followed by Medina in her adaptation. Likewise, Jones and Medina wished their audiences to believe that they were watching true historical stories of pre-Revolutionary France and the early American West when they applauded the revenge of a carpenter and the exploits of the Jibbenainosay in *The Carpenter of Rouen* and *Nick of the Woods.*[9]

This shift from conservative romance to the near-allegory of symbolical meanings results in transcendental villainy in these melodramas. While most of the villains of apocalyptic melodrama remain aristocrats, their power transcends the mundane spheres of politics and economics—the domains of Lords Say and Crassus, for instance—to embrace the spiritual. In *The Carpenter of Rouen*, the Duke De Saubigne disguises himself as a Catholic monk and uses the rituals of the church to enhance his power. Standing astride the decadence of Pompeii is Arbaces, a colossus of villainy, who practices black magic and consorts with witches. Referring to the gladiators and aristocrats of Pompeii, the Egyptian priest exults, "They are my tools—I read their passions, guide their wills, employ their services, and laugh them all to scorn" (I,1). The villains of Forrest's plays used the power of the state to tyrannize the people; the monsters and their minions in apocalyptic melodramas strive to hold the people in their thrall through religious rituals as well as political repression.

Consequently, these apocalyptic plays rely much less on the roomy rhetoric of political freedom than did Forrest's vehicles. Some of the set speeches of the carpenter hero of Rouen pack the kind of hortatory punch delivered by Forrest as Spartacus or Jack Cade, but none of the heroic characters in *Nick* or *Pompeii* serve up his kind of generalized, republican oratory. In part, this is because the evil the heroes strive to overcome is more religious than political. It is also because honor and revenge are of more immediate concern than political freedom in these apocalyptic melodramas. Forrest and his playwrights folded the hero's personal motives of avenging his own and his family's honor into his larger political goals; Metamora's and Cade's attempts to save their wives from villainous violation were a part of their drive to win their people's freedom. Even in *Carpenter*, the most overtly political of these three apocalyptic plays, personal honor provides the main motive for Marteau's revenge against De Saubigne, with freedom a very distant second. "A murdered wife, one of the sinless victims of St. Bartholomew, beckons the way," shouts the carpenter at the climax of the play, referring to the villain's participation in the historical massacre of the Huguenots. "Blood for blood!" (IV,3). Although the show ends with a tableau of De Saubigne hanging from a gibbet constructed by Marteau, the artisans of France remain under the control of the aristocracy and the church at the play's conclusion. Marteau's vindication of his honor is not translated into political freedom.

The breach between personal honor and politics widens in *Pompeii*. Lyndon the gladiator strives to win "the palm crown and purse of gold" in the arena to buy the freedom of his father, a dishonorable slave. "Thou wilt yet live in thine own native land, to see the little rosy cherubims climb thy kneee and call thy Lyndon father. . . . We are Thessalians! We cannot live in bondage," he tells his father (III,1). Despite this Spartacus-like speech and Lyndon's disgust at the injustice of gladiators murdering each other, he kills in the arena to restore his family's honor; rallying the gladiators and slaves to revolt against their Pompeian oppressors is never an option. Fighting oppression and gaining freedom are not feasible choices in the world of *Pompeii* because everyone is doomed by the imminent eruption of Mount Vesuvius, foreshadowed from the start of the show. Under such a fate, all the good characters can do is salvage personal honor.

The Jacksonian conflict of the people versus the aristocrats is even further removed from the Hobbesian wilds of *Nick of the Woods.* Although beginning somewhat like *Metamora* by invoking the desire of a liberal Arcadian utopia in the West, the play finally centers on the contest between honor and nature, with indigenous Americans as the chief exemplars of the assumed savagery of nature. Initially, to the heroine, nature seems peaceful and promising:

How bright and beautiful it is, all around us! The sweet song of the blackbird and the cry of the whippoorwill seem to invite us to their leafy homes. The fresh, green turf spreads a fragrant carpet for our feet; and the breeze which stirs the forest leaves whispers on my ear a most enchanting music. (II,1)

But nature is more brutish than bountiful in this play. Because wild panthers stalk children and native Americans ravage settlers, *Nick* requires several heroes to save heroines and avenge American Indian massacres. Among them is Roaring Ralph Stackpole, "a ring-tailed squealer" of the Davy Crockett type, "a strange medley of the bully and the hero" (I,3), who twice rescues the settlers from the Indians. The primary hero, however, is Reginald Ashburn—a.k.a. Bloody Nathan, Nick of the Woods, the Avenger, the Spirit of the Waters, and the Jibbenainosay—a crazed yeoman farmer who stalks Indians to avenge the death of his wife and child in a massacre. "As the green leaves turn crimson, and then fall to earth, so pass all things through my brain—gorgeous of hue, but withering, withering away," moans Ashburn, his images of nature in striking contrast to those of the heroine (II,1). After gaining his revenge, the hero "laughs wildly and exit[s], dragging the body" (III,4). Ashburn's vengeful defense of his family's honor has no direct connection to the republican defense of freedom.

The emphasis on traditional male honor in apocalyptic melodrama reduces the female characters to little more than counters in the male exchange of insult and vindication between villain and hero. All of the women characters accept their role as vessels of family honor. When a villain in *Nick* sneers that he will marry Edith to acquire her estate, the heroine knows what to say: "Death is more welcome than the title of wife to thee" (I,2). Madelon, daughter of Marteau, counters the advances of the lecherous duke with a like rebuff: "My course is thine, but not my honor" (IV,1). One of the most affecting scenes in *Pompeii* occurs when Nydia, a blind flower girl, affirms her virtue to her father and brother: "Here I stand before the face of heaven—that heaven I cannot see—and offer thee my breast if guilt defile it. Strike! I do not fear to die" (II,1). This subjugation of women to a patriarchal code of honor is more oppressive in these shows than in Forrest's vehicles.

The extent of this rigid sexism is also apparent in several of the comic scenes of these plays. Apocalyptic melodramas place young women on a pedestal—Stackpole refers to the heroine in *Nick* as an "angeliforous crittur"—but generally depict older married women as shrews. In comic scenes between a bickering middle-aged couple in *Carpenter*, the husband always gets the better of the wife: "Marteau makes the only suit of clothes husbands never begrudge their wives the expense of," states M. Grander, adding, "he's a coffin maker, my dear" (I,1).

Partial program of The Carpenter of Rouen, *1848 (Billy Rose Theatre Collection, New York Public Library for the Performing Arts, Astor, Lenox, and Tilden Foundations). Note the emphasis given to Antoine's initiation scene in this production featuring Edward Eddy, later a popular Bowery actor, at the National Theatre in Boston. Comic actors in working-class theatres frequently chose the role of Nykin for their benefit.*

Pompeii features a similar comic couple, Burbo, a retired gladiator, and his sharp-tongued wife, Stratonice. In their scenes together, the comedy is aimed at Burbo because he boasts of honors he never won and allows his wife to browbeat him mercilessly. So committed is he to getting rid of her that he allows Nydia to escape Arbaces' prison by tricking him into believing that she can conjure devils who will tell him "how long that cancerous old wife of mine will live to spoil my honors" (III,2). Traditional honor, rung in comic as well as heroic changes, defines the patriarchal construction of gender roles in these shows.

Apocalyptic melodramas subject young men of honor to several tests of their courage and fortitude. Although this occurs too in Forrest's heroic plays, the trials of honor are both more numerous and seem more extreme in apocalyptic shows because they are inflicted on mere mortals, not charismatic supermen. In *Nick*, the young hero Roland is captured by the Indians and threatened with torture to reveal the plans of the settlers. He does not submit. The Confrérie, a secret group of artisan Huguenots, tests the loyalty and fortitude of Antoine, a young aristocrat apprenticed to Marteau in *Carpenter*. In this initiation rite, the Confrérie constructs a situation through playacting and props in which they convince Antoine that he is about to be hung for the murder of a fellow Huguenot. They urge him to confess his crime, but Antoine is adamant: "I will not lie, though death is certain." When offered his life if he will reveal the secrets of the Confrérie, Antoine still refuses:

> I shall not betray my friends, even for my life. My head is yours, for I am in your power. To punish the usurpations of tyrant powers, to stop unlawful murders such as these, I joined the order of the Confrérie. Their secret is mine; it dies with me.

At this climactic moment, the brothers reveal their true identities and welcome Antoine into full membership: "The ordeal is passed; we hail thee as a brother" (II,2). Tests of honor are often crucial rites of passage in apocalyptic melodrama.

Apocalyptic melodrama's legitimation of traditional male honor is consonant with the centrality of honor in the lives of its audience. Tradition-directed American men accorded their peers honorable social worth on the basis of their group loyalty, fortitude, and physical prowess, as Forrest knew when he caned Willis at the time of his divorce. In honor-bound societies, the usual arena for testing honor was the dueling ground for the upper class or the town square for the rough-and-tumble of the lower; all classes of men looked to the battlefield as the ultimate social space for the vindication of honor. Lacking opportunities in these locales, a man might prove himself in competitive sports, in games of chance, in drinking bouts, or even in boasting matches. These competitions were events intended for public display—social performances whose outcomes both opponents knew would be widely circulated. Group solidarity in the face of the enemy was also important, with the consequence that rituals of fraternity involving oath taking, initiation rites, and male bonding activities occupied an important place in traditionalist male culture. Since a man's self-identity was tied to the honor of his family and of his immediate social group, honor-bound men perceived an insult to a sister, a cousin, or a comrade as a direct challenge to themselves. Instead of self-control, inner dignity, and self-reliance, the tradition-directed male worker who was concerned to demonstrate his honor committed himself to brave action, group solidarity, and male integrity.[10]

The type of honor current among urban male workers in the antebellum era might best be designated as Bowery honor after the New York neighborhood where it was most widely practiced and best understood. The beliefs and behavior of men in the volunteer fire companies of New York, Boston, and Philadelphia exemplified this code. Composed mainly of tradition-directed workers by 1840, these tightly knit clubs competed among themselves for the honor of being the first to arrive at city fires and the bravest in putting them out. The fire companies sponsored other competitions among workingmen, including engine races on Saturday nights and prizefighting between representatives of various companies. Each company was a quasi-secret organization with its own insignia, secret oaths, and private rites of initiation. Often cementing the solidarity of company members was a heroic leader, typically the best pugilist of the group, who inspired worshipful awe from the younger men and led his company in brawling and fighting fires. So esteemed were brave firefighters among tradition-directed workers that an entire series of heroic comedies, the "Mose" plays made famous initially at the Chatham Theatre by the star Frank Chanfrau, gained widespread popularity in the urban theatres of the Northeast in the late 1840s.[11]

By then, however, most volunteer fire companies had become fiercely ethnic in their antagonisms. The code of Bowery honor in the 1840s drew sharp distinctions among groups on the basis of class and ethnicity. As immigration increased in the 1840s and urban land values kept rents high, Irish- and German-Americans were crowded into tenements and slums next to native-born workers. The population density of major northeastern cities was never higher than in the late 1840s and 1850s before streetcar and railway systems allowed business-class urbanites to sprall into the surrounding countryside. Given their proximity to one another, their ongoing competition for similar jobs, and the general level of frustration caused by low wages and crowded living conditions, ethnic conflict was nearly inevitable. Philadelphia was the first scene of widespread violence between nativist and Irish groups when the riots of 1844 took the lives of at least twenty persons and injured over a hundred others. Ethnic antagonism spawned nativist political movements which attracted widespread working-class support throughout the Northeast.

The adult gangs which evolved to protect the turf of numerous ethnic enclaves threatened the peace of working-class neighborhoods in the 1840s. Similar to the volunteer fire companies in their commitment to Bowery honor but more deviant in social behavior, the gangs also whispered private oaths and enforced physical tests of manliness among their members. Indeed, the distinction between a fire company and a gang was not always clear-cut, since these fraternal orders were increasingly polarized along ethnic lines and several company "musses" turned into deadly territorial battles. Instead of putting out fires, however, gangs functioned as informal neighborhood police, concentrating their muscle on private betrayals and ethnic vendettas. Like the fire companies, urban gangs also continued to exclude women, relegating them to spectatorship at fires and fights. Some gangs, like the Empire Club and the Bowery B'hoys in New York, turned to political action and worked against or in tandem with the urban political machines emerging in the forties. Like the gladiators in *Pompeii* and the Huguenot artisans in *Carpenter*, these gangs constructed a world of "us" against "them" and defended their honor through rituals and recriminations.

Gang members also cultivated images of deviance to enhance their belligerence. The best known of this type was the Bowery B'hoy himself, a working-class dandy bristling with class and nativist antagonism whose black suit, soaped-back hair, and swaggering defiance was meant to frighten rich folks and Irish immigrants. Working-class journalists and novelists like George Foster and Ned Buntline softened the b'hoy's pugnacious persona in their *New York in Slices* (1849) and *The B'hoys of Boston* (1850), but the historical b'hoys were crude, racist, and violent. More typical of the social masks worn by gang members were the images in a report on the Killers, an Irish-American gang in Philadelphia. According to a contemporary, the Killers

> were divided into three classes: Beardless apprentice boys who after a hard day's work were turned loose upon the street by their masters and bosses; young men of nineteen and twenty who, fond of excitement, had assumed the name and joined the gang for the mere fun of the thing and who would either fight for a man or knock him down, just to keep their hand in; and fellows with countenances that reminded of the brute and devil intermingled. These last were the smallest in number, but the most ferocious of the three.[12]

Little wonder that business-class reformers and journalists began to brand tradition-directed workers as the "vicious" poor in the late 1840s. Equally dangerous and deviant, from the point of view of the corrupt society within which they lived, were the avenging heroes of apocalyptic melodrama. Not even a Philadelphia Killer, third class, could command the fear and respect of the Jibbenainosay.

The degradation of most working-class males at their places of employment induced many of them to embrace the deviant status of gang membership. The rise of workingmen's advocates in the urban political machines of the 1840s also provided a channel of expression for traditionalist frustration with capitalism. In New York, for instance, Mike Walsh dominated Democratic working-class politics for most of the decade, despite repeated attempts by Tammany regulars to kick him out. His political base was the Spartan Association, founded in 1840 as a secret Irish society and political gang. Walsh also published a newspaper from 1843 to 1847, *The Subterranean*, which proclaimed itself "uncompromising in its support of the working class and merciless in its exposure of corruption." Among his regular targets was John Jacob Astor, whose name, like his opera house, came to be synonymous to *Subterranean* readers with robbery and exploitation. "What is capital," Walsh asked his readers, "but that all-grasping power which has been wrung by fraud, avarice, and malice from the labor of this and all ages past?" Walsh's deviant actions frequently matched his explosive republican rhetoric. In 1842, his Spartans muscled their way into a Tammany convention and carried Walsh on their shoulders to the podium, where he mocked the regulars and railed against Democratic hypocrisy. His belligerent deeds and cocky denunciations made this b'hoy politician a hero among tradition-directed workers. "Our Napoleon," as the Spartans called him, demonstrated his Bowery honor through brave acts, class and ethnic loyalty, and rhetorical flourish. How the Spartans must have enjoyed the similar rhetoric and revenge of Marteau in *Carpenter* when they went to the Bowery Theatre![13]

Although the conjunction of Bowery honor in the theatrical and social lives of many urban workers rested on traditional customs and codes, significant changes in the social and economic position of American artisans explain the belligerence of its expression in the late 1830s and 1840s. Through the eighteenth and into the nineteenth century, Americans generally viewed craftworkers as occupying the middle rungs of the social ladder, below the merchant and professional elite but well above unskilled laborers and servants. Community leaders praised mechanics, as all artisans were called, for their yeoman virtue, their love of republican liberty, and their sacrifices in American wars. Trade workers were encouraged to think of themselves, in words used by the Butchers' Guild of Philadelphia, as a "fraternity of men essential and indispensible to the body politic." In 1842 a labor newspaper complained, "The capitalists have taken to bossing all the mechanical trades, while the practical mechanic [i.e., the master artisan] has become a journeyman, subject to be discharged at every pretended 'miff' of his purse-proud employer." Other masters abandoned their traditional obligations to their workers and joined the ranks of the capitalists to sweat profits from their employees. Especially galling to the wageworker was the wide gulf that had opened between his or her status and that of the new business class by the 1840s. Instead of enjoying the fruits of early industrialization—larger homes, indoor plumbing, and public education for his children—the journeyman saw himself sinking to the position of an English factory worker, becoming a permanent member of a dependent, proletarian class. As an 1845 editorial in *The Voice of Industry* noted, echoing similar rallying cries in heroic melodrama, craftworkers yearned to be "reinstated into the bonds of nature's brotherhood."[14]

What had happened? In brief, the rapid growth of cities in the 1820s forced a greater demand for handicraft products than traditional craft organizations could produce. Entrepreneurs, either outside capitalists or opportunistic master artisans, gathered together the isolated shops of specific crafts into a unified putting-out system geared to quantity production. This economic rationalization reduced other masters and many journeymen and apprentices to piecework and then to working for wages. The traditional web of obligations and loyalties binding together workers in the same trade—a system which was already unraveling in the eighteenth century—further deteriorated, exacerbated by economic rivalry between master and journeyman and by the ethos of commercialization. With the pressure for quantity production came the introduction of simple machinery in several trades, increasing the pace of work and occasionally making obsolete crafts which had flourished for centuries. Worker fears of economic exploitation and lower social status increased during the depression years of the late 1830s and early 1840s and remained high into the 1850s. Nor were these fears unfounded; while the average wage between 1830 and 1850, adjusted for inflation, rose for some skilled artisans, it declined for most workers. In addition, the number of skilled craftworkers as a percentage of all workers declined dramatically—from around 60 percent in 1820 to only 20 percent in 1855 in New York City. The traditional ladder up which the ambitious and skillful worker had risen to become a master artisan, gaining a measure of economic independence and social prestige along the way, had been flattened by the forces of market capitalism.[15]

Tradition-directed workers responded in religious as well as political ways to these changes in their lives. Indeed, apocalyptic melodramas mobilized fears and raised expectations that were more forthrightly religious than directly political in nature. Their edge-of-the-seat, apocalyptic climax, especially, warned their spectators to look to their souls and prepare for God's wrath. This does not mean, of course, that the quasi-religious experience induced by watching these plays was devoid of political implication. But it does mandate a focus on the kind of religious revitalization inscribed in these scripts and realized in their performance.

The nature of this religious experience was primarily millenarian in orientation and goals. By definition, millenarian movements condemn the present world as unregenerately evil; they look forward to an imminent, divinely ordained catastrophe in which God will destroy villainy forever and establish a utopia of the virtuous lasting, in conventional Christian belief, for a thousand years. All millenarian movements center in a prophet, often an alienated wanderer with charismatic power. Typically, this prophet and his or her loyal group of followers separate themselves from the perceived corruption around them, prepare for Judgment Day through ritual purification, and reject their lack of power and prestige in the present society to celebrate their status as God's chosen. Historians, sociologists, and anthropologists have discerned these basic characteristics and goals in millenarian movements in a variety of periods and cultures, from the early Christians of Roman times to Seventh-Day Adventists in the United States. Some, following Max Weber, classify millenarianism as a subspecies of charismatic authority but most prefer to type it as a related but distinct movement.[16]

Apocalyptic melodramas went a long way toward fulfilling millenarian expectations, beginning with their depiction of a world ripe for destruction. Not only is wickedness individualized in villains with apparently superhuman powers; it pervades the social norms of everyday experience in all three plays. Greed, lust, cruelty, and indifference are presented as a normal part of life on the American frontier, in Reformation Rouen, and in Roman Pompeii. The following dialogue from *Pompeii* typifies these plays' moral judgment of immoral norms:

[A patrician]:	The brave boys [i.e., the gladiators] are preparing for to-morrow and, as there is no criminal to fight the lion, the conquering gladiator must.
Glau[cus]:	A man to fight the lion! Why, 'twould be instant death.
[Another patrician]:	. . . 'Tis fine to mark the writhings of the man compared with the brute monarch's giant force,—and hear his dying groans drowned in one tremendous roar.
Glau[cus]:	You sicken me. (II,1)

Likewise, Ashburn in *Nick* says that men are "ravening tigers" and the melodrama's incidents prove him correct (I,3). In such a Calvinistic world, mere political reform or even revolution will not wash clean the indelible stains of sin and corruption.

A prophet-avenger, however, can temporarily check the spread of evil against the day when God will end the rule of Satan. Typically, millenarian prophets in late eighteenth- and early nineteenth-century England and America were mystically inspired men and women alienated from the present social order who worked in a traditional profession or trade. According to anthropologist W. La Barre, "In every age sensitive, aberrant, creative individuals, in their personal anguish with life and defrauded somehow of the comforts to be expected from old beliefs, come close to an awareness of the dire contingency of all symbols." Marteau, Ashburn, and Lyndon fall within this general description; all are dispossessed, defrauded men who break with the institutions and symbols of an evil order to forge, with others, their own identities and lives. Conventional society in these melodramas judges these charismatic prophet-avengers either deviant, the situation of Marteau and Lyndon, or insane, as in the case of Reginald Ashburn.[17]

But how are the faithful to know whether a man is a genuine prophet inspired by God, a madman whose visions are false, or perhaps even a tool of Satan? To this difficult but vitally important question, *Nick* addresses several scenes in which the power and goodness of Reginald Ashburn is gradually revealed. Initially, however, the Jibbenainosay seems as savage as the Indians he murders. As a reliable character explains in the second scene, the Jibbenainosay, who may be "man, beast, or devil," tomahawks his victims with "a regular cross on the breast and a good dig through the skull" (I,2). It is not until the end of the second act that the audience learns that this avenging yeoman is on the side of right. Savages pursue Roland and his fiancé, who are stopped in their flight by a raging river below a waterfall. Suddenly, "the Jibbenainosay is precipitated down the cataract in a canoe of fire. The Indians all utter a yell of horror and fall on their faces" (II,5). Near the end of *Nick*, the prophet-avenger reveals his true identity to his band of settler followers, a revelation of revenge which presages the revelation of divine wrath at the climax of the action.

A similar revelation occurs at the end of *Carpenter* with Marteau's admission of his true motive for stalking De Saubigne to the gibbet.

Advertising woodcut depicting the Jibbenainosay in Nick of the Woods, *ca. 1870 (Dover Pictorial Archive Series). The already-dead Indian with a cross on his chest (to the right of the settlers) suggests that this woodcut was intended to represent several moments in the play, not just the cataract scene.*

The link between Lyndon's revenge and God's vengeance is more ambiguous in *Pompeii*. Lyndon, by participating in a system he abhors, is tarred with the decadence of Pompeii, but his blind sister Nydia is not. After her brother's death from his wounds in the arena, she appears as the goddess Truth at the acme of the gladiatorial arena (III,6). Following the customs of Pompeii, Arbaces must swear before the goddess and the Pompeian public that Glaucus, the secondary hero, killed one of his priests, even though the villain knows that he himself did the deed. Nydia produces a witness to the murder and thus completes her family's vengeance against the Egyptian priest. In effect, brother and sister work together as avenger and prophet, combining—as do Marteau and Ashburn—muscular revenge with transcendental justice.

In millenarian movements, prophets and their followers celebrate their separation from the dominant society through rites of solidarity.

Typically, this involves distinguishing true rituals from false ones. Nydia's distribution of flowers, freely given to the good characters as symbols of Christian love, and her emergence as Truth are in contrast to the complex "mummery," as one of Arbaces' priests calls it, of worshipping the false gods of Pompeii. *Carpenter* also unveils the religious fakery of the powerful. Following the opening of a scene in a convent with "an organ heard playing" and "a procession of nuns" carrying a coffin into a crypt, "the black drapery is removed and the scene appears a splendid banquet room. What seemed altars are banquet tables, chandeliers are lowered, the walls are filled with pictures of amatory subjects" (IV,2).[18] To counteract the false rituals of De Saubigne and the Catholic church, Marteau and his fellow mechanics spend an entire act in the initiation of Antoine into the Confrérie. This primal scene climaxes in a tableau elevating banners depicting symbols of genuine solidarity and the tools of the carpenters' trade: "Arms of France [with] Bare Arm and Banner, Arms of Rouen [with] Hammer and Saw, Cross of Rome [with] Plumb-line and Chisel" (II,2). These ritual props not only contravene the power of Catholic censers, crosses, and relics, they also serve as rallying points in the mechanics' attack on De Saubigne's palace at the end of act 3.[19]

Envisioning an imminent apocalypse, of course, is the sine qua non of millenarian movements. The closest in these three plays to the biblical model is the earthquake in *Pompeii* which follows Arbaces' defiance of the crowd in the arena after he admits to murdering his priest. "At this moment, the fire breaks forth from the mountain and the walls of the [gladiatorial] arena fall. Everybody cries, 'The earthquake! The earthquake!' Curtain falls on a grand tableau" (III,6). Apparently, the audience assumed that Vesuvius buried good and evil alike, leaving the Almighty to sort out the saved from the damned. In *Nick*, Ashburn leads an attack on the Indians and dies during the grand tableau accompanied by music and burning wigwams. The climax of *Carpenter* is similar: "Music. Crash! The whole scene at back falls and discovers the convent yard, with gibbet, upon which hangs De Saubigne, dead. Coffin at the foot. General Tableau" (IV,4). In terms of its apocalypse, *Carpenter* fits the millenarian model less well than the other two, since only the villain (and probably some of his Catholic minions) dies in the catastrophe. Further, history doesn't end for Marteau and his Confrérie; nor, for that matter, for the western settlers in *Nick*.

In other ways too, these plays shy away from fully embracing millenarian desire. For the true millenarianist, the period preceding the apocalypse is a time of no rules, a condition of being, states K. Burridge, "in which humans become free-movers, in which there are no obligations, in which all earthly desires are satisfied and therefore expunged."[20] Many western millenarian movements have involved periods of anarchy, property destruction, and sexual license. The deviant outcasts of apocalyptic melodrama may destroy property and even lives in preparation for the end of history, but they continue to live by one important set of rules, the code of Bowery honor. Even Roaring Ralph Stackpole, who comes the closest to freewheeling anarchy in these plays, never turns his omnivorous appetite against the good white folks of the play. Also, no thousand-year rule of goodness takes the place of the reign of Satan, as it does in genuine millenarian movements. If the prophet-avenger doesn't die in the struggle, neither does he rejoice in the establishment of a God-given utopia. Although the wish for a heaven on earth had been a staple of melodramatic desire since Pixérécourt, it is nearly absent in these plays.

Instead, apocalyptic melodramas concentrate all of their considerable energy and ingenuity on revenge, allowing no contradictions or qualifications to cut into its cathartic satisfaction. Avenging honor is more important than political freedom, the solidarity of true believers, or even life itself, since the avenger often dies in the successful accomplishment of his task. And the final judgment of God through an apocalypse, of course, only links the honor of the revenger to the wrath of the Almighty. Apocalyptic melodrama's prophet-avenger neither promulgates a new set of commandments for the chosen who survive nor does its final tableau depict a promised land in which justice will reign for a thousand years. While several millenarian prayers had been induced and answered for the tradition-directed workers in the audience—allowing them to imaginatively separate themselves from the pervasive wickedness of the world, to cleanse and solidify their ranks through potent rituals, and to bear witness to God's judgment of wickedness—the plays did not move their auditors to become millenarians. Apocalyptic melodramas stopped short at revenge.

Retribution rather than transcendent revelation was also central to these plays in production. J. Hudson Kirby and John R. Scott, popular working-class stars celebrated for Forrest-like excesses in performance, emphasized the vengeful, fated aspects of Marteau and Lyndon on Bowery stages and occasionally at the Boston National and Walnut Street theatres in the 1840s. Kirby was especially celebrated for his lengthy and tempestuous stage deaths; so renowned, in fact, that the audience expected him to walk through the early scenes of his melodramas to save himself for the agonies of his characters' expirations. "Wake me up when Kirby dies" was a standing jest for years among Bowery spectators. Some audience members in New York preferred Scott's magnetic stage presence to Forrest's. "Ned Forrest is some but he ain't a touch to Scott when he wraps hisself in the star-spangled banner and goes for to die," professed one stalwart of the Bowery Theatre. Scott's florid and forceful acting style was well enough known to be celebrated in a verse of the popular song "The Boys of the Bowery Pit":

> But presently the actors are seen looking at the wings,
> As if they were awatching for somebody or something,
> The Gallus boys are wide-awake, they know what's coming now
> For J. R. Scott is coming, and then there's such a row.

Kirby and Scott died alcoholics in 1848 and 1856, respectively.[21]

Workers expected to applaud these stars at their neighborhood playhouse, but it was primarily the spectacle of apocalypse that kept them coming back for more. Hamblin, knowing the tastes of his audience, spent more on scenery and effects than he ever did on acting or playwriting. An 1837 Bowery Theatre program carried the following typical announcement: "*The Bronze Horse, or The Spell of the Cloud King, or The Enchanted Flying Steed,* which has been four months in preparation, at the enormous expense of $5,000 and the manager has every confidence that it will be pronounced the most gorgeous spectacle ever produced." Sometimes Hamblin used spectacular advertising devices to call attention to his spectacles on stage. To fan the fires of popular enthusiasm for Medina's adaptation of *Rienzi*, another of Bulwer-Lytton's novels, he covered the entire front of his theatre with a transparency depicting "the vast conflagration of the Palace of Constantine, with the fall of the Basalt Lion."[22]

Indeed, spectacle was the chief theatrical agency for putting across scenes of apocalypse. Oftentimes, the final catastrophe involved practical, three-dimensional scenic units of surprising complexity for their

time. A prompter's copy of *The Butchers of Ghent*, a melodrama similar to *The Carpenter of Rouen*, makes explicit the protorealistic scenic
conventions that are only implied in other apocalyptic shows. The
script specifies that the hero's home and shop "should be a built house,
perforated for the discharge of musquetry [*sic*], with a flat roof capable
of [holding] four or five men." *The Butchers of Ghent* set Bowery carpenters the further task of constructing the door of the shop so as to
withstand the blows of a battering ram and to rig a way for the entire
structure to blow up and collapse at the end of the scene.[23]

Protorealistic catastrophes reached their dubious acme in Hamblin's
staging of several melodramas of aquatic apocalypse in 1840. For *The
Pirates of Signal*, Hamblin boasted, "To give the full effect of this novel
drama, a large body of water, covering the whole of the stage, will be
exhibited throughout the last act, upon which a great portion of the
scene takes place." Indeed, the apocalyptic ending of this spectacle involved an exploding powder magazine, the destruction of two ships,
and moans of despair from several actors playing drowning pirates.
Yankees in China, Hamblin's next sail into aquatic melodrama, launched
"two frigates, colors flying, decks and yards crowded with men, battering a fortress. . . . The crews mount the walls and hurl the besieged into
the waves." Although real water had soaked American stageboards
before (briefly at the Lafayette Theatre in 1828), Hamblin's nautical
productions broke completely with the old scenic conventions and put
him in the forefront of managers experimenting with protorealistic
techniques.[24]

Hamblin was not alone among working-class theatre managers in
striving to make the final calamities of his shows as realistic as possible. In 1840, Francis Wemyss, nearing the end of his tenure at the
Walnut Street Theatre, hired a master machinist from London to mod-
ernize the gaslighting of his playhouse. Gas was crucial to the success
of apocalyptic melodrama. By illuminating much more of the upstage
area than had been possible before, gas increased the playing depth of
the stage and allowed actors to perform within the scenery, not just in
front of it. Medina, Jones, and other playwrights of apocalyptic melodrama took full advantage of the new lighting technology to achieve
weird and startling images. The following effect from *Pompeii* would
have been impossible to realize without gas: "Gong. Thunder and lightning. Red fire. The cave opens and discovers the witch in the midst of

flames" (I,5). Gas illumination, especially when aided by the firework-like displays of red and blue fire, made the burning convents and the exploding volcanoes at the climax of these plays especially effective; indeed, gas made manifest the power of God to control human life. Without this technology, it is doubtful that apocalyptic melodrama would have been written or produced.[25]

From the mid 1830s to the Civil War, tradition-directed workers joined thousands of other Americans to revel in visions of apocalypse provided by the popular culture of the day. An 1836 panoramic display, for example, advertised "The Deluge," "Storm and Shipwreck," and "The Conflagration of Moscow." Many works of fiction, written in what literary historian David Reynolds calls the mode of "Dark Adventure," featured pirates, monsters, orgies, the macabre, and other sensational topics with apocalyptic endings. As Reynolds reports, these pamphlet novels "constituted nearly 35 percent of all fiction volumes published in America between 1830 and 1860." Some workers joined millenarian sects, such as the Millerites and the Shakers, during the depression years of the early forties. More of them at this time were frightened by the apocalyptic fears induced by evangelical preachers—a kind of preaching that labor historian E. P. Thompson has called "religious terrorism." Others applauded the speeches of labor radicals who, although they did not support gang vendettas and most other expressions of Bowery honor, liked to summon up images of a coming catastrophe to warn the powerful of what might happen if workers were denied their rights. John Commerford, head of the General Trades Union in New York during the 1830s, wrote of a "day of retribution" for workers. Like prophet-avengers, labor leaders often spoke as though the days of decadence were numbered; surely some apocalypse would occur to sweep evil from the world and avenge the wrongs suffered by the industrious mechanic.[26]

The closest many urban Americans got to an apocalyptic experience was a working-class riot. As labor historian Herbert Gutman notes, "Both the form and the content of much expressive [antebellum] working-class behavior . . . often revealed the powerful role of secular and religious rituals." Gutman's general conclusion can be carried a step further and applied more specifically. The structure, imagery, and rhetoric recurring in most working-class riots in the theatre and elsewhere made them potent symbolic events for their producers and spectators. According to historians George Rudé and Eric Hobsbawm, these preindustrial riots typically involved the following scenario: finding a villain perceived to be the cause of a specific social injustice; rallying to the call of a hero who inspires his followers to brave acts of revenge; making use of inflammatory slogans, stirring rhetoric, and a panoply of mystically charged symbols to increase group solidarity; and, finally, destroying machinery, buildings, and other symbols of villainous power. The obvious parallel between the formula of apocalyptic melodrama and the usual scenario of preindustrial riots suggests the strong possibility of cultural circulation and mutual legitimation, especially since working-class theatregoers and rioters were often the same people. The experiences of applauding apocalyptic melodrama and performing a theatre riot reinforced Bowery honor for their working-class participants.[27]

The Farren riot of 1834 and the Astor Place riot of 1849 began as theatre riots but rippled outward to encompass the racial or class tensions of New York City. A disgruntled actor began the Farren riot to avenge his firing and a mob of workers joined in its later antiabolitionist phase to oust blacks from jobs they wanted for themselves. Rioters at the Astor Place Opera House were avenging the treatment of their democratic hero, Edwin Forrest, at the hands of William Macready, a symbol, to them, of aristocratic villainy. As rituals of honor and vengeance, the Astor Place and Farren riots were generally representative of other acts of working-class mob violence during the 1830 to 1855 period.

Riot burned over American cities in 1834, scorching New York thirteen times in that year alone, the worst outbreak of mob violence since the days of the Revolutionary War. Similar political, nativist, and antiabolitionist disturbances in Philadelphia, Baltimore, Boston, and twelve other cities paralleled the violence in New York. The worst of the riots in Gotham, which destroyed over sixty buildings and caused numerous injuries (though few deaths), occurred during several days in July. A remark made by William Farren, the English-born stage manager at the Bowery Theatre, helped to precipitate the incident. According to reports, Farren stated: "Damn the Yankees; they are a damn set of jackasses and fit to be gulled." D. D. McKinney, an actor fired by Hamblin for refusing to learn his lines, used newspaper announcements and other means to gather together a group of men intent on avenging Farren's and Hamblin's purportedly unpatriotic behavior. At a benefit performance for Farren on July 9, a mob of more than a thousand people, no doubt including McKinney and his gang, broke down the front doors of the theatre, stopped the performance, and demanded Farren's dismissal and an apology from Hamblin. Hamblin complied, but most of the mob, many of whom had gathered initially to protest an antislavery meeting in the nearby Chatham Street Chapel, proceeded to the home of abolitionist leader Lewis Tappan, where they broke doors and windows and burned much of the furniture. Meanwhile, Thomas "Daddy" Rice performed his racist contortions as Jim Crow at the Bowery to keep Hamblin's crowd amused. During the next two days, mob violence against the homes, churches, and businesses of New York African-Americans and abolitionists burned out of control. Finally, the mayor called out the National Guard to quell the violence.[28]

The Astor Place riot of 1849 topped other disturbances of that year in lives lost. Beginning in the dispute between Forrest and Macready, it culminated when Forrest's Tammany friends and Bowery followers decided to avenge the wrongs suffered by their hero at the opera house. On May 10, 1849, some of the b'hoys stopped Macready's *Macbeth* while others outside threw rocks at the building. An ineffective show of force by the New York police further inflamed the mob, which set fires inside the opera house and began throwing paving stones through the windows. The arrival of the militia and their initial volley over the heads of the rioters momentarily quelled the crowd, but they surged forward again in the mistaken belief that the military was using blanks. The next volley left twenty-two dead, many of them onlookers, and scores wounded. Crowds gathered the next day to protest this "murderous outrage," but military preparedness kept them at bay.[29]

Although a demographic profile of the mob in the Farren and Astor Place riots is difficult to draw, enough evidence exists to conclude that most rioters were of the same class, age, and sex as the typical Bowery theatregoer. Of the twenty-two males who died in the 1849 riot, sixteen were listed in an anonymous account of the violence—a synthesis of several newspaper reports—whose occupations were working-class, with only two who were not workers, while the rest were not identified by occupation. Also, at least thirteen were under twenty-five years of age (out of nineteen whose ages were listed). Although many of those who died were onlookers, the presence of such a great proportion of young male workers in the surrounding crowd in an upper-class square of the city suggests that many spectators came to cheer on their working-class friends and gang members. Newspaper accounts, too, stressed the involvement of the b'hoys in the violence.

Regarding the Farren riot, the friends of the ousted actor McKinney were doubtless Bowery Theatre regulars. The man who swore out a statement that Farren had damned the Yankees was a butcher, a trade the New York members of which were often involved in rioting. Further, the Chatham Street Chapel near the Bowery Theatre was an initial target of violence, and most of the destruction of African-American homes and establishments occurred in a predominately working-class neighborhood. Sufficient circumstantial evidence exists, then, to conclude that the mobs in the Farren and Astor Place riots were predominately young, working-class men. The typical rioter also had "ties to the Jacksonian equivalent of the modern urban gang, the firehouse company," notes one historian.[30] The audience for apocalyptic melodrama was virtually identical.

In both riots, as in apocalyptic melodrama, the mob perceived a conspiratorial web of villainy to be the root cause of the problem. For several weeks preceding the Farren riot, many New York newspapers spread rumors linking abolitionism to "amalgamation," that is, interracial marriage. They alleged that abolitionist ministers were regularly conducting such ceremonies, that the prominent abolitionist Arthur Tappan had married an African-American, and that black "dandies" were attempting to attract white females. Even the *Evening Post*, generally a defender of antislavery activities, reported that abolitionists "had entered into a conspiracy against the human species by promoting marriage between the blacks and whites." As historian Paul Gilje notes, racism mixed with patriotism to attach Farren to this chain of amalgamationist evil: "Since middle-class abolitionists like the Tappan brothers were popularly associated with the British abolition movement, the crowd may have focused on Farren to express their resentment at British abolitionist intrusion into America." Breaking this chain which threatened to crush "the human species" and avenging the insults of Tappan and his British-born minions became the patriotic duty of every full-blooded white American.[31]

Class antagonism between the rich and poor defined conspiratorial villainy for the rioters in 1849. Macready, with his aloof acting style and English aristocratic connections, came ready-made for artisan nomination to villainy. An anonymous but typical "American citizen," for example, dubbed the English star "the pet of princes and nobles— the stately but frigid representative of kings." Macready, like Farren before him, became a transparent target through which the rioters perceived a more pervasive evil—in this case, the threat of aristocratic domination. "Working men: Shall Americans or English rule in this city?" demanded posters put up before Macready's arrival in New York. With no basis in fact, the poster also claimed:

> The crew of the *British Steamer* have threatened all Americans who shall dare to express their opinion on this night at the English Aristocratic Opera House!!!
>
> We advocate no violence, but a free expression of opinion to all public men!
>
> WORKING MEN! FREEMEN!
Stand by your
LAWFUL RIGHTS.
>
> American Committee.

The American Committee, a group of nativist politicians and their gangs, fired broadsides of posters, pamphlets, and newspaper statements at "aristocrats" before and during the rioting. And the day after the riot, the committee urged citizens to "own yourselves sons of the iron hearts of '76" by protesting the killings. When police officers were stationed at the opera house to stop further mob violence, one Tammany politician told the assembled crowd that they had been placed there "to avenge the aristocrats of this city against the working classes." As the anonymous *Account* reported after the riot, "Macready was a subordinate personage, and he was to be put down less on his own account than to spite his aristocratic supporters. The question became not only a national, but a social one. It was the rich against the poor—the aristocracy against the people. Forrest's advocates looked upon it as a piece of retributive justice."[32]

Both riots featured wronged avengers in starring roles, with McKinney attempting to play the millenarian part of prophet as well. As Rudé notes, the heroes embraced by preindustrial mobs were themselves often reluctant to riot; they usually stayed nearby to watch the spectacle of their vindication.[33] Forrest lurked in the wings while the American Committee led the attack. Though no doubt pleased that his Democratic worshippers were avenging the Englishman's insults, he apparently stopped short of planning or participating in the riot itself.

Like Forrest, McKinney was an active avenger before the fighting began, but then disappeared offstage during the riot. Somewhat like Marteau in *The Carpenter of Rouen,* the disgruntled actor gathered with his compatriots to counter Hamblin's evil power with a resolution ringing with the republican rhetoric of the Revolutionary War. McKinney's resolution damned Hamblin's managerial regulations for the Bowery Theatre as "tyrannical and arbitrary in the extreme," excoriated Hamblin's disposition as "despotic, aristocratic, and unprincipled," and demanded that the Bowery manager reverse his support of "the illegal and despotic conduct of Mr. Farren, the stage manager, towards Mr. McKinney." By thus wrapping himself in the flag, McKinney identified his own honor with that of the country. His rhetoric of patriotic vengeance also set him apart as a self-appointed prophet; he certainly knew that calling Hamblin an unprincipled tyrant would conjure up images of the revolution-to-come for his followers.[34]

Separated from the pervasive evil they saw around them and inspired by a charismatic avenger, the rioters of 1834 and 1849 sought solidarity in ritually charged acts of defiance. According to a contemporary, minutes before the start of Macready's *Macbeth* the b'hoys inside the opera house began their "regular 'tramp' warning peculiar to the Chatham and Bowery," a cacophony of clapping and banging which signaled their desire to start the show. They increased this racket to a crescendo to force Macready's appearance. This minor rite trumpeted the power of the b'hoys and their contempt for the kid-glove manners of the "aristocrats" in the audience. The 1834 rioters adopted a system of biblical semiosis to distinguish white from black homes by spreading the word that white families were to keep candles lighted in their windows so that the riotous "plague" might pass over them. In the theatre part of the Farren riot, wealthy New Yorker Philip Hone reported in his diary that "poor Hamblin" was "hissed and pelted" at the Bowery despite "the talisman which he relied upon, the American flag, which he waved over his head." The rioters' respect for objects of ritual significance (Hamblin's pelting notwithstanding) occasionally took an ironic turn. In the midst of destroying the house and possessions of Lewis Tappan, a few of the rioters paused to rescue a portrait of

George Washington from the flames, gently setting it aside to guard it from accidental harm.[35]

Both riots culminated in the ritual desecration of symbols of aristocratic oppression. In addition to burning and wrecking Tappan's belongings, the 1834 rioters fired or pulled down over sixty African-American residences and churches. In 1849, the b'hoys broke windows, chairs, and other furnishings in the opera house, set fires in the basement, and attempted to batter down the front doors. As in the earlier riot, the mob's vengeance was directed against symbols of evil, not against the aristocratic spectators or even against Macready. This tradition of rioting, carried over from the eighteenth century, separated most antebellum mob violence from apocalyptic melodrama, where a vengeful God slaughtered the wicked as well as burning their property. Clearly, however, what the rioters of 1834 and 1849 had in mind was staging the same sort of spectacular destruction they had seen so often in Bowery theatres: an all-consuming fire that would burn away their bitterness by destroying an image of villainy.

Although the rioters gained their imitation apocalypse in 1834, the intervention of the militia cut short their ritual in 1849. From a dramaturgical point of view, the Astor Place riot was a failure, arousing expectations of a spectacular finale—a burning opera house—and then frustrating them when the militia's deadly response truncated the pyramid of dramatic action. This, perhaps as much as anything, accounted for the barricades, bonfires, and further assaults on the hated opera house on the night following the principal riot. The American Committee, like their counterparts in 1834, had carefully planned the riot, but it did not foresee and certainly did not welcome the arrival of the military. Rudé remarks that traditional riots rarely happened entirely according to plan; instead, they often assumed "a dimension and momentum that no one, not even the most experienced of leaders, could have planned or expected."[36] The leaders of the 1834 and 1849 mobs may have designed a scenario roughly similar in its structure to apocalyptic melodrama, but accident and chance insured that their riots would never match their artistry.

In other ways, too, the fit between the melodramas and the mob violence was inexact. The plays were both more extreme and less complex than the riots. Both the amalgamationists and their abolitionist allies and Macready and his aristocratic minions may have been secretive and decadent from the rioters' point of view, but the mob did not assume that their powers encompassed religious as well as social and economic authority. Further, McKinney and Forrest, both more avengers than prophets in their social melodramas, did not lead the assault on their oppressors, further separating their roles from those of Marteau or the Jibbenainosay. Nonetheless, these plays and riots shared two massive congruences: both were motivated by Bowery honor and both climaxed ideally in a spectacle of destruction. Given these factors, it is likely that the actions and ideology of apocalyptic melodramas and preindustrial working-class riots legitimated each other in the minds of their primary participants and spectators, traditionalist male workers.

In considering antebellum riots and play performances as similitudes, the historian must note that participants in neither event were fully conscious of the meanings of their actions for themselves. Thus, in 1834, the white mob was doing much more than avenging an insult to their racial pride and ousting some blacks from their jobs; they were also celebrating an avenger, solidifying their social group, and reaching for a kind of millennial catharsis—motives and meanings generally beyond the consciousness of most rioters. In effect, the conscious intentions and planned structure of their riots provided a necessary framework for their irrational, cathartic affect. Just as the rhetoric of theatrical performances must be structured to achieve a desired response, so too was it necessary to plot out a riot to excite the participants and spectators and perhaps partly to purge them of their bitterness and fear. The rioters, then, not only did the acting but also the playwriting and a bit of the directing for their performances. Although theirs was mostly an amateur production, the rioters of 1834 and 1849 who frequented the Bowery theatres certainly understood the emotional satisfaction that the pursuit of vengeance and destruction could bring.

By 1849, workers were becoming the primary audience for their riots. Of course mobs had always enjoyed their own handiwork, but in 1834 a wide variety of New Yorkers, including wealthy businessmen and middle-class women, enjoyed the show of looting, destruction, and burning in the Farren riot. In the Astor Place riot, in contrast, the performance admired by working-class spectators was meant to overturn the norms of respectability and horrify the elite. Philip Hone reported in his *Diary*, "I walked up to the corner of Astor Place but was glad to make my escape." George Templeton Strong, another New York patrician, attended the opera house on the night of the riot and confided to his diary the next day:

> Prospect of a repetition of the [b'hoys'] performances tonight on a larger scale, for the blackguards swear they'll have vengeance. The houses of the gentlemen who signed the invitation to Macready to perform last night threatened. Judge [William] Kent and Mr. Ruggles and some six or seven others of them live on Union Square and that will, therefore, very probably be a scene of disturbance. I'm going up now to clean my pistols, and if possible to get my poor wife's portrait out of harm's way.

Strong, generally a levelheaded and ironically humorous man, was not overreacting. He knew that his economic class and public reputation made his house a possible target for an encore performance of the b'hoys' ritual vendetta.[37]

This contrast between the intended audiences in 1834 and 1849 is sharpened by focusing on those to whom the promotional campaign for each production was directed. In 1834, newspaper editorials enjoined all white Americans (minus the Tappans and other abolitionists) to protest the purported outrages. And McKinney addressed his declaration of independence to a presumed general audience of republicans throughout the city. Tammany satraps and their gangs appealed primarily to a working-class audience of Democrats in 1849, a much narrower group. This evidence, plus the rising number of complaints about riotous workers and the establishment of a municipal police department in 1845, suggests that most urban Americans were coming to view mob violence as the deviant behavior of a distinct minority, perpetrated by an underclass and enjoyed by them alone.

This conclusion is borne out by the shifting social base of justification for working-class mob violence, a shift that also helps to explain the quasi-millenarian values of apocalyptic melodrama. The Anglo-American mob tradition growing out of the eighteenth century had rested on the legitimacy of paternalistic, elite authority. In the typical preindustrial riot, the elite granted the mob a "kind of temporary license," in the words of one historian, to protest a wrong that most citizens of the town agreed was unjust, but which remained, for whatever reason, be-

The Attack upon the Astor-Place Opera House, *woodcut in newspaper, 1849
(Harvard Theatre Collection). This print, like most contemporary images of
the riot, emphasizes the threatening deviancy of the mob, not the use of
military force.*

yond the reach of the law. Once the limited goals of the mob had been met, the elite reestablished its fatherly control. The outline, if not the entire substance, of these traditional rioting conventions remained in 1834 as New York patricians watched working-class rioters destroy African-American homes and churches but did not oppose them because the rioters were acting within the consensus of community values. Although these traditional rules of the game were already breaking down in the 1820s, they retained sufficient social strength, when backed by patrician resolve, to stop a riot at the Park Theatre in 1838. According to *The Spirit of the Times*, elite theatregoers faced down a working-class mob, apparently convincing them that "any attempt to incite a disturbance would be promptly put down."[38] Of course the Park, unlike the Bowery and Chatham, continued to attract substantial elite patronage during the 1830s.

These consensual conventions specifying working-class deference to limits set by the elite carried no force whatever by 1849. Workers looked to their own increasingly distinctive culture for justification for their riotous actions; they found it partly in productions of apocalyptic melodrama. In this regard, it is significant that representatives of elite power in these plays are invariably villains, conspiring to rob the innocent outcast of his bread, his wife, and his freedom. If the protomillenarian symbology of apocalyptic melodrama figured centrally in the minds of rioters in 1849, the mob was not simply redressing the balance of an unjust social order but, from its own perspective, seeking transcendent vengeance on all the villains in their lives. As Eric Hobsbawm, historian of European mob violence, remarks, "There are moments [in a riot] when the apocalypse seems imminent; when the entire structure of existing society, whose total end the apocalypse symbolizes and predicts, actually looks about to collapse in ruins, and the tiny ray of hope turns into the light of possible sunrise."[39] Rioters responsive to the formula of catastrophic melodrama would likely have found several such moments of imminent apocalypse in 1849. That there is no direct historical evidence for this is not surprising. Participants in working-class mobs not fully conscious of their motives and desires cannot be expected to have spoken of or written about all the hopes and fears animating their actions.

Taken together, the riots and melodramas chart a pessimistic, belligerent, and Calvinistic ideology underlying the actions of the workers who participated as actors and/or spectators in both kinds of events. At the center of this nexus of action and belief was the imperative of avenging insults to Bowery honor by wreaking vengeful destruction against symbols of villainy. Also central was the confluence of proto-millenarianism and Jacksonian Calvinism, which together justified human-made terror by linking it to the strong arm of a wrathful God. Like other Jacksonians, these tradition-directed workers desired a republican revolution to destroy aristocratic oppression, but unlike many Democrats, they turned their backs on the hope of utopian freedom in a liberal, Lockean Arcadia. These workers looked to deviant avengers as role models, but expected that group solidarity would be just as important as Napoleonic leadership in avenging past wrongs. Given this balance between their attraction to charismatic leadership and their conformity to traditional group norms, these workers were probably more inclined to support egalitarian democracy than some other Democratic groups; certainly most men of Bowery honor believed that they were the political equals of anyone, regardless of wealth or class. Their truculent or aggressive assertion of republican equality, however, stopped far short of endorsing equal rights for all individuals; villains had no rights when honor was at stake, and women could never be the equals of men. While the practices of Bowery honor in the theatre and elsewhere frame this working-class society within the general confines of yeoman culture, apocalyptic melodrama paints their specific ideology in deeper values and darker hues.

Heroic and apocalyptic melodramas continued to attract tradition-directed workers after 1850, but in dwindling numbers. This was partly because workers had other kinds of entertainments from which to choose. Since over half of the working-class populations in Boston, New York, and Philadelphia were recent immigrants, theatre managers began to tailor their shows to the tastes and needs of specific immigrant groups. Thus, Irish-American plays and, to a lesser extent, German-language productions began to crowd out apocalyptic melodramas on working-class stages. These and other workers also turned to tent circuses, minstrel shows, variety acts, and equestrian spectacles in the 1850s. Some traditionalist workers abandoned their Bowery haunts to cultivate a more respectable self-image by patronizing moral reform melodrama at one of the new museum theatres.

In his history of bare-knuckle prizefighting in New York City in the 1850s, Elliott J. Gorn remarks,

> Working-class men adopted their own forms of expressive culture and prize fighting symbolically affirmed their distinct ethos. If not a political threat to new alignments of social and economic power, the ring at least offered cultural opposition; if not a challenge to evangelical and bourgeois authority, here at least was a denial of the values that undergirded oppressive social relations.

Similarly, traditionalist workers used theatre riots and apocalyptic plays in the 1840s to flaunt their opposition to emerging Victorian norms of domesticity, moral character, and contractual economic relations. Both their plays and their riots, like their prizefights, affirmed the reality of violence and the importance of cunning and manliness in their daily lives. Most workers in the audience rejected glib assertions of liberal progress and probably questioned their own republican virtue, but Bowery honor still prompted them to celebrate their independence. Winning a boxing match, setting a fire in a riot, conquering a girlfriend, and cheering for a prophet-avenger at the playhouse offered immediate and palpable rewards. And knowing that their actions and values deviated from the social and legal norms of the new bourgeois culture made their behavior all the more vengeful and sweet.[40]

PART III

Business-Class Theatre for

the Respectable, 1845–1870

By 1870, northeastern urbanites saw two kinds of theatre in their cities: respectable and unrespectable. Respectability, defined by midcentury Americans as self-control, principled behavior, and virtuous affection, had not constructed most playgoing before 1840. Patrician and plebeian urbanites alike had assumed that they would encounter prostitutes, drunkards, noisy spectators, and occasional riots, as well as risqué spectacles on stage, when they went to the theatre. Business-class moralists, however, increasingly ruled such behavior out of bounds for respectable folks, and the result was a minor revolution in the theatre. Leading the way were the owners of the new museum theatres, who promised their patrons chaste entertainment in environments closer to the church and the front parlor than to traditional playhouses. Other theatre managers incorporated many museum theatre innovations in the 1850s, excluding prostitutes and liquor and encouraging family attendance. Melodrama changed too. As heroic and apocalyptic melodrama declined in popularity, moral reform plays took their place with many of the same spectators. The sensation melodrama which emerged after 1855 confirmed the dominance of the new business class.

The expansion of capitalism after 1845 generated these changes and led to the proliferation of new occupations for men and new economic roles for women, creating a more modern and diverse bourgeoisie. The role of the general merchant who bought, shipped, and marketed goods gave way to more specialized positions involving managerial as well as entrepreneurial skills. These new commission merchants, jobbers, salespeople, retailers, clerks, and others earned yearly salaries, not weekly wages. They and their families joined others with occupations in the emerging communication, transportation, and entertainment fields to buy the products of early industrialization for themselves and their homes, including broadcloth suits and dresses, wool carpeting, and indoor toilets. Mass production and new marketing techniques drove down the prices of most consumer goods during the period as women took the place of men as the primary shoppers for the family. Bourgeois consumption in this liberal market economy made Alexander T. Stewart and Horace B. Claflin, the owners of the first two general department stores in New York City, millionaires by 1860. By then, roughly 35 percent of the urban families in the Philadelphia and New York regions belonged to one or another stratum of the new business class.[1]

The new bourgeoisie challenged the beliefs and behavior of the traditional patrician and artisan classes. Their market-oriented competitiveness undermined the older elite notions of property and patriarchy and destroyed the possibility of yeoman self-sufficiency for traditional workers. The acquisitive and rationalistic individualism of the new business class undercut the ideals of republican citizenship believed in by both artisans and patricians. Joining together the different strata of the bourgeoisie, from the wealthy manufacturer to the aspiring clerk, was the ideology of respectability, forged in the class conflicts of the antebellum city. And separating them from the working-class below was the fundamental distinction between mental and physical labor. As the Reverend Jonathan F. Stearns explained in 1857, "the business class" included "not the merchant or the trader only," but "all those whose vocation it is to organize and direct the industrial forces of the community—the manufacturer, the master mechanic, the contractor, or the superintendent, in the various enterprises of production, accommodation, or improvement." Noted another moralist of the business class, "The man who carries on any business must have others to carry out his plans. He must contrive, others must execute. . . . Hence he advertises for *hands*, not heads—for manual labor, and not for mental."[2]

The distinction between manual and mental labor spilled into nearly all aspects of urban life, figuring prominently in class differences relating to family income, habits of consumption, work environment, and even home décor after 1850. By midcentury, several social barricades segregated the respectable from the unwashed in northeastern cities: housing patterns kept the poor in their own neighborhoods or back alleys, architectural divisions separated manual from nonmanual workers in places of employment, and new metropolitan police forces maintained order on city streets. Those with the economic means could demonstrate their gentility through the trappings of sentimentality. But the families of many shopkeepers, artisans, clerks, and others near either side of the class margin unable to afford the costumes and rituals of the emergent culture had to look elsewhere to convince their neighbors of their respectability. Many male workers gave up traditionalist habits and adopted "the new industrial morality" of hard work, temperance, and perseverance in the hope of achieving self-made success. Following the dictates of respectable society, many women near the class line turned to sentimental domesticity to cultivate a respectable self-image.[3]

As the theatre changed to fulfill these new social needs, many families of moderate means found in playgoing both instruction in the norms of respectability and release from their pressures. After midcentury, this theatrical formation shifted from emergent to dominant, as the new business class established its own theatres and patronized a kind of melodrama which consolidated its hegemony. Enjoying these sensation melodramas helped the new bourgeoisie to make sense of altered class relations, eased the definition of respectability for men, broadened the notion of virtue for women, and empowered audiences to play their new social roles without hypocrisy or embarassment. Such innovations as the long run and darkened houselights during performance turned playgoing into an extension of consumer culture; audiences retreated from public interaction toward private enjoyment in their theatres. When the network of itinerant starring joined to stock company production could no longer deliver popular stars after the panic of 1873, the bourgeoisie abandoned the stock system for the combination mode of production. In this new system, stars hired actors and rented theatres, like other manager-capitalists, reducing former stock actors to proletarian status. The dynamics of capitalism during the 1870s nearly eliminated a mode of production that had dominated the American theatre since its inception over a hundred years before.

6. "We Will Restore You to Society"

In 1865, following the destruction of his American Museum by fire, P. T. Barnum wrote a stinging response to a letter in the *Nation* charging that his lecture room theatre had presented immoral plays to pander to degraded spectators. "No vulgar word or gesture and not a profane expression was *ever* allowed on my stage," he insisted. "Even in Shakespeare's plays, I unflinchingly and invariably cut out vulgarity and profanity." To the accusation that "it had been many years since a citizen could take his wife or daughter to see a play on that stage," Barnum countered that his productions had educated and uplifted many families in New York City. Admitting that the taste of his audience "was not elevated," that "millions of persons were only induced to see [his educational plays] because, at the same time, they could see whales, giants, dwarfs, Albinos, dog shows, et cetera," Barnum nonetheless defended the respectability of his establishment. He had even hired detectives, he pointed out, to keep his museum above reproach:

> I would not even allow my visitors to "go out to drink" and return again without paying the second time, and this reconciled them to the "icewater" which was always profuse and free on each floor of the Museum. I could not personally or by proxy examine into the character of every visitor, but I continually had half a score of detectives dressed in plain clothes, who incontinently turned into the street every person of either sex whose actions indicated loose habits. My interest ever depended upon my keeping a good reputation for my Museum.[1]

Barnum was right to be concerned. The proprietary museums that flourished from the mid 1840s through the 1850s in the urban centers of the Northeast depended upon their reputation for respectability. At a time when class consciousness was segregating nearly all forms of urban entertainment, museums drew their audiences predominately from those just above or below the class line. Because mixed-class patronage was vital to their success, Moses Kimball at the Boston Museum and Barnum at the American developed entertainments respectable enough to preserve and enhance the reputations of their establishments, yet affordable enough to attract the millions. No doubt these museum curiosities and performances produced a variety of effects and responses in the hearts and minds of antebellum spectators. On the whole, however, three distinct rhetorics were at play in the exhibit sections of these museums: sentimental, gothic, and rational. While these rhetorics, in their different ways, helped to fold thousands of status-anxious urbanites into the embrace of the emergent business-class culture, the rationalism of the exhibits gained added force in museum performances of moral melodrama. The disparate meanings generated by these experiences contained contradictions, both within and among themselves, that would partly undermine even as they legitimated bourgeois values.[2]

While there is little direct evidence concerning the class, gender, and cultural orientation of most museumgoers in Boston and New York in the 1840s and 1850s, it is likely that the popularity of museums cut across most lines distinguishing social groups. Given the low admission prices at both museums—25¢ for adults and 12½¢ for children before 1860—plus the preponderance of low- and moderate-income people in both cities before the Civil War, most of their patrons must have come from moderate-income groups, citizens especially vulnerable to status anxiety.[3] William W. Clapp noted in his history of theatre in Boston that

> [Kimball's] museum attracted all classes, and it was the resort not only of the middling and lower classes, but of the more wealthy residents, for the pieces were well put upon the stage and the actors above mediocrity. The museum was then and is now patronized by a large class who do not frequent theatres.

A British traveler in the mid 1850s echoed Clapp's allusion to unsophisticated spectators: "Those who would shudder at the base idea of witnessing a play, be it even *Hamlet* or *The Rivals*, . . . will yield to the fascinations of some third-rate 'moral drama' on the boards of the 'Museum.'"[4]

With regard to working-class patronage, Barnum regularly featured Bowery stars who were already popular with working-class theatregoers; he hired J. R. Scott, the king of Bowery bombast, for a season in the mid fifties, for instance. Similarly, Kimball paid J. S. Jones, best known for his *Carpenter of Rouen*, to construct *Old Job and Jacob Gray* for his museum audience. *Old Job* "pictured so perfectly a Boston mechanic's life that the characters were real," stated one contemporary; it became one of the museum's most successful productions in the late forties. To reach the several communities of these artisans living on the outskirts of Boston, Kimball arranged special omnibuses and, later, trains, so that respectable workers and their families living in Roxbury or Cambridge could be sure of a ride home after the show. During the 1850s when New York managers were moving their business-class theatres uptown beyond Astor Place, Barnum remained at Broadway and Ann Street, a reputable neighborhood below City Hall but within easy walking distance from the Lower East Side and nearby moderate-income districts.[5]

Barnum and Kimball also encouraged the patronage of women and children. Noting the numerous women spectators at New York museums, one contemporary commented, "Thousands who, from motives of delicacy, cannot bring themselves to attend theatrical representations in a *theatre* find it easy enough to reconcile a *museum*, and its vaudevilles and plays, to their consciences." The museum impresarios encouraged this distinction to attract female customers. In a printed letter widely circulated before the opening of his much-enlarged lecture room in 1850, Barnum stated:

> My whole aim and effort is to make my museums [he owned a smaller museum uptown] totally unobjectionable to the religious and moral community, and at the same time combine sufficient amusement with instruction to please all proper tastes and to train the mind of youth to reject as repugnant anything inconsistent with moral and refined taste.

Kimball, who operated his lecture room as a complete theatre six years before Barnum, began scheduling matinee performances on Wednesday and Saturday afternoons (when children were out of school) to accommodate and increase female attendance. Other managers had tried matinees before, but as long as the theatre was a predominately male ritual few afternoon performances had been profitable. By the 1850s, with Barnum offering five matinees a week, afternoon performances for women and children had become a theatregoing convention.[6]

Further, these men and women of moderate means were predominately Protestant in cultural orientation, if not in religious practice. Neither manager produced the kinds of entertainment popular primarily with Catholic Irish- and German-American working-class audiences. Rather, they featured moral reform melodramas like *Rosina Meadows* and *The Six Degrees of Crime*, which derived from the traditions of Calvinism and appealed mostly to native-born workers and lower-strata members of the business class from Protestant backgrounds. Both managers also trumpeted their endorsement of temperance, a cause offensive to most Catholic immigrants, and enforced their teetotalism throughout their establishments. Some Protestants continued to view even moral plays and exhibits as immoral temptations, of course. Harriet Beecher Stowe feared that "if the barrier which now keeps young people of religious families from theatrical entertainments is once broken down by the introduction of respectable and moral plays, they will then be open to all the temptations of those which are not such." But most urban Americans had few such scruples. An anonymous *History of the Boston Museum* published in 1873 declared that since its founding "not a single piece has been produced that has reflected discredit upon the management or offended the moral sense of the audience."[7] Museum audiences, then, were predominately native-born family members of moderate means, were oriented toward Protestantism, and may have included almost as many women as men.

Concern for their position in midcentury urban society led to a variety of responses among these city dwellers. Most of the workers who patronized museums were not traditionalists bound by Bowery honor, but "revivalists," historian Bruce Laurie's term for men and women workers who looked to religion for guidance, practiced frugality and perseverance in their lives, and saw their own success as a matter of respectability and individual effort, not working-class solidarity. Many of the male artisans owned a little property and joined conservative trade organizations, such as the American Institute and the Mechanics Institute in New York City, where they heard lectures praising the maxims of Benjamin Franklin and the virtues of free-market competition. During the depression years of the early 1840s, some traditionalist workers rejected Bowery culture as sinful and embraced movements such as temperance and health reform which promised social status and economic success through a regimen of self-control. One temperance society, the Washingtonians, attracted a substantial working-class membership through cathartic "experience meetings" and raucous (but cold-water) picnics and dances. In the mid 1840s, many revivalist workers turned to the antiforeign, Protestant politics of nativism and joined mutual aid societies designed to help each other and restrict immigrant access to jobs. Listening to a lecture at a mechanics' institute, taking the temperance pledge, and denouncing Catholic immigrants gave these workers a sense of controlling their own lives and perhaps winning a measure of social respectability.[8]

These same motives also led many in the lower strata of the business class to join benevolent societies, temperance groups, and nativist political parties. Nativism, in fact, exerted its strongest appeal among shopkeepers, contractors, and other petite bourgeoisie in Philadelphia, Boston, and New York near the class line. (Interestingly, Moses Kimball ran for the Boston mayoralty on the nativist ticket in the late 1850s.) Many clerks, salespersons, bookkeepers, and other nonmanual employees who identified with the values of their employers filled the lower ranks of the religious tract, temperance, and Sunday school societies of their cities. These mostly young men gave speeches at local gatherings and distributed monthly journals like the *Temperance Recorder*, which featured melodramatic tales of businessmen whose moderate drinking led them, step by fateful step, to ruin and infamy. From the mid forties through the fifties, this group defined itself as a class more by its fear of losing respectability than by its hope of rising into the elite.[9]

Although women of moderate means could do less than men to work for the moral reform of their cities, many female revivalists attended lectures on self-help, religion, and domesticity. Charles Dickens reported in his *American Notes* (1842) that "[Boston] ladies who have a passion for attending lectures are to be found among all classes and conditions." Some of these lecturegoers joined missions and visited the homes of the poor to distribute religious tracts and urge temperance, industry, and frugality on their inhabitants. For the most part, as historian Christine Stansell concludes, evangelical bourgeois women did little to help the poor; their presence may even have convinced some working-class women to stop working for wages and practice domesticity. The emergent culture defined respectable women as wives and mothers, not workers. Concerned to train their children in habits of discipline and morality which might aid their later success, many women near the class margin enrolled them in the new public and Sunday schools, significant agents of socialization in the culture of gentility.[10]

Families of moderate income also turned to the ideology of domesticity to enhance their status. Though generally sentimental in orientation, domesticity limited the objects and goals of sentimental compassion to those approved by the emerging culture. According to the advocates of domestic values in the pulpit, the government, and the publishing industry, men should control the institutions of worldly power while women exercised their more spiritual expertise in home and family matters. Genteel propriety mandated that self-control and spirituality restrain and purify the tensions of home life. Family members, led by the mother, should treat one another with sincerity and "sensibility," a term which midcentury Americans took to mean sensitivity to and concern for the feelings and morals of others. Thus if her home were a place where "heart meets heart, in all the fondness of a full affection," the sentimental wife might believe she was performing her duty to her husband and children. The central values of respectable domesticity—self-control, spirituality, sincerity, and sensibility—helped to shape several of the social institutions and reform movements of the antebellum era. Like revivalism, however, domesticity turned the problems of social order and economic justice back onto the family and the individual. Neither led status-anxious urbanites toward a questioning of the emergent culture of respectability.[11]

The backgrounds and personalities of Moses Kimball and P. T. Barnum inclined both men to seek to profit from the social anxieties of their audiences. Like other New England children growing up in small towns during the early national period, Kimball and Barnum had learned to stitch the remnants of Puritan spirituality and sincerity to the quilt of Yankee cunning and competitiveness. Kimball tried real estate, newspaper publishing, and a printing company before he and his brother purchased the collections of the indebted New England Museum in 1838. Barnum, too, trained himself to become a museum impresario through various short-lived enterprises combining hucksterism, managerial skills, and the appearance of sincerity and sensibility. Contemporaries of Kimball remembered him for his "quick intelligence, his strong good sense," his habits of "methodical and systematic hard work," but also for a "certain impatience of opposition and a lack of the disposition to conciliate." Barnum was more flexible and outgoing, freely admitting his materialism in his autobiographies, but insisting that the humbugs from which he had profited educated and uplifted the public. Both advocated temperance, education, and health reform. As Barnum explained in public lectures with such titles as "The Art of Money Getting," self-improvement was a key to economic success. Both were also active in civic affairs: Kimball ran twice for the Boston mayoralty in the late 1850s and Barnum became the mayor of Bridgeport, Connecticut, after the Civil War. New England–born, competitive, reform-minded, and politically active, Kimball and Barnum knew firsthand the desire of their audiences for respectability.[12]

Seeing no contradiction between their profits and the public good,

Kimball and Barnum catered to their spectators with a clear conscience. The two showmen built their businesses partly on the impeccable reputations, but poor profitability, of earlier institutions dedicated to educating the public in the arts and sciences. Charles Willson Peale had established a museum in Philadelphia in 1786 where, as he observed, "every art and every science should be taught by plans, pictures, real subjects, and lectures." By 1840, proprietary museums in several cities of the Northeast featured scientific displays, waxwork figures, small menageries, landscape and portrait paintings, and magic lantern shows in lecture rooms. When Kimball and Barnum began their museums in 1841, however, interest in these leftovers from the American Enlightenment had waned. The museum impresarios understood that the public's desire to witness past scientific discoveries and artistic achievements could not sustain their operations. Charles Willson Peale had exhibited few "human curiosities," preferring instead to emphasize the rationality of nature. From the outset, Kimball and Barnum made most of their profits from their highly touted dwarfs, albinos, Siamese twins, and giants.[13]

Barnum and Kimball advertised to attract entire families to their museums. *Tom Pop's First Visit to the Boston Museum with His Grandfather, Giving an Account of What He Saw There and What He Thought,* a pamphlet distributed by Kimball and evidently intended to be read to children, demonstrates the impresario's use of the sentimental rhetoric of domesticity. Following notices on the inside cover that boast both the quality and the exoticism of the exhibits, Tom, his sister, and their grandfather make their sentimental entrance:

> And when they found themselves inside—my!—didn't they catch
> their breath and hold on tight by grandfather's coattail, and stare at
> the beautiful ceiling and the huge pillars and the long high galleries
> and the pictures and the marble women and the dear little children
> running about and peeping into the great glass windows and gig-
> gling and chirping like fun.

Having established this tone of breathless, innocent delight, the anonymous writer has grandfather instruct the children on the specifics of the stuffed birds and fossils, not neglecting to correct the children's minor (and lovable) mistakes in grammar and etiquette. At an exhibit of monkeys, grandfather ties the superiority of Christian culture to the value of a dollar. These monkeys, he tells Tom, "are worshipped in some parts of India; and when the Portuguese pillaged Ceylon, they found a poor monkey's tooth in a temple there which the poor simpletons offered 700,000 ducats for!—more than $1,500,000 dollars. What d'ye think o' that, my lad?"[14]

In the course of their sentimental education, Tom and his sister discover that nature, like human society, has its villains and victims. Grandfather points to a stuffed anaconda crushing a "poor little antelope." The children discover an orangutan that "refuse[d] to eat after his wife died" and a female polar bear that "kept pawing her cub and moaning over him after he was shot." Grandfather frequently links such pathetic domestic scenes to a religious sensibility. Indeed, he says, the entire museum is "a kind of Noah's ark . . . , bigger than the biggest church you ever saw." The pamphlet presents the museum as a series of object lessons in a domestic culture which has colonized religion, society, and nature. The exhibits have only to be interpreted by a sincere teacher like grandfather to reveal homey truths and induce a sensible reaction.[15]

Barnum and Kimball provided domestic environments for their exhibits to encourage and enhance such sentimental effects. Both impresarios surrounded their rows of artifacts, stuffed animals, and mechanical marvels with many of the attributes of a well-to-do parlor. Kimball placed his exhibits in alcoves off "a spacious and lofty hall of Grecian design," positioning several chairs where his visitors might relax in the midst of their moral education. Adorning the walls of this hall were pictures of "a chasteness and propriety . . . that cannot but please the most fastidious taste," including Sully's painting of Washington crossing the Delaware.[16]

Barnum eschewed Greek Revival for the ornamental style then coming into vogue. Writing to Kimball in the summer of 1844 about refurbishing his museum, Barnum stated his desire for "plenty of gold leaf, rich chandaliers [sic], looking glasses, etc., to make it look novel." The showman even added a domestic touch to the housing for part of his menagerie. No doubt Tom Pop and his grandfather would have applauded Barnum's "Happy Family": natural enemies—owls and mice, eagles and rabbits, cats and rats—caged together and trained to tolerate each other. In 1872, looking back over thirty years of enjoyment at the Boston Museum, a reporter for the *Boston Journal* remarked, "Indeed, the place has seemed to many more like a cozy home, abounding in pleasant conversation and lively humor, than as a temple of public amusement." In the Boston and American museums, working-class families could experience the environment of upper-strata domesticity—surroundings they might wish to emulate but could never afford.[17]

This cozy environment no doubt influenced spectator response to the displays mounted by Barnum and Kimball which miniaturized and domesticated mechanization and industrialization. Signor Vivaldi's "wonderful mechanical figures," robotlike dancing dolls, appeared frequently at the Boston and American museums. Barnum exhibited a sewing machine, "Barnum's Self-Sewer," powered by a dog on a treadmill. For two weeks during the summer of 1849, Kimball displayed "The Beauties of Mechanism, or Lowell in Boston," which featured "the manufacture of cloth from raw material using miniature machines." Such exhibits anticipated the celebration of technological progress in the world's fairs later in the century. Most museum technological wonders, however, were right at home in the parlorlike environment of their exhibit halls. Barnum and Kimball tended to downplay the appeal of new technology—its rhythms of order and efficiency and its implicit promise of progress and power—by folding its rhetoric of rationality into the rhetoric of sentimental domesticity. Moderate-income customers could see that progress enhanced domestic bliss, but they may have wondered when their own or their neighbor's experience of mechanization would be as beautiful.[18]

Museumgoers' fascination with miniatures carried over into their adoration of Barnum's most profitable attraction during the antebellum era, General Tom Thumb. By endowing the dwarf whose real name was Charles Stratton with "status-enhancing characteristics," notes sociologist Robert Bogdan, Barnum exhibited his "freak" to the public in the "aggrandized mode." Soon after signing a contract with the boy's parents in 1842, Barnum advertised the four-year-old as eleven, changed his place of birth from Bridgeport, Connecticut, to London, and rechristened him Tom Thumb, adding the title "General" to further aggrandize his status. Audiences usually laughed with Tom Thumb, rarely at him. In the vehicle crafted for his public performance, Charles played the role of an upper-class gentleman, jocular with the men and decorously flirtatious with the women in the audience. Taking his spectators into his confidence, he dressed up as different characters—a fellow at Oxford, Napoleon Bonaparte, and other high-status roles—sang popular songs, and danced with animation. His "levees," as Barnum advertised them, ended with the General assuming the poses of several familiar statues.[19]

Audiences were enchanted. One critic who had little good to say about the American Museum conceded, nonetheless, that General Tom Thumb "was really worth seeing, not only for the remarkable minuteness and perfection of his physical composition, but for the precocity and brightness of his mental attributes." Another commentator called the General "one of Nature's Indices, in which the principal features of the race may be looked at with one glance." Barnum toured his prime attraction around the country, eventually assenting to Kimball's letters entreating the showman to allow him to exhibit the General in Boston. "My receipts in New York were over $16,000—so help me God—in four weeks," bragged Barnum to his friend. Were he managing Tom Thumb's royal entry into Boston, P. T. continued, "our miniature equipage would be . . . perambulating the streets daily." Barnum had puffed Charles Stratton's introductions to the elite of New York to increase his status with the American public; after the impresario took him to England and France and advertised his audiences with Queen Victoria and King Louis Philippe, the dwarf's popularity skyrocketed.[20]

For the thousands of museumgoers anxious about their own status, aggrandized freaks like Tom Thumb offered sentimental reassurance as well as amusement. The giants, living skeletons, bearded ladies, and other human curiosities that Barnum exhibited in the aggrandized mode demonstrated the apparent democracy of the norms of respectability. If such freaks of nature commanded the respect and attention of the elite, surely all Americans who could afford to enter a museum could count themselves among the genteel. Barnum's presentations of this sort projected the aesthetics of sentimentality into the display of human oddities. By extending their compassionate concern to these freaks rather than laughing at them, spectators could celebrate their own sincerity and their sensitivity to the wonders of God's nature.[21]

Barnum and Kimball exhibited other freaks designed primarily to induce gothic horror. The "exotic" mode of freak presentation which, states Bogdan, "cast the exhibit as a strange creature from a little-known part of the world," probably thrilled and repulsed most antebellum spectators. Typically, these were nonwestern people with physical differences whom the showmen presented as bizarre by costuming them in animal skins, emphasizing the strangeness of their place of origin, producing pseudo-scientific explanations for their deformities, and occasionally staging them behind bars. Their exotic freaks included Hervey Leach, a "monkey man" presented as a "missing link," the original Siamese twins, Chang and Eng, a Negro with vitiligo, cast as a "leopard-spotted slave," and the "Aztec children," two microcephalics or "pinheads," supposedly "captured" from the wilds of Central America.

These freaks joined other gothic horrors at both museums. Chief among them was the "feejee mermaid," apparently the upper torso of a monkey joined to the lower half of a large fish, a "black, shriveled thing," according to Barnum, which both impresarios exhibited in a jar. Some of the waxwork tableaux also induced gothic responses from museum visitors. The actor Otis Skinner remembered his "horror" as a boy when viewing "Three Scenes in a Drunkard's Life." Many adults, too, probably experienced a secret thrill at the sight (in the third cabinet) of the drunkard killing his wife with a gin bottle while their "moron son" looked on.[22]

By presenting an image of otherness that was primitive, erotic, or bestial, these gothic exhibits probably recalled fears of Calvinistic sin and damnation for their mostly Protestant spectators. According to critic Joel Porte, gothic fiction was often a form of "religious terror" which represented "for its producers and consumers alike a genuine expression of profound religious malaise." For viewers who knew *Pilgrim's Progress* (next to the Bible, the most popular book of the antebellum era), attended temperance meetings and religious revivals, and believed along with their contemporaries that external physiognomy reflected internal character, gothic exhibits at museums may have induced a kind of liminal experience: viewers were both relieved to discover their own normality through the contrast to "pinheads" and drunkards and appalled to see nightmarish images of what they might become if they gave way to temptation. Struck by the physical malformation or irregularity, strange customs, and indecorous behavior of exotic freaks, museum spectators could congratulate themselves on their own ordinariness, civilization, and decorum. In this sense, the exotic otherness of these exhibits induced smug satisfaction by encouraging even the humblest working-class family to feel respectable through the contrast. The same exhibits, on the other hand, were also radically unsettling because they suggested the mutability of human forms; ordinary Dr. Jekylls might become fiendish Mr. Hydes. Both responses probably worked to reaffirm the dictates of respectable domesticity for most spectators most of the time—inducing the belief that they were already normal or the fear that they had better become more so.[23]

In their modes of exhibit presentation, Kimball and Barnum for the most part continued previous traditions; their primary innovations were in centralizing and marketing their displays. They broke with tradition, however, in attempting to convince the public that their moral lecture rooms differed substantially from immoral playhouses. Liquor and prostitution had been a part of playgoing since the eighteenth century; theatre architects even designed semiprivate bars and separate entrances to the third tier of boxes for "unescorted ladies." One reporter recalled that the third tier of the Park Theatre "was at one time the most valuable part of the house." At the Chatham, he said, "it was the rule for the girls—especially those well known to the doorkeepers—to lay off their bonnets or cloaks, and sit or walk about as much at home as if in some private parlor." (Such statements may not be wholly reliable since business-class reporters sometimes mistook working-class Bowery g'hals, who also sat in the third tier, for prostitutes.) By 1840, some spectators were objecting to "the open and shameless manner in which [the theatre] has encouraged vice." In one journalist's opinion, the fact that "a portion of each house has been set aside for public prostitutes, has been converted into an arena of assignation, a sort of vestibule to the bagnios" was the main reason for the decline of theatregoing in the early 1840s.[24] Such "shameless vice" kept most respectable women and nearly all children out of the theatre.

Despite the clear risk to his own and his museum's gentility, Kimball opened his lecture room as a theatre in 1843, at the same time publicly puffing his ban on spiritous refreshment and unescorted ladies. Soon named "the deacon's theatre" because Kimball gave free tickets to all the clergy in Boston, the first museum playhouse seated twelve hundred in rows of plain, hard chairs. As one reporter later recalled, "The 'lecture room' was in another building similar in shape and size to the first, standing parallel to it, separated from it by a wide court, and connected with it by a few bridges and corridors, so that they who had

Interior View of the Lecture Room of the American Museum, New York, *anonymous engraving* (Gleason's Pictorial, *January 29, 1853). The relative isolation of this respectable family in parlorlike surroundings—the woman is even reading a magazine—in the midst of a theatrical production suggests that Barnum may have had a hand in this promotional illustration.*

conscientious scruples about the propriety of theatrical shows need not even set foot within the four walls that contained them." Following the phenomenal success of *The Drunkard*, adapted by his ingenious stage manager William S. Smith, the impresario expanded his lecture room in 1846 to seat twenty-five hundred. The new theatre featured an orchestra with rows of padded chairs, a parquette circle around it of more chairs in short rows divided by aisles, and first and second balconies above the parquette. Gone was the hierarchical box, pit, and gallery division and in its place a seating arrangement that assured his public that all audience members were equally respectable. Kimball also abandoned the usual hierarchy of ticket prices. In fact, Kimball sold no theatre tickets at all; spectators were charged nothing extra to walk from his exhibit halls into his lecture room.[25]

Barnum used his lecture room to exhibit Tom Thumb and other freaks, but did not open it for fully staged productions right away. He feared that his American Museum was too close to the nearby Park Theatre to offer plays at a profit. After the Park burned in 1849, Barnum expanded his lecture room, hired the experienced Francis Wemyss as his stage manager, and opened with *The Drunkard.* To accommodate its successful run, Barnum expanded again in 1850, enlarging the house to seat three thousand spectators. Although no architectural plan of the theatre remains, it is likely that Barnum followed Kimball's lead in abolishing the pit and boxes; a contemporary illustration of the interior suggests this conclusion. Barnum's theatre, however, may have been more richly appointed than Kimball's. Sensing the public's desire for mixing morality and luxury, Barnum puffed on his *Drunkard* program that his "new and gorgeous lecture room [was] fitted up in the most voluptuously luxurious style and is really surpassed in its elegance, taste, refinement, delicacy, and superb finish by no royal saloon in the world." Like his friend Kimball, Barnum allowed his museumgoers to enter the lecture room for free. Although both men were soon charging an extra twenty-five cents for reserved seats, they retained the appearance of nonhierarchical pricing, evidently an important consideration for their status-conscious patrons.[26]

The showmen's theatrical success hinged on their personal reputations and on their production of moral drama. In the first ten years of his lecture room, Kimball's stock company produced farces, spectacles, working-class plays, and moral reform melodramas, and jobbed in Yankee comedians, melodramatic stars, and minstrel shows. Barnum staged fewer spectacles and hired fewer visiting stars than his Boston ally; he made up the difference with more farces, minstrel shows, and moral reform melodramas. Although these repertoires did not differ substantially from those of conventional playhouses during the same period, Protestant families came to trust museum theatres because of their long runs of moral reform plays like *Uncle Tom's Cabin* and the chasteness of all of their productions. The theatres were also known for the moral respectability of their owners. Although he disliked his humbugs, theatre critic W. K. Northall admitted that "Barnum himself is one of the curiosities [of his museum] and we scarcely know which people would go further to see—Barnum, the sea serpent, or a real mermaid." In the past, most elite owners had left the business and promotion of their theatres up to their managers. But Barnum and Kimball kept their managers, Wemyss and Smith, backstage and invented numerous opportunities to place themselves at the center of public acclaim. The museum impresarios, stars of their own enterprises, moved the competitive, self-aggrandizing practices of starring into their show business. Barnum and Kimball constructed a new role for themselves as professional theatrical capitalists.[27]

Their theatrical success spawned numerous imitations. Beginning in 1849, the Beach Street Museum in Boston competed with Kimball's curiosities. In Philadelphia, Edmund Peale, grandnephew of Charles Willson, followed Kimball's lead when he expanded the family business to include a theatre for exhibitions, farces, and minstrel shows. According to one contemporary, the refurbished museum was "a moral bijou in all respects. It had neither seats for cyprians nor bars for drinkers." Another museum theatre, the Athenaeum and National, opened in Philadelphia in 1848. Barnum bought out its owners and was soon advertising a "full company" of actors "all pledged to temperance" for performances there of *The Drunkard*. A third establishment, the City Museum, began in Philadelphia in 1854. A program for one of its plays bragged that their "museum department" was "fitted up on the most extensive plan and great care has been taken to render it both interesting and instructive."[28]

In New York, Barnum opened a Chinese Museum with a small concert hall in 1849. The showman's strongest competition in the New York area was probably the Brooklyn Museum, which began in 1850 and continued for most of the decade. Like the American, the Brooklyn Museum boasted live animals, stuffed birds, wax figures, and a lecture room devoted to "the representation of chaste and strictly moral and pleasing entertainments." Its list of acting company members read like a who's who of minor museum troupes in the Northeast: actors hailing from the Baltimore, the Albany, the Providence, and the Troy (New York) museums played in Brooklyn during the 1850s. So great was the rage for museum theatres around the turn of the decade that the manager of the Franklin Theatre began advertising his little playhouse as the Franklin Museum in 1848 even though he had no curiosities at all on display.[29]

Moral reform plays, the primary melodramatic genre at museum theatres, drew on many of the same sentimental and gothic inducements as museum exhibits, but shaped the experience of playgoing primarily through the rhetoric of rationality. Their form and subject matter derived from the bourgeois tragedies of the eighteenth century. George Lillo's *The London Merchant* (1731), the most popular of the type, centered on the fate of George Barnwell, a young apprentice driven by sexual desire to lie, cheat, and finally murder his benevolent employer. Edward Moore's *The Gamester* (1756) was directed toward the slaves of a related passion; the gamester of the title, duped by a villain, gambles away his friends and reputation and finally kills himself to avoid exposure and shame. These and other early moral dramas warned the worldly of the entanglements of temptation and preached the bourgeois, Calvinistic virtues of industry, honesty, frugality, and deference to one's superiors.

As part of eighteenth-century humanitarian reform, bourgeois tragedy was a manifestation of the rationalistic cognitive style resulting from the rise of early market capitalism. In his influential essay, "Capitalism and the Origins of the Humanitarian Sensibility," Thomas Haskell argues that the experience of market relations taught capitalists to value conscience as well as calculation. "Men of principle," having profited from the promise-keeping and future orientation of contractual relations, were led, "by subtle isomorphisms and homologies," to embrace humanitarian reforms like temperance, sexual self-control, and even the abolition of slavery. Habits trained in the marketplace led to a style of thinking which suggested the possibility of moral progress and guided capitalist reformers in shaping their strategies. Bourgeois tragedy, which legitimated this rationalistic ideology, centered on the breaking of a moral contract between a promising youth and the respectable society of the bourgeoisie. George Barnwell and the gamester were negative examples meant to instruct potential men of principle in the virtues of promise keeping and self-control as the path to prudent success and eventual salvation.[30]

As market relations penetrated into more areas of social interaction in the nineteenth century, the cognitive style of humanitarian reform shaped the needs and expectations of many more theatrical spectators. American playgoers near the class margin attracted to revivalism continued to witness *The Gamester* and *The London Merchant*, the latter usually presented under the title *George Barnwell*. More frequently, however, they applauded the nineteenth-century spin-off of bourgeois tragedy, moral reform melodrama. These included such gothic and sentimental thrillers as *Thirty Years, or The Gambler's Fate*, by William Dunlap, *The Crock of Gold*, by Silas Steele, and *The Six Degrees of Crime, or Wine, Women, Gambling, Theft, Murder, and the Scaffold*, by F. S. Hill, whose categories of sin indicate that notions of bourgeois temptation had changed little since Lillo penned *The London Merchant* in 1731. Temperance plays, however, did alter the focus, if not the underlying moral calculus, of this tradition. By midcentury, melodramas centering on temperance reform were ubiquitous in working-class and museum theatres: *The Bottle, Another Glass, Life, or Scenes of Early Vice, The Curate's Daughter, Aunt Dinah's Pledge, The Drunkard's Warning, The Fruits of the Wine Cup,* and *Ten Nights in a Barroom,* to mention some of the most popular. Like their predecessors, moral reform melodramas continued to trace their victim's temptation and downfall from modest position and public esteem to the depths of ruin and shame, sometimes, however, ending with their reformation and success.

Rosina Meadows (1843) by Charles H. Saunders, *The Drunkard* (1844) by William H. Smith, and *Uncle Tom's Cabin* (1852) by Henry J. Conway typify moral reform melodramas popular at museum theatres between 1845 and the Civil War. Following an initial run at Pelby's National Theatre in Boston, *Rosina Meadows* played frequently at the Boston and American museums, as well as at other working-class and museum playhouses in the Northeast. *The Drunkard* reeled for an astounding 101 performances at Kimball's museum in 1844, establishing it as the model for most subsequent dramas of dipsomania. Teetotaler Barnum opened his lecture room with 150 evenings and matinees of the melodrama, and managers at such diverse playhouses as the Bowery, the Arch Street Theatre in Philadelphia, and the Brooklyn Museum turned regularly to *The Drunkard* to revive sagging seasons. Regarding *Uncle Tom's Cabin,* Moses Kimball hired Conway to put together a script that mingled "the grave and gay" aspects of Stowe's novel, and the playwright complied, fashioning a show that played throughout the Northeast in the mid 1850s. In New York City, competition between Barnum's production of Conway's version of *Uncle Tom's Cabin* and an adaptation written by George Aiken at the National Theatre sparked a notorious theatre war that led to street disturbances among spectators partial to one of the rival productions.[31]

All three plays exemplify what Haskell understands as the two main lessons taught by the dynamics of the market and celebrate rational men of principle as the model of male behavior in a capitalist society. Haskell notes that the regimen of the market taught entrepreneurs the necessity of keeping their economic promises. Mutual promise making and promise keeping provided the basis for rational contractual relations, without which commerce and banking could not develop. Because fulfilling a contract presupposed some human control over nature and historical circumstances, capitalism also "expanded the range of causal perception and inspired people's confidence in their power to intervene in the course of events," Haskell's second lesson. This magnification of a sense of personal power and responsibility led capitalists both to elaborate techniques for manipulating others for their own profit and to apply many of those same rationalistic techniques to humanitarian purposes. Together, the two chief lessons of the market created the man of principle, the dominant model of liberal bourgeois behavior by the late eighteenth century. An inner-directed man concerned to act on principle and focused on future consequences, this historical type thrived best in the United States between the Revolution and the Civil War, when, says Haskell, "the future was at once open enough to the individual to be manipulable and yet closed enough to be foreseeable."[32]

Each of the three moral reform melodramas uses the man of principle as the rational norm against which to judge the actions of its major characters. At the start of *The Drunkard*, Edward Middleton is a principled, respectable, college-educated young man with a promising future. Even as he begins his slide into dipsomania, lured to the bottle by a vengeful villain, he recognizes his responsibility for his moral condition: "Why, surely I have eyes to see, hands to work with, feet to walk, and brain to think, yet the best gifts of Heaven I abuse, lay aside her bounties, and with my own hand, willingly put out the light of reason" (II,4). Despite these misgivings, he continues to drink, losing his wealth, his domestic happiness, and his self-esteem. "You were respectable once and so was Lucifer; like him you have fallen past rising," a callous landlord tells Edward in his slough of despond (IV,1). But no: Arden Rencelaw, a temperance philanthropist, finds him near suicide and promises "to raise [Edward] once more to the station in society from which [he has] fallen." "We will restore you to society," says Rencelaw (IV,1). His rational self-control revived by this timely intervention, the protagonist regains his principles and soon rejoins his wife and child to celebrate his worldly salvation. Rencelaw, of course, is the very model of a modern man of principle; unctuous, fatherly, and sensible, he makes moral contracts with others ("I administer the

Pledge . . .") and points them toward a future they can control. Modeling himself on Rencelaw, Edward becomes his surrogate prodigal son.

Rosina Meadows features a more patriarchal, Calvinistic man of principle. In the first scene, Old Meadows, Rosina's father, sends his daughter off to Boston with stern orders for her to preserve her honor. But the temptations of city life blight the sweet innocence of the country rose, and Old Meadows must go to Boston to search for his wilted flower. Finding her abandoned and betrayed, the patriarch finally forgives the dying Rosina, then strangles her seducer. Old Meadows' injunctions to beware of temptation and plan for the future are contrasted to the carefree, dissipated life of Harry Mendon, who promises to marry Rosina and then seduces her. Minor men of principle dot the action of *Rosina Meadows*. When Rosina is seeking lodgings in Boston, a kindly father figure admonishes her not to take the room suggested to her by a villain. And George Milton, his name redolent of both patriotic and puritanical connections, keeps his promise to marry Rosina and accompanies Old Meadows to rescue her.

Several humanitarian reformers animate the plot of *Uncle Tom's Cabin*. After learning that his father has sold Tom to a slave trader, young George Shelby makes this pledge:

> I am only a boy, but listen to me and remember: if I live to be a man you shall be free. See, Uncle Tom, I have bored a hole through this dollar and I now put it around your neck. Kneel, Uncle Tom, and listen to the promise of a boy who will redeem it if he lives to be a man. (I,3)

Sure enough, George grows up to be a man of principle and keeps his promise. And the token of his pledge, in proper melodramatic fashion, figures significantly in the action, at one point saving Tom from Legree's wrath. Following the novel, Conway has a principled Quaker plan the escape of George and Eliza from the slave catchers and then defend them when they are cornered. To Stowe's story Conway also added a Yankee character, Penetrate Partyside, who acts on humanitarian principles throughout. Taking notes for a book on slavery, Penetrate comments, "Niggers chained like dogs ginerally because they are going to be sold according to law particularly. Quere! Who deserves to be chained most, the niggers to be sold or the owners who sell them?" (II,2). Partyside tries to rescue Tom at a slave auction and later searches for a legal way to free him from Legree. These minor heroes of *Uncle Tom's Cabin* are not scrupulous and respectable merchants or farmers, like Arden Rencelaw and Old Meadows, but they all embody what Haskell terms the defining characteristic of the principled man: "his willingness to act on principle no matter how inconvenient it might be." [33]

The villains of these melodramas act out of irrational passion and urge immediate gratification on their victims; in effect, they embody the opposite attributes of the man of principle. Whereas in Stowe's novel Simon Legree's actions are rooted in rational economic considerations, Conway's arch villain is motivated by cruelty and revenge. Disregarding profit and loss in the auction scene, Legree sneers to Tom: "I will buy you and the dearer you cost me, the dearer I'll make you pay for it" (IV,3). In *Rosina*, Harry Mendon lures the village rose with a vision of idle luxury and, implicitly, sexual enjoyment: "I am rich and influential and can raise you from the poor, secluded seamstress that you are to a fine lady. . . . I can give you gold and fine dresses—take you to balls and parties" (II,5). Lawyer Cribbs in *The Drunkard* represents a kind of temptation even more specifically geared to the individualistic ideology of bourgeois respectability. Finding Edward Middleton without money on a city street, Cribbs offers to give him a dollar as "charity," knowing he will drink it up. Edward is tempted, but finally throws the money back at the villain: "Take back your base bribe, miscalled charity; that maddening drink that I should purchase with it would be redolent of sin and rendered still more poisonous by your false hypocrisy" (III,1). In moral reform melodrama, charity threatens the principles of self-control and self-reliance. With the exception of Simon Legree, the major villains of these plays are less agents of external oppression than bad angels of internal temptation, sitting inside the heads of their victims and urging them to give way to passion and desire. The moral is clear: only rational men of principle can resist and persevere.

There are no women of principle in these plays. Lacking the ability to project their will in the world, female characters may protect their honor and sanctify the domestic nest, but the respectable among them do not make contracts or intervene to alter significant events. If they attempt such undomestic tasks, moral reform melodrama dismisses them as villains or fools, legitimating the sentimental norm of wife and mother found in the ideology of domesticity. As her last name suggests,

Alice Warren in *Rosina* uses her millinery shop as a front for a brothel. "So child, you wish to get employment in my shop? You'll soon change the roses of your cheeks to lilies, if you keep housed up as much as your work will require you" (II,5), she tells Rosina. So much for the only woman shopkeeper encountered in these plays.

Most female characters who stray beyond the confines of respectable domesticity are treated comically. *Uncle Tom* and *Drunkard* invite their audiences to laugh at "old-maid" characters who act like men and lack the self-control and sensibility to win husbands. Miss Spindle, the grotesque inversion of sentimental domesticity in *Drunkard*, is discovered at her "toilette table" reading and making up her aging face:

> "Age cannot wither me nor custom stale my infinite *vacuity*." But time is money, then money is time, and we bring back, by the aid of money, the times of youth. I value my beauty at fifty dollars a year, as that is about the sum it costs me for keeping it in repair year by year. . . . Woman was made for love. They suppose that my heart is unsusceptible of the tender passion. But the heart can be regulated by money, too. I buy all the affecting novels and all the terrible romances, and read them till my heart has become soft as maiden wax. (I,3)

The old maid is a figure of mockery in moral reform melodrama because she confuses the values of domesticity with the norms of marketplace behavior, muddling the spheres of home and business kept separate in the ideology of respectability. Villainous women shopkeepers and foolish old maids confirm the rationality of men of principle by inversion and contrast; the rhetoric of sentimentality plays domestic drudge to the masculine power of rationality.

Because they can never be men of principle or women of honor, the African-American characters in *Uncle Tom* are pictured as childish buffoons, their characterizations taken directly from the stereotypes of the minstrel show. Conway's Sam on the Shelby farm is a pretentious bumpkin; he and Tom's wife, Chloe, dance a minuet "with the greatest extravagance and politeness" while the other slaves form a "half circle" to watch them (I,1). St. Clare's Adolph is a minstrel dandy; he speaks "foppishly," owns a "half pair of specs," and is "all scented over too," notes a surprised Partyside (III,1). After she gains her freedom, Topsy delivers a stump speech promising to join "a benevolence s'ciety" in the North to "lucidate to dat s'ciety de necessity ob doin' somethin' for dere coloured brethren in bondage" (IV,1). All of these minstrel characterizations effect their comedy by the implicit contrast between the rational, respectable white man of principle and the unrespectable black fool attempting to ape his betters.[34]

As several critics have noted, the sentimental heroine in Stowe's novel, female in gender construction if not in sex, is Uncle Tom.[35] Conway's adaptation keeps him sincere, domestic, and sensible, also the chief attributes of genteel female characters in *Rosina* and *Drunkard*. Rosina, whose main problem is the absence of a father figure to guide her in the city, mouths the values of sentimental domesticity even as she abandons the hope of attaining it by giving her hand to the villain: "Mr. Mendon, I cannot give you riches, but if the possession of a devoted heart you can accept in lieu of these, I give it to your keeping" (II,6). Mary Middleton shows the loyalty of a true bourgeois wife by following her husband to the city and striving to keep the family together until Edward can conquer temptation. The stage directions of act 3, scene 5, testify to their poverty:

A wretched garret—old table and chair with lamp burning dimly. Mary in miserable apparel, sewing on slop work; a wretched shawl thrown over her shoulders. Child sleeping on a straw bed on the floor, R[ight], covered in part by a miserable ragged rug. Half a loaf of bread on the table. The ensemble of the scene indicates want and poverty.

When Cribbs tells her that Edward is carousing with fallen women, Mary defends him: "The only fault of my poor husband has been intemperance, terrible, I acknowledge, but still a weakness that has assailed and prostrated the finest intellects of men who would scorn a mean and unworthy action" (III,5). Respectable women in these plays are home-loving, loyal, patient, and sincere—such unaggressive characteristics that they are unobjectionable even in a black slave.

Not surprisingly, the prayers and justifications of sentimental characters save neither themselves nor their families in these melodramas. One writer reported in an 1847 preface to *The Drunkard* that in episodes "depicting the distress of the family, it was no uncommon thing to see scores of men and women weeping like children."[36] To weep for a family in distress, however, is to recognize that the moral influence of family members on each other and family affection as the model of societal relations of power—the essential basis of sentimentalism—is ineffective. Families are victims in these plays; rationality, not moral influence, reforms the drunkard and frees the slave. Although these plays do use sincerity and sensibility to tug at the heartstrings, their rationality undercuts their sentimentality, a shift in emphasis with significant implications. While anyone could claim respectability on the basis of his or her membership in the human family, all members of society were clearly not equal in rationality. Moral reform melodramas prepared Americans to accept an undemocratic social order, based not on charismatic leadership, as in Forrest's melodramas, but on rational respectability in a liberal economy.

This shift changed the attitudes generated by these plays toward the urban poor. Audiences applauding moral reform melodrama believed that male principle and female domesticity were easier to preserve and practice in the country than in the city. At the start of *Rosina*, before Harry Mendon becomes a villain, he says, "Here is a village apparently enjoying its primitive simplicity; but I fear that the frequent and easy communication with the city by the railroad's iron arm may even now have tinctured it. . . . God made the country; man made the town" (I,1). This introduction sets up the main action of the melodrama, the corruption of village innocence by city temptation. In *Uncle Tom's Cabin*, the slave plantation is the rough equivalent of the city, offering up the same temptations of idle luxury and sexual desire to weak-willed scoundrels like Simon Legree. In neither play is it suggested that the environment causes vice; an immoral city or plantation can tempt the unwary, but individuals, prone to sin from the time of Adam's fall, are wholly responsible for their moral failures.

Like other temperance plays, *The Drunkard* suggests that inebriation is primarily an urban (and male) vice. To underline Edward's slide toward the pit, the play moves him from his cottage home in a country village to the slums of New York City, finally depicting his attack of "the snakes" in front of a "wretched out-house" in the Five Points district of the Bowery (IV,1). After his salvation, Edward returns with his family to the country, a kind of neoplatonic return to wholeness couched within the terms of bourgeois respectability. The stage directions for the last scene of the play enshrine the manufactured materialism of the genteel parlor:

Interior of Cottage as in Act Ist, Scene Ist. Everything denoting domestic peace and tranquil happiness. The sun is setting over the hill
at back of landscape. Edward discoverd near music stand, R[ight].
Julia [his daughter] seated on low stool on his L[eft]. Mary sewing
at handsome work table, L[eft]. Elegant table . . . with astral lamp
not lighted. Bible and other books on it. Two beautiful flower stands
with roses, myrtles, etc., under window, L[eft] and R[ight]. Bird
cages on wings, R[ight] and L[eft]. Covers of tables, chairs, etc., all
extremely neat and in keeping. (V,3)

This setting pointedly contrasts the family's country surroundings with
their wretched circumstances in the city witnessed in act 3, scene 5.
Each of the above props, especially the music stand, astral lamp, Bible,
flower stands, and birdcages, signifies the union of respectable domesticity and country living. The perception of this moral connection would
help to drive middle-income families to the periphery of cities and
eventually to the suburbs after 1850.

The moral chasm separating city from country in these melodramas
echoes through much of the moral reform literature of the period as
well—a literature likely read by many of the spectators at museum
theatres. Before it was a stage play, *Rosina Meadows* was a popular
novel, one of several antiseduction thrillers depicting the immoral
blandishments of city life. In another of this genre, *Mary Beach, or The
Fulton Street Cap Maker,* the Rosina-like heroine believes the brothel
she has moved into is really a boardinghouse. Much of Catherine Sedgwick's popular fiction hinged on the city/country dichotomy, including
The Poor Rich Man and the Rich Poor Man, which contrasts the pretentiousness and materialism of city life to the frugal virtue of country
living. T. S. Arthur, Susan Warner, Maria Cummings, and others wrote
similar novels in which principled men join temperance societies and
rescue widows and orphans from urban poverty while virtuous women
find peace by withdrawing from the temptations of the city into the
privacy of home and family. Literary historian Janice Stout notes that
"Mrs. Sedgwick and others working in the same vein exalt domesticity
and espouse humanitarian and moral causes while reinforcing an acquisitive social system with encomiums of hard work and virtuous
poverty." In many of these books, the rationality of male principle effectively underwrites the female world of sentimental domesticity. As

in moral reform melodramas, the city is a testing ground for individual morality, a crucible in which only the most principled and virtuous will not be ground down.[37]

Such literature was part of a larger bourgeois revulsion, dating from the eighteenth century, against urban wickedness. According to the Reverend John Todd in his *Moral Influence, Dangers, and Duties, Connected with Great Cities* (1841), urban centers were "gangrenes on the body politic," purveyors of prostitution, "licentiousness," gambling, crime, and "all that demoralizes and pollutes." Especially troubling to Protestant moralists was the rapid increase in immigrants from Catholic Germany and Ireland. One Boston newspaper summarized the prevailing stereotype of the Irish as "idle, sloth-loving, improvident, and intemperate," the moral opposite of the rational man of principle. Nativist antagonism to immigrants sparked anti-Irish riots in Boston in 1834 and Philadelphia in 1844 and led to numerous gang fights in all the cities of the Northeast. Emory Washburn, reforming governor of Massachusetts, spoke for many evangelically oriented Americans when he complained in 1848 about the "hosts of foreigners crowding to our shores, and bringing with them the habits and associations of foreign lands; with intemperance, that great mother of poverty and vice, and crime, spreading out her lures on every side." For many humanitarian reformers, antebellum cities were both symptoms and partial causes of a vast moral depravity and irrationality threatening to swamp the righteous in a turbulent sea of temptation.[38]

Neither the moralists nor their devotees in museum theatres, however, understood their cities as the logical if unforeseen results of an expanding market economy and its concommitant urbanization. Cities grew at a faster rate between 1820 and 1860 than at any other time in American history—more than three times the rate of the burgeoning national population. Driven by increasing property values and high rents, slums appeared in New York City as early as 1815. By 1850, the average density of the seven lower wards in Manhattan was 163.5 persons per acre, nearly double the density of 1820 and more closely packed than it would ever be again after streetcars and eventually commuter trains allowed the business class to sprawl outward from the center. Few self-employed artisans after the mid 1830s could afford to purchase a modest house for their families. While artisan families settled into tenement rooms, day laborers, seamstresses, and wage-workers fared even worse. In the mid 1850s, roughly half of the people in Boston, New York, and Philadelphia were foreign-born, attracted to the United States by the booming economy and casually exploited by American capitalists soon after they got off the boat. Like many native-born workers at midcentury, immigrant families moved between cities frequently in search of better housing and work. In Boston, for instance, nearly half of the population left the city during any given two-year period in the 1840s and 1850s. Cholera epidemics ravaged northeastern cities in 1849 and 1854. The mortality rate in New York City in 1856 was a shocking 1 in 29, twice the rate of London in the same year. In 1860, seven out of every ten children born to immigrant parents in New York died before reaching the age of two.[39]

Living in these degrading and dangerous circumstances, many urbanites near the class margin turned to behaviors that labeled them as deviants in the eyes of the respectable. Many men drank in excess because liquor was cheap and intoxication relieved stress. Many women who turned to prostitution did so out of economic necessity, not usually because they were seduced and abandoned, as the melodramas taught. Some bourgeois moralists knew these facts, but hypocritically hid from their implications. Most, blinkered by the ideology of respectability and increasingly isolated from the city poor, suffered from a massive failure of social and moral imagination.[40]

The emergence of the man of principle as the social norm for judging cities as unregenerate sinkholes of depravity rested upon the replacement of a moral economy by a contractual one. As Haskell notes, contract making was the logical extension of promise keeping among businessmen, a rational and legal method of binding strangers to ties of mutual trust and responsibility. Contracts fostered the rapid expansion of market relations in the late eighteenth and nineteenth centuries by allowing people "who shared no tie of blood, faith, or community" to do business together.[41] When linked to the market, contractualism meant that workers would no longer be paid what the community might regard as a fair wage, nor would food and housing be sold or rented at a consensual fair price—contracts between individuals settled such matters without recourse to community values. Because contracts were fundamental to the expansion of capitalism, business owners and those influenced by bourgeois culture began to believe that other areas of social life might also be ordered along rational contractual lines. In politics, for instance, many of the advocates of a national U.S. government understood the Constitution as a contract among the people which established and legitimized state power. And by the mid nineteenth century, temperance leaders typically viewed the pledge as a contract between man and respectable society.

Beyond the obvious example of taking the pledge, contractual relationships and their homologies recur frequently in moral reform plays; promise making and promise keeping, whether legally binding or not, is idealized as the path to virtue for men. In *Uncle Tom's Cabin*, Conway is able to arrange a happy ending by having his good characters expose the illegality of Legree's contracts. "We are prepared to prove that [Uncle Tom] was sold unlawfully," states George Harris (V,1). This assertion follows a scene in which Penetrate Partyside had outbid Legree to buy Tom at the auction, but was foiled by an illegal prior agreement between Legree and the auctioneer. He and George Harris also discover that Legree kidnapped Eliza and kept Cassy "by a false bill of sale" (V,1). The contractualism of the law effects the freeing of all the slaves that the audience has any reason to care about. This plot convenience, of course, allowed Conway to oppose slavery for three of its victims, but to uphold the legal structure of slavery, including the Fugitive Slave Law.

Several kinds of contractual promises are legitimated in *The Drunkard* and *Rosina Meadows*. George Milton remains faithful to his marriage contract with Rosina while Harry Mendon breaks his matrimonial promise. The scene in which Alice Warren tricks Rosina into agreeing to work for her underlines the morality of true contracts of employment through contrast. An early scene in *The Drunkard* legitimates rental contracts when Edward gives his wife-to-be a little extra time to pay the rent. "We recognize a benefactor in our creditor," says Mary (I,2), who soon falls in love with her landlord. When Cribbs suggests that Edward help him to forge documents to ruin Arden Rencelaw (so that the villain may ruin Edward as well), the playwright terms forgery a "revenge on society"—in effect, the breaking of a social trust which underwrites the operations of capitalism. The complicated plot of *Drunkard* is finally resolved and the villainy of Cribbs exposed when a mentally ill woman regains her sanity and reveals the truth about Edward's grandfather's will, another type of contract involving the legal fulfillment of a promise.

Various kinds of contracts and promises had been used by play-wrights as plot devices for centuries, of course. What finally distinguishes moral reform melodrama from earlier types of plays is partly the greater number of these devices in their content, but mostly the extent to which contracts are embedded in their form. Simply put, *Drunkard, Uncle Tom,* and *Rosina* are allegories of contract keeping or contract breaking. Edward Middleton signs the pledge and rescues himself from urban misery to enjoy village respectability. George Shelby promises to free Uncle Tom and gains a just reward for both of them: Tom is freed and George gains Tom's gratitude. Rosina Meadows vowed to keep her virtue, but breaks her promise to her father and her village fiancé and goes to her death in the city. The protagonist's rational will power to keep promises determines the dramatic shape of his or her fate.

As representations of broken or kept contracts, these plays exhibit all the mechanistic rigidity of allegory. Like characters out of *Pilgrim's Progress,* the major figures in moral reform melodrama embody abstract categories of moral behavior: Uncle Tom and Mary Middleton are Patient Endurance, Lawyer Cribbs and Harry Mendon are Sinful Temptation, Old Meadows and Arden Rencelaw are Judgment and Forgiveness, and George Shelby, Rosina Meadows, and Edward Middleton are Everyman (or Everywoman) on the Path of Life to Salvation or Damnation. Subtract the moral categories behind these characters and there is little left of them. Likewise, the action of these plays is locked into a cause-effect logic that nearly freezes their form: Loss of Control in the presence of Temptation causes Sin, which leads to Retribution and Remorse, which in turn causes more Loss of Control and Sin in a spiraling down to eventual Degradation and Failure—*unless* Judgment and Forgiveness intervene to prompt Rationality and Repentance which leads, with the same clockwork inevitability, to Respectability. As critic Elder Olson notes, "The allegorical incident happens, not because it is necessary or probable in the light of other events, but because a certain doctrinal subject must have a certain doctrinal predicate." The result is a didactic universality which drives out all contradiction and ambiguity by excluding the historically specific and the psychologically complex. The only flexibility of form in these plays occurs in their humorous scenes, which, because of the rigidity of the rest of the melodrama, are indeed scenes of comic relief. Nineteenth-century melodrama from Pixérécourt onward relied on typological characters who stood in symbolically for moral and social attributes, but only moral reform melodrama locked typological understanding into allegory, the most rationalized form of expression available to writers of fiction.[42]

For all of their concern with individual volition as the key to respectability and success, these allegories allowed their audience members little room for individual reaction. With its abstract typology of characterization and lockstep representation of social cause and effect, allegory attempts to control the response of spectators and critics much more tightly than do other forms of drama. As Northrop Frye argues, the allegorist's concern to "indicate how a commentary on him [or her] should proceed" leads the commenting critic to become "prejudiced against allegory without knowing the real reason, which is that continuous allegory prescribes the direction of his [or her] commentary, and so restricts its freedom." William K. Northall said as much in objecting to the evident didacticism of many of Barnum's shows: "The morality of a play is to be inferred by the spectators, not intruded upon their attention by the author." The rationalistic rhetoric of allegorical theatre implicitly bullies its audience into believing that there is only one correct interpretation; either you get the point or you don't.[43]

But why would audiences pay to see such melodramas? Presumably, Barnum's and Kimball's spectators wanted to be told "the morality of the play," *pace* Northall; they wanted to know what to believe, rather than to have to decide for themselves. Critic Angus Fletcher finds a number of similarities between the rationalistic rhetoric of allegory and the syndrome psychoanalysts term obsessive-compulsive:

> In both cases, therefore, we find an authoritarian sort of behavior, rigid, anxious, fatalistic; the hero of an allegorical epic will be presented to us doing things the way a compulsive person does things, regularly, meticulously, blindly. In both cases there is a great play for magical influence, psychotic possession, taboo restrictions. In both cases we shall expect events to be isolated from each other into highly episodic forms, thereby "encapsulating" particular moments of contagion and beatitude. The compulsive pattern of behavior often shows a use of oracular omens, which are felt to be binding, and this provides the overall sublime pattern for a sublime

literature, where the hero is compelled ever onward and is held on his path by these predestinating omens and oracles.[44]

The historian need not believe in the ultimate validity of psychoanalysis to find significant insight in Fletcher's comments.

"Magical influence, psychotic possession, [and] taboo restrictions" occur at several moments of great emotional intensity in moral reform melodramas. These plays coated their mechanistic rhetoric with a general layer of sentimental syrup, but relied on gothic terror to push their allegorical messages in scenes of extreme dramatic crisis. In such moments, characters become possessed, the power of the Almighty is implored, ghosts appear on stage to haunt the living, and villains may even die by unseen hands. These effects, the "predestinating omens and oracles" noted by Fletcher, reveal the legacy of Calvinistic rhetoric in these plays. Unlike the rhetoric of sentimentalism, gothicism strove to terrorize its spectators into a dread of their own sinfulness and a resolve to suppress their emotions. Yet it, too, largely worked within the confines of rationalistic control.

Fletcher's analysis suggests that several good characters become possessed by evil in these plays. Driven to distraction by her life of poverty and sin, Rosina bursts into Mendon's rooms and shrieks, "I want money! I am famishing, houseless and friendless—give me money!" (III,2). Evil possesses Mendon himself near the end of the melodrama and drives him to robbery, an act that leads to his final fall. Alcoholic abandon also possesses St. Clare in *Uncle Tom's Cabin*, a substantial change from Stowe's depiction of the character which was probably due to W. H. Smith's influence in shaping Conway's adaptation for Boston Museum audiences. The museum "programme of scenery and incidents" for act 3, scene 7, charts the downward path of this character's decline and demise: "Saloon in St. Clare's house. Grief and desolation. Agony of the wife and child. DEATH OF ST. CLARE. Apotheosis of his mother! Tableau." The tableau at the end encapsulates, to use Fletcher's wording, the ghost's doleful warning, thus folding the previous sentimental and gothic effects into the rationalized meaning of the scene.

The extreme physicality of the acting conventions for Edward Middleton's descent into delirium tremens indicates that this scene in the melodrama was also played as if the character were possessed. Writhing on the ground, he yells, "These snakes, how they coil around me.

Oh! How strong they are—there, don't kill it, no, no, don't kill it; give it brandy, poison it with rum" (IV,1). The d.t.'s continue to torment him until Rencelaw enters soon after. Actors performing Edward were expected to throw themselves on the ground and appear to be injuring themselves in their agony; sometimes the injuries they sustained were genuine. Managers tried to cast the role with men who were in top physical condition. At Barnum's Museum, Wemyss hired William Goodall, who apparently threw himself into the part so effectively that one fellow thespian found his performance "almost painful in its startling truth to nature." The actor Harry Watkins, who had written earlier of his run-in with Forrest, noted in his journal that the audience for his Edward Middleton at the Beach Street Museum in Boston in 1849 was relatively lifeless until the delirium tremens scene, when they called him out after the curtain, gave him "nine cheers," and demanded a speech. The next day Watkins wrote in his journal, "My body is very sore from the effect of the delirium tremens in the scenes of *The Drunkard.*" Later at the Arch Street Theatre in Philadelphia, Watkins continued his sucess as Edward Middleton but admitted, "Fifth night of *The Drunkard.* I wish they would discontinue it—my body is sore enough." So popular was the d.t.'s scene that it was occasionally performed, probably in parody, as a solo act in minstrel shows.[45]

While *The Drunkard*'s happy ending precludes a gothic finale, the death scenes of the villains in *Rosina* and *Uncle Tom* revel in moral terror. With Rosina dead at his feet and Mendon begging him for mercy, Old Meadows intones, "Her spirit is even now hovering over thee, impatient to denounce thee at the judgment-seat! 'Tis time for the sacrifice. Villain! Seducer! Murderer! Die! Die!" After strangling the wretch, the patriarch stands center stage for the tableau "with one hand pointing to heaven, the other to Rosina" (III,7). Legree's death scene contains a similar evocation of heavenly justice. An illuminated window in Legree's haunted plantation house shows Eliza dressed like the villain's murdered mother "with a long white dress, bosom bloody, and a long white veil. [She] points to Legree with her left hand and to heaven with her right hand." Legree, beset by "demons," writhes on the ground in agony and is strangled by "unseen hands" (V,3). Cassy and Eliza have staged this ghoulish masquerade, but the spectators, knowing that the monster killed his mother and prompted by Eliza's gesture heavenward, would surely have understood that an angry God effected Legree's death. Likewise, the evangelical families in the audience for *Rosina* would have seen Mendon's death as a warning; Old Meadows becomes the agent of an avenging God—his action a binding oracular omen symbolizing the power of the Almighty to punish sin.

The use of gothic rhetoric in these popular melodramas, particularly at emotion-packed moments, suggests that fears of personal guilt, social shame, and eternal damnation were still very much alive in evangelical urbanites, however much Calvinism may have softened since Puritan times. In this regard, *Rosina* seems a more Calvinistic show than *Drunkard*, since one misstep sends Rosina and Harry to their doom while Edward sees the light of reason and repents. Yet if the God of temperance is primarily a deity of love rather than of judgment, he is also a cog in the cosmic, contractual machinery guaranteeing such mundane materialism as astral lamps and caged birds for the restored. For that matter, the God who damns Mendon and Legree is a function of the same cause-and-effect logic; though more judgmental, he altogether lacks the inscrutability of the Calvinist deity. In moral reform melodrama, as in many other intersections of theology and experience in the antebellum era, the rational, individualistic doctrine of human perfectability replaced Calvinist predestination as the underlying ground of meaning. These plays obligate the Almighty to save or damn protagonists depending on their ability to conquer temptation and to perfect their character. The God of moral reform melodrama works not in mysterious ways but within the rational rules of human contractualism; man proposes and God lives up to his end of the bargain.

By emphasizing human volition in the making and fulfilling of contracts, Haskell links the culture of contractualism with the self-reliance of bourgeois individualism. But men of principle and women of virtue are actually given very few positive choices in moral reform melodrama. Only refusals are required to maintain their morality and, once fallen, they quickly become possessed, thus losing the capacity for rational choice. Even their decision to reform, if it occurs, is prompted by an outside agent of greater rationality than themselves. And apparently their moral reformation need be followed by no other conscious action to be effective. Edward Middleton does not win back his well-stocked cottage in the country through old-fashioned hard work or modern decision making; taking the pledge is enough. Overall, will power plays a much more central role in Forrest's vehicles than in these allegories, which promise self-reliance but actually fix action to rational rails and push it along their predetermined tracks through sentimental affection and gothic terror. Alfred Habegger asserts that "allegory is the literature of exiles, prisoners, captives, or others who have no room to act in their society. . . . Allegory is one of many human artifacts expressing a sense of human powerlessness." In this important sense, moral reform melodrama broke ranks with the culture of contractualism. Embracing the morality of men of principle and the legitimacy of capitalistic contracts, these plays nonetheless expressed the powerlessness of their marginalized antebellum viewers to swim against the rationalizing currents of their society. Perhaps they covertly recognized that most forms of contract making and keeping would empower others at their own social and economic expense. Mandating repression and self-control, moral reform melodrama promised material rewards for the respectable, but the price was self-reification, the remaking of the self into a cog in a rational machine.[46]

On another level, the passivity that these plays induced in their audience—coupled with the weeping, applauding, and terror that accompanied their performance—probably reminded many of their spectators of the experience of a revival meeting. "In pre–Civil War America, there was an almost obsessive concern with exorcising spiritual deadness," asserts a historian of antebellum popular culture. As a dynamic social movement, revivalism waned after the mid 1830s, but the general form and rhetoric of revivals—evident in temperance meetings, Sunday worship services, many public speeches, and in revivals themselves—persisted through the 1840s and 1850s. Like moral reform melodramas, revivals worked on the principle that God had given men and women the ability to perceive their sinfulness, but that surrendering one's will was necessary to be saved. Because they believed they could perfect themselves, conscientious Americans frequently experienced wrenching guilt. Camp meetings offered evangelicals an emotional catharsis through hymn singing, exhortation, weeping, prayer, shouting, and confession. These experiences bombarded guilt-laden men of principle and women of virtue with sentimental and gothic stimuli designed to lead these inner-directed folk to a rigorous examination of their consciences which would compel a conversion experience and exorcise their anxieties, leaving them physically exhausted but spiritually revived.[47]

The cultural historian R. Laurence Moore notes that critics of revival methods regularly compared the techniques and responses found at camp meetings to similar strategies and reactions in the theatre. In most revivals an "anxious bench" would be put near the middle of the minister's platform so that the congregation could focus their prayers and songs on the bench sitters about to be converted. Said one critic: "The movement of coming to the anxious bench is always more or less theatrical" and, like watching a play, it usually produced "transient excitement," not permanent conversion. Some revival preachers took the comparison to heart and turned it back on their opponents. Urging that effective stage acting provide the model for revival preaching, Charles Grandison Finney asked, "Now what is the design of the actor in a theatrical representation?" The actor, he said, was "to throw himself into the spirit and meaning of the writer, as to adopt his sentiments, make them his own, feel them, embody them, throw them out upon the audience as living reality." In short, actors provided ministers with the "best way of diffusing the warmth of burning thought over a congregation." Finney's theatrical techniques were widely imitated by other preachers in the 1840s and 1850s. Trained in the law, Finney preached that God would surely honor the sinner's promise to repent. From Finney's point of view, the Almighty had set up a contract with humanity: "He has enacted laws wisely calculated to promote [the greatest practicable amount of happiness in the universe], to which he conforms all his own conduct, and to which he requires all of his subjects perfectly and undeviatingly to conform theirs."[48] As social-religious ritual and ideology, revivals and performances of moral reform melodrama had much in common.

Why did so many midcentury Americans retreat from the possibilities of democracy to the haven of commodified, repressed respectability in rituals at camp meetings and museum theatres? Fear of immigrants and cities and fear of being caught on the wrong side of the class line were potent inducements, to be sure, but part of the answer also lies in the transparency of character that respectable culture taught its initiates to see in each other and in themselves. As Robert Wiebe points out, conventional midcentury morality left "men and women with no place to hide their flaws. The human formed a simple whole [from their point of view], with body, mind, and soul merged into a single expression of character, and a weakness anywhere permeated the entire person." The exhibits and plays at the American and Boston museums underlined this unitary notion of human character and provided their customers with strategies for preventing their slip from upright and moral to bestial and degraded. Barnum and Kimball made it easy for their worried customers to rationalize their enjoyment of museum exhibits and performances as allegorical lessons in self-improvement.[49] After such edification, how could museumgoers doubt that they had a greater claim to respectability than the exotic freaks, minstrel blacks, and melodramatic villains they saw on stage?

On the other hand, such claims encouraged social hypocrisy. "If the stage be distasteful, in [Barnum's] judgment, to the habits and morals of the audience who visit his establishment," demanded W. K. Northall, "why not eschew them altogether, not wheedle the public into his trap and thus oblige them to patch up their damaged consciences with the paltry excuse that it was the museum and not the play they came to see."[50] Museum hypocrisy went far beyond the claim that lecture rooms were not playhouses, however. In the name of propriety, the impresarios helped their customers to believe that the cause of self-control led inevitably to the effect of respectability and success, that women's natural domesticity made her a sensible mother but a villain or a fool outside of the home, that unrespectable deviants below the class line fully deserved their lives of toil, sickness, and misery, and that the mechanical marvels of Lowell cotton mills fitted comfortably within domestic parlors. In their eagerness to patch up their own damaged consciences, museum spectators closed their eyes to the realities of capitalism in their cities.

Perhaps the museums' most hypocritical claim was their implicit assurance that temporary respectability meant social equality. Barnum and Kimball did all they could to erase the traditional markers of class distinction within their museums: all paid the same admission price, all sat in the same lecture hall seats (except for some, later on, who paid an extra twenty-five cents for reserve seating), and all saw the same curiosities and melodramas. While inside the Boston and American museums, customers could believe that they were just as respectable as the wealthier patrons among them and much more genteel than the deviant classes of Catholic immigrants, free blacks, and urban poor who either could not afford the twenty-five cents admission or preferred less moral entertainment. As historian Peter Buckley remarks, Barnum "appropriated the assets of conventional bourgeois morality and placed them on a cash basis."[51] But audience involvement in what might be called lowest-common-denominator respectability masked an important reality. Most museum spectators had exercised little conscious choice in establishing the ideology of respectability that limited and channeled the the kinds of entertainment and edification they enjoyed. Nor could these members of moderate-income families effectively challenge or change the cognitive and normative boundaries of respectability as they were being shaped by the arbiters of the emergent culture. Finally, the price of respectability was not only hypocrisy but disempowering reification. Maybe this contradiction between the promise of social equality and the reality of increasingly hegemonic subjection led some museumgoers to reject bourgeois propriety. But the experience of museumgoing for the majority of spectators enrolled them unknowingly in a culture that was shifting from emergent to dominant. Indeed, in retrospect, museum entertainment partly served to effect this transition.

7. "How Her Blood Tells"

In productions at museum theatres and else-where, moral reform melodrama had helped to establish the legitimacy of business-class domination among the marginally respectable by the mid 1850s. Its allegorical chains of cause and effect had excluded the city poor from sympathetic concern. Its just-say-no policy to temptation had advanced the values of bourgeois industry and self-control. And its focus on respectability had effectively substituted rationality for republicanism as the moral basis of society. Overall, moral reform melodrama set the stage for business-class progress through rationality, conformity, and obedience.

Nonetheless, the social effects of moral plays left some unfinished business and even created some problems for bourgeois hegemony. Partly because allegories of moral reform had been produced for audiences near the class margin, the relations between classes and within the business class were not clear in these plays. How were business-class families to be sure that their servants were their inferiors, if rationality was the primary basis for judgment? And what was the relation between those new to the business class and the old-moneyed elite? Moral reform melodrama had forged links of iron between self-control and economic success. But what if a capitalist lost his wealth or a clerk lost his position through no fault of his own—through the vagaries of the marketplace? Were he and his family still respectable?

Perhaps the biggest problem for the bourgeoisie deriving from the legacy of moral melodrama was the need to protect one's respectability and, at the same time, to maintain the moral transparency of one's actions. For if a businessman were even to consider fashioning his own social image, his self-concern and lack of sincerity would show through his character and condemn him in his own eyes and those of others as a hypocrite. This had not been a problem for playwrights depicting drunkards and wayward young women struggling to gain respectability, since there was no distance between self and social role in these protagonists. But for melodramatists interested in showing men and women who had already attained respectability, the transparency of the self left them with rational heroes and virtuous heroines too constricted by self-consciousness to effectively save themselves from villains attacking their respectability. This dramaturgical problem reflected a larger social difficulty. Ruling classes, from Renaissance aristocracy through eighteenth-century gentry, had always been able to separate themselves from their social masks; the necessary hypocrisy of ritual and role-playing had served a variety of hegemonic uses. How could respectable men and women intent on demonstrating their transparency gain sufficient social flexibility to exercise their considerable power?

The mid nineteenth-century bourgeoisie overcame this impediment to their hegemony by redefining respectability for men and naturalizing femininity for women. The sensation melodramas of Dion Boucicault and Augustin Daly, in conjunction with new rules of etiquette and decorum, helped them to make these adjustments and achieve cultural dominance. In the process, the business class and their playwrights transformed the structure and ideology of nineteenth-century melodrama.

Before these changes could occur, however, the bourgeoisie needed its own theatres. While the middling classes had been going to the theatre all along, managers before the mid forties had largely taken them for granted, gearing their policies and their seasons to attract either elite or working-class spectators. The initial effect of itinerant starring had been to encourage larger playhouses to pack in as many urbanites as possible, regardless of their class. By the early 1850s, however, museum theatres in the Northeast had demonstrated the profitability of women auditors, cold-water playhouses, and lowest-common-denominator respectability. Their popularity suggested the likely success of smaller, more exclusive theatres catering to the business-class desires and concerns of both genders—playhouses distinct from working-class theatres but less elitist than the opera houses beginning to be planned or built in New York, Philadelphia, and Boston.

To attract the bourgeoisie, theatre entrepreneurs after 1850 continued to ban liquor and prostitutes, replaced the lascivious third tier with a balcony usually termed the family circle, and created a new space for business-class seating, initially termed the parquette but finally called the orchestra. These trends were already evident to one columnist in 1861: "The pit is to be broken up and fine parquette seats put down; the boys are expected to go aloft, while lorgnettes and crinoline take their vacated seats."[1] By the panic of 1873, most urban playhouses had eliminated the pit, shoved the remaining boxes nearer the proscenium, and adopted orchestra/balcony seating for most spectators. The pricing and reserve seating policies of the bourgeois theatres kept most of the orchestra and first balcony seats within the reach of modest business-class households, but beyond the means and the planning of most workers, who sat in the upper balcony if they attended at all. By gradually cutting back the number of side boxes, bourgeois owners and managers also insured that most elite theatregoers would sit with the rest of the business class. In the place of the three-part hierarchy of box, pit, and gallery seating was a two-class theatre catering primarily to the needs of the business class with a marginal space set aside for respectable workers and the impecunious bourgeoisie. These class-related architectural developments paralleled similar changes in European theatres at the same time.

The parquette emerged in the late 1840s as a means of segregating business-class spectators from the increasing rowdiness of the pit. Borrowed from the opera house (which borrowed the term from the French theatre), the parquette area of seating was initially at the rear of the pit in front of the first row of boxes. Playgoers in the first parquettes sat on long padded benches with backs, akin to church pews—a seating arrangement that had proved popular at the Boston Museum as well as at the opera.[2] The enormous Broadway Theatre featured a small parquette when it was finished in 1847 and William E. Burton kept the parquette in Palmo's Opera House when he refurbished that playhouse for his own company in 1848. By the early 1850s, the Arch and Walnut Street theatres in Philadelphia and the Howard Athenaeum in Boston had joined several other New York theatres in adding a parquette for business-class spectators. From the beginning of the trend, parquette seating was priced at or near that of seats in side boxes, thus undermining the previous class distinction between box and pit. The prices at the Broadway Theatre in 1854, soon after the parquette was expanded to eliminate the pit, for instance, were fifty cents for box and parquette seating and twenty-five cents for the family circle and upper tier. At the Broadway and other fashionable theatres in the mid fifties, the bourgeoisie was assured of equality of respectability with the elite.

Most new theatres built after 1854 continued to expand the number of seats for the business class and lavished increased attention on bourgeois comforts. The 1854 Boston Theatre was the first to install folding theatre seats. With some surprise, *Ballou's Pictorial* reported:

> The chairs in the parquet and [first] balcony have iron frames, and are cushioned with leather on the back, seat, and arms, the seat being so balanced as to rise to a perpendicular when not in use, affording a place to stand in the area occupied by the frame.

Uniform parquet chairs allowed for the possibility of numbered seating in the former pit. The playbill of the new Boston Theatre was pleased to announce that "a corps of ushers . . . will conduct ladies and gentle-

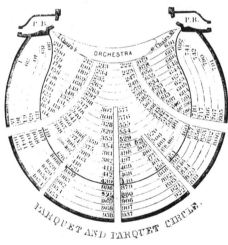

Auditorium and seating plan of the Boston Theatre, anonymous engravings, 1854 (from Eugene Tompkins and Quincy Kilby, The History of the Boston Theatre, 1854–1901, *1908). Reduced to little more than decoration, separate boxes have taken the place of proscenium doors in earlier auditoriums. Individually numbered seats facilitated reserved seating, further enhancing the rationalization of theatregoing.*

men to their seats." The commodious house also featured a second balcony and a family circle above the first balcony, but only four private boxes, continuing the practice of mixing most of the elite with the rest of the business class. Rich panels and draperies decorated the interior, and a large clock, symbol of bourgeois rationalization, crowned the space above the proscenium. Theatre historian Weldon Durham notes that "the circularity and size of the auditorium and negligible seating for aristocrats were emblems of the purpose of the theatre: to provide quality entertainment for Boston's burgeoning middle class and liberal profits for the theatre's managers."[3]

The opulence and seating arrangements of Laura Keene's 1856 theatre quickly made it a favorite among business-class theatregoers in New York. Keene had performed with her company at a different playhouse a year earlier, but it burned down. At the opening of her second theatre, the *Spirit of the Times* gushed that the "sculpture, fresco, and gilding" of the mostly white and gold interior created "a glow and warmth [that] seem to pervade and temper the atmosphere." Of the nearly 2,500 seats in the 1856 playhouse, about 1,000 were in the parquette, with 750 in each of the dress circle and family circle balconies. There were only two private boxes, and Keene kept the parquette and dress circle prices the same at fifty cents. In 1857, she announced the availability of "reserved orchestra seats," a practice begun two years earlier in New York by William E. Burton at his playhouse.[4]

James William Wallack opened his Lyceum Theatre in 1852 and soon established his company as the most respectable in New York. By 1858, its parquette already provided a "synopsis of the most valuable portion of the New York people," according to *Frank Leslie's* magazine. Wallack's new uptown theatre in 1861 incorporated many of the architectural innovations developed in the previous decade. Like his earlier house, Wallack's Theatre on Broadway at Thirteenth Street was small but elegant, continuing the trend toward more intimate playhouses. The seating capacity was around 1,600, with 600 in the parquette, 455 and 512 in the first and second balconies, and only 42 in the box seats. Within the parquette, however, was another area near the stage known as the orchestra stalls. Such seating arrangements, begun in London, had been tried before by Laura Keene at her 1855 theatre and in 1856 at the Broadway, but Wallack's decision to install luxurious seats near the orchestra and to double their price above the seating in the dress circle and the rest of the parquette established the orchestra as the new bourgeois mode. His 1861 prices were fifty cents for the dress circle and parquette, twenty-five for the family circle, and a dollar for a chair in an orchestra stall. Apparently all members of the business class were equal in respectability at Wallack's, but some were more equal than others.[5]

By the 1870s, matinee ladies, fashionable latecomers, commuting early-leavers, serious-minded businessmen, and other bourgeoisie dominated theatregoing in the Northeast. A patronizing writer for the *Spirit of the Times* in 1866 congratulated the matinee-goer for relieving "the biped man from the bore of attending dull or even good performances for the sole purpose of escorting their Mary Janes. The dear creatures can go to afternoon performances all alone by themselves, and stop on the way home for ice punch and cream cakes." Other male journalists complained of ladies at evening performances drawing attention to themselves by entering late and "disturbing unfashionable playgoers, who go early and try to enjoy themselves." Leaving before the final curtain was also a problem. "Every minute beyond half-past ten that you keep the curtain up is doing you harm," warned an 1861 critic. "My cousins in Brooklyn and the Jerseys want time to get home." Most play reviewers congratulated the bourgeoisie on their gentility and decorum, but a few were already criticizing them for their unimaginative self-involvement:

> These matter-of-fact, realistic, unpoetical audiences, who can enjoy the contemplation of no ideal above that realized by themselves, who chiefly delight in seeing the likenesses of their own petty intrigues and their own trivial acts represented upon the stage; who, forsooth, are so serious, and so earnest, and so benevolent, and so sympathetic in actual daily life that their feelings will not bear the additional strain produced by a tragedy or serious play.

This realistic business class would transform melodrama as radically as it had changed midcentury playhouses.[6]

To attract this audience, Augustin Daly continued the conventions of seating and décor standardized by 1870, but also added some new touches to his 1869 and 1873 theatres. His tiny 1869 theatre, which seated only nine hundred, used the entire lower floor for orchestra seating. The interior side walls of this narrow theatre were plated with mirrors, partly to give the illusion of a larger space, but also to allow his audience to watch themselves and others playing their social roles. He continued to adorn his walls with mirrors at his 1873 theatre, located on Twenty-eighth Street near Broadway (but named, like his first playhouse, the Fifth Avenue Theatre). The mirrors "framed in walnut and crimson satin," the ceiling frescoes "done by Gariboldi," and the "softly carpeted" floors presented "a scene of rich and impressive magnificence" to a New York *Tribune* reporter on opening night. The playhouse seated about 1,500, with 530 in an undivided main floor (without separate orchestra stalls), 364 in the first balcony, and the rest in 12 private boxes and the family circle. The general size, décor, and seating arrangements of the bourgeois theatre came together in Daly's second playhouse. These features would change very little over the next forty years.[7]

Augustin Daly's early career combined the aggressiveness and respectability needed to succeed in theatrical management during the 1860s and early 1870s. Although Daly would continue as a manager until 1899, most of his later practices maintained the hard work, autocratic control, close attention to public image, and rationalization of production that made him successful in his early years. Involved in producing popular theatrical illusions for the business class, Daly's professional life epitomized the tensions that resulted from the bourgeois production of the illusion of gentility. Behind the scenes of graciousness, morality, and naturalness in Daly's business-class theatre lurked the backstage reality of cutthroat competition, dictatorial domination, and repressive self-control.

Daly moved to New York City in 1856 at the age of eighteen and was soon working as a newspaper reporter and writing scripts for women stars. As a press agent for Adah Isaacs Menken and Kate Bateman, he learned the importance of Barnum-like publicity. By the mid 1860s, Daly was a drama critic on five different newspapers and had developed a lifelong cynicism about the integrity of reviewers. Daly's frequent evenings at New York theatres led him to despise Bowery audiences, uphold the importance of conventional morality in drama, and appreciate the smooth play-carpentry and sensational effects of Dion Boucicault, whom Daly believed to be the best playwright of his generation. His ambition was boundless. "I have the will and disposition to ride over every puny obstacle," Daly wrote to his brother in 1865.

His competitiveness, rationalization, and self-control would take this man of principle to the top of his profession as a manager-capitalist in the theatre.[8]

Daly gained modest success with *Griffith Gaunt*, a comedy he wrote and staged in 1866. The following year he struck it rich with *Under the Gaslight*, his sensation melodrama that played for a thirteen-week run in New York, four weeks in Boston, and seven in Philadelphia, and enjoyed numerous revivals at Daly's own theatres and elsewhere over the next two decades. As one critic wrote later, *Gaslight* "made more money than any play Mr. Daly ever had any interest in." Daly had rehearsed the show for two weeks, double the usual time in that era, and his attention to detail paid off. A reviewer for the *Leader* praised Daly's "most perfect familiarity with managerial details . . . extracting the most perfect climaxes out of every extension of his plot." At the sensational climax of the piece, the heroine saves a man strapped to railroad tracks by the villain. Crashing through a locked shed with an axe, she unties him just as the "Express"—terrific steam-engine sound effects and the blinding headlight of the locomotive—roars across the stage. "Not only was *Under the Gaslight* played in every city," wrote Joseph Daly in his 1917 biography of his brother, "but for many months the vaudevillists, 'sketch artists,' variety performers, and minstrel troupes were inventing burlesque 'acts' of the railroad scene." Joseph concluded that "these travesties were so many evidences of the wide and strong impression" of his brother's melodrama.[9]

Daly capitalized on his *Gaslight* success by opening his own theatre in 1869. "I went upon the stage [of the Fifth Avenue Theatre]," he wrote to his brother, "and felt as one who treads the deck of a ship as its master." To gain mastery, however, he had first to control the stars. Daly had threatened to discharge E. L. Davenport from his cast of *Gaslight* for mocking the actress who played the heroine during rehearsals, but the young manager, knowing the star's drawing power and needing a hit show, had been forced to back down. After 1869, however, it was the stars who relented—or left. Several starring women did leave Daly's company in the early years: Agnes Ethel in 1872, Clara Morris and Linda Dietz in 1873, Fanny Morant and Ada Dyas in 1874. While their individual conflicts with Daly varied, all fought the Governor, as he was called by his company, over control of their careers. Headstrong stars, he admitted to Clara Morris, would easily counter all his "commands, threats, or reasons." Moreover, with female stars, Daly's possible loss of control threatened his masculinity. Augustin wrote to Joseph that giving in to the demands of Ada Dyas "meant nothing more than the subjugation of my manhood." [10]

Daly used other means to enforce his authority. He had his actors agree to a long list of rules and fines hedging in their actions when they signed their contracts. Actors had long been accustomed to some modest restrictions on their behavior, especially since many of the traditional rules, like refusing to play a role or appearing drunk on stage, affected company morale and collective artistry. But several of Daly's restrictions were vague, petty, and demeaning. He fined his actors for gossiping, for lack of courtesy, and "for addressing the manager on business outside of his office." In rehearsal, Daly treated his actors like puppets, often insisting that they read a line or perform a bit of business exactly as he instructed them. The critic William Winter, who reviewed Daly's shows throughout his career, noted that his direction tended to "efface individuality in an actor and convert him into a machine." Another critic recalled that Daly was a "despot" in his theatre during the seventies: "Everything that happened between the box-office and the stage door was subject to his personal supervision." The Governor instructed his scene painters on technique, prompted his actors on opening night, and even helped his machinists move scenery during the run of a show. Otis Skinner worked for Daly in the 1880s, but his observation applies to the "martinet," as he called him, throughout his career: His only hobby, said Skinner, "was the perfect running of the machinery of his organization." [11]

Such severe rationalization was necessary on the inside of his theatre, believed Daly, to protect its outer public image. The Governor reserved the highest fine in his list of regulations for "the giving to outsiders of any information whatsoever; touching the plays in rehearsal, their names, scenery, length, or story." To insure good publicity, he paid off newspaper editors and bought critics. Daly typically let stars go rather than risk a public court battle which might harm his respectability. When Morris broke her contract and left, Daly threatened to enjoin her from performing elsewhere, but her lawyer told her not to worry because Daly would not cross public opinion; he was right. Daly's careful attention to image continued on opening night. As Skinner recalled:

First nights at Daly's [in the 1880s] were such sought-after events that he could select his audience from the representative names in town. All Gotham was sure to be there. He invariably stood at the ticket taker's wicket, with a word of greeting for the illustrious ones. At his back was the inviting lobby, hung with paintings, engravings and historic playbills, warm and homelike, where well-groomed people kept up a buzz of talk. . . . The lights were subdued and the curtain went up. There was a little flurry of music to bring the members of the cast on the scene, and each received his greeting as an old friend. It was all very much like a huge family party, well-ordered, sympathetic.

Daly's construction of such homelike bourgeois conventions at his theatre had begun in the early seventies. His audience little guessed, nor probably much cared, that the illusion of a "huge family party" on opening night required the autocratic subjection of Daly's entire company all the time.[12]

Something of the personal price Daly paid for maintaining a high gloss on his theatre's reputation may be gleaned from his correspondence with his brother. Struggling to raise capital for his 1873 theatre, Daly considered taking on a partner who had plenty of money but a poor reputation because of his ties to Tammany Hall scandals. Joseph cautioned Augustin about such an alliance: "The point about the Fifth Avenue Theatre is its impregnable respectability. It is managed by you who are spotless in fame and unconnected with any failures whatever. It wouldn't do to give the helm to the head of an exploded institution like Tammany Hall." Augustin took his brother's advice and raised sufficient funding elsewhere, but it cost him constant worry. His undercapitalized theatre struggled during the depression years after 1873 and finally folded in 1877. Joseph had continually to reassure his brother that their policy of no stars and frequent change of bill would keep the theatre in the public eye and assure their eventual success, if only Daly would persevere. "You have an iron will, an iron constitution, iron perseverance, and the rebound of a steel spring," wrote Joseph in the summer of 1874. Since reputation was everything and failure unthinkable, Daly had little to fall back upon except the repression and industry of his "iron will."[13]

And his family. Like most other bourgeois capitalists of his era, Daly publicly segregated his family from his business life. He leaned heavily on the confidence and support of his brother and his wife, Mary Duff Daly, who "knew her husband's business thoroughly and never told a word of it," according to the memoirs of one company member. Neither his brother, who had a hand in most of his projects, including his playwriting, nor his wife, the daughter of theatre entrepreneur John Duff, who financed many of his son-in-law's early ventures, gave interviews or even suggested that they had any influence on Augustin; to do so might have compromised his reputation by suggesting some chink in his iron resolve. Apart from his brother, his wife, and his two sons, however, Daly was usually taciturn, obsessive, and aloof. "It was almost impossible to get Mr. Daly to laugh at an actor's joke," remembered Clara Morris. "He was too generally at war with them and he was too often the object of the jest." Striving mightily to enhance his power and respectability, Daly could seldom relax long enough to laugh at the distance between his occasional foolishness and his vaunted public image. Seeking to rationalize his theatre, he had become machinelike himself; a governor not only exercises political authority, but also acts mechanically to control the speed of a steam engine. Perhaps his company's name for him carried this intentional double meaning.[14]

Daly's desires and anxieties may have helped him to succeed with his business-class patrons since most of his problems reflected their own. Like many of the new bourgeoisie after 1850, Augustin and Joseph Daly were the first generation of their family to achieve modest wealth and social position. And like many arrivistes, Augustin sometimes felt that he was passing as genteel, attempting a social role that he was ill-suited to play. His fear of being exposed and embarrassed was apparent both in the regimen of rules he used to protect himself from his acting company and in the care he took to prepare his theatre for the gaze of society. No doubt this latter fear was exacerbated by the still-questionable status of theatre as a profession. But then, there were many new business-class occupations—salesperson, retailer, manager—whose social position was unclear.[15]

Behind the general anxiety of the parvenu was a fear more specifically related to Daly's and to the business class's historical circumstances. As historians of American Victorianism have noted, bourgeois propriety mandated rigorous self-control in public but it also enjoined its initiates to represent themselves sincerely and naturally. This double bind seems to have led Augustin Daly into two parallel difficulties. On the one hand, Daly's repression and self-control tended to alienate him from his own feelings, a rationalization of the self common among business-class men and women of his era. On the other, his need to project an image of sentimental sincerity clashed with the aggressiveness and duplicity he needed to run his business, thus threatening to reveal him to society as a hypocrite. Both problems enmeshed Daly in one of the central concerns of the midcentury bourgeoisie, the authenticity of the self. The codes of bourgeois respectability, notes social historian John Kasson, "extended deep into the individual personality. The rituals of polite behavior and interaction helped to implant a new, more problematic sense of identity—externally cool and controlled, internally anxious and conflicted—and of social relationships." By undermining "a sense of personal coherence," states Kasson, business-class society "led the way toward the 'anticipatory self,' which continually depends upon the products of the consumer culture for its completion." Bourgeois audiences came to their theatres burdened with the psychosocial problems of authenticity. Aware of his own desires and concerns, Daly may have been particularly well attuned to the burdens of his audience.[16]

Like Daly, Dion Boucicault understood the problems of class and authenticity troubling bourgeois theatregoers well enough to profit from them as a playwright. Before arriving in America in 1853, Boucicault had worked in London and Paris, learning his craft by adapting French well-made plays and farces for the English stage and even scoring several comic and melodramatic hits in London, including *Old Heads and Young Hearts*, *The Corsican Brothers*, and *London Assurance*. In the United States, Boucicault first managed and wrote star vehicles for his young wife, Agnes Robertson. Soon other stars were requesting scripts from his facile pen. Painfully familiar with the poverty of most playwrights from his hackwork in London, Boucicault joined with Robert Montgomery Bird and poet-playwright George Henry Boker to push for copyright protection, which passed Congress in 1856. Seeing the possibility of deriving a handsome income from playwriting, Boucicault began writing scripts with more general appeal.[17]

The legal protection of the copyright law made playwrights the potential equals of touring stars and manager-entrepreneurs in theatrical moneymaking. Boucicault reached for this gold ring and hung on. For the next twenty years, he churned out hits in London and New York, most of them owing more to the paste pot and to a keen sense of theatrical effect than to innovative conception. Following his death in 1890, the critic William Winter remarked that the playwright had "possessed an exceptional faculty for devising dramatic machinery." To this dramaturgical rationality, Boucicault added what A. C. Wheeler called "the swift instinct which apprehends the aberrations of the public pulse." Boucicault fitted his plays "to the restless and superficial needs and moods of the public," said Wheeler, "not by being abreast of the thought of our time, but by being abreast of its desires." [18]

The first of his sensation melodramas to succeed in the United States was *The Poor of New York*, adapted from *Les Pauvres de Paris*, by Brisbarre and Nus. It opened in early December 1857 at Wallack's Theatre and ran almost uninterruptedly until January of the following year. The reviewer for the *New York Times* praised its "powerful local interest"—Boucicault had worked in a wealth of local details, from the slums of the Five Points district to the Academy of Music opera house—and the play's "entire grasp of the emotions of the moment." This was a reference to the fear and helplessness generated by the panic of 1857 which, together with the 1837 panic, motivates much of the action. Altering the local referents to suit the city, Boucicault pieced out new scripts entitled *The Streets of Philadelphia* and *The Rich and Poor of Boston*; later, the same show became *The Poor of Liverpool*, *The Streets of London*, and, much later, *The Streets of New York*. "I localize it for each town and hit the public between the eyes," said Boucicault with characteristic bravado. [19]

Opening at Laura Keene's Theatre in March of 1860, *The Colleen Bawn, or The Brides of Garryowen* enjoyed greater popularity than any of Boucicault's previous hits in America. He took the double plot and most of the characters of his melodrama from *The Collegians*, a turgid Irish novel by Gerald Griffin. The playwright starred himself in the comic role of Myles-na-Coppaleen, an Irish peasant who saves the heroine. Crafting a vehicle for his wife but also needing to please his actor-manager, Boucicault put two excellent roles for women in the show, the fair-haired Colleen, played by Agnes Robertson, and the spunky Irish heiress Anne Chute, performed by Laura Keene. A sensation drama, *The Collen Bawn* featured the special effects of a water cave with the illusions of an attempted drowning and a headfirst res-

Advertising woodcut of the water cave scene in The Colleen Bawn, *ca. 1875 (Dover Pictorial Archive Series). As in other sensation plays, the audience enjoyed the stage illusionism—and the offstage sound effects—of such scenes but did not assume that they were realistically achieved.*

cuing dive. The *Times* reviewer called it "the most intense drama of the season" and the *Tribune* pronounced it "one of Boucicault's masterpieces." *The Colleen Bawn* played throughout the Northeast in the 1860s and 1870s.[20]

Despite the initial long run of *The Colleen Bawn*, Boucicault had not been confident of the play's success with business-class spectators. One section of his opening night speech (prepared before Boucicault could have known the audience's reaction to the show) suggests the reason for his apprehension:

> I think it will be admitted by you all that Irishmen do most of the hard work in this country—I mean real hard manual labor. I myself have worked very hard for the past seven months and I don't believe that for the next three months you could get another idea out of me with a derrick. I have written an Irish drama for the first time in my life.

This was premeditated blarney. Apart from the coy comparison of his labors with those of recent Irish immigrants, Boucicault wrote the melodrama rather quickly and it was at least his fourth play with Irish characters. He compounded these minor social lies with a whopper. Expressing his hope that other playwrights "may hereinafter give you plenty of Irish plays," he added, "which I am certain will be appreciated by you, from my experience of your intelligence as American citizens and of the hearty welcome you have ever extended to everything Irish since the country has been a country."[21]

A section of the *Times* review suggests an explanation for Boucicault's bootlicking. The critic was gratified to find *The Colleen Bawn* much better than the usual Irish melodrama. "A certain class of [play] remarkable for its stupidity, passes muster as the Irish drama," he stated. "[It] exhibits rather too liberally the virtues of an agrarian peasantry, the depravity of cultivated classes, and the supreme reformations that are effected on the latter by the free use of the shillelah." Thankfully, the critic continued, "this fashion of fun has gone out of date. . . . Boucicault has opened new ground." Unlike such melodramas as *Ireland as It Is*, in other words, Boucicault's play had not induced the audience to weep over Irish poverty and celebrate Irish revenge against the British. Boucicault had kept social injustice and ethnic hatred out of his play! The critic's sigh of relief is almost audible. Boucicault had been treading on the thin ice of class and ethnic antagonism in America and he knew it; that he did so without falling through made the play even more popular.[22]

The Poor of New York and Daly's *Under the Gaslight* also acknowledged the reality of ethnic and class conflict in Anglo-American society and, like *The Colleen Bawn*, smoothed over the problem. Historically, hegemonic cultures have generally admitted inequalities and antagonisms among social groups; their dominance derived not from denial, but from strategies of representation whereby social conflicts could be contained and explained. For the business class to achieve dominance in the social formation of melodramatic theatre, it needed a more adequate representation of society than that provided by moral reform melodrama, yet one which maintained the values of rationalization and respectability propagated in those productions. The sensation melodramas of Daly and Boucicault and their imitators filled the bill. From the mid 1850s through the early 1870s, sensation plays packed business-class theatres in Boston, New York, and Philadelphia; *The Poor of New York*, *The Colleen Bawn*, and *Under the Gaslight* were representative of this popular genre.[23]

Moral reform melodrama insisted on a cause-and-effect relationship between individual respectability and social success. The message was clear: economic well-being reflected inner sincerity and sensibility; lose the outer markings of the bourgeoisie and you descend below the class line. Sensation melodrama decoupled this linkage by acknowledging that chance often interferes with the best-laid plans of business-class heroes and heroines to maintain their social position. Accidents, misunderstandings, and circumstances beyond human control abound in these melodramas and, in large measure, determine their outcome. A string of mishaps in *The Colleen Bawn*, for example, leads Anne Chute to believe that Kryle Daly is already married; hence, she hesitates to pursue wedlock with the shy collegian. A more serious problem arises when Danny, the hunchbacked boatman, mistakenly thinks that Hardress Cregan has given him the signal to kill his secret wife. Another accident occurs when Myles-na-Coppaleen mistakes Danny for a swimming otter and wounds him, thus accidentally saving Eily O'Connor from drowning. More misunderstandings occur as the major characters bounce from one mishap to another, never achieving a clear perception of their situation until the end of the show.

The implications of this kind of plotting for the class position of bourgeois characters are best exemplified in *Under the Gaslight* and *The Poor of New York*. Society brands Laura Courtland an outcast when it discovers (wrongly, as it turns out) her lowly origins as an orphan. Between acts 1 and 2, she descends from living in an elegant bourgeois townhouse to a poor basement apartment. Similar misfortune—at least from within the orientation of sensation melodrama—strikes the respectable characters of *The Poor of New York* when the panic of 1857 causes them economic hardship. "Three months ago, I stood there the fashionable Mark Livingstone," says the hero, "owner of the Waterwitch yacht and one of the original stock-holders in the Academy of Music. And now, bust up, sold out, and reduced to breakfast off this coat" (II,1). When the panic hits the Fairweather family, Paul loses his job as a clerk, and Lucy, the heroine, must take a low-paying position as a milliner's apprentice. But has their economic descent hurt the respectability of these business-class heroes and heroines? Not at all. Having carefully established that they had no responsibility for these apparent acts of God, these melodramas do not blame them for their fall. These characters deserved their wealth and position, it seems, but not their misfortune.

To preserve the class line, all three melodramas shift the definition of respectability from inner qualities of character and morality to "natural" attributes resulting from birth and upbringing. To be sure, most of their heroines, though few of their heroes, are more than unusually principled and loyal. But language and ethnicity are the fundamental markers dividing the genteel from the unrespectable in these plays. Augustin Daly parades a variety of lowlife types, all with distinguishing accents and colors—newsboys, "a colored citizen," a slum dweller, "an Italian organist from Cork," and others—across his *Gaslight* stage, and none of them speaks the standard English of his hero and heroine. When Puffy in *The Poor of New York* tells of his descent into poverty, a tale which parallels Mark Livingstone's ("Down in the world, now sir—overspeculated like the rest on 'em . . ."), the audience has no doubt about the class of each. The language of class is at the center of *The Colleen Bawn*, with the respectable Hardress attempting to teach his peasant-born wife Eily proper English. "I'm gettin' claine of the brogue, and learnin' to do nothin—I'm to be changed entirely," says this Irish Eliza Doolittle (I,3). The melodrama affirms that only suffering can result when representatives of different language groups fall in love. The language of one's birth and early life creates apparently natural and nearly insuperable barriers.[24]

Likewise, the affection that many working-class characters show toward their betters seems entirely natural, the result of good-hearted friendliness, not submissiveness or opportunism. Snorkey, a one-armed veteran from the Civil War, runs messages around New York City for the villain at the start of *Gaslight*, but changes his colors when he sees that the heroine is in danger. Refusing to take Laura's money, he promises to save her for free: "I stood up to be shot at for thirteen dollars a month, and I can take my chances of a lickin' for nothing" (II,1). Similarly, Myles-na-Coppaleen rescues the Colleen Bawn and hides her from her husband, motivated by his previous love for the heroine, not by the hope of gain. In *The Poor of New York*, the Puffys are lower-class, but for much of the action they have more money than their business-class boarders, the Fairweathers. Nonetheless, when Lucy, Paul, and their mother invite Mark Livingstone to dine with the Puffys, Mrs. Puffy insists on cooking and serving the meal. "Wouldn't think of sitting at the same table with them," she remarks (II,3). These earnest veterans, carefree peasants, and urban workers are permanent members of the lower class, with no thought of rising into the bourgeoisie. And, luckily for the respectable, they not only assist their heroes and heroines, they genuinely admire them. Lower-class helpers and servers are business-class wish fulfillments come to life; there's no servant problem in sensation melodrama.

The relations within the business class between families of moderate income and people of great wealth are not as predictable. These plays assert that the power of the rich breeds arrogance, pretentiousness, and exclusivity. In *Gaslight*, Mrs. Van Dam, her claim to aristocratic position evident in her name, organizes all the women in Delmonico's to snub Laura Courtland when she discovers her lowly origins. This leads the hero to compare high society to a pack of wolves. Lucy Fairweather in *The Poor of New York* is victimized by the daughter of a rich banker who pays off Mark Livingstone's debts to trap him into marriage. Corrigan, the villain of *The Colleen Bawn*, tries the same strategy to marry the widowed and temporarily impoverished Mrs. Cregan.

Despite these intraclass wrangles, however, the plots of all three plays underline the unity of the business class, often by an alliance between respectable families of moderate means and the old-moneyed elite. Anne Chute, a representative of the Protestant Ascendancy in Ireland, uses her money to save the Cregan estate from foreclosure, thus joining the Chutes and the Cregans to foil Corrigan's villainy.[25] Saved in the nick of time from a forced alliance with Alida Bloodgood, the banker's daughter, the elite Mark Livingstone marries the respectable Lucy Fairweather. *Gaslight* features no moderate-income families, but it does seal the division between rich and poor, ruptured by the lower-class villain's attempts to blackmail Laura's fiancé with the promise of keeping quiet about her humble birth. Even the female villain, a woman from the slums named Old Judas, recognizes the "natural" difference between the two classes. Ruefully admitting Laura's stoic nobility after she and Byke, the villain, kidnapped her, she says, "How her blood tells—she wouldn't shed a tear" (III,3). Blood tells in each of these plays. The pretentious and wolfish qualities of high society cannot finally divide a bourgeoisie united by nature.

Chance-ridden plays with the survival of business-class heroes and heroines weighing in the balance had obvious appeal for midcentury bourgeois audiences. Many business-class men and women in the 1850s and 1860s believed that their economic and social success was due more to luck than to their own self-control and industry. The popular books of Edwin T. Freedley, most of them published in the 1850s, for example, taught that the economy did not necessarily reward individuals for morally correct behavior. His *Practical Treatise on Business, Leading Pursuits and Leading Men*, and *Opportunities for Industry and the Safe Investment of Capital* dispensed specific advice on handling investments and developing markets, but recognized that risk was an inherent part of any business enterprise. And most Horatio Alger novels, already popular by the mid sixties, coupled confidence and respectability with the lucky break as the path for youths eager to rise from newsboy to millionaire. As social historian Richard Sennett points out,

> The businessmen and bureaucrats of the last century had little
> sense of participating in an orderly system. The new principles of
> making money and directing large organizations were a mystery
> even to those who were very successful. . . . [Most pictured] their
> activities in terms of the gamble, the game of chance—and the ap-
> propriate scene was the stock exchange.

For the American bourgeoisie, economic panics, estate foreclosures, and embarrassing questions about their social origins—the chance events that structure these sensation melodramas—were believable accidents of fate that could happen to them.[26]

All the more reason, then, to construct a social order based on nature rather than on the historical contingencies of wealth, environmental conditioning, or traditional social position. This construction was made easier for bourgeois moralists by the increasing distance of the business class from the lives of urban workers and poor people. In their places of business, managers and clerks rarely came into contact with manual laborers. Many moderate-income business-class families lived on the peripheries of Boston, New York, and Philadelphia by the time of the Civil War, their flight from the inner city motivated by a desire to own their own homes and enabled by a rapidly improving commuter system of transportation. By 1870 in New York, most business-class men saw life in the Bowery only through the windows of city omnibuses taking them to and from their homes in Brooklyn or northern Manhattan. Business-class women might come to know working-class neighborhoods and families firsthand through their social and religious work, but most shopped at different stores and socialized at different restaurants, hotels, and theatres.[27]

At the same time that business-class families of modest income were defining themselves in opposition to workers, they were also drawing closer to the elite. To be sure, many bourgeois moralists remained critical of the extravagance and pretentiousness of the wealthy, and moderate-income families taught their children to value prudence and sensibility rather than the aggressive self-assertion of the rich. Nonetheless, salaried clerks thought of themselves as "businessmen in training," joined many of the voluntary associations run by the elite, and voted for politicians who would perpetuate and enhance the power of their class. Social historian Stuart Blumin speaks of an "axis of respectability" uniting upper- and moderate-income families, generated primarily by the interaction of women and clerks in downtown retail stores. While the urban elite continued to maintain separate clubs, schools, and places of amusement, the price of joining the "upper ten thousand" was increasingly mere money. Any business-class family, regardless of past social position or even current financial distress, could aspire to elite status.[28]

How "natural," in these circumstances, to regard manual laborers as inherently inferior creatures. Historian Robert Wiebe notes the shift in American culture from "inner convictions to outward appearances" as the primary means of classifying groups of people. This shift, he adds, "gave the nineteenth century its distinctiveness as the age of ethnic awareness." Increasingly, the American bourgeoisie identified poverty with ethnicity and ethnicity with natural traits of behavior and belief. This was especially true of stereotypes of Irish-Americans, which gravitated during the antebellum period from conceptions of Irishness based on environmental factors to differences believed to be matters of race. Historian Dale T. Knobel concludes:

By midcentury, language had built into American folk culture a sense that "Americans" and "Irish" were innately and permanently—physically—different from one another and that intelligence, morality, religious inclination, political affiliation, social conduct, and economic behavior were all derivatives of "race."

While this stereotype could never exclude Irish-Americans from respectable society as thoroughly as it segregated out African-Americans—passing for the Irish was much easier than for blacks—it clearly retarded their assimilation and social progress.[29] Little wonder that Boucicault was worried about the success of *The Colleen Bawn* with business-class spectators.

As for the native-born worker—the real Puffys and Snorkeys of the 1855–70 period—bourgeois moralists tended to divide them between the respectable and the naturally dependent. "The labor of a single year gives to every laborer, if he choose to save his earnings, a very considerable capital," Nathan Appleton assured his business-class readers. "He takes at his pleasure a place in society." If a native-born American worker did not elevate himself to the business class, in other words, he had only himself to blame. Appleton's remarks echoed hundreds of similar assurances from the pulpit, from newspapers, and from political halls, and most members of the business class believed these absurdities. Workers who did not succeed were somehow defective. Abraham Lincoln had genuine sympathy for poor workers, as did many other Republicans, but it was not unmixed with condescension: "It is not the fault of the system [if a man remained a wage earner], but because of either a dependent nature which prefers it, or improvidence, folly, or singular misfortune." Singular misfortune could be explained in an economy of chance, but improvidence and folly were likely to be a part of a person's dependent nature. As Robert Wiebe notes, by the Civil War many business-class moralists were concluding that "nature had bestowed [morality and respectability] only on some humans and that society now must reckon with a fundamental separation between those who did have a moral sense and those who did not."[30]

If nature created such differences between ethnic groups and classes, perhaps it also divided the sexes along more than biological lines. The bourgeoisie believed that respectable men could rise above their selfish natures and act on principle in matters of politics and economics, but what about women? Their lack of political and economic power suggested that they might derive their rights and duties from nature rather than business contracts and civil law. By 1860, most Americans believed that woman's nature produced the social benefits of child care and domestic virtue; it was a small step from there to argue that women were incapable of transcending their biological roles. Medical opinion, eager to replace midwifery with the new sciences of obstetrics and gynecology, took that step, and others followed. One well-known gynecologist wrote in 1847 that "[woman] is a moral, a sexual, a germiferous, gestative and parturient creature." The construction of maternal affection, emotional excess, and familial loyalty as natural to women was not without its dangers to the dominant culture, however. As John Frost explained in his *Daring and Heroic Deeds of American Women*, natural women could meet any attack on their domestic happiness with ferocity and violence, "sparing neither sex nor age."[31] Merely socialized women had tended to be meek and passive; naturalized women could transcend these social conventions and act with passion.

As women became more natural in bourgeois culture, men became more self-controlled, less able to exercise their natural instincts in mixed company. An 1856 article in *Harper's* on "Domestic Society in Our Country" commented:

> No civilized man is so helpless and dependent in certain respects as an American gentleman and the reason is obvious: our wives do our thinking in these matters, and we are perfectly content to follow their lead. A large part of our social system is under their control and they legislate for our dress, etiquette, and manners without the fear of a veto. . . . It is, indeed, the subtlest and most pervasive influence in our land.

Harper's was exaggerating; numerous other accounts, some in the same magazine, complained of men putting their boots on the furniture, eating with their knives, and swearing in the parlor. But the norms of polite society, as reflected in etiquette books, novels, and plays, had changed, and masculine behavior in the presence of respectable women was not far behind. In the man's world of politics and business, however, rationality and self-aggrandizement remained the dominant values. Bourgeois males were increasingly pulled in two directions: the sincerity and repression of parlor life, if practiced in business, hobbled his success; calculating rationality, pursued in mixed company, turned him into a vulgar boor.[32]

The heroes and heroines of sensation melodrama helped to legitimate these new constuctions of gender roles. Although allowed to act defensively, the heroines of Forrest's plays and even moral reform melodramas initiate no action to save themselves or their families. This changes with sensation melodrama. To release their family from having another mouth to feed when they are starving, Lucy Fairweather and her mother, both unbeknownst to each other, attempt suicide. Only by discovering and convincing each other of the futility of death do they decide not to go through with their desperate acts. *The Colleen Bawn* features no female heroism, but Anne Chute's pursuit of Kryle Daley is indicative of the more active role allowed to natural women in sensation melodrama. Of course the most dramatic act of heroism in these three plays occurs when Laura rescues Snorkey from the onrushing train. She is initially agitated when she sees him tied to the tracks, but when Snorkey tells her that Byke and Judas are "on the way to your cottage . . . to rob and murder," the threat to her family and loved ones steels Laura's determination. As she is battering through the stationhouse door with an axe, racing the thundering train to reach Snorkey, he cries "Courage!" and "That's a true woman!" (IV,3). With her family in danger, Laura's "natural" feelings triumph over her socialized reserve.[33]

The bourgeois heroes of sensation plays are more conflicted than the heroes of any previous type of melodrama. Caught between the sentimental urge to behave correctly to their wives or sweethearts and the competitive need to improve their economic and social positions, all three heroes float passively through their plays. Ray Trafford continues to love Laura throughout *Gaslight*, but vacillates between rejecting and pursuing her because of the effect her questionable past has on his social position. Hardress Cregan has much the same problem in *The Colleen Bawn*. If he stays wedded to Eily, he and his mother will lose their estate and compromise the family name through his alliance with a peasant. If he voids their marriage, either through Eily's cooperation or her death, he sacrifices his true love for opportunistic gain. Trafford and Cregan do careless and even despicable things during the course of the action—Hardress is even partly responsible for Eily's near drowning—but each is sincerely embarrassed and apologizes for his vacillation and moral turpitude. Luckily for her, other characters untangle the accidents and misunderstandings of the plots and all three heroes get both the money and the girl. In effect, sensation melodrama winks at the moral compromises made by the bourgeois hero, allowing him to maintain his respectability as long as he continues to profess his sincere good intentions.[34] Such hypocritical behavior was the mark of villainy in earlier melodramas.

In its reconstruction of gender roles, sensation melodrama no longer demands that the inner reality of respectable men and women match their outward behavior. Given the right circumstances, heroines can drop their domestic self-control and fight like tigers. Heroes, allowed more latitude, can turn their backs on loved ones as long as they later repent their folly. Sacrificing the moral transparency of the self for social role-playing has its price, however. These business-class characters are sometimes at a loss to know who they are. Hardress Cregan, aware that his manservant believes he would kill Eily to preserve his social position, doubts his moral sanity. "Begone!" he orders Danny:

> I have chosen my doom; I must learn to endure it—but, [my] blood! and hers! Shall I make cold and still that heart that beats alone for me?—quench those eyes that look so tenderly in mine? Monster! am I so vile that you dare to whisper such a thought. (II,1)

Dragged into court by Byke, who claims her as his daughter, Laura says, "I am—I dare not say it. I know not who I am, but I feel that he [i.e., Byke] cannot be my father" (III,1).

Business-class nervousness about role-playing scapegoats the working class in *The Poor of New York*. Upset that the poor are getting more sympathy after the 1857 panic than people like himself who have been forced by society to hide their poverty to preserve their reputations, Mark Livingstone demands:

> The poor! Whom do you call the poor? Do you know them? Do you see them? They are more frequently found under a black coat than under a red shirt. The poor man is the artist who is obliged to pledge the tools of his trade to buy medicines for his sick wife. The

lawyer who, craving for employment, buttons up his thin paletot to hide his shirtless breast. These needy wretches are poorer than the poor, for they are obliged to conceal their poverty with the false mask of content. Smoking a cigar to disguise their hunger, they drag from their pockets their last quarter to cast it with studied carelessness to the beggar at home whose mattress is lined with gold. These are the most miserable of the poor of New York. (II,1)

Such are the demands of keeping up a false mask, that the business-class players of these roles have a greater claim on public sympathy than the truly needy. Underlying this bourgeois self-pity is contempt for and even fear of the red shirts and beggars because, like the business class itself, they are no longer morally legible—their mattresses at home may be lined with gold. If the bourgeoisie could not trust themselves to live morally transparent lives, whom could they trust?

Having separated hypocrisy from respectability by endorsing the wearing of social masks, sensation plays cannot treat their villains with the usual severity of previous types of melodrama. Further, in a world dominated by chance, circumstances seemingly beyond anyone's control cause most of the evil in these plays, relegating villainy to a more benign role. Corrigan still does some nasty things, but the most dastardly deed in *The Colleen Bawn* results from a misunderstanding. Appropriately enough, Corrigan's comeuppance at the end of the play is a simple dunking in the horse pond, hardly a fit fate for a traditional villain. In *The Poor of New York*, Bloodgood reforms at the end when Paul Fairweather promises not to put him in jail if only he will return his father's money; the banker leaves the stage in tears. And Byke walks away from his crimes. Trafford promises not to prosecute him for robbery and murder as long as Byke keeps silent about the birth of Laura's half-cousin, Pearl, the real foundling of the play. The ending of *Gaslight* endorses the social hypocrisy of the bourgeoisie.[35]

To separate villainy from happenstance requires careful detective work in these plays. Myles-na-Coppaleen is the first to unravel the web of accident and misunderstanding that led to the near drowning of the Colleen Bawn. He hides Eily in his cottage and then produces her at the climax of the show, foiling Corrigan's attempt to arrest Hardress for the murder of his wife. Snorkey dogs Byke's trail and discovers his intention of murdering Laura and robbing Pearl at their country house—information that eventually results in the villain's capture. The most perceptive and persevering of these protodetectives is Tom Badger, the reformed villain of *The Poor of New York*. Intent in 1837 on blackmailing the banker Bloodgood for absconding with Captain Fairweather's deposit in his bank (the captain dies and Badger is the only other witness to the transaction), Badger reforms after befriending Lucy Fairweather in 1857 and joins the police department to gain justice for the Fairweather family. He has carefully hidden the receipt proving Bloodgood's crime in a rooming house. When Bloodgood sets fire to the premises to burn up the evidence, Badger rushes into the burning building and appears, receipt in hand, at an upper-story window—the sensation moment of the play! In the final scene, he interrupts the wedding of Alida Bloodgood and Mark Livingstone (much as Myles stops the marriage of Anne Chute to Hardress Cregan) and arrests the villain.

Significantly, contemporary reviewers singled out the actors playing the two Boucicault protodetectives for special notice. Dion himself, of course, played Myles and won this review from the *Tribune*: "[He] displays alarming symptoms of a most capital talent for playing Irishmen—a talent hitherto unsuspected and latent; he is excellent." Boucicault's Myles-na-Coppaleen was the first of his many shrewd and whimsical Irishmen to gain popular and critical acclaim. Although the *Herald* thought Lester Wallack's Badger "too fierce, gruff, and melodramatic," the *Times* termed him "excellent," and fashionable New Yorkers enjoyed the opportunity of watching Mr. Lester, as he was known, in a role beyond his usual romantic-lead line of business.[36]

Wallack's and Boucicault's success in these roles is not surprising. Apart from their acting, the roles themselves are the protagonists of each melodrama, since the heroes of each are too self-divided and too ignorant to push to resolution the plots which entangle them. Moreover, these detectivelike characters, Snorkey included, are shrewder than previous heroic protagonists, their success depending as much on perceptive reasoning as on a strong will and a good heart. Myles, Badger, and Snorkey are not Sherlock Holmes, to be sure, but their vigilance and analytical ability mark them as precursors of this later theatrical type. Since these characters are lower-class but aligned to the bourgeoisie through friendship, their detective skills pose no threat to the class system. Indeed, by helping to solve the mystery at the heart of each of these plays—who stole the Fairweathers' money in 1837, what happened to the Colleen Bawn, and who were Laura Courtland's parents—they restore authenticity to the hero and heroine. Their trials now over, the business-class couples can finally relax and behave according to their true feelings. Moral transparency remains the goal of the bourgeoisie, but it takes role-playing and the help of a detective to achieve it.

The reconstruction of the hero and heroine, the reduction of the role of the traditional villain, and the emergence and centrality of a detectivelike character in the plot signal a fundamental shift in melodramatic form away from Pixérécourt's neoplatonic structure and toward the formula of the well-made play. Eugène Scribe began writing his *pièces bien faite* in Paris in the 1820s, and other comic playwrights soon borrowed his formula. By the 1840s, Parisian dramatists were freely mixing elements of Pixérécourt and Scribe to create what might be termed well-made melodrama. Boucicault and others imported these hybrids to the English stage and they soon made their way to the United States.[37]

Traditional melodrama and the well-made play share some similarities, but differ in significant ways. Villainy motivates the plots of melodrama; even in heroic and apocalyptic plays, the heroic protagonist is only attempting to restore what the villains have violated. Evil intent may also shape parts of well-made plays, but chance is more fundamental to their internal causation. Whereas melodrama tends toward an episodic arrangement of plot incidents, alternating between scenes of villainy, heroism, and comedy, the incidents of a well-made play are arranged in a chain of cause-and-effect relationships. Since each incident is motivated by the incident preceding it and the characters do not have all the information they need to make sense of their situations, well-made plays often generate a sense of mechanical inevitability. In melodrama, where the characters generally know the cause of their distress, human agency is accorded greater efficacy.

Nor do characters usually require protodetectives to act on their behalf in melodramas, as often occurs in well-made dramas. In Scribean kinds of plays, as in detective fiction, a rational specialist is necessary to analyze and bring order to an increasingly illegible world. Yet, well-made plays and detective stories rarely explore the underlying causes ˙of the social disorder their characters confront; a specific crime may have an explanation, but the past is made to seem largely accidental. As cultural historian Stephen Knight states, "The crime and the resolution [of detective fiction] are without history, without recurring roots. This powerful and frighteningly delusive notion is still with us that desocialized, unhistorical understanding can, by deciphering isolated problems, resolve them." In melodrama, on the other hand, God-given intuition or heroic action in history, not an ahistorical skill in reasoning, is usually more important in resolving the action.[38] In general, melodrama pulls its audience back to the beliefs and communal relations of the past, while the more highly rationalized form of the well-made play fosters the illusion of an objective perspective which prepares its spectators to exercise individual power in the present and future.

The formal differences of these two dramatic types are related to the historical context of their origins. Pixérécourt's melodramas were a reaction against what he and others took to be the moral chaos of the Enlightenment and the French Revolution. Scribe perfected the well-made play in the 1830s, riding the wave of optimism about the apparent order and possibilities for progress in French bourgeois society after the Revolution of 1830. Neil C. Arvin, Scribe's biographer, is struck by the playwright's embrace of the cash nexus: "Probably in no other dramatic literature does one find so many discussions of bank accounts, investments, loans, mortgages, dividends, and business failures." Consequently, money in Scribe's plays becomes a respectable concern of the major characters and, says Arvin, "a real motive force in the plot."[39] In traditional melodrama, on the other hand, only villains focus on money; high finance usually divides daughters from fathers and the people from their freedom.

Within the range of structural possibilities between the ideal types of traditional melodrama and the well-made play, Daly's and Boucicault's pieces are clearly at the well-made end of the continuum. Each play does require villains to motivate its action; Byke's duplicity and greed have a particularly important impact on the shape of Gaslight, for instance. And, while both playwrights tend to structure their sequence of scenes in a cause-and-effect rather than an episodic pattern, both are rather casual in connecting their comic interchanges to the preceding action, especially when they need a short scene played downstage to effect a change of scenery behind it. On the other hand, dropped letters, old receipts, and similar devices of accident figure prominently in these dramas. *The Colleen Bawn* has more misunderstandings than many a Scribe play, and all three dramas need proto-detectives to unravel and resolve their complicated plots.

Finally, Daly and Boucicault bid farewell to the transcendental, often neoplatonic underpinnings of the traditional melodramatic tableau. From Thérèse's final triumph to Old Meadows' revenge, these concluding poses had reminded audiences of the ties binding human action to divine will. Following Scribe, the well-made melodramatists retained the final tableau but oriented them horizontally, cutting their vertical ties to transcendental realities. At the ends of their plays, Daly's and Boucicault's reunited families exist solely in a secular world where respectability and role-playing have no spiritual reverberations. Unlike the earthquake in *Pompeii* or even the Drunkard's "snakes," their sensations were based on rational and materialistic premises; the Almighty had been stripped of power.

Daly and Boucicault knew they were breaking tradition to develop a new type of play. In his newspaper reviews written in the 1860s, Daly used the yardstick of "faithfulness to nature" to measure the "drama of everyday local life" against more traditional plays like *Virginius*:

> Judged by this standard, where [in nature] are the stilted and impossible declamations and allegories, fates, furies, and divine machinery of the classic tragedies compared with the easy flow of language, the natural and varied incidents in the local scenes of modern plays?

Daly made it clear that he preferred "ideality" to literal reality on the stage, however. "We hold it to be in keeping with the theory of theatrical representation to produce [a] cunningly contrived imitation of the original," said Daly, "so that we should have to admire both in the acting and the accessories of the scene the same ingenious counterfeit." With such goals in mind, believed Daly, "it is not impossible that the 'sensational melodrama' may sublime itself to be tragedy." Such bourgeois sublimity could not transcend an imitation of the material world, however, and remain believable.[40]

In articles written in the late 1870s and early 1880s, Boucicault proclaimed his allegiance to dramaturgical rationality: "No art becomes respectable until its principles are acknowledged, methodized, and housed in a system." Like Daly, he favored the "drama of ordinary life" over "unreal, poetic . . . transcendental drama." Reading the structure of the well-made play into Aristotle's *Poetics*, he stressed the need for plays to give pleasure "by exciting in the mind of the spectator a sympathy for fellow creatures suffering their fate." The right way to engineer this sympathy, said Boucicault, was to arouse expectation, suspense, and reflection:

> Expectation is aroused by the beginning, suspense is maintained by the process of development, and reflection is invited by the repose to which the action is conducted. But the feelings must be excited in this order. For the spectator must not be induced to reflect at the beginning, but rather to be looking forward with curiosity.

In Boucicault's recipe, plotting was chiefly a means of building suspense and sympathy, the primary rhetorical inducements of the well-made play. He even indirectly acknowledged his debt to Scribe. "French writers and painters excel in the composition of their pictures, being cunning draughtsmen," he noted.[41]

Performances of well-made sensation melodramas served many of the same social purposes for their business-class audiences in the 1850s and 1860s as practicing the new bourgeois code of manners. In magazines, novels, and especially in the many manuals on etiquette published after 1830, bourgeois moralists assured their mostly urban readers that they could acquire, rehearse, and perfect the manners of polite society. This advice literature was primarily directed at readers new to business-class status—"for persons who had not the advantages of polite learning in youth, but . . . [who now] find themselves possessed of wealth to command the luxuries and elegances of society, but have not the polish to make themselves agreeable," according to the 1856 *Guide to Good Behavior*. Following the rationalistic basis of bourgeois culture, most etiquette books justified the legitimacy of good manners on legalistic, contractual grounds. Just as "no one questions the right" of people in a nation "to make laws for themselves," noted an 1868 manual, so those in society have "a perfect right to make laws which shall be binding upon all of its members." The analogy was misleading, however: the arbiters of polite culture never intended that those below the class line should exercise any vote on the laws of society. As in sensation melodramas, the mix of rationality and respectability in etiquette manuals crowded out democracy and republicanism.[42]

The code of genteel manners not only kept the poor in their place; it also relieved the respectable of having to accept responsibility for social inequality. As Kasson asserts:

[The] apostles of civility battled for far bigger stakes than how best to eat asparagus. Their enterprise must be viewed within the larger concern of how to establish order and authority in a restless, highly mobile, rapidly urbanizing and industrializing democracy. Seeking to avoid overt conflict, they turned issues of class and social grievance back upon the individual. They redefined issues of social conflict to questions of personal governance, social propriety, and "good taste."

Within this framework, lower-class people simply didn't know how to behave themselves: they walked boldly and immodestly, used crude expressions, and even laughed out loud in public. Unrespectable workers exercised little of the physical and emotional self-control—what Kasson terms "the psychological defense mechanisms of repression, displacement, and denial"—of the bourgeoisie. No wonder such people would never rise in the world! Although etiquette books did not define manual laborers as inferior by nature, the fact that workers could learn proper behavior, but didn't, certainly suggested some inherent flaw. Like the division of labor in sensation melodrama, the bourgeois code of behavior tended to naturalize the class division in the Gilded Age. Some people were intended for head-work and heroics, others for hand-work and comic relief.[43]

Despite this separation, the mix of classes and the jostlings of urban life led bourgeois men and women into frequent embarrassing situations in public. Further, the mandate of self-control generated its own sense of social shame, simply because the difficulty of maintaining it led to frequent lapses. The new advice books helped these Hardress Cregans to diffuse the problem of an unrespectable spouse and these Laura Courtlands to avoid the gaze of society intent on segregating "us" from "them." "Etiquette is the machinery of society," cooed one Miss Manners. "It prevents the agony of uncertainty, and soothes even when it cannot cure the pains of blushing bashfulness. If one is certain of being correct, there is little to be anxious about." To avoid embarrassing oneself and others, these writers advised tact and respect for the privacy of others. "All rights and the exercise of true politeness are

contained in the homely maxim, 'MIND YOUR OWN BUSINESS,' "
stated an 1855 manual bluntly. Minding one's own business conveniently excluded questions of social class from polite society.[44]

It also heightened anxieties about the authenticity of the self. Earlier
moralists had been concerned that the self-conscious performance of
good manners would undermine one's inner sincerity. The newer writers of etiquette manuals assumed that one's identity was little more
than a succession of social roles and urged the manipulation of the
outer mask to alter inner feelings. Advised one: "An admirable method
of controlling feeling is to maintain by effort the serenity and suavity of
the countenance. It is impossible for a man to have a rage in his breast
who has a smile on his countenance." The arbiters of gentility, however, had no suggestions for defusing the burden of repression necessary to keep the forced smile on the lips of the bourgeoisie. Such advice
was of little help to the Augustin Dalys of the period mired in the rationalization of the self.

Sensation melodrama also generated fears about business-class identity, but it eased these burdens by assuring its concerned audience that
repression and role-playing would be rewarded in the end with a new
alignment of inner desire and outward repose. In this sense, its performance departed from the immediate psychosocial consequences of
business-class manners, even as it prepared its spectators to endure
the next round of repression and release. On the other hand, the plays
promised an authenticity that their rhetoric denied. Male spectators
especially were encouraged to identify with characters who triumphed
in the end by denying their inner feelings throughout their struggles.
Finally, neither the plays nor the etiquette offered the audience an
imaginative utopian alternative to the social realities of the bourgeois
world. When it excluded the Christian God from its materialistic universe, business-class theatre and decorum also ruled out a nexus of
hopes and beliefs that had animated some to oppose the hegemony of
industrial capitalism. Although perhaps a positive development in the
long run, the death of an active God in melodrama primarily allowed
"nature" to take "his" place. If polite behavior in society were mostly
a matter of following one's natural inclinations, alternatives to bourgeois propriety might not be ungodly, but they were surely unnatural.[45]

8. "Built to Endure"

For historian John Higham, the decade of the 1850s marks a fundamental shift in American culture from a sense of boundlessness to a yearning for consolidation: "In the United States, as well as England and much of Europe, the 1850s witnessed a subsidence of the radical hopes and reactionary fears of the early nineteenth century and the formation of a more stable, more disciplined, less adventurous culture." Higham charts a decline in the reform effort to perfect American society, a shift from the romantic to the practical in matters of business, religion, and government, and a new awareness of limits in city planning, political oratory, and westward expansion. In the mid-century American theatre too, the popularity of Forrest's aggressive heroics and of apocalyptic visions in working-class melodramas waned as Barnum's mix of domesticity and rationalization and Boucicault's well-made melodramas took their place. These sea changes in American culture suggest a fundamental shift in the productive relations driving American society, a shift both reflected in and facilitated by the bourgeois consolidation of American culture beginning in the late 1840s. By 1870 this transition was mostly complete; a culture legitimating the interests of the new business class of industrialists and financiers had passed from emergence to dominance. In the theatre as in the rest of society, the new bourgeoisie consolidated and strengthened its immense power.[1]

Control over the state and over productive economic relations helped the American business class to achieve cultural hegemony. With its primary base in the new Republican party, the bourgeoisie won the 1860 election in the North, extended federal power during the Civil War, and expanded the reach of capitalism into the South through its reluctant abolition of chattel slavery. The state helped the new industrialists to free themselves from the financial power of merchant capital by subsidizing railroads, liberalizing immigration and tariff laws, and rationalizing the currency. Wartime profiteering gave an added boost to the power of the northern industrialists. By driving weaker competitors into bankruptcy as well as crushing a revived labor movement, the economic depression of the late 1850s increased the concentration of wealth and power, a process that continued into the 1860s. The *New York Times* reported in 1869 that "the greater establishments, [with their] larger purses, labor-saving machines, etc., refused to allow the small manufacturers a separate existence." The 1873–79 depression furthered the consolidation of economic power in the hands of the industrial bourgeoisie. Increasingly, industrial production drove overall economic growth; in the 1860s, employment in manufacturing in Boston, New York, and Philadelphia rose by 53 percent. Throughout the United States during the decade, the percentage of the total labor force engaged in nonagricultural production jumped from 41 to 47 percent.[2]

The political and economic dominance of the industrial bourgeoisie gave them substantial power in defining and containing the social relations resulting from their dominance. The chief barrier for protecting themselves and their property from the toiling masses in northeastern cities was the police department. By the Civil War, the bourgeoisie of Boston, Philadelphia, and New York had substantially modernized and expanded police protection. On the next line of defense—though few urban moralists thought of their work in this way—were the benevolent societies, providing assistance and moral education to "deserving" slum dwellers. The Association for Improving the Condition of the Poor (AICP), begun in 1843, won bourgeois support for its rationalized system of relief and reform. In the words of one enthusiastic divine, the AICP was marshaling a "vast machinery of moral forces" geared to "the regeneration of the bad." The Children's Aid Society, begun by Charles Loring Brace in 1853 to focus attention on the "idle and vicious children" of the poor, concentrated its efforts on sending city boys to live with families in the West. Brace admired the pugnacity and opportunism of his urchins and hoped that the West would allow them freer rein for these impulses. He also acknowledged that scattering streetwise children throughout the country would inhibit the growth of urban class consciousness. The bourgeoisie also supported the rapid growth of the Young Men's Christian Association, although this organization had little impact on immigrant populations. After the war, urban moral reform efforts flagged until the late 1870s, when the threat of continuing industrial warfare again spurred the bourgeoisie to action.[3]

These institutions of social control sometimes failed to contain urban unrest. The Draft Riots exploded for four days in July of 1863, leading some prominent New Yorkers to fear that the complete collapse of the bourgeois order was imminent. Initially objecting to the class basis of the draft law (which allowed the wealthy to buy their way out of the fighting), the rioting quickly engulfed racial and ethnic hatreds, a range of class antagonisms, and antiauthoritarian resentments. Mobs numbering in the thousands attacked symbols of bourgeois hegemony, including the mayor's house, the Negro Orphan Asylum, elegant homes and shops on Lexington Avenue, the New York *Tribune* building, and the police. With police and local army units overwhelmed, the authorities called in regular troops, many of them fresh from the Union victory at Gettysburg. The soldiers brought up cannon and fired point-blank into the mob; more than a thousand people died in the rioting. To one bourgeois moralist, William O. Stoddard, the mob was a "whooping, yelling, blaspheming, howling, demonic" mass, an eruption of "social volcanic forces." Stoddard feared that such forces would soon erupt again.[4]

Some bourgeoisie believed that educating the urban poor to appreciate business-class culture might help to keep the lid on the volcano and perhaps even diffuse some of its disruptive pressure. John Pintard, secretary of the Academy of Arts and Sciences in New York, argued that the creation of "Theatres, Operas, Academies of Arts, Museums, etc.," could counter "the growth of vice and immorality" among urban youth; "gross dissipation always prevails where refinement is not cultivated," he urged. Frederick Law Olmsted, designer and superintendent of New York's Central Park in the 1850s, supposed that his park facilitated "a distinctly harmonizing and refining influence upon the most unfortunate and most lawless classes of the city—an influence favorable to courtesy, self-control, and temperance." In 1872, the founder of the Children's Aid Society, Charles Loring Brace, restated the conventional wisdom of the era in his observation that "one of the best modes of driving out low tastes in the masses is to introduce higher." Galleries, libraries, museums, and respectable theatres, he argued, were "formidable rivals of the liquor shops." Buoyed by their optimistic faith in the reforming powers of culture, as well as driven by their fears of revolutionary eruption from below, the northeastern bourgeoisie founded several cultural institutions in the 1850–70 period, including the Boston Public Library and the New York Academy of Music (the opera house) in 1854, the Philadelphia Academy of Music and the Astor Library in New York in 1857, and the Metropolitan Museum of Art and the Boston Museum of Fine Arts in 1869 and 1870, respectively.[5]

Reforming the morals of the lower class through culture encountered difficulties from the start, however. Following a New York Philharmonic concert in 1858, elite Gothamite George Templeton Strong complained in his diary: "Crowded and garrulous, like a square mile of tropical forest with its flocks of squalling paroquets and troops of chattering monkeys." For Strong and others, excluding the barbarous natives from the temples of culture was preferable to welcoming and uplifting them. Joseph Henry, first director (1846–78) of the Smithsonian Institution, agreed. Henry claimed that the chief aim of his museum, despite its public funding, was for "study and investigation" to "advance to a higher civilization," not "to gratify an unenlightened curiosity."[6]

Strong and Henry were the antebellum avatars of what historian Lawrence Levine terms "the sacralization of culture," a bourgeois movement occuring mostly after the Civil War to separate high culture from low and to purify artistic experiences so as to achieve aesthetic and spiritual elevation rather than mere entertainment. Levine traces the gradual transformation of Shakespeare, the fine arts, symphonic music, and other cultural expressions into "high art," suitable only for refined tastes, from the 1850s to the end of the century. He remarks that the social construction of high and low culture helped the members of the business class to believe themselves superior to their servants and factory hands and thus to justify "the disparate conditions in which the various classes lived and worked." Levine's account, however, also underlines the significant tension in bourgeois ideology concerning the proper use of high culture, especially in the 1855–70 period. Should the purveyors of sacralized culture make such experiences available to the urban masses to reform them, or should they exclude the barbarians to further purify their own cultural domains?[7]

In the theatre for business-class audiences, bound more closely to the vagaries of the marketplace than most libraries, museums, and symphonic orchestras, the role of high culture was tied to the bottom line. Sometimes popularization seemed to promise higher profits than sacralization; sometimes the reverse. Augustin Daly played it both ways, boasting of his respectable audiences and refined offerings, but taking care to inject enough thrills into his plays to keep the b'hoys in the upper tier buying tickets. Earlier in his career as a critic, Daly had complained that the "eager faces of young and impressionable boys" at the Bowery Theatre "needed better mental food . . . than they got." *Under the Gaslight* and similar fare, he believed, would elevate their sentiments while filling their hunger for melodramatic effects. In retrospect, sensation melodrama was built to walk the line between the sacred and the popular.[8]

The tension between excluding the masses to sanctify the theatre and including them to elevate their sentiments is evident in the writing of William Winter, the foremost drama critic of his day by 1870. A reviewer first for the *Albion* in the early sixties and, after 1865, for the New York *Tribune* (where he remained until 1909), Winter championed both positions during the decade, apparently unaware of their contradictory implications. For the *Albion* he wrote in 1862: "The sole refuge of this age is art; and that should be kept white, pure, peaceful and beautiful. What we need on stage is what will cheer, comfort, and strengthen." In 1865 at the *Tribune* he saw reforming popular morality as his own and the theatre's chief task:

> By thus disseminating true ideas, we shall continually affect and gradually elevate the standard of popular taste, until at last that taste, which is now content with merely vulgar farce and gaudy commonplace, shall suddenly find itself disgusted with these trivial matters.

Exacerbating these contradictions, Winter was also concerned that the atmosphere of the theatre, onstage and off, "should be that of the drawing room where refinement prevails and where oaths and innuendoes and coarse jokes are never permitted." Winter never bothered to explain how the bourgeoisie might seek refuge in "white" art while those with vulgar tastes were being uplifted; nor why the populace might wish to pay money to be made uncomfortable by the drawing-room atmosphere of a respectable theatre. Indeed, Henry Clapp, Jr., one of his fellow critics, complained in 1866 that Winter's crusade for theatrical "High Art" forced him to look down his nose at more popular forms of entertainment. But Winter's chilly moralism was more in touch with the times than the fading "bohemianism," as historian Tice Miller terms it, of Clapp.[9]

Similarly, theatre architecture and interior décor moved toward an ambiguous embrace of high art, divided between a desire to imitate aristocratic tastes from the past and the need to meet expenses in the future. Imitations of classical Greek statuary and Italian Renaissance painting, plus allusions to past geniuses of the English stage (usually Shakespeare), crowded the décor of Laura Keene's, Wallack's, and Daly's theatres. The interior of the new Chestnut Street Theatre, which opened in Philadelphia in 1863, typified many bourgeois playhouses. According to historian Mari Fielder, the auditorium "was decorated in a florid mixture of Victorian and neoclassic design elements: gold-leafed moldings ornamented with leaves, brackets, and scrolls; a white, gold, and red color scheme; a proscenium arch busily decorated with wreaths and classical figures; and a central medallion head of Shakespeare done in relief." So shoddy was the décor, however, that when

Laura Keene took control of the theatre in 1869, she had to completely refurbish the playhouse to increase bourgeois attendance.[10]

Perhaps the most substantial theatrical edifice connecting the bourgeoisie to their construction of "the great tradition" was Edwin Booth's Theatre in New York, completed in 1869. Built of granite, the playhouse presented an elaborate French and Italian Renaissance façade with white marble statues of Shakespeare, Comedy, and Tragedy to passersby on Twenty-Third Street. Inside, the lobby floor was paved with Italian marble tiling, its ceiling adorned with Michelangelo-like frescoes. Ornamenting the proscenium were marble pillars and another statue of Shakespeare. According to the New York *World*, the opening night audience "swarmed into the blazing lobbies, breathing sighs of astonishment at the wealth of color and perfection of luxuriant decoration." To the mind of one critic, all the details of Booth's Theatre "combine into a perfect whole and constitute the fulfillment of an exalted ideal." "It has been built to endure," intoned William Winter. It didn't. Constructed as a sanctuary of high culture, Booth's playhouse proved too expensive to maintain during the depression years of the 1870s; he sold it to an attorney who eventually converted it into that symbol of low culture, a variety theatre. It was torn down in 1888.[11]

Critics from the mid 1850s into the 1870s looked to acting as well as architecture to elevate the theatre into the realm of the genteel ideal. Most critics followed Winter in believing that stars who uplifted their art also insured themselves of wide popularity, since they assumed that theatregoers of all classes would respond to idealized depictions of bourgeois morality. They praised Laura Keene, for example, who played before a variety of audiences as a touring star in the sixties after losing her New York theatre. Celebrated for her statuesque beauty, her sparkling repartee in comedy, and her passion and pathos in melodrama, Keene called forth special praise for her restraint and naturalness. According to the *Evening Journal* in 1862, Miss Keene "sends terror quivering to its inmost depths or steeps it in the sunlight of joy. You weep with her and laugh with her. This is the highest reach of art." Unlike earlier women stars like Charlotte Cushman, Keene did not thrill audiences with grotesquerie and sublimity; rather, affirmed her fondest critics, she aroused the bourgeois emotions of sensibility and sincerity. Little wonder, from their point of view, that Keene attained both gentility and popularity.[12]

Given the construction of womanliness in American Victorian society, theatre critics tended to praise women stars for embodying either the homebound virtues of simplicity and loyalty or the natural passions of the protector of her race. For many Victorian critics, Agnes Robertson, the wife of Dion Boucicault and the originator of many of his best ingénue roles, typified the ideal young wife. "It was this winsome womanliness, shining softly and subtly out through every environment of costume and character, which made an unconscious but imperative demand on all sympathies," recalled critic Benjamin Ellis Martin. For him, Agnes Robertson was "the ideal embodiment of innocence, artlessness, sweetness, simplicity." Rose Eytinge, the first to play Daly's Laura Courtland, on the other hand, evoked praise that idealized, even as it reveled in her sexual energy. Said a *New York Times* critic of her work in two different roles at Wallack's Theatre in 1868: "Her best characteristic is that she is intensely womanly, whether in her devotion, her sacrifice, or her hatred. To find anyone natural in these days—largely, humanely, sobbingly, even violently natural—is a rare thing." Probably many a bourgeois male's response to Rose Eytinge involved a similar tension between sexual excitement and idealization. In the respectable theatre of the late fifties and sixties, critics tended to locate women stars on a continuum from innocent sweetness to idealized passion. In the unrespectable theatre, the body-stockinged form and overt sexuality of Adah Isaacs Menken, first seen in Bowery theatres in 1859, extended the continuum considerably.[13]

American business-class culture enjoined its males to become men of principle, but admitted that the sincere effort to achieve honesty, sobriety, and compassion in the midst of social pressures and business reversals was good enough to preserve respectability. Joseph Jefferson's mixture of comedy and pathos in the title role of *Rip Van Winkle*, a play revised for the star by Dion Boucicault, induced the bourgeoisie to sympathize with this difficulty. As early as 1857, a critic for the New York *Herald* praised Jefferson for combining farce and gentility: "His performance was racy and laughable, without vulgarity, and he is a low comedian, to use a seeming paradox, who is not the least low. He established himself in the favor of the audience at once." Jefferson characterized Rip as a compassionate drunkard, sincerely attempting to put right a situation over which he has very little control. "There is a depth of pathos, tenderness, and beauty that charms like music and attunes the heart to the finest sense of pity," wrote a reviewer in the *Atlantic Monthly* on Jefferson's Rip in 1867. A critic for the *New York Times* in 1869 was even more emphatic: "[Jefferson's] Rip Van Winkle holds high rank among the purest, the truest, and the noblest illustrations of human nature and human sentiment that the present stage affords." Watching Jefferson play Rip in the 1860s induced American business-men to laugh at and cry away the tensions of maintaining the image of principled respectability while simultaneously encouraging them to re-produce the culture that caused these tensions.[14]

No other actor was as sanctified by the American bourgeoisie in the 1860s as Edwin Booth. That his brother shot Lincoln, forcing Edwin into a brief retirement, only increased his stature by seeming to lend his acting added tragic sensitivity. Even before 1865, American busi-ness-class critics were constructing Booth as the bourgeois answer to the plebeian but still mighty Forrest, who continued performing nearly up to his death in 1872. The reviewer for the *Herald* complained that a persistent "clique" of critics was already set "against Forrest" in 1860. One member of this clique, George William Curtis, the editor of *Harper's*, compared Forrest and Booth in terms of audience and acting style in his "Easy Chair" column in 1863. Forrest moved the crowded house of "coarse" and "unrefined" theatregoers, wrote the editor, with the "boundless exaggeration of all the traditional conventions of the stage." In Forrest's case, these included "the muscular school; the brawny art; the biceps aesthetics; the tragic calves; the bovine drama; rant, roar, and rigmarole." In contrast, noted Curtis, "a more cultured and intellectual audience," with "an air of refined attention rather than of eager interest," appreciated Booth, "pale, thin, intellectual, with long black hair and dark eyes," and his more spiritual, less athletic performance. In his eagerness to separate high art from low along the line of the class divide, Curtis probably exaggerated the differences between the tragedians and their spectators. Historical understanding of Booth's acting has been hampered because so much of his relation to his bourgeois critics and audiences hinged on their need to sacralize representatives of high culture.[15]

Booth's most acclaimed character was Hamlet, a role Forrest had rarely attempted and no longer played after the mid 1850s. At the Win-ter Garden Theatre in 1864, Booth performed the tragic Dane for one hundred straight performances, a box-office record. In a clear rebuff to

Edwin Booth as Hamlet, photograph, ca. 1870 (author's collection). The pho-
tographer emphasized Booth's large eyes, high forehead, and long curly hair
to suggest the character's (and actor's) intellectual and "feminine" qualities.

Forrest, the *Tribune* called it "the most picturesque and refined example of American tragic art." Winter at the *Albion* ignored the Jacksonian star and placed Booth in the wider pantheon of Anglo-American theatrical greats:

> Side by side with the figures of Garrick as Richard, Kemble as Coriolanus, Kean as Othello, the verdict of taste and culture in our time will place the Hamlet of Edwin Booth. . . . [To see Booth's *Hamlet*] with appreciation and sympathy is to comprehend the genius of Shakespeare and to witness its most spiritual ideal realized and produced in form, substance, color, and meaning.

Booth continued to refine his Hamlet during the sixties, making the character more soft-spoken, intellectual, and sensitive. By 1870, when he produced *Hamlet* at his own theatre, all one reviewer could do was thank the star for the "magnificent honor" of his performance, "not only to the American stage, but to the drama of the entire civilized world." Unlike Jefferson, who clearly broadened his popularity by "purifying" his art, Booth may have narrowed his appeal by working so exclusively within the business-class values of sensibility, spirituality, and idealization. He achieved only modest success, for example, at the Walnut Street Theatre in Philadelphia, a less exclusively bourgeois house than the Winter Garden, which he starred at and co-managed during the late 1860s.[16]

Given the desire of the business class to elevate Shakespeare to the pinnacle of high culture, it may seem surprising that the percentage of the Bard's dramas of all plays produced actually declined during the 1855–70 period. While precise figures are not available for the total number of performances of plays by specific authors in New York City during the period, the figures for all Philadelphia theatres, albeit between 1856 and 1878, are revealing: Shakespeare, 2,314; Boucicault, 1,587; Tom Taylor, 934; J. B Buckstone, 839; John Brougham, 829; and J. M. Morton, 652. In the decades before 1855, Shakespearean performances in all cities of the Northeast easily outnumbered those of any contemporary playwright by three to one. For roughly twenty years after 1855, however, Shakespeare's relative popularity was cut nearly in half, with Boucicault's success far outdistancing the popularity of any previous nineteenth-century playwright on the Anglo-American stage. Impressionistic evidence suggests that the kinds of Shakespearean plays done at first-rate playhouses changed after 1855 as well. Some of the more muscular tragedies, including *Macbeth, King Lear,* and *Coriolanus,* declined in popularity, while *Hamlet, Romeo and Juliet,* and *Othello* remained strong. Significantly, one critic praised Booth for the "feminine quality" of his genius, a remark which was intended and understood as a compliment. Also, managers and stars produced a higher proportion of comedies over tragedies than before.[17]

A variety of relatively new genres, including sensation melodramas by Boucicault and others, gradually took the place of Shakespeare in bourgeois playhouses after 1855. Domestic melodrama, which centers dramatic interest on the breakup and later reunion of a family, had appeared before midcentury, but rose to new heights of popularity. *East Lynne, Rosedale, The Ticket-of-Leave Man,* and *The Sea of Ice* were some of the more successful plays in this half-child of moral reform melodrama and kissing cousin to sensation melodrama. Domestic comedy, involving much the same dramatic conflict but inducing more laughter than bated-breath suspense, also flourished, largely taking the place of the classical comedies of Sheridan, Goldsmith, and others in the repertory. Two of the more popular were *Fanchon,* a star vehicle for Maggie Mitchell, and *Our American Cousin,* by Tom Taylor. One spin-off of domestic comedy, the "cup and saucer" plays of Tom Robertson, so called because of their careful attention to the details of domestic life, achieved immense success with bourgeois audiences in the late sixties. For most of the decade, Wallack's Theatre had exclusive rights to mount the first productions of the plays of Tom Taylor and Tom Robinson in the United States. These popular genres, like sensation melodrama, embraced the bourgeois values of domesticity, sensibility, and principled and virtuous behavior.

As the previous list of popular playwrights in Philadelphia suggests, the farces of Morton and Buckstone and the parodies of Brougham continued on the boards. Built upon the popularity of these genres, with the added attractions of spectacle and ballet, was a new genre, the musical extravaganza. Laura Keene billed one of the first of these American pieces, *The Seven Sisters,* as an "operatic, spectacular, diabolical, musical, terpsichordian, farcical burletta," a fair summation of the extravaganza's polyglot construction. *The Seven Sisters* ran for 253 performances during the 1860–61 season, beginning a trend that ran through the war years and culminated in the 475-performance run of *The Black Crook*, with its mix of mortal and immortal characters, lavish spectacle and transformations, and scantily clad troupe of ballerinas. The popularity of musical extravaganza spurred the success of related genres during the sixties, including Offenbach operettas, the burlesques of Lydia Thompson and her British Blondes, and the knockabout pantomimes of George L. Fox, who emerged from the Bowery onto Broadway with *Humpty Dumpty* in 1867 and played it for over a thousand performances. *The Spirit of the Times* huffed that *Humpty* was "a medley of concert saloon, minstrel hall, and country circus attraction." Nonetheless, many New York bourgeoisie clearly preferred Fox's "farrago of nonsense" to Shakespearean tragedy in the late sixties, perhaps an indication that the elevation of high culture in the market-sensitive theatre could not prevent the occasional return of the repressed at the box office. With extravaganza and related genres, the business class dumped spirituality and sensibility for the vulgar pleasures of lavish spectacle, masculine knockabout, and feminine flesh.[18]

Apart from the types of entertainment popular on business-class stages and their relation to the sacralization/popularization tension, a significant trend of the 1855–70 period was the rise of the long run. The continuous run of a single production had occurred before—*The Last Days of Pompeii, The Drunkard,* and *Uncle Tom's Cabin* had established earlier records of duration—but Laura Keene was the first to deploy the practice as managerial policy. She ran *Our American Cousin* for over a hundred performances in 1858–59 and *The Colleen Bawn* for nearly fifty nights after its premiere in 1860. By the mid sixties, most business-class theatres structured their seasons around a series of hoped-for long runs and only reverted to repertory scheduling when their new productions fell flat. Even Wallack's Theatre, one of the last companies to continue the repertory system, gradually succumbed; instead of the usual two-week run for a new show, Wallack's played Robertson's *Ours* forty times in a row in 1867. And several stars backed into long runs on their tours when they discovered that the public preferred them in a single character instead of enjoying their range of roles. Maggie Mitchell, Joseph Jefferson, and Lucille Western attained such great popularity in *Fanchon, Rip Van Winkle,* and *East Lynne* that they often performed the starring roles in these vehicles to the near exclusion of other parts. Jefferson, for instance, probably the most versatile comedian in the country, played only Rip for an astounding twelve weeks at the Boston Theatre in 1868–69.

The long run signified an important shift in the social psychology of playgoing. Patrician and plebeian spectators had gone to the theatre as much for social interaction as to see a show; oftentimes, the play itself was secondary since the audience already knew it as an old favorite or could count on seeing it again soon. With the advent of the long run and its counterpart the hit show, the experience of playgoing became more of a fashionable commodity. Audiences had to purchase the product during its run or possibly go without; they could not be sure that the play would be available for their enjoyment at a later date. In effect, the shift from repertory to long run reduced the sociality of playgoing and further commodified audience enjoyment. Two examples from productions of Booth's *Hamlet* make the point. Anticipating competition rather than sociability among spectators, one publicist in 1870 warned, "Not to have seen *Hamlet* will be an unenviable distinction." Five years earlier, George William Curtis of *Harper's* commented that Booth's playing had "an exquisite tone, like an old picture." He then elaborated at some length on the similarity in the spectator's experience between the impressions and emotions evoked by Booth and by looking at the "finest portraits" of the Italian Renaissance. Such portraits and their cheaper imitations, of course, were prized commodities in bourgeois homes in the 1860s. Watching a play was becoming less like attending a political rally and more like purchasing the latest fashion in hat design.[19]

The commodification of playgoing in the 1855–70 period worked hand in glove with the privatization of the bourgeois theatrical experience, as the mandates of self-control and sincerity in public changed audience behavior after midcentury. In 1854 the *Spirit of the Times* approvingly quoted the *New Orleans Picayune*:

> The privileges alike of applauding and hissing must be exercised with a due regard for the proprieties of the occasion that excites either; it is the delicate point to be ascertained when the line of propriety has been overstepped.

Increasingly, applauding during a scene or hissing an actor overstepped the bourgeois line of propriety. Historian of audience behavior Ben Graf Henneke reports that the practice of giving an actor three cheers at his or her entrance, a common occurrence in Forrest's performances of the 1830s and early 1840s, fell out of fashion during the Civil War and was revived "only on very special occasions such as Edwin Booth's return to the stage in 1866." Likewise, hissing became so unusual that one reporter in the early sixties tried to revive its practice as an effective "brake to carelessness." By 1870, wrote the actor Olive Logan, "New York audiences [were] for the most part extremely sedate, decorous, and, save at the Bowery, seem[ed] devoid of the decidedly plebeian element." Having kicked most of the b'hoys upstairs or out of their theatres, the business class clamped down on its own theatregoing behavior.[20]

As audience members pulled back from overt expressions of enthusiasm and censure, the lights in the auditorium, previously ablaze during the performance, gradually dimmed. As early as 1856, one critic complained of Laura Keene's "great error" in keeping her auditorium lights brightly lit during performances. By the mid 1860s, the question of houselights during the show had become a matter of public discussion. A reporter at the Boston Theatre had this to say in 1868:

> Many persons argue that if the front of the theatre is very light, it tends to detract from the stage effect; that argument might prove good, if the full force of light was thrown upon the audience when the curtain was up. But it is only between the acts, and when the curtain is down, that it is necessary to have the auditorium light; then it is that the audience wish to amuse themselves by seeing each other.

For centuries, amusing themselves by seeing each other had been fun throughout the performance. Why was it no longer?[21]

Exactly how low the gasman dimmed the house cannot be known and probably varied from theatre to theatre, perhaps even from show to show. The houselights could not be turned off and then brought back up because relighting the lamps had to be done by hand. Certainly the house had to be nearly dark for the climax of *Under the Gaslight*, since Daly's locomotive effect depended on the engine's headlight partly blinding the audience so that they wouldn't see the two stagehands pushing the contraption across the stage. No doubt a dimmed house also allowed bourgeois males to enjoy the fleshly delights of musical extravaganza in the privacy of their own fantasies. But managers may also have lowered the houselights to save an increasingly anonymous audience from the awkwardness of social interaction. Spectators unsure of themselves and their social roles did not want strangers looking at them; they must have appreciated the respite of near darkness from society's gaze, the retreat into the privacy of the self provided by the dimming of the house. Booth's 1869 theatre, the first to install wiring which provided an electric spark to relight the gas, became the first to allow the audience complete privacy during the show.

The commodification and privatization of bourgeois theatregoing produced an increasingly pacified audience. Writing in the 1880s, Joseph Jefferson remembered when "hissing and jeering" greeted a mistake he had made on stage in the 1840s, early in his career. He contrasted those spectators to "the well-dressed, decorous audience of today [who], when an accident occurs, sit quietly, bearing it with patience and consideration." For the sake of this restrained audience, Jefferson urged that the contemporary performer be doubly conscientious:

> Should a picture in an art gallery be carelesssly painted, we can pass on to another, or if a book fails to please us, we can put it down. An escape from this kind of dullness is easily made, but in a theater the auditor is imprisoned. If the acting be indifferent, he must endure it, at least for a time. He cannot withdraw, making himself conspicuous; so he remains, hoping that there may be some improvement as the play proceeds, or perhaps from consideration for the company he is in. It is this helpless condition that renders careless acting so offensive.

Ideally, Jefferson suggests, watching a play should be a private, commodified experience, akin to looking at a picture or reading a book. But playgoing could also "imprison" a spectator and put him in a "helpless condition," a situation that would have been unthinkable forty years before. Clearly, the private manners of the genteel parlor, which began to be enforced in museum theatres in the late forties, overtook the public behavior of traditional theatregoing by 1870.[22]

Although theatre capitalists had little more control than their audiences over the commodification and privatization of their products, they profited from these trends. Not only were pacified audiences more malleable, they were also more predictable—a bonus for the stars, who specialized their repertories and standardized their touring circuits during the 1860s. Playwrights also profited from the rise of the long run and the increasing predictability of audiences by cranking out formulaic pieces. Most, however, attained only modest success unless they, like Boucicault, also turned to management. For the entrepreneur-managers, the long run increased competition for new pieces and, coupled with the price of mounting spectacles, managerial risks. Several extravaganzas cost more than ten thousand dollars to produce, leaving capitalists a longer wait before they could recoup their investment and turn a profit. The *New York Times,* for instance, estimated that *The Black Crook* cost its producers "a total outlay of $25,400" before opening. On the other hand, the long run was a potential gold mine for theatre capitalists. *Humpty Dumpty* netted over thirty thousand dollars a month in 1867–68, and Daly made enough from *Under the Gaslight* to put together his first permanent company and open a first-class theatre.[23]

Most actors, however, fared worse than before during the consolidation of business-class theatrical production under stars and managers in the 1855–70 period. With the rise of the long run, the size of several repertory companies decreased during the 1860s, leaving actors with fewer positions at the better-paying theatres. The Arch Street Theatre company, for example, shrank from thirty-three to twenty-six actors in the last five years of the decade. Managers relying on touring stars and occasional opera troupes could get along with even smaller troupes; the Boston Theatre company employed thirty-four actors for the 1856–57 season, but only nineteen in 1867–68. The advent of the long run also led to managers' hiring "job actors" when the casting demands of a show exceeded the size of their company. Unlike the repertory performer hired for a full season, the job actor's employment was subject to the run of the play. Comic actor Willaim Davidge complained of "the measure of misery [the job actor] system is fraught with" in 1866. As if in ironic acknowledgment of the job actor's situation, the park in Union Square where New York managers hired job actors and other unemployed performers became known by the late sixties as "the slave market."[24]

These and other problems for stock actors came to a head in the summer of 1864 when several New York performers established the Actors' Protective Union to protest managerial exploitation, the first major labor dispute in the American theatre. Low salaries and managerial contract breaking were the immediate causes of the dispute. Many New York managers, anticipating smaller houses after the outbreak of the Civil War, had lowered the salaries of their stock actors for the 1861–62 season. Although attendance did dip initially, most theatres were doing excellent business by the 1863–64 season, but managers were reluctant to restore the old salaries because wartime inflation had increased their production and rental costs. Of course the stock actors were suffering from inflated costs too, but lacked the leverage to regain their previous salaries, much less a cost-of-living increase. Meager salaries were especially hard on the women actors. The theatrical reporter for the *Tribune* noted "the almost incredible fact" that "the conditions under which women are engaged at New York theatres reduces their payment to about one half of that received by men holding equal professional rank." Not only were their salaries lower by roughly a third, but the women, unlike the men, had to provide their own costumes and "the dresses of even well paid actresses consume above one fourth of their regular salary."[25]

New York actors were also incensed in July of 1864 because several managers, their long runs having closed in the spring, called an early end to their season and released their stock actors without pay well before the usual summer interim. The *Tribune* reported, however, that one woman actor, "dismissed from one of our Broadway theatres on the fictitious declaration of a close of 'season,'" sued her former manager "to recover the balance of her salary for forty weeks, and, we rejoice to add, gained it without difficulty." Despite their legal victory, many of the dismissed actors resented their treatment and sought to check their declining ability to gain equitable contracts and just wages. No doubt they were also emboldened by the recent success of theatrical musicians to force a pay increase from the managers.[26]

The Theatrical Protective Association, as the actors initially named their group, met twice in July to vote on resolutions and discuss future plans. William Davidge, who had worked in the stock companies of the Broadway, Winter Garden, and Brooklyn Park theatres, presided. After noting the decline of their salaries and the recent success of the musicians, those in attendance (purportedly representing all theatres in the city) unanimously adopted the following:

Resolved, It now becomes a duty to themselves and their fellow artists elsewhere for the actors and actresses of the municipal cities
[of New York] to appeal to the liberality and sense of justice of their
managers for a prompt and adequate increase in salaries, placed on
a specie basis.

Resolved, That we establish, for the future welfare of the profession, a Protective Association or Union, having for its principal object the following:

> *First*—A fixed minimum salary for each distinct line of business,
> from leading to utility, to be determined by artists from each de-
> partment and of acknowledged ability therein.
>
> *Second*—A return to the old system of engaging members of the
> profession for definite lines of characters, thus obviating all pro-
> fessional misunderstandings and preventing any artist from un-
> dertaking any more than his or her legitimate business, and by
> such means keeping another professional out of an engagement.
>
> *Third*—A regular and careful systemization of all business mat-
> ters between managers and artists.

Davidge appointed one committee to draft rules for the new organization and a second to seek alliances with other trade unions in New
York. He adjourned the meeting following the resounding approval of
a motion to "invite all artists throughout the country to cooperate in
the movement."[27]

The actors' concern to reestablish the contractual legitimacy of old
lines of business, which traditionally specified the kind of roles an actor
must play (and others he or she could refuse), centered on preserving
job security and professional rights. By shrinking the size of their stock
companies and employing job actors, managers were proletarianizing
their performers, forcing them to become utility players who could be
cast in any role. In the public discussion that followed the publication
of the Protective Association's resolutions, one letter writer, probably
a manager, complained that a return to traditional lines of business
would "inflict a large surplus company on the manager." "In the present state of drama," he added, "an actor's versatility determines his
value." The actors understood this, but wanted to reverse the trend;
they believed their value should reflect their professional line within a

traditional company hierarchy, not their general utility. If returning to old lines of business meant more positions (and an end to employing job actors), so much the better.[28]

Reestablishing these traditional arrangements on a sound contractual basis was also connected to the actors' desire to systematize actor-manager relations. In a letter to the *New York Times*, one performer, perhaps Davidge himself, explained how managers had used the ambiguity of the present understanding of lines of business to fire unwanted actors:

> The plan of operation is simple enough. A manager desires to get rid of an artist; he instructs the stage manager to proffer to said artist a part which he or she cannot by any possibility perform. It must be remembered that what is technically termed "business" is more understood than defined. The artist declines the part, which he knows will compromise him with the public. For this he is at once dismissed. The manager then sneaks down to this meeting and denounces the artist for breach of contract.

By legalizing the status of traditional lines of business, the association hoped to return actor-manager relations to the days of William B. Wood, before managerial capitalism had destroyed the paternalistic basis of company hierarchy and cohesion. Like many early workers' unions in industrializing America, the Protective Association fought the leveling effects of capitalism. As shoemakers had opposed the elimination of their craft hierarchy by capitalists bent on industrialization, so stock actors sought to preserve their traditional crafts and republican rights.[29]

At their fourth meeting on August 18, the performers changed the name of their organization to the Actors' Protective Union. Despite this seeming step toward solidarity, the union members also claimed a "conscientious regard for the interests of the managers as well as the actors and actresses." Boasting that over a hundred actors had joined the union, Davidge delivered a pep talk about the need to persevere in pressuring the managers. But it must have been apparent to most of those attending that the union had failed to win its goals. The other trade unions in the city could give them little help, the managers had not met with them, and most actors had already signed contracts for the upcoming season. Apparently some managers were paying slightly better salaries—they had conducted a newspaper campaign during the summer to prepare the public for higher ticket prices to accommodate these increased costs—but the managers continued to handle salary negotiations on an individual basis, not through the union. And the problems surrounding the loose definition of lines of business remained. Union members agreed to meet again in September, but their meeting was apparently of such little importance, if it occurred at all, that the newspapers did not cover it. The available evidence suggests that managerial manipulation, competition among actors for work, and the lingering effects of traditional inequalities among actors—ironically a hierarchy the union was attempting to reestablish—killed the Actors' Protective Union. Theatre capitalists had beaten back the first attempt at unionization, further enhancing their economic power.[30]

The emergence of the first theatre district in the Union Square area in New York City also facilitated the consolidation of theatrical capitalism. By the early 1870s, the Rialto, as it was called by its theatrical inhabitants, boasted several of the most prominent bourgeois theatres in the city—the Academy of Music opera house, Wallack's Theatre, the Union Square Theatre, and Daly's Fourteenth Street Theatre. Intersected by Broadway, Union Square was part of the "Ladies' Mile" of fashionable shops and restaurants along the city's main artery of business-class retail commerce. Among the attractions of the district were several of New York's best hotels, providing lodging for visiting musical and theatrical stars as well as other business-class travelers. The Rialto also housed several concert-lecture halls, including Irving Hall, constructed in 1860 for balls, concerts, lectures, and diorama productions, and the more exclusive Steinway Hall, built in 1866 by Steinway and Sons to sanctify high culture and sell pianos. At the other end of the sacralization/popularization continuum in Union Square in the late 1860s were Tammany Hall and the Hippotheatron, which housed minstrel troupes, equestrian shows, and circus productions. By 1870, a respectable bourgeois couple could enjoy an afternoon and evening of shopping, minstrelsy, dining, and theatregoing, all within easy walking distance, and catch a trolley and ferry back to Brooklyn before midnight.[31]

Theatre capitalists built the Rialto for business as well as pleasure. In the midst of establishments dedicated to bourgeois enjoyment were the offices and shops of theatrical booking agents, printers, newspapers, photographers, and manufacturers of scenery, costumes, and properties. The popularity of extravaganza and related genres in the 1860s led to increased specialization in scenery and costume building, as theatre capitalists, unable to build these shows in their own shops, contracted with separate companies to furnish their spectacles. The Eaves Costume Company, which opened in the Union Square area in 1867, made costumes for Booth's *Hamlet* soon after starting business, for instance. The long run also led to the rise of ticket brokers in the Rialto and their logical extension in a commodified theatre, the scalper. Davidge knew one scalper who "cleared nearly four hundred dollars by premiums on boxes and seats" in one night.[32]

Several of the theatrical businesses on the Rialto were regional and national in scope. Managers in the Northeast increasingly contracted with Union Square agents to fill their acting troupes, rather than hiring performers directly on the "slave market." Other agents like T. Allston Brown plotted national itineraries and booked theatres for the stars they represented. Photographers like Napoleon Sarony, who began taking theatrical pictures in 1866, also profited from the solidity of the star network. As pictures of stars and their hit shows became popular collectors' items for scrapbooks in bourgeois parlors, Sarony and other photographers peddled their products in a national market. By turning plays into the private property of the writer, the 1856 copyright law spurred the profitability of playscript publishing as well as dramatic authorship. South of Union Square, Samuel French, who had begun printing plays in 1846, established a near monopoly on the publishing rights to British and American scripts in the United States. By 1870, French was selling hit shows, minstrel skits, and parlor comedies to the nation. One historian estimates that roughly two hundred thousand people were involved in theatre and related businesses in the United States in 1870. While New York City probably contained less than a quarter of these people, many of them across the country were already looking to the theatrical capitalists of the Rialto for information, direction, and manufactured goods.

Increasingly specialized, centralized, and consolidated, bourgeois theatre boomed during the 1860s. In contrast, theatre catering to the tastes of working-class audiences declined in the urban centers of the Northeast after 1850 and into the 1860s. In Philadelphia, the closing of the gallery saloon at the Arch Street Theatre in 1844 and the introduction of parquette seating at the Walnut Street Theatre in 1852 signaled the gradual transformation of those playhouses into bastions of business-class respectability. Pelby's National Theatre in Boston struggled on after the manager's death in 1850, but failed in 1855. Workers in these cities—as in Providence, Baltimore, Albany, and elsewhere in the Northeast—turned to minstrel halls, equestrian and circus tents, museum theatres, and variety shows in saloons for their entertainment. They also filled the family circle balconies of many of the bourgeois playhouses. With the exception of saloon variety, however, these entertainment venues served mixed-class needs; outside of New York City, theatrical companies no longer addressed the class-specific concerns and desires of workers.

New York was the exception not only because of its enormous laboring population, but because working-class culture in Gotham remained more geographically concentrated than in other cities. Other forms of entertainment also drew off New York workers, but did not completely shut down Bowery theatres. Nonetheless, several companies catering primarily to working-class tastes had already closed by 1852, including Mitchell's Olympic and Brougham's Lyceum theatres. Despite the enormous profits he garnered from the Aiken adaptation of *Uncle Tom's Cabin* and the pantomimes of George L. Fox, A. H. Purdy and his company could not last out the decade at the National Theatre. Even the profitability of the Bowery Theatre, the recognized leader of working-class entertainment in New York, fell off after 1850. Following Hamblin's death in 1853, a variety of managers ran the company, including G. L. Fox in 1858–59 and from 1862 to 1867. For roughly two years between his actor-manager turns at the Bowery, Fox co-managed the New Bowery Theatre, built just two blocks from its namesake and opened in September 1859. Unlike business-class playhouses in the 1855–70 period, the New Bowery, like the old, featured a pit with backless benches which, said one reviewer, were "jammed with the democracy, unwashed and unterrified, to the number of a couple of thousand" on opening night. But two large playhouses in the Bowery were no longer economically feasible. In 1861, Fox and his co-manager at the New Bowery replaced the pit with a parquette of cushioned seats to attract uptown theatregoers. "The demands of upper twenty-five-cent-dom could no longer be resisted," explained one critic; the b'hoys were once more moved to the upper balcony. After Fox skipped back to the old Bowery, taking most of his troupe with him, the new house languished and finally burned in 1866. It was not rebuilt.[33]

Bowery companies in the 1855–70 period borrowed from several traditions as well as creating new plays and spectacles to fill their repertories. Although occasionally reliant on long runs or traveling stars, most Bowery managers maintained a repertory system, sometimes grinding three shows a night out of their overworked companies. These included spin-offs of moral reform plays, such as *Orion, the Gold Beater* and *The Gun-Maker of Moscow*, and the genteel melodramas of Boucicault. Under Fox's management in the mid sixties, the old Bowery continued to produce some of the more popular apocalyptic melodramas from the 1830s, including *The Last Days of Pompeii* and *The Carpenter of Rouen*. "Pepper's Ghost" illusion spooked New York audiences during the same years, especially on the Bowery, leading to a spate of ghost plays at the old and New Bowery. Far and away the most popular of the Bowery shows in the 1860s were Fox's pantomimes. As theatre historian Laurence Senelick notes, Fox perfected a form of panto that altered the traditional English harlequinade to emphasize knockabout high jinks and topical parody in a setting that was recognizably urban American. His *Little Boy Blue*, for instance, used the rough-and-tumble of flying brickbats and billy clubs to topple such bourgeois symbols as police officers and mothers with babies. With *Humpty Dumpty* in 1867, however, Fox moved out of the Bowery to the uptown Olympic Theatre and largely abandoned his assault on business-class propriety to perform for respectable theatregoers.

Fox's flight from the Bowery underlined the waning of an alternative theatrical tradition that had thrived earlier among working-class audiences. Apocalyptic melodramas had legitimated a kind of honorable deviancy in the Bowery and similar neighborhoods in Boston and Philadelphia. But the values of abstinence, individualism, and competition cut into the rough camaraderie of old. Such qualities, of course, were the prime ingredients of *The Poor of New York, The Colleen Bawn*, and *Under the Gaslight*, shows popular in the Bowery as well as uptown. Workers probably identified more closely with the actions of characters near the class divide in these melodramas than with their men-of-principle heroes; the plight of an Irish lass afflicted with a brogue and the success of a marginal detective figure may have appealed to audience members conflicted about their own respectability. Nonetheless, for these shows to gain popularity in the Bowery, working-class audiences must have hoped that their business-class characters would find happiness and security by play's end. Similarly, *Orion, the Gold Beater, The Gun-Maker of Moscow,* and other near relations of moral reform melodrama popular in the Bowery after 1855 generally ignored problems of class to focus on working-class heroes who save the deserving poor from petty villains. These popular plays and the theatrical life of which they were a part were no longer alternatives to the dominant culture. Outside of occasional revivals, the early pantos of Fox, and some variety and minstrel skits, bourgeois culture both pervaded and contained working-class theatre in New York during the 1855–70 period.[34]

The panic of 1873 and the five years of depression which followed further consolidated the hegemony of business-class theatrical culture by ending the era of stock company production in the United States. Since the founding of the American Company in 1752, local stock companies run by a manager with a fixed number of actors for a season of plays had provided the backbone of American theatrical entertainment. Traveling stars and manager-entrepreneurs had pushed stock actors into more proletarian relationships, but the stock company itself continued as the base of productive operations. In 1870, playwrights were still writing shows to fit within stock company limitations, actors continued to shape their careers in terms of traditional lines of business, and managers planned seasons, not single shows, to make the most profitable use of their troupes. All of this changed rapidly after 1873. In the the first three years of the depression, the number of stock companies in the major cities of the country dropped from over fifty to fewer than twenty. By 1880, only seven remained.[35]

To take their place, theatre capitalists formed combination companies, a star in combination with a troupe of actors usually engaged for only the run or tour of a single show. Combinations had occurred before. James W. Wallack and Laura Keene had hired separate groups of actors to perform with them on the road in 1862 and 1863, respectively. But these and most other early ventures in combination touring resulted from special circumstances; it made little economic sense for a star to take along a full troupe when there were stock companies to provide support in all of the major cities. The collapse of several stock companies outside of New York soon after the panic, however, created a snowballing effect which changed the economic realities of touring for the stars. As more stars hired their own troupes, local managers with less use for their stock companies laid them off, creating an even greater need for more combinations. From a half-dozen or so combination companies in 1873, the number skyrocketed to over a hundred by the end of the decade. Some stars initially attempted to produce several different shows with their touring companies, but most settled into single productions of their best hit. By 1886, with the long run firmly linked to combination touring, there were 282 companies on the road.[36]

The chief beneficiaries of this shift in the mode of theatrical production were the theatre capitalists on the Rialto and their class, the national industrial bourgeoisie. After 1873, decisions made in New York increasingly affected theatre workers and audiences across the country. Playwrights also profited from this centralization of theatrical power, since it gained them greater access to a national audience. Under combination production, stars had either to become full-fledged capitalists by hiring their own companies and charting their own tours or to give up economic control of their careers. Local managers could move to New York to launch combination companies with minor stars or stay put and work for the owners of the local theatre to provide booking for road shows. Former stock actors lost the remnants of their rights in traditional companies and had to pay agents to find them temporary work on a per-show basis; in effect, most performers were reduced to the status of job actors.

The panic of 1873 was a significant turning point in the transformation of the American theatre under capitalism. The relative independence of local stock companies had facilitated the emergence of an alternative theatrical culture on the Bowery and elsewhere from the mid 1830s through the early 1850s. The expansion of combination production after 1873, however, further marginalized local pockets of theatrical resistance to the dominant culture. James A. Herne's difficulties in producing his *Margaret Fleming* and the outraged responses to most American productions of Ibsen suggest the pervasiveness of business-class ideology in the theatre by the 1890s. Stock production of a revolving repertory revived in the 1890s and again in the 1920s, but it would never again provide the primary mode for the production and delivery of theatrical entertainment to the American public. The combination shows touring out of New York after 1873 primarily consolidated the hegemony of the American bourgeoisie.

Notes

The following notes emphasize the social-historical context of melodramatic theatre during the 1820–70 period. In addition to providing the necessary citations for all material quoted in the text, they attempt to relate the most important sources, in my estimation, for understanding the historical meanings generated within each melodramatic formation. I am indebted to many other scholarly works of theatre history, dramatic criticism, and social and cultural history which, for reasons of space and economy, I am unable to cite.

The notes also use the following abbreviations throughout: NYPL for the New York Public Library of Performing Arts at Lincoln Center; HTC for the Harvard Theatre Collection; BPL for the Boston Public Library; *TJ* for *Theatre Journal*; *QJS* for the *Quarterly Journal of Speech*; and *AHR* for the *American Historical Review*. Unless otherwise noted, all plays cited are available from Readex Microprint in one of two series: Three Centuries of Drama (to 1830) and English and American Drama of the Nineteenth Century (1830–1900).

Introduction

1. Joseph R. Roach, "Theatre History and the Ideology of the Aesthetic," *TJ*, 41 (May 1989), 155. Roach states in a footnote that Eagleton used the term "the ideology of the aesthetic" in a lecture delivered at Northwestern University, and later as the title for his book *The Ideology of the Aesthetic* (Cambridge, MA: Basil Blackwell, 1990). For an overview of theatre historians using aesthetic categories to organize their texts, see Thomas Postlewait, "The Criteria for Periodization in Theatre History," *TJ*, 40 (October 1988), 299–318.

2. Jameson borrows the term "symbolic act" from Kenneth Burke to "dramatize the ambiguous status of art and culture" in *The Political Unconscious: Narrative as a Socially Symbolic Act* (Ithaca: Cornell Univ. Press, 1981), p. 81. On Burke's use of the term, see his *The Philosophy of Literary Form* (Berkeley and Los Angeles: Univ. of California Press, 1973), pp. 5–6. For Jameson's largely positive assessment of Burke, see "Symbolic Inference; or, Kenneth Burke and Ideological Analysis," *Critical Inquiry*, 4 (Spring 1978), 507–23. This point of view is also implicit in Raymond Williams'

insistence that a work of art be seen as a "practice," not as an object. See his "Base and Superstructure in Marxist Cultural Theory," in *Problems in Materialism and Culture* (London: NLB, 1980), p. 47.

3. On the theoretical and practical difficulties of a positivist approach to theatre history, see my "Towards a Postpositivist Theatre History," *TJ*, 37 (December 1985), 465–86.

4. Fredric Jameson, "Ideology, Narrative Analysis, and Popular Culture," *Theory and Society*, 4 (Winter 1977), 553.

5. "Texts in History: The Determinations of Readings and Their Texts," in *Post-Structuralism and the Question of History*, ed. Derek Attridge, Geoff Bennington, and Robert Young (Cambridge: Cambridge Univ. Press, 1987), p. 72. Bennett, however, would have historians look at relations among texts; even, in his attempt to synthesize aspects of deconstruction with Marxism, to consider social realities and events as kinds of texts. On this important matter of epistemology, I draw back from a "strong" notion of the linguistic construction of reality to side with the Realism of Frederic Jameson, Raymond Williams, and others. Modes of economic production, political events, and theatrical performances are not discursive constructions, even though they are often inaccessible to us except in textual form.

6. On cultural hegemony, see Antonio Gramsci, *Selections from the Prison Notebooks of Antonio Gramsci*, ed. Quinton Hoare and Geoffrey Nowell-Smith (New York: International Publishers, 1971); Williams, "Base and Superstructure in Marxist Cultural Theory"; T. J. Jackson Lears, "The Concept of Cultural Hegemony: Problems and Possibilities," *AHR*, 90 (June 1985), 567–93; and my "Using the Concept of Cultural Hegemony to Write Theatre History," in *Interpreting the Theatrical Past: Essays in the Historiography of Performance*, ed. Thomas Postlewait and Bruce A. McConachie (Iowa City: Univ. of Iowa Press, 1989), pp. 37–58.

7. See Raymond Williams, *Marxism and Literature* (Oxford: Oxford Univ. Press, 1977), pp. 121–27, for a discussion of these terms; specific quotations on pp. 122, 123.

8. On the popularity of different types of plays for the first half of the century, see David Grimsted's tabulations in the appendices of *Melodrama Unveiled: American Theater and Culture, 1800–1850* (Chicago: Univ. of Chicago Press, 1968), pp. 249–61. No one has taken on the much larger task of assessing the popularity of specific types and nationalities of plays for the second half of the century.

Part I. The Waning of Paternalistic Theatre for the Elite, 1820–1835

1. Richard Sennett, *Authority* (New York: Random House, 1980), pp. 71, 84. On paternalism in general, see Eugene D. Genovese, *Roll, Jordan, Roll: The World the Slaves Made* (New York: Vintage, 1974), pp. 3–6, passim. Regarding early American paternalism, see Robert H. Wiebe, *The Opening of American Society: From the Adoption of the Constitution to the Eve of Disunion* (New York: Knopf, 1984), pp. 1–125.
2. Philip Hone, quoted in the *New-York Mirror* (January 24, 1826), p. 32.

1. "A Spirit of Locomotiveness"

1. Quoted in David Grimsted, *Melodrama Unveiled: American Theater and Culture, 1800–1850* (Chicago: Univ. of Chicago Press, 1968), pp. 27, 26.
2. George Combe, *Notes on the United States of America* (Edinburgh: MacLachlan, Stewart and Co., 1841), 1: 28–29; and Louis Fitzgerald Tasistro, *Random Shots and Southern Breezes* (New York: Harper and Brothers, 1842), 1: 65–66. For further evidence of elite theatregoing, see Ben Graf Henneke, "The Playgoer in America (1752–1952)," Ph.D. diss., Univ. of Illinois, 1956, pp. 97–104.
3. See *Documents of American Theatre History: Famous American Playhouses, 1716–1899*, ed. William D. Young (Chicago: American Library Association, 1973), 1: 65; and Robert Montilla, "The Building of the Lafayette Theatre," *Theatre Survey*, 15 (November 1974), 105–29. William B. Wood's discussion of the founding of the Arch Street Theatre on pp. 345–51 of his *Personal Recollections of the Stage, Embracing Notions of Actors, Authors, and Auditors, during a Period of Forty Years* (Philadelphia: H. C. Baird, 1855) is probably the most complete account. The quote by Clapp is on p. 249 of his *A Record of the Boston Stage* (Boston: James Monroe, 1853).
4. James S. Buckingham, *America*, 3 vols. (London: Fisher, Son and Co., 1841), 3: 485; *New-York Mirror* (March 31, 1832), p. 310.
5. William Dunlap, *History of the American Theatre*, 2 vols. (London: J. J. Harper, 1832), 1: 358; *American Athenaeum*, 1 (November 17, 1825), 307; Henry Bradshaw Faron, *Sketches of America* (London: Longman, Hurst, Rees, Orme, and Brown, 1818), pp. 86–87.

6. Frances Trollope, *Domestic Manners of the Americans*, ed. Donald Smalley (New York: Vintage Books, 1949), p. 74; Tyrone Power, *Impressions of America during the Years 1833, 1834, and 1835* (1836; rpt., New York: Benjamin Blom, 1971); Francis Anne [Kemble] Butler, *Journal* (London: John Murray, 1835), 1: 2–3; Philip Hone, *The Diary of Philip Hone, 1828–1851*, ed. Bayard Tuckerman, 2 vols. (New York: Dodd, Mead, 1889), 1: 39; Wood, p. 321.

7. Wood, p. 299; Joseph N. Ireland, *Records of the New York Stage* (1866; rpt., New York: Benjamin Blom, 1965), 1: 522.

8. Both citations from *Documents of American Theatre History*, pp. 66, 73.

9. *New-York Mirror* (August 23, 1828), p. 49.

10. Quoted from *Documents of American Theatre History*, p. 74.

11. Wood, p. 291.

12. Clapp, pp. 269–70.

13. Quoted in Theodore Shank, "Theatre for the Majority: Its Influence on a Nineteenth-Century American Theatre," *Educational Theatre Journal*, 11 (October 1959), 189.

14. "Cracked and dingy" quotation and mention of the Lafayette chandelier in Montilla, pp. 121, 122.

15. *New-York Mirror* (August 23, 1828), pp. 49, 50.

16. *Columbian Sentinel* (January 13, 1821), [n.p.]; *New-York Mirror* (January 24, 1826), p. 32.

17. Quoted by Grimsted, p. 59.

18. Egging quotation cited by Lawrence W. Levine, *Highbrow/Lowbrow: The Emergence of Cultural Hierarchy in America* (Cambridge, MA: Harvard Univ. Press, 1988), p. 28. *American Monthly Magazine and Critical Review* (November 1817), p. 62; quoted by Grimsted, p. 63; *American Monthly Magazine and Critical Review*, pp. 62–63.

19. See Peter G. Buckley, "To the Opera House: Culture and Society in New York City, 1820–1860" (Ph.D. diss., SUNY, Stony Brook, 1984), pp. 120–25, for his discussion of the implications of this definition of "public," which he takes from definition 10 in the *Oxford English Dictionary*.

20. Wood, pp. 198, 316–17.

21. Chestnut company intermarriages are fully discussed in "The Warren Family," an anonymous pamphlet in the Harvard Theatre Collection.

22. Wood, pp. 296–97, 138, 402. William Warren, in his Journal entry for April 23, 1822 (MS, Howard University), noted the repeat performance. The artisan-patrician relation continued as the model for actor-audience

relationships at the Chestnut even after Wood left the theatre. In 1827, Richard Peters, a stockholder in the Chestnut company, instructed Francis Wemyss, Wood's replacement, to remember in hiring new actors "that with the audience who are to be amused at the Chesnut [sic] St. Theatre, polished manners, good exterior, and a guarded sense of decorum are all important. . . . An actor who does not appear as a gentleman will never succeed here" (Wemyss, *Theatrical Biography; or, The Life of an Actor-Manager* [Glasgow: R. Griffin, 1848], p. 109).

23. *Boston Gazette* quoted in *Recorder* (June 2, 1821), p. 91; Kean quoted in Buckley, p. 178.
24. *Boston News Letter and City Record* (December 21, 1825), pp. 16–17. See also Clapp, pp. 183–93.
25. On conventional rioting behavior, see David Grimsted, "Rioting in Its Jacksonian Setting," in *The Underside of American History: Other Readings,* ed. Thomas Frazier, 3rd ed. (1972; rpt., New York: Harcourt, Brace, 1978); Theodore Hammett, "Two Mobs of Jacksonian Boston: Ideology and Interest," *Journal of American History,* 62 (1976), 845–68; and George Rudé, *The Crowd in History: A Study of Popular Disturbances in France and England, 1730–1848* (New York: John Wiley and Sons, 1964). Most of the theatre riots in New York in the 1820s occurred at the Amphitheatre, a minor playhouse built like a circus, which drew mostly working-class crowds and never enjoyed widespread elite patronage. See Paul Gilje, *The Road to Mobocracy: Popular Disorder in New York City, 1763–1834* (Chapel Hill: Univ. of North Carolina Press, 1987), p. 249.
26. Quoted by George C. D. Odell, *Annals of the New York Stage,* 15 vols. (New York: Columbia Univ. Press, 1927–49), 2: 257.
27. On the Wood-Warren management of the Chestnut, see Charles Durang, *History of the Philadelphia Stage between the Years 1749–1855,* ed. Westcott Thompson, 7 vols. (1868; rpt., Ann Arbor, MI: University Microfilms, [n.d.]); Reese D. James, *The Old Drury of Philadelphia* (Philadelphia: Univ. of Pennsylvania Press, 1932); Calvin Pritner, "A Theatre and Its Audience," *Pennsylvania Magazine of History and Biography,* 91 (January 1967), 72–79; Pritner, "William Warren's Financial Arrangements with Traveling Stars—1805–1829," *Theatre Survey,* 6 (November 1965), 83–90; William Warren, Journal; Wemyss; and Wood's *Personal Recollections.* See also my "William B. Wood and the 'Pathos of Paternalism,' " *Theatre Survey,* 23 (May 1987), 1–14, from which much of my discussion is taken.
28. Wood, p. 332; Warren quoted in James, p. 49.

29. Wood, p. 349.

30. Wemyss, p. 139; Warren (December 6, 1828); and Wood, p. 353. Also see James, pp. 55–59, for more details of managerial problems during the two depressed seasons.

31. Warren (April 25, 1828). See James, pp. 57–63, and Pritner's article on Warren and the stars for more details of the 1827–31 period.

32. Wood, pp. 343, 393, 391.

33. Ibid., p. 267.

34. Ibid., pp. 451, 436, 446, 438.

2. "Wert Thou Not Born in Fairy-land?"

1. Gordon S. Wood, "Ideology and the Origins of Liberal America," *William and Mary Quarterly*, 44 (January 1987), 635; Robert H. Wiebe, *The Opening of American Society: From the Adoption of the Constitution to the Eve of Disunion* (New York: Knopf, 1984), pp. 143–67. On the rise of economic liberalism in the early nineteenth century, see Steven Watts, *The Republic Reborn: War and the Making of Liberal America, 1790–1820* (Baltimore: Johns Hopkins Univ. Press, 1987).

2. Quoted by Fred Somkin in *The Unquiet Eagle: Memory and Desire in the Idea of American Freedom, 1815–1860* (Ithaca, NY: Cornell Univ. Press, 1967), p. 14. See W. Elliott Brownlee, *Dynamics of Ascent: A History of the American Economy* (New York: Knopf, 1974), pp. 85–132, for a recent history of the take-off period of American economic growth. Douglas T. Miller, in his *The Birth of Modern America, 1820–1850* (New York: Pegasus Paperbacks, 1970), p. 14, notes the types of jobs Americans had in 1815 and 1840.

3. See Wiebe, pp. 146–56.

4. Somkin, p. 16; Dwight quoted by Somkin, p. 39.

5. New York visitor and Stafford quoted in Paul Boyer's *Urban Masses and Moral Order in America, 1820–1920* (Cambridge, MA: Harvard Univ. Press, 1978), pp. 5, 9.

6. Haddock, Clay, and Hone in Somkin, pp. 102, 99, 128.

7. The theoretical basis for these statements is a synthesis of the rhetoric of Kenneth Burke and object-relations psychology within the psychoanalytic sociology of Gerald Platt and Fred Weinstein. See Burke, *A Rhetoric of Motives* (1950; rpt., Berkeley and Los Angeles: Univ. of California Press,

1969); Harry S. Guntrip, *Psychoanalytic Theory, Therapy, and the Self* (New York: Basic Books, 1971); Gerald Platt and Fred Weinstein, *Psychoanalytic Sociology: An Essay on the Interpretation of Historical Data and the Phenomena of Collective Behavior* (Baltimore and London: Johns Hopkins Univ. Press, 1973). Michael Ryan uses these ideas for film analysis in "The Politics of Film: Discourse, Psychoanalysis, Ideology," in *Marxism and the Interpretation of Culture*, ed. Cary Nelson and Lawrence Grossberg (Urbana and Chicago: Univ. of Illinois Press, 1988), pp. 477–86.

8. Cooper quoted in David Grimsted, *Melodrama Unveiled: American Theater and Culture, 1800–1850* (Chicago: Univ. of Chicago Press, 1968), p. 112; William B. Wood, *Personal Recollections of the Stage, Embracing Notions of Actors, Authors, and Auditors, during a Period of Forty Years* (Philadelphia: H. C. Baird, 1855), p. 433.

9. These plays are available in the Readex series, Three Centuries of Drama, ed. Henry W. Wells (New York: Readex Microprint, 1960). I have also consulted a promptbook for *Clari* MS, NYPL [184?]. All quotations from the three plays are noted in the text. Other American fairy-tale melodramas include *The Mountain Torrent* and *The Rose of Arragon* [*sic*], by Samuel B. H. Judah; *Accusation, or The Family of D'Anglade, Adeline, the Victim of Seduction, Ali Pacha, or The Signet Ring*, by John Howard Payne; and *The Forest of Rosenwald*, by John Stokes.

10. Quoted in George C. D. Odell, *Annals of the New York Stage*, 15 vols. (New York: Columbia Univ. Press, 1927–1949), 3: 146–47.

11. Payne's preface quoted in Gabriel Harrison, *John Howard Payne* (1855; rpt., New York: Benjamin Blom, 1969), p. 101.

12. Jack Zipes, *Breaking the Magic Spell: Radical Theories of Folk and Fairy Tales* (Austin: Univ. of Texas Press, 1979), pp. 3, 20–40.

13. Ibid.

14. Louis Bergeron, *France Under Napoleon*, trans. R. R. Palmer (Princeton, NJ: Princeton Univ. Press, 1981), p. 198. Châteaubriand quoted in Bergeron, p. 199. Critic Charles Nodier quoted in Peter Brooks, *The Melodramatic Imagination: Balzac, Henry James, Melodrama and the Mode of Excess* (New Haven, CT: Yale Univ. Press, 1976), p. 43.

15. For discussion of the origins and history of neoplatonism, see M. H. Abrams, *Natural Supernaturalism: Tradition and Revolution in Romantic Literature* (New York: W. W. Norton, 1971), pp. 146–63; Philip Merlan, "Neoplatonism," *The Encyclopedia of Philosophy* (New York: Macmillan, 1967), 5: 473–76; Philip Merlan, "Plotinus," *The Encyclopedia of Philoso-*

phy, 6: 351–59; R. T. Wallis, *Neoplatonism* (London: Duckworth, 1972); and Plotinus, *The Six Enneads,* trans. Stephen MacKenna and B. S. Page (Chicago: Univ. of Chicago Press, 1952), II.ix.1; V.i.1. Manicheanism, which understands good and evil as equal forces in the world, may be an appropriate framework for analyzing modern melodrama, but it does not structure the plays of Pixérécourt and his imitators.

16. "Plotinus," p. 354. Merlan also notes a "pessimistic" notion of emanation involving human sinfulness which occurs less frequently, however, than the optimistic one (6: 354).

17. Charles Durang, *History of the Philadelphia Stage between the Years 1749–1855,* ed. Westcott Thompson, 7 vols. (1868; rpt., Ann Arbor, MI: University Microfilms [n.d.]), 2: 205; *New-York Mirror* (November 8, 1823), p. 132.

18. Odell, 3: 419; Cox's summary quoted in *Famous Actors and Actresses of the American Stage,* ed. William C. Young, 2 vols. (New York: R. R. Bowker, 1975), 1: 373–74. Regarding Clara Fisher's early success, also see Durang, 3: 249–50; and [Clara Fisher Meader], *Autobiography of Clara Fisher,* Dunlap Series, no. 3, ed. Douglas Taylor (New York: Dunlap Series Publications, 1897), pp. 10–47.

19. The Misses Vincent, Twibill, and Riddle were three other pretenders to Clara Fisher's crown. *New-York Mirror* (June 6, 1829), pp. 382–83, and (November 10, 1832), p. 151. Joseph Cowell, *Thirty Years Passed among the Players in England and America* (1844; rpt., Hamden, CT: Archon, 1979), p. 82.

20. Undated newspaper clipping in Joseph N. Ireland, *Extra-Illustrated Records of the New York Stage* (MS, HTC), vol. 2, pt. 2, p. 63.

21. William H. Akins, Jr., in his "Three Melodramas by Guilbert de Pixérécourt" (Ph.D. diss., Univ. of Denver, 1971), provides fine translations (as well as useful introductions) to each of the three Pixérécourt plays. Pixérécourt recorded 1,476 performances of *Coelina,* 1,022 performances of *The Man with Three Faces,* and 1,158 of *The Dog of Montargis* during his lifetime (he died in 1844). In the United States, *Coelina* typically went under Holcroft's title, *A Tale of Mystery. The Man with Three Faces* was generally known as *Abaellino,* an anglicized spelling of the original German title. American managers usually produced translations of *The Dog of Montargis* under its subtitle, *The Forest of Bondy.* For the popularity of these plays in the United States, see Grimsted, pp. 249–55; Reese D. James, *The Old Drury of Philadelphia: A History of the Philadelphia Stage,*

1800–1835 (1932; rpt., New York: Greenwood Press, 1968), pp. 637–82; and Odell, 2–5, passim.

22. German visitor quoted in Floyd M. Martinson, *Family in Society* (New York: Dodd, Mead, 1970), pp. 49, 51; Marryat quoted in Frank E. Furstenburg, "Industrialization and the American Family: A Look Backward," *American Sociological Review*, 31 (June 1966), 333. Furstenburg makes the significant point that changes in American family structure preceded rather than followed the rapid industrialization of the United States.

23. See Peter Dobkin Hall, "Family Structure and Economic Organization: Massachusetts Merchants, 1700–1850," in *Family and Kin in Urban Communities*, ed. Tamara K. Hareven (New York: Franklin Watts, 1977), pp. 40–50.

24. Quotations in John and Virginia Demos, "Adolescence in Historical Perspective," in *The American Family in Social-Historical Perspective*, ed. Michael Gordon (New York: St. Martin's Press, 1969), pp. 211–12; and Stow Persons, *The Decline of American Gentility* (New York and London: Columbia Univ. Press, 1973), p. 79. See also Martinson, pp. 48–50, for a discussion of the different kinds of discipline recommended by child guidance writers of the period.

25. Steven Mintz, *A Prison of Expectation: The Family in Victorian Culture* (New York: New York Univ. Press, 1983), pp. 36, 33.

26. Ibid., p. 37.

27. Bernard W. Wishy, *The Child and the Republic: The Dawn of Modern American Child Nurture* (Philadelphia: Univ. of Pennsylvania Press, 1968), p. 4.

28. Michael Fellman, *The Unbounded Frame: Freedom and Community in Nineteenth-Century American Utopianism*, Contributions in American History, no. 26 (Westport, CT: Greenwood Press, 1973), and Dolores Hayden, *Seven American Utopias: The Architecture of Communitarian Socialism, 1790–1975* (Cambridge, MA: MIT Press, 1976), are especially perceptive on the paternalism at the heart of many antebellum utopias. Their studies also tend to echo Somkin's hunch that "the proliferation of communitarian settlements [may be] the most striking testimony on a spatial level to the powerful longing for the temporal community" (p. 7). "Home" quotation in Hayden, p. 24.

29. David J. Rothman, *The Discovery of the Asylum: Social Order and Disorder in the New Republic* (Boston: Little, Brown, 1971), p. 214.

30. Ibid., p. 107. Rothman is speaking specifically about asylums for the insane

here, but he reaches virtually the same conclusions for orphanages, alms-houses, and prisons.

31. Michel Foucault, *The Order of Things: An Archaeology of the Human Sciences* (New York: Pantheon, 1970), pp. 17–30. The "circulation" of similitudes, of course, is Stephen Greenblatt's master trope of historical explanation for his *Shakespearean Negotiations: The Circulation of Social Energy in Renaissance England* (Berkeley and Los Angeles: Univ. of California Press, 1988). I have adapted Foucault and Greenblatt to my own, somewhat different, purposes.

32. Tremont Committee quoted by Lawrence Levine, *Highbrow/Lowbrow: The Emergence of Cultural Hierarchy in America* (Cambridge, MA: Harvard Univ. Press, 1988), p. 56. Visitor quoted in Ben Graf Henneke, "The Playgoer in America (1752–1952)," Ph.D. diss., Univ. of Illinois, 1956, p. 110. Fashionable lady quoted in Grimsted, *Melodrama Unveiled*, p. 56.

33. On elite operagoing, see Peter Buckley, "To the Opera House: Culture and Society in New York City, 1820–1860," Ph.D. diss., SUNY, Stonybrook, 1984; and my "New York Operagoing, 1825–1850: Creating an Elite Social Ritual," *American Music*, 6 (Summer 1988), 181–92.

34. See Fredric Cople Jaher, *The Urban Establishment: Upper Strata in Boston, New York, Charleston, Chicago, Los Angeles* (Urbana: Univ. of Illinois Press, 1982); Edward Pessen, "The Lifestyle of the Antebellum Urban Elite," *Mid-America*, 55 (1973), 163–83; and Persons. Amy Beth Bridges, "Another Look at Plutocracy and Politics in Antebellum New York City," *Political Science Quarterly*, 97 (Spring 1982), makes a strong case for her thesis that "wealthy men did not abandon local politics in the antebellum years and that city politics in that period makes most sense when the political activity of these wealthy men is taken into account" (p. 57).

Part II. Theatre of Yeoman Independence for Jacksonians, 1830–1855

1. Allan Kulikoff, "The Transition to Capitalism in Rural America," *William and Mary Quarterly*, 46 (January 1989), 140–42. For the urban variant of yeoman culture, see Rex Burns, *Success in America: The Yeoman Dream and the Industrial Revolution, 1825–1860* (Amherst: Univ. of Massachusetts, 1976).

2. Joyce Appleby, "Introduction: Republicanism and Ideology," *American*

Quarterly, 37 (Fall 1985), 470. Appleby is paraphrasing J. G. A. Pocock's assessment of republicanism in his *The Machiavellian Moment: Florentine Republican Thought and the Atlantic Republican Tradition* (Princeton: Princeton Univ. Press, 1975). On eighteenth-century republicanism, see Linda Kerber, "The Republican Ideology of the Revolutionary Generation," *American Quarterly*, 37 (Fall 1985), 474–95; Gordon S. Wood, *The Creation of the American Republic, 1776–1787* (Chapel Hill: Univ. of North Carolina Press, 1969); Steven Watts, *The Republic Reborn: War and the Making of Liberal America, 1790–1820* (Baltimore: Johns Hopkins Univ. Press, 1987); and Sean Wilentz, *Chants Democratic: New York City and the Rise of the American Working Class, 1788–1850* (New York: Oxford Univ. Press, 1984).

3. Kenneth Greenberg, *Masters and Statesmen: The Political Culture of American Slavery* (Baltimore: Johns Hopkins Univ. Press, 1985), p. xi; Bertram Wyatt-Brown, *Southern Honor: Ethics and Behavior in the Old South* (New York: Oxford Univ. Press, 1982), pp. 25–61. Although drawing most of his examples from the Old South, Wyatt-Brown defines a generic type of "primal honor" that derives from feudal relations and remains pervasive in several western historical cultures. On antebellum honor, see also Peter Berger and Hansfried Kellner, *The Homeless Mind: Modernization and Consciousness* (New York: Random House, 1973); and Elliott J. Gorn, "'Gouge and Bite, Pull Hair and Scratch': The Social Significance of Fighting in the Southern Backcountry," *AHR*, 90 (February 1985), 18–43. The quotation distinguishing honor from dignity is Gorn's summary of Berger's position, p. 39.

4. E. P. Thompson, "The Moral Economy of the English Crowd in the Eighteenth Century," *Past and Present*, 50 (1971), 76–136. On the clash of republicanism and liberalism, see Appleby, Burns, Kerber, Watts, Wilentz, and Wood, plus Amy Beth Bridges, "Becoming American: The Working Classes in the United States before the Civil War," in *Working-Class Formation: Nineteenth-Century Patterns in Western Europe and the United States*, ed. Ira Katznelson and Aristide R. Zolberg (Princeton: Princeton Univ. Press, 1986), pp. 157–96.

5. See Marvin Meyers, *The Jacksonian Persuasion: Politics and Belief* (1960; rpt., Stanford: Stanford Univ. Press, 1970); Bryan D. Palmer, "Social Formation and Class Formation in North America," in *Proletarianization and Family History*, ed. David Levine (New York: Academic Press, 1984), pp. 229–302; and Robert H. Wiebe, *The Opening of American Society: From the*

Adoption of the Constitution to the Eve of Disunion (New York: Knopf, 1984), pp. 234–52.

3. "The People's Verdict"

1. Curtain speech quoted in full by Montrose J. Moses in *The Fabulous Forrest: The Record of an American Actor* (Boston: Little, Brown, 1929), p. 296.
2. Noah Ludlow, *Dramatic Life as I Found It* (St. Louis: G. I. Jones, 1880), p. 691; Lawrence Barrett, *Edwin Forrest*, American Actor Series (Boston: Osgood, 1881), pp. 44–45; obituary in *Philadelphia Sunday Dispatch* (December 15, 1872), quoted in Joseph N. Ireland, *Extra-Illustrated Records of the New York Stage*, 1867 (MS, HTC), vol. 1, pt. 13, p. 112.
3. Quoted from Richard Moody, *Edwin Forrest: First Star of the American Stage* (New York: Knopf, 1960), pp. 260, 262; and Moses, pp. 280, 281.
4. Quoted in Moses, pp. 287, 288.
5. Ibid., p. 279.
6. See Greenberg, pp. 144–46, on Brooks's caning of Sumner.
7. For the blow-by-blow of the trial, see Moody, pp. 299–324. New York *Herald* quoted on p. 321.
8. Quoted in Moody, p. 326.
9. Carlyle quoted in Walter L. Reed, *Meditations on the Hero: A Study of the Romantic Hero in Nineteenth-Century Fiction* (New Haven: Yale Univ. Press, 1974), p. 1.
10. Liszt quoted by Richard Sennett, *The Fall of Public Man: On the Social Psychology of Capitalism* (New York: Vintage Books, 1974), p. 200. William R. Alger on Kean, quoted by Garff B. Wilson, *A History of American Acting* (Bloomington: Indiana Univ. Press, 1966), p. 22. Morse Peckham, "The Dilemma of a Century: The Four Stages of Romanticism," in *The Triumph of Romanticism* (1964; rpt., Columbia: Univ. of South Carolina Press, 1970), p. 43. For Weber on charisma, see *The Theory of Social and Economic Organization*, trans. A. M. Henderson and Talcott Parsons (New York: Oxford Univ. Press, 1947), pp. 358–64. Turner quoted by Chris Rojek, *Capitalism and Leisure Theory* (New York: Methuen, 1985), p. 20.
11. George Vandenhoff on Cushman, quoted in Barnard Hewett's *Theatre U.S.A., 1668–1957* (New York: McGraw Hill, 1959), p. 127; William Winter on Wallack, quoted in *Famous Actors and Actresses of the American*

Stage, ed. William C. Young, 2 vols. (New York: R. R. Bowker, 1975), 2: 1114.

12. Quotations in Ben Graf Henneke, "The Playgoer in America (1752–1952)," Ph.D. diss., Univ. of Illinois, 1956, pp. 166, 167.

13. *The Spirit of the Times: A Chronicle of the Turf, Field Sports, Literature, and the Stage* (April 15, 1837), p. 65, and, quoting a Washington, D.C., reviewer, (November 17, 1855), p. 480.

14. Critic (from the New Orleans *Picayune* in 1856) quoted in Henneke, p. 167. For Thomas Carlyle's views on hero worship, see his *On Heroes, Hero-Worship, and the Heroic in History* (1841; rpt., New York: Scribner's, 1900).

15. Quotations in David Grimsted, *Melodrama Unveiled: American Theater and Culture, 1800–1850* (Chicago: Univ. of Chicago Press, 1968), p. 148.

16. Anna Cora Mowatt, *Autobiography of an Actress* (Boston: Ticknor, Reed, and Fields, 1854), p. 227.

17. Francis Wemyss, *Theatrical Biography; or, The Life of an Actor-Manager* (Glasgow: R. Griffin, 1848), pp. 151, 152; Bird quoted in Clement Foust, *Life and Dramatic Works of Robert Montgomery Bird* (1919; rpt., New York: Burt Franklin, 1971), p. 40; review quoted in Richard Harris, "An Analysis of the Serious Dramas of Robert Montgomery Bird," Ph.D. diss., Indiana Univ., 1966, p. 37.

18. Maude and Otis Skinner, *One Man in His Time: The Adventures of H. Watkins, Strolling Player, 1845–1863, from His Journal* (Philadelphia: Univ. of Pennsylvania Press, 1938), p. 65.

19. Quotations in Grimsted, *Melodrama Unveiled*, p. 84; and the *New-York Mirror* (April 21, 1832), p. 335.

20. See Raymond Williams, *The Sociology of Culture* (New York: Schocken, 1982), pp. 45–47. Otis Skinner, *Footlights and Spotlights: Recollections of My Life on the Stage* (1923; rpt., Westport, CT: Greenwood Press, 1972), p. 52.

21. See the 1881 obituary on Marshall in the New York *Clipper* included in Ireland, *Extra-Illustrated Records*, vol. 3, pt. 13, p. 35.

22. See the obituary cited above; the entries on the Broadway and Walnut companies in *American Theatre Companies, 1749–1887*, ed. Weldon Durham (Westport, CT: Greenwood Press, 1986), pp. 121–25, 530–47; and William Davidage, *Footlight Flashes* (New York: American News Company, 1866), pp. 124–98, for an actor's view of Marshall's management of the Broadway during the 1850s.

23. See, for instance, the Cushman and Marshall exchange of letters quoted by Joseph Leach, *Bright, Particular Star: The Life and Times of Charlotte Cushman* (New Haven, CT: Yale Univ. Press, 1970), p. 232.

24. John Foster Kirk quoted in *Actors and Actresses of Great Britain and the United States*, ed. Brander Matthews and Laurence Hutton (New York: Cassell, 1886), p. 58. Obituary in the *Brooklyn Daily Eagle* (December 12, 1872) quoted in Ireland, *Extra-Illustrated Records*, vol. 1, pt. 13, p. 121. See also Garff Wilson, pp. 19–29, who finds many similarities between Forrest's style and Kean's, and Fanny Ellsler, *The Letters and Journal of Fanny Ellsler* (New York: H. G. Daggers, 1845), p. 39, who was particularly impressed by Forrest's voice.

25. William R. Alger, *Life of Edwin Forrest, the American Tragedian*, 2 vols. (Philadelphia: J. B. Lippincott, 1877), 2: 172; Forrest's note to Alger quoted in Grimsted, p. 69.

26. *New-York Mirror* (October 24, 1829), p. 126; *Democratic Review* (1845), p. 386.

27. Quoted in Alger, 2: 837.

28. *New-York Mirror* (March 8, 1828), p. 279; Bird quoted by Harris, p. 249.

29. Forrest on Napoleon quoted in Alger, 2: 274. Many Napoleonic plays were popular with Forrest's audience, including *The Battle of Waterloo, Napoleon the Exile and Death of Napoleon the Great*, and *Napoleon Buonaparte's Invasion of Russia, or The Conflagration of Moscow*. See also Theodore Gross, *The Heroic Ideal in American Literature* (New York: Free Press, 1971), pp. 3–17.

30. Alger quoted in Alan S. Downer, "Early American Professional Acting," *Theatre Survey*, 12 (November 1971), 89.

31. Harrison quoted in Alger, 2: 543.

32. John William Ward, *Andrew Jackson: Symbol for an Age* (1966; rpt., New York: Oxford Univ. Press, 1971), p. 208.

33. See Greenberg, pp. x–xi, for the quotation from Hobbes and his own comments on the "compatibility and tension" evident in southern conceptions of honor and republicanism.

4. "Freedom! Revenge or Death!"

1. James Murdoch, *The Stage, or Recollections of Actors and Acting from an Experience of Fifty Years* (1880; rpt., New York: Benjamin Blom, 1969),

p. 296; *The Diary of Philip Hone*, ed. Bayard Tuckerman, 2 vols. (New York: Dodd, Mead, 1889), 1: 270; [Anonymous], *Account of the Terrific and Fatal Riot at the New York Astor Place Opera House on the Night of May 10th, 1849* (New York: H. M. Ranney, 1849), p. 19.

2. Both quotations in Montrose J. Moses, *The Fabulous Forrest: The Record of an American Actor* (Boston: Little, Brown, 1929), p. 329.

3. See Theodore Shank, "The Bowery Theatre, 1826–1836, Ph.D. diss., Stanford Univ., 1956, on the mid 1830s Bowery Theatre. Whitman quoted in *The American Theatre as Seen by Its Critics, 1752–1934*, ed. Montrose Moses and John Mason Brown (New York: W. W. Norton, 1934), p. 85.

4. Francis Wemyss, *Twenty-Six Years of the Life of an Actor and Manager*, 2 vols. (New York: Burgess, Stringer, and Co., 1847), 2: 234–35. For the Hamblin-Wemyss correspondence, see Joseph N. Ireland, *Extra-Illustrated Records of the New York Stage*, 1867 (MS, HTC), vol. 2, pt. 1: 177, and vol. 2, pt. 9: 149.

5. T. Allston Brown, *A History of the New York Stage from the First Performance in 1732 to 1901*, 3 vols. (1903; rpt., New York: Benjamin Blom, 1964), 1: 367–68.

6. See *Account* . . . , pp. 28–30, for the composition of the riot, and Stuart Blumin, *The Emergence of the Middle Class: Social Experience in the American City, 1790–1900* (Cambridge: Cambridge Univ. Press, 1989), pp. 3–15, 108–21, on the relative proportions of population by class in the antebellum city.

7. See Sean Wilentz, *Chants Democratic: New York City and the Rise of the American Working Class, 1788–1850* (New York: Oxford Univ. Press, 1984), pp. 117, 405. As Blumin notes, "Wilentz's income estimates are very similar to those provided for Philadelphia by Bruce Laurie, Theodore Hershberg, and George Alter" (p. 110). Ticket prices at the Bowery, Walnut, and Broadway theatres generally ranged from twenty-five to seventy-five cents during the 1835–55 period, with some prices halved during the depression years of the late thirties and early forties.

8. George G. Foster, *New York by Gas-Light: With Here and There a Streak of Sunshine* (New York: Dewitt and Davenport, 1850), p. 87. Christine Stansell, *City of Women: Sex and Class in New York, 1789–1860* (Urbana: Univ. of Illinois Press, 1987), pp. 89–100.

9. Paul Faler and Alan Dawley first used the terms radical, loyalist, and traditionalist in their "Working-Class Culture and Politics in the Industrial Revolution: Sources of Loyalism and Rebellion," *Journal of Social History*,

9 (June 1976). I agree with Wilentz that the terms, though useful as general groupings, are poor predictors of loyalty or rebellion. See also Bruce Laurie, *The Working People of Philadelphia, 1800–1860* (Philadelphia: Temple Univ. Press, 1980).

10. Lawrence Kohl, *The Politics of Individualism: Parties and the American Character in the Jacksonian Era* (New York: Oxford Univ. Press, 1989), p. 15. My notion of the Jacksonians merges Kohl's emphasis on social psychology with the political analysis of John Ashworth, *"Agrarians and Aristocrats": Party Political Ideology in the United States, 1837–1846* (Cambridge: Cambridge Univ. Press, 1987). Despite their different points of view toward the Jacksonians, Ashworth's emphasis on Jacksonian agrarianism and egalitarianism meshes rather closely with Kohl's focus on their traditionalist orientation. Richard L. McCormick, *The Party Period and Public Policy: American Policy from the Age of Jackson to the Progressive Era* (New York: Oxford Univ. Press, 1986), provides a recent overview of interpretations of Jacksonian political culture.

11. See, for example, *The Ancient Briton* by Stone, *Oralloosa* and *The Broker of Bogotá* by Bird, and *Caius Marius, Sertorius, or The Roman Patriot*, and *Conrad, King of Naples*, by Richard Penn Smith, David Paul Brown, and Robert T. Conrad, respectively. Not all of these plays were motivated directly by Forrest's success. His heroic melodramas were a part of a general dramatic interest in romantic subjects which also supported *Marmion*, by James N. Barker, *Ugolino*, attributed to Junius Brutus Booth, *Pocahontas*, by George W. P. Custis, and many other so-called Indian plays.

12. Michael D. Bell, *The Development of American Romance: The Sacrifice of Relation* (Chicago: Univ. of Chicago Press, 1980), p. 15. For Bell's elaboration of the conventions of conservative romance, see pp. 7–22. For Forrest's three prize plays, I have used the following editions: *The Gladiator* and *Metamora* in *Dramas from the American Theatre, 1762–1909*, ed. Richard Moody, New World Literature Series (1966; rpt., Boston: Houghton Mifflin, 1969), pp. 241–75 and 305–77; *Jack Cade* in *Representative Plays by American Dramatists: From 1765 to the Present Day*, ed. Montrose J. Moses, 3 vols. (1925; rpt., New York: Benjamin Blom, 1964), 2: 462–519. Subsequent citations to these plays are taken from these editions.

13. I have used the following editions of these plays: *Brutus, or The Fall of Tarquin* in Moses, *Representative Plays by American Dramatists*; *Virginius* in *The Dramatic Works of James Sheridan Knowles*, 2 vols. (London: G. Routledge and Co., 1856); and *Pizarro, A Tragedy in Five Acts, Taken*

from the German Drama of Kotzebue, 4th ed. (London: James Ridgeway, 1799), Special Collections, Swem Library, William and Mary.

14. Samuel Young, Amos Kendall, and *The Young Hickory Banner* (August 24, 1844) quoted in Ashworth, pp. 11, 24, 31. Ashworth takes the Jacksonian advocacy of republicanism a step further by arguing that Democratic ideology rested on a precapitalist concept of equality. Certainly some Democrats thought this way, especially some of the Locofocos in New York City. But Democrats drew too much from Locke, Ben Franklin, and Adam Smith to be called precapitalist. On the durability of republican thinking in the Democratic party, on the other hand, see Jean Baker, *Affairs of Party: The Political Culture of Northern Democrats in the Mid-Nineteenth Century* (Ithaca: Cornell Univ. Press, 1983), pp. 143–76.

15. Quoted in Ashworth, pp. 40, 38. Bancroft quoted in Marvin Meyers, *The Jacksonian Persuasion: Politics and Belief* (1960; rpt., Stanford: Stanford Univ. Press, 1970), pp. 4–5. On charisma, see Weber, *The Theory of Social and Economic Organization*.

16. Kohl, passim. Camp quoted in Rush Welter, *The Mind of America, 1820–1860* (New York: Columbia Univ. Press, 1975), pp. 91–92. Welter, pp. 92–93.

17. Michael Kreyling, *Figures of the Hero in Southern Narrative* (Baton Rouge: Louisiana State Univ. Press, 1987), p. 5. Kreyling uses Sidney Hook's *The Hero in History: A Study in Limitation and Possibility* (New York: John Day, 1943) to point up the antidemocratic assumptions of these novels.

18. John L. O'Sullivan, "The Democratic Principle," reprinted in *Notions of the Americans, 1820–1860*, ed. David Grimsted (New York: George Braziller, 1970), pp. 95–96.

19. Baker, pp. 292–93, 271. Baker cites other pre-election rituals, such as pole raising and defending, and notes that the soldiers of these ceremonies were expected to fulfill their military duty of obedience by voting the party ticket (p. 300).

20. Howard Martin, "The Fourth of July Oration," *QJS*, 44 (December 1958), 393–401; "Style in the Golden Age," *QJS*, 43 (December 1957), 374–82; and Richard Weaver, *The Ethics of Rhetoric* (Chicago: H. Regency, 1953), pp. 164, 169.

21. Lewis O. Saum, *The Popular Mood of Pre–Civil War America* (Westport, CT: Greenwood Press, 1980), p. 138.

22. Leman Thomas Rede and Francis C. Wemyss, *The Guide to the Stage* (New

York: Samuel French, 1859), p. 34. Rede published the initial *Guide* in London in 1827; Wemyss updated the work by adding information useful to the young actor interested in the possibility of a professional career. T. W. Erle, an English stage manager, on the villain's skulking walk quoted in Michael R. Booth, "The Acting of Melodrama," *University of Toronto Quarterly*, 34 (October 1964), 34. Donald C. Mullin, "Methods and Manners of Traditional Acting," *Educational Theatre Journal*, 27 (March 1975), 7, on melodramatic stage movement as ritual. See also Gilbert B. Cross, *Next Week— East Lynn: Domestic Drama in Performance, 1820–1874* (London: Associated University Presses, 1977), pp. 106–67; and Alan Downer, "Player and Painted Stage: Nineteenth-Century Acting," *PMLA*, 61, 2 (June 1946), 522–76.

23. Weaver, p. 176.

24. Rede and Wemyss, p. 32. Cross, pp. 124–27, is especially good on the conventions of point making.

25. *The Spirit of the Times* quoted in *Famous Actors and Actresses of the American Stage*, 1: 398; *Arcturus* (June 1841), 63; "The New York Stage: The New Tragedy of *Metamora*—A Bird's Eye View of Mr. Forrest's Performance," *Irish Shield and Monthly Milesian*, 1 (1829), 468.

26. See p. 161 and the discussion of these modes, pp. 157–206, in Bert O. States, *Great Reckonings in Little Rooms: On the Phenomenology of Theater* (Berkeley and Los Angeles: Univ. of California Press, 1985).

27. Murray Edelman, *The Symbolic Uses of Power* (Urbana: Univ. of Illinois Press, 1964), pp. 137, 138, 125.

28. Whitman and Bird quoted in Curtis Dahl, *Robert Montgomery Bird* (New York: Twayne, 1963), pp. 58, 59. Richard Moody ("Introduction to *The Gladiator*," in *Dramas from the American Theatre*, p. 239) also agrees with Whitman and Bird on slavery and the play.

29. Murdoch, pp. 298–300, reported the *Metamora* episode in Georgia. He quotes a Georgia judge at the time as stating, "Any actor who could utter such scathing language and with such vehemence must have the whole matter at heart. . . . I insist upon it: Forrest believes in that d——d Indian speech and it is an insult to the whole community" (pp. 299–300). A more representative response occurred in an 1837 article in the New York *Herald*, which perceived an unbridgeable gulf between Forrest's performance in the role and the situation of real Native Americans: "[Forrest-Metamora] is truly the impersonation of the Indian of romance. The Indian in his *true* character never *can* find a representative among the whites." Cited by

Jeffrey D. Mason, "The Politics of *Metamora*," in *The Performance of Power: Theatrical Discourse and Politics*, ed. Sue-Ellen Case and Janelle Reinelt (Iowa City: Univ. of Iowa Press, 1991), p. 105.

5. "The Earthquake! The Earthquake!"

1. See Rosemarie K. Bank, "Bowery Theatre Company," *American Theatre Companies, 1749–1887*, ed. Weldon Durham (Westport, CT: Greenwood Press, 1986); Theodore Shank, "The Bowery Theatre, 1826–1836," Ph.D. diss., Stanford Univ., 1956; Thomas S. Hamblin, "Last Will and Testament," MS [1836], HTC; and a note on Hamblin's final will (in which he was rumored to have left over $100,000) in Joseph N. Ireland, *Extra-Illustrated Records of the New York Stage*, 1867 (MS, HTC), vol. 1, pt. 12, p. 100. Bowery Theatre fires occurred in 1836, 1838, and 1845. Hamblin managed the playhouse throughout the period except for two years between 1837 and 1839 when William Dinneford ran the company. "Stir-em-up" quote in the *Spirit of the Times* (Sept. 23, 1837), [n.p.].
2. Mary C. Henderson, *The City and the Theatre: New York Playhouses from Bowling Green to Times Square* (Clifton, NJ: James T. White, 1973), p. 69.
3. *Brother Jonathan*, 6 (May 9, 1843), 47; William K. Northall, *Before and Behind the Curtain, or Fifteen Years' Observations among the Theatres of New York* (New York: W. F. Burgess, 1851), p. 152.
4. *Spirit of the Times* (February 6, 1847), p. 590.
5. On deviancy, see Howard S. Becker, *Outsiders: Studies in the Sociology of Deviance* (New York: Free Press, 1963); Nanette Davis, *Sociological Constructions of Deviance: Perspectives and Issues in the Field* (Dubuque, IA: William C. Brown, 1975), pp. 192–224; David Downes and Paul Rock, *Understanding Deviance: A Guide to the Sociology of Crime and Rule Breaking* (Oxford: Clarendon Press, 1982); and Edwin M. Schur, *The Politics of Deviance: Stigma Contests and the Uses of Power* (Englewood Cliffs, NJ: Prentice Hall, 1980).

For studies of Bowery culture in the 1840s, I have relied primarily on Elliott J. Gorn, *The Manly Art: Bare-Knuckle Prize Fighting in America* (Ithaca, NY: Cornell Univ. Press, 1986); Christine Stansell, *City of Women: Sex and Class in New York, 1789–1860* (Urbana: Univ. of Illinois Press, 1987); and Sean Wilentz, *Chants Democratic: New York City and the Rise of the American Working Class* (New York: Oxford Univ. Press, 1984). See also Stuart Blumin, *The Emergence of the Middle Class: Social Experience in the American City, 1790–1900* (Cambridge: Cambridge Univ. Press, 1989), who comments on Bowery fashion: "There is a suggestion here not only of defiance but of parody as well—Mose and Lize may have deliberately combined some of the elements of middle- and upper-class dress to create a counterstyle that expressed contempt for bloodless gentility" (pp. 143–44).

6. *Spirit of the Times* (June 28, 1838), p. 1; M. Clarke, *A Concise History of the Life and Amours of Thomas S. Hamblin, Late Manager of the Bowery Theatre, As Communicated by His Legal Wife, Mrs. Elizabeth Hamblin* (New York: [n.p.], [n.d.]). As this title indicates, Hamblin may not have divorced his first wife before marrying Louisa Medina; the legal record is unclear. On Hamblin and Medina, see also Rosemarie K. Bank, "Theatre and Narrative Fiction in the Work of a Nineteenth-Century American Playwright, Louisa Medina," *Theatre History Studies*, 3 (1983), 54–67.

7. *New-York Mirror* (April 28, 1838), p. 351; Lester Wallack, *Memories of Fifty Years* (New York: Scribner's, 1889), p. 90; see also Bank on Medina. I used the following editions of Medina's plays: *The Last Days of Pompeii: A Dramatic Spectacle*, French's Standard Drama, Acting Edition no. 146 (New York: S[amuel] French, [n.d.]), and *Nick of the Woods* MS, NYPL, the promptbook of E. H. Taylor (based on the V. W. Spencer edition of the script, [n.d.]). These plays and the melodramas of Jones, noted below, were similar in formula to the type of play popular with midcentury English working-class audiences. See Michael R. Booth, "East End Melodrama," *Theatre Survey*, 17 (May 1976), 57–67.

8. Jones's statement in the preface to his *Moll Pitcher, or The Fortune Teller of Lynn* (1855; rpt., New York: Readex Microprint, 1966). I used the following edition of Jones's play: *The Carpenter of Rouen*, MS, NYPL, the promptbook of J. B. Wright (prompter for Pelby's National Theatre). Subsequent editions of *Carpenter* by Samuel French delete two pointedly anti-Catholic scenes in the play and add the subtitle *The Massacre of St. Bartholomew*, a publishing error since the massacre actually occurs in another of Jones's plays, *The Surgeon of Paris*. The quoted pamphlet was intended to puff both of these plays with National Theatre audiences: *Original Dramas: Surgeon of Paris and Carpenter of Rouen* (Boston: E. G. House, 1837), p. 3.

Some notion of the ongoing popularity of *Pompeii, Nick*, and *Carpenter* may be gained from the Bowery Account Book (MS, HTC) recording daily performances and gross receipts between August 4, 1845, and March 4, 1848. Hamblin presented *The Carpenter of Rouen* sixteen times for a total of $5,719, *The Last Days of Pompeii* nine times for $2,344, and *Nick of the Woods* seventeen times for $5,558. These and several other apocalyptic melodramas seem to have accounted for about half of Hamblin's performances during these years.

Other apocalyptic melodramas include *The Three Brothers, or Crime Its Own Avenger* by Nathaniel Harrington; *The Shoemaker of Toulouse, or The Avenger of Humble Life* by Frederick S. Hill; *Captain Kyd, or The Wizard of the Sea* and *Wacousta, or The Curse* by Jones; *Ernest Maltravers* by Medina; *The Evil Eye* by Jonas B. Phillips; *Yankee Jack, or The Buccaneer of the Gulf* by James Pilgrim; *The Pirates' Legacy, or The Wreckers' Fate* by Charles H. Saunders; and *The Brazen Drum, or The Yankee in Poland* by Silas Steele.

9. Bulwer-Lytton quoted in Edwin Eigner, *The Metaphysical Novel in England and America: Dickens, Bulwer-Lytton, Melville, and Hawthorne* (Berkeley and Los Angeles: Univ. of California Press, 1978), pp. 146, 157. Ironically, Bulwer-Lytton abandoned his "symbolical" aims when he began to write plays. His *Richelieu*, immensely successful in the 1840s, bore little resemblance to the still-popular dramatizations of his novels.

10. In addition to Gorn, *The Manly Art*, and Wilentz, see Bertram Wyatt-Brown, *Southern Honor: Ethics and Behavior in the Old South* (New York: Oxford Univ. Press, 1982); and Kenneth Greenberg, "The Nose, the Lie, and the Duel in the Antebellum South," *AHR*, 95 (February 1990), 57–74.

11. See Bruce Laurie, "Fire Companies and Gangs in Southwark: The 1840s," in *The Peoples of Philadelphia: A History of Ethnic Groups and Lower-Class Life*, ed. Allen F. Davis and Mark H. Hall (Philadelphia: Temple Univ. Press, 1973), pp. 71–87; and Wilentz, pp. 259–62. Stephen F. Ginsberg's "Volunteer Firemen in N.Y.C., 1836–1837," *New York History*, 50 (April 1969), 165–86, is also helpful. Benjamin Baker's *A Glance at New York* and Samuel Johnson's *The Firemen* are representative examples of fire-company plays. For a recent explanation of the popularity of these dramas, see Richard B. Stott, *Workers in the Metropolis: Class, Ethnicity, and Youth in Antebellum New York City* (Ithaca and London: Cornell Univ. Press, 1990), pp. 223–26, 251–65.

12. On the Bowery B'hoy and his social image, see Wilentz, p. 263; David S. Reynolds, *Beneath the American Renaissance: The Subversive Imagination in the Age of Emerson and Melville* (New York: Knopf, 1988),

pp. 464–66; and Stansell, pp. 76–102. Quotation on the Killers in David R. Johnson, "Crime Patterns in Philadelphia, 1840–70," in *The Peoples of Philadelphia*, p. 98.

13. Quotations from Walsh in Amy Beth Bridges, *A City in the Republic: Antebellum New York and the Origins of Machine Politics* (Cambridge: Cambridge Univ. Press, 1984), p. 111; and Wilentz, pp. 332, 334. See also Reynolds, pp. 458–59.

14. See Howard B. Rock, *Artisans of the New Republic: The Tradesmen of New York City in the Age of Jefferson* (New York: New York Univ. Press, 1979), pp. 135–43; and Wilentz on artisan life before industrialization. Quotations from Michael Feldberg, *The Philadelphia Riots of 1844: A Study of Ethnic Conflict*, Contributions in American History, no. 43 (Westport, CT: Greenwood Press, 1975), p. 68; Norman Ware, *The Industrial Worker, 1840–1860: Reactions of American Industrial Society to the Advance of the Industrial Revolution* (Cambridge, MA: Houghton Mifflin, 1924), p. xiv; Rex Burns, *Success in America: The Yeoman Dream and the Industrial Revolution, 1825–1860* (Amherst: Univ. of Massachusetts Press, 1976), p. 118.

15. Blumin, drawing on the research of several labor historians, provides a good overview of the average income, wealth, and mobility of antebellum workers, pp. 109–21.

16. See Kenelm Burridge, *New Heaven, New Earth: A Study of Millenarian Activities*, Pavilion Series in Social Anthropology (New York: Schocken Books, 1969); J. F. C. Harrison, *The Second Coming: Popular Millenarianism, 1780–1850* (New Brunswick, NJ: Rutgers Univ. Press, 1979); and Bryan R. Wilson, *Magic and the Millennium: A Sociological Study of Religious Movements of Protest among Tribal and Third-World Peoples* (New York: Harper and Row, 1973). Burridge is especially useful on the social dynamics of millenarian movements.

17. La Barre quoted in Vittorio Lanternari, "Nativistic and Socio-Religious Movements: A Reconsideration," *Comparative Studies in Society and History*, 16 (September 1974), 495. Also see Burridge, pp. 110–14; and Harrison, pp. 12–38.

18. This transformation scene occurs only in the J. B. Wright copy of *Carpenter*, cited above, used at Pelby's National Theatre; it is absent from the French edition, published later. Bowery and Walnut productions of *Carpenter* probably also employed this nativist appeal to anti-Catholic sentiments, but direct evidence of the scene's inclusion is lacking.

19. Wilentz makes several comments on the iconography of actual banners used by New York artisans, pp. 91, 96, 246. Apparently the banner used on stage in *Carpenter* was not the same as the one usually displayed by New York carpenters at parades and rallies.

20. Burridge, p. 165.

21. Quoted in Alvin F. Harlow, *Old Bowery Days* (New York: D. Appleton, 1931), pp. 262, 191; song quoted by Shank, p. 262.

22. Program in Scrapbook of Newspaper Clippings Relating to the Drama in the U.S., MS, NYPL, [n.p.]; review in the New York *Sun*, quoted by George C. D. Odell, *Annals of the New York Stage*, 15 vols. (New York: Columbia Univ. Press, 1927–49), 4: 83.

23. *The Butchers of Ghent*, promptbook, MS, NYPL (III,2).

24. Ireland, vol. 2, pt. 8, pp. 40–41. Hamblin's four aquatic shows in 1840, however, were the last he attempted.

25. On the new machinist at the Walnut, see Charles Durang, *History of the Philadelphia Stage between the Years 1749–1855*, ed. Westcott Thompson, 7 vols. (1868: rpt., Ann Arbor, MI: University Microfilms, [n.d.]), 4: 166. On gaslighting, see Wesley Swanson, "Wings and Backdrops: The Story of American Scenery from the Beginnings to 1875," *Drama*, 18 (1927), 78–80; and John R. Wolcott, "The Genesis of Gaslights," *Theatre Research*, 12, no. 1 (1972), 74–86.

26. Panoramic advertisements cited by Douglas E. Branch, *The Sentimental Years, 1836–1860* (1934; rpt., New York: Hill and Wang, 1965), p. 161. Reynolds quote, p. 189; see pp. 188–210 for Reynolds' discussion of Dark Adventure and Subversive fiction, which has much in common with apocalyptic melodrama. See E. P. Thompson, *The Making of the English Working Class* (New York: Pantheon, 1963), pp. 351–400. Commerford quoted in Edward Pessen, *Most Uncommon Jacksonians: The Radical Leaders of the Early Labor Movement* (Albany: State Univ. of New York Press, 1967), p. 194. On apocalyptic imagery in the antebellum era generally, see Curtis Dahl, "Bulwer-Lytton and the School of Catastrophe," *Philological Quarterly*, 32 (October 1953), 428–42, and "The American School of Catastrophe," *American Quarterly*, 11 (Fall 1959), 380–90.

27. Herbert G. Gutman, *Work, Culture and Society in Industrializing America: Essays in American Working-Class and Social History* (New York: Vintage Books, 1976), p. 63. See George Rudé, *The Crowd in History: A Study of Popular Disturbances in France and England, 1730–1848* (New York: John Wiley and Sons, 1964); and Eric J. Hobsbawm, *Social Bandits and*

Primitive Rebels: Studies in Archaic Forms of Social Movement in the Nineteenth and Twentieth Centuries (Glencoe, IL: Free Press, 1959), pp. 108–25, 150–74.

Interpretations of American antebellum urban riots include Paul A. Gilje, *The Road to Mobocracy: Popular Disorder in New York City, 1763–1834* (Chapel Hill: Univ. of North Carolina Press, 1987); David Grimsted, "Rioting in Its Jacksonian Setting," in *The Underside of American History: Other Readings,* ed. Thomas Frazier, 3d ed. (1972; rpt., New York: Harcourt Brace, 1978); Theodore Hammett, "Two Mobs of Jacksonian Boston: Ideology and Interest," *Journal of American History,* 62 (1976), 845–68; Leonard L. Richards, *"Gentlemen of Property and Standing": Anti-Abolition Mobs in Jacksonian America* (1970; rpt., New York: Oxford Univ. Press, 1977); and Paul O. Weinbaum, *Mobs and Demagogues: The New York Response to Collective Violence in the Early Nineteenth Century,* Studies in American History and Culture, no. 3 (Ann Arbor, MI: UMI Research Press, 1979); and Wilentz.

28. See Richards, pp. 113–22, for a brief account of the Farren riot. Shank, pp. 378–84, emphasizes the significance of Hamblin, Farren, and McKinney in the riot. Gilje, pp. 248–51, and Weinbaum, pp. 2–41, place the riot in the context of other similar acts in New York in 1834. While it is not clear that the riot against Farren at the Bowery and the one against the Tappan brothers were linked, Wilentz cites a "multitude of associations" connecting the rioters (pp. 265–66).

29. See Richard Moody, *The Astor Place Riot* (Bloomington: Indiana Univ. Press, 1958); and Peter Buckley, "To the Opera House: Culture and Society in New York City, 1820–1860," Ph.D. diss., SUNY, Stony Brook, 1984. The anonymous *Account of the Terrific and Fatal Riot at the New York Astor Place Opera House, on the Night of May 10, 1849* (New York: H. M. Ranney, 1849) is also useful.

30. Grimsted, "Rioting in Its Jacksonian Setting," p. 178.

31. *Evening Post* quoted in Richards, p. 115. See also his note on the same page for Richard's assessment of the extent of the rumors. Gilje, p. 251.

32. "American Citizen," in *A Rejoinder to "Replies from England," Together with an Impartial History and Review of the Lamentable Occurrences at the Astor Place Opera House* (New York: Stringer and Townsend, 1849), p. 68. Other quotations in Northall, p. 143; Montrose J. Moses, *The Fabulous Forrest: The Record of an American Actor* (Boston: Little, Brown, 1929), p. 260; Moody, p. 187; and *Account,* p. 19.

33. Rudé, pp. 247–48.

34. Quoted in full by Shank, pp. 379–80.

35. See Northall, pp. 133–36, on the "tramp warning" of the rioters. Philip Hone, *The Diary of Philip Hone*, 2 vols., ed. Bayard Tuckerman (New York: Dodd, Mead, 1889), 1: 100.

36. Rudé, p. 242.

37. Hone, 2: 361; excerpts from Strong's diary in *Notions of the Americans*, ed. David Grimsted (New York: George Braziller, 1970), p. 276.

38. *Spirit of the Times* (September 22, 1838), p. 249. Regarding rioting conventions, see Paul Gilje, "The Baltimore Riots of 1812 and the Breakdown of the Anglo-American Mob Tradition," *Journal of Social History*, 13 (Summer 1980), 547, passim; also, Gilje's *Road to Mobocracy*.

39. Eric Hobsbawm, *Bandits* (New York: Delacorte Press, 1969), p. 22. See also his *Social Bandits and Primitive Rebels*, pp. 57–174, for related comments on millenarianism and labor sects in Britain.

40. Gorn, pp. 145–46.

Part III. Business-Class Theatre for the Respectable, 1845–1870

1. Stuart M. Blumin, *The Emergence of the Middle Class: Social Experience in the American City* (Cambridge: Cambridge Univ. Press, 1989), p. 74, combines the estimates of several other historians to arrive at a general figure of 40 percent, but notes that it was lower in New York and Philadelphia. Blumin makes a case for a tripartite class division—working, middle, and upper classes—emerging around midcentury. Ironically, most of the information he presents suggests that the division between manual and nonmanual was more fundamental and pervasive by 1850 than the divide between an elusive "middle class" and the elite. In this regard, Michael B. Katz's distinction between class and stratum is significant: Class refers to the social relations deriving from the structures of production, while strata are distinctions within a class relating to differences of income, ideology, etc. See Michael B. Katz, *The People of Hamilton, Canada West: Family and Class in a Mid-Nineteenth-Century City* (Cambridge, MA: Harvard Univ. Press, 1975), pp. 44–93. Also Katz, Michael J. Doucet, and Mark J. Stern, *The Social Organization of Early Industrial Capitalism* (Cam-

bridge, MA: Harvard Univ. Press, 1982). In this sense, clerks, foremen, and salespeople were in the lower strata of the business class.

2. Blumin, p. 136. I borrow the term "moralists" from Daniel T. Rodgers, *The Work Ethic in Industrial America, 1850–1920* (Chicago: Univ. of Chicago Press, 1978), p. 16, who defines these ministers, journalists, teachers, and others as the "keepers of their countrymen's conscience."

3. On class division in antebellum northern cities, see Paul Boyer, *Urban Masses and Moral Order* (Cambridge, MA: Harvard Univ. Press, 1978); Anne Norton, *Alternative Americas: A Reading of Antebellum Political Culture* (Chicago: Univ. of Chicago Press, 1986), chaps. 1–3; Robert H. Wiebe, *The Opening of American Society: From the Adoption of the Constitution to the Eve of Disunion* (New York: Knopf, 1984), chap. 16; and Sean Wilentz, *Chants Democratic: New York City and the Rise of the American Working Class, 1788–1850* (New York: Oxford, 1984). See Paul Faler, "Cultural Aspects of the Industrial Revolution: Lynn, Massachusetts, Shoemakers and Industrial Morality, 1826–1860," *Labor History*, 15 (Summer 1974), 367–94, on "the new industrial morality." This Victorian bourgeoisie was emergent, but not yet fully hegemonic in the 1840s and early 1850s, in the sense of Raymond Williams' notion of emergent culture as "active and pressing, but not yet fully articulated" (*Marxism and Literature* [Oxford: Oxford Univ. Press, 1977], p. 126).

6. "We Will Restore You to Society"

1. The *Nation* published the original letter on July 27, 1865. Barnum's reply appeared in the August 10 issue. Both recent biographers of Barnum underline his concern with propriety and decorum at his museum. See Neil Harris, *Humbug: The Art of P. T. Barnum* (Boston: Little, Brown, 1973); and A. H. Saxon, *P. T. Barnum: The Legend and the Man* (New York: Columbia Univ. Press, 1989).

2. Regarding class divisions in midcentury urban entertainment, see my articles on operagoing and Bowery theatre: "New York Operagoing, 1825–1850: Creating an Elite Social Ritual," *American Music*, 6 (Summer 1988), 181–93; and "'The Theatre of the Mob': Apocalyptic Melodrama and Preindustrial Riots in Antebellum New York," in *Theatre for Working-Class Audiences in the United States, 1830–1980*, ed. Bruce A. McConachie and Daniel Friedman (Westport, CT: Greenwood Press, 1985), pp. 1–46. Also

useful are Mary C. Henderson, *The City and the Theatre: New York Playhouses from Bowling Green to Times Square*, (Clifton, NJ: James T. White, 1973); Lawrence W. Levine, *Highbrow/Lowbrow: The Emergence of Cultural Hierarchy in America* (Cambridge, MA: Harvard Univ. Press, 1988); and George C. D. Odell, *Annals of the New York Stage*, 15 vols. (New York: Columbia Univ. Press, 1927–49).

3. Barnum reported in later editions of his autobiography that he sold 38 million admission tickets between 1841 and 1865. See, for instance, *Struggles and Triumphs* (Hartford, CT: J. B. Burr, 1889), p. 314. Since the total population of the U.S. in 1865 was only 35 million (and allowing for Barnumesque inflation of his ticket sales), it is clear that Barnum drew in the lowest common denominator of theatre patron. Further, at twenty-five cents, Barnum's and Kimball's admission prices in the 1850s were as low as any in either city.

4. William W. Clapp, *A Record of the Boston Stage* (Boston: James Munroe, 1853), p. 471; visitor quoted in Ben Graf Henneke, "The Playgoer in America (1752–1952)," Ph.D. diss., Univ. of Illinois, 1956, p. 110.

5. Critic on *Old Job* quoted by Claire McGlinchee, *The First Decade of the Boston Museum* (Boston: Bruce Humphries, 1940), p. 130. On the respectability of the neighborhoods near Barnum's museum, see Henderson. The popularity of moral reform melodramas, such as *The Drunkard* and *Uncle Tom's Cabin*, at working-class playhouses in Boston and New York also suggests that workers were attending museum theatres, where these kinds of plays were more frequent and generally enjoyed longer runs, in large numbers.

6. Critic quoted in Henderson, p. 80; circular letter (c. June 1850) reprinted in *Selected Letters of P. T. Barnum*, ed. A. H. Saxon (New York: Columbia Univ. Press, 1983), p. 43.

7. Stowe quoted in Oral S. Coad and E. Mims, *The American Stage* (New Haven, CT: Yale Univ. Press, 1929), p. 87. *History of the Boston Museum with a Description of the Alterations and Improvements* (Boston: Lincoln and Co., 1873), p. 5.

8. On revivalist workers, see Bruce Laurie, "Nothing on Compulsion: Life Styles of Philadelphia Artisans, 1820–1850," *Labor History*, 15 (Summer 1974), 337–66; and Laurie, *The Working People of Philadelphia, 1800–1860* (Philadelphia: Temple Univ. Press, 1980), pp. 35–53, 117–35, 140–46. On working-class institutes and temperance, see Stuart Blumin, *The Emergence of the Middle Class: Social Experience in the American City, 1760–*

1900 (Cambridge: Cambridge Univ. Press, 1989), 202–4; Jill Siegel Dodd, "The Working Classes and the Temperance Movement in Antebellum Boston," *Labor History*, 19 (Fall 1978), 510–31; and Sean Wilentz, *Chants Democratic: New York City and the Rise of the American Working Class, 1788–1850* (New York: Oxford Univ. Press, 1984), pp. 271–86, 306–25, 343–49. See also Herbert Gutman, "Protestantism and the American Labor Movement: The Christian Spirit in the Gilded Age," *AHR*, 72 (October 1966), 71–101; and Ian R. Tyrrel, *Sobering Up: From Temperance to Prohibition in Antebellum America, 1800–1860* (Westport, CT: Greenwood Press, 1979).

9. On nativism, see Dale Baum, "Know-Nothingism and the Republican Majority in Massachusetts: The Political Realignment of the 1850s," *Journal of American History*, 64 (1978), 959–86; and Eric Foner, *Free Soil, Free Labor, Free Men: The Ideology of the Republican Party before the Civil War* (New York: Oxford Univ. Press, 1970), pp. 226–60. Blumin, pp. 67–107, 192–230; and Paul Boyer, *Urban Masses and Moral Order in America, 1820–1920* (Cambridge, MA: Harvard Univ. Press, 1978), pp. 67–122, comment on the middle-class response to urban problems. Carrol Smith-Rosenberg, *Disorderly Conduct: Visions of Gender in Victorian America* (New York: Knopf, 1985), p. 86, notes that the middle class was far more conscious of maintaining its distinctiveness from the working class than envious of elite wealth and prerogative. David Leverenz, *Manhood and the American Renaissance* (Ithaca: Cornell Univ. Press, 1989), p. 78, echoes this insight.

10. Dickens quoted in *Dickens on America and the Americans*, ed. Michael Slater (Austin: Univ. of Texas Press, 1978), p. 151. Regarding bourgeois evangelicals' presence in the slums, Christine Stansell, *City of Women: Sex and Class in New York, 1789–1860* (Urbana: Univ. of Illinois Press, 1986), notes, "Their sympathy for the collectivity of women, real indeed in some cases, took the form of an imagined womanhood which had little to do with the actual difficulties of women and their working-class neighborhoods" (pp. 75, 64–75). See also Carroll S. Rosenberg, *Religion and the Rise of the American City: The New York City Mission Movement, 1812–1870* (Ithaca: Cornell Univ. Press, 1971).

11. *The Mother's Assistant* (July 1845) quoted by Karen Halttunen, *Confidence Men and Painted Women: A Study of Middle-Class Culture in America, 1830–1870* (New Haven, CT: Yale Univ. Press, 1982), p. 59. Sentimentalism did not necessarily support domesticity; see, for example,

Blanche G. Hersh, *The Slavery of Sex: Feminist-Abolitionists in America* (Champaign-Urbana: Univ. of Illinois Press, 1978). On sentimental culture, see Nancy Cott, *The Bonds of Womanhood: "Woman's Sphere" in New England, 1780–1835* (New Haven, CT: Yale Univ. Press, 1977); Mary Kelley, *Private Women, Public Stage: Literary Domesticity in Nineteenth-Century America* (New York: Oxford, 1984); Mary P. Ryan, *Cradle of the Middle Class: The Family in Oneida County, New York, 1790–1865* (Cambridge: Cambridge Univ. Press, 1981); Stansell; and Jane Tompkins, *Sensational Designs: The Cultural Work of American Fiction, 1790–1860* (New York: Oxford, 1985).

Mary P. Ryan concludes that domestic values undercut the possibility of fundamental social change: "The doctrine of domesticity sundered the more inclusive social organizations necessary to uphold human rights and to exercise human freedom. . . . Individual family units could be relied upon to secure the common welfare and maintain social order. No intermediary institutions, no combination of critical citizens, no collective action by the oppressed were necessary to secure social justice" (*The Empire of the Mother: American Writing about Domesticity* [New York: Institute for Research in History and Haworth Press, 1982], p. 140).

12. Kimball's contemporaries quoted by Charles A. Cummings in *Memoir of Moses Kimball* (Boston: David Clapp and Son, 1902), p. 10. Cummings' *Memoir* is the only biography of Kimball. On Barnum, see Harris and Saxon.

13. Peale quoted in Harris, p. 56. On Peale's museum, see Charles C. Sellers, *Mr. Peale's Museum: Charles Willson Peale and the First Popular Museum in Natural Science and Art* (New York: W. W. Norton, 1980).

14. *Tom Pop's First Visit to the Boston Museum with His Grandfather, Giving an Account of What He Saw and What He Thought* (Boston: [n.p.], 1848), pp. 6, 14.

15. Ibid., pp. 15, 1.

16. Howard M. Ticknor, "The Passing of the Boston Museum," *New England Magazine*, 28 (June 1903), 384.

17. The illustration is in *Gleason's Pictorial Drawing-Room Companion*, January 29, 1853; Barnum to Kimball, June 17, 1844, Barnum-Kimball Letters, Boston Atheneum; "Boston Museum, An Interesting Retrospect," reprinted in *The Golden Jubilee of William Warren: His Life and Reminiscences* ([Boston]: James Daly, 1918), p. 27, BPL. On the differences between working- and business-class home environments, see Blumin, pp. 138–91.

18. Vivaldi noted in Boston Museum program for December 26, 1845 (BPL Collection); "Lowell in Boston" noted by McGlinchee, p. 314.

19. Robert Bogdan, *Freak Show: Presenting Human Oddities for Amusement and Profit* (Chicago: Univ. of Chicago Press, 1988), p. 97. Saxon, pp. 126–28, presents excerpts from Barnum's script for Stratton.

20. William K. Northall, *Before and Behind the Curtain, or Fifteen Years' Observations among the Theatres of New York* (New York: W. F. Burgess, 1851), p. 20; James Watson Webb of the *Courier and Enquirer* quoted in Harris, p. 93; and Barnum to Kimball, p. 38, in *Letters*.

21. On the aesthetics of sentimentality, see Gregg Camfield, "The Moral Aesthetics of Sentimentality: A Missing Key to *Uncle Tom's Cabin,*" Nineteenth-Century Literature, 43 (December 1988), 319–45; and Philip Fisher, *Hard Facts: Setting and Form in the American Novel* (New York: Oxford Univ. Press, 1985).

22. Bogdan, p. 97. Regarding Barnum's exotic freaks, see pp. 97–103 in Saxon. Skinner in Young, *Documents of American Theatre History: Famous American Playhouses, 1716–1899* (Chicago: American Library Assn., 1973), p. 105.

23. Porte, "In the Hands of an Angry God: Religious Terror in Gothic Fiction," in *The Gothic Imagination: Essays in Dark Romanticism*, ed. G. R. Thompson (Pullman: Washington Univ. Press, 1974), pp. 42–64. Gothic freaks and exhibits functioned like trickster figures in the mythology of many cultures; socially marginal, the freak, like the trickster, could induce liminality through his or her powers of contamination. See Mary Douglas, *Purity and Danger: An Analysis of the Concepts of Pollution and Taboo* (New York: Praeger, 1966), p. 102. Halttunen uses Douglas to understand the threat of the confidence man in antebellum cities, pp. 24–32.

24. Reporter quoted in Henneke, p. 84; spectators and journalist quoted in Vera Brodsky Lawrence, *Strong on Music: The New York Music Scene in the Days of George Templeton Strong* (New York: Oxford Univ. Press, 1988), p. 130. See also Claudia Johnson, "That Guilty Third Tier: Prostitution in Nineteenth-Century American Theatres," *Victorian America*, ed. Daniel Walker Howe (Philadelphia: Univ. of Pennsylvania Press, 1976), pp. 111–20; and Stansell, pp. 169–92, who points out that occasional prostitution among young working-class women at midcentury probably accounted for more solicitation than that from prostitutes. I am also indebted to Rosemarie K. Bank, "Hustlers in the House: The Bowery Theatre as a Mode of Historical Information," *The American Stage: Social and*

Economic Issues from the Colonial Period to the Present, ed. Ron Engle and Tice Miller (Cambridge: Cambridge Univ. Press, 1992). As Bank notes, solicitation occurred in most neighborhoods near theatres and in all parts of the playhouse, not just in the "guilty third tier."

25. Ticknor, "The Passing of the Boston Museum," p. 385; 1846 architectural plan in "The History of the Boston Museum" by Ticknor included in *The Golden Jubilee of William Warren,* p. 10.

26. *Gleason's Pictorial Drawing-Room Companion,* January 29, 1853; *Drunkard* program in Joseph N. Ireland, *Extra-Illustrated Records of the New York Stage,* 1867 (MS, HTC), vol. 2, pt. 13, p. 163.

27. For Kimball's repertoire, see McGlinchee; for Barnum's, see Odell, vols. 5, 6. Also useful is *American Theatre Companies, 1749–1887,* ed. Weldon Durham (Westport, CT: Greenwood Press, 1986), pp. 38–44, 68–75. Northall, p. 158. Like the protocapitalist stars, Barnum exploited playwrights outrageously. Journeyman actor and playwright Harry Watkins reported in his diary that, following a successful play of his at Barnum's museum in 1858, the impresario hired him to adapt "a five act play in eight days" from a popular novel. "I am working myself to death here," said Watkins (Maude and Otis Skinner, *One Man in His Time: The Adventures of H. Watkins, Strolling Player, 1845–1863, From His Journal* [Philadelphia: Univ. of Pennsylvania Press, 1938], p. 228).

28. Sellers, p. 308, on Peale's Museum; Charles Durang, *History of the Philadelphia Stage between the Years 1749–1855,* ed. Westcott Thompson, 7 vols. (1868; rpt., Ann Arbor, MI: University Microfilms [n.d.]), 3: 331, on Barnum's *Drunkard* in Philadelphia; and Ireland, vol. 2, pt. 13, p. 163, on the City Museum.

29. See Odell, 5: 596, for the Brooklyn Museum program.

30. Thomas Haskell, "Capitalism and the Origins of the Humanitarian Sensibility," *AHR,* 90 (April–June 1985), 339–61, 547–66.

31. A promptbook copy of Conway's adaptation may be found in the General Theatre Collection, Hoblitzelle Library, University of Texas at Austin. This promptbook, used in a Boston Museum production in 1876, is incomplete: missing are nearly all of scenes 3 through 7 of Conway's act 3. In place of these five short scenes, I rely on a Boston Museum program for *Uncle Tom's Cabin* dated December 7, 1852 (Boston Museum Collection, BPL). It is clear from the detailed descriptions of scenes in this program that the 1876 MS was not substantially altered from Conway's version as performed in the 1850s, except for those five scenes. Conway also did an adaptation of

Stowe's novel, *Dred, A Tale of the Great Dismal Swamp.* For a comparison between Conway's adaptation and George L. Aiken's *Uncle Tom's Cabin,* see my "Out of the Kitchen and into the Marketplace: Normalizing *Uncle Tom's Cabin* for the Antebellum Stage," *Journal of American Drama and Theatre,* 3 (Winter 1991), 5–28.

The Drunkard, or The Fallen Saved is in *Dramas from the American Theatre, 1762–1909,* ed. Richard Moody (Boston: Houghton, Mifflin, 1966), pp. 277–308. For Charles H. Saunders, *Rosina Meadows, the Village Maid, or Temptations Unveiled,* consult the series English and American Drama of the Nineteenth Century ([185-]; rpt., New York: Readex Microprint, 1967), which features a copy of a promptbook of the play based on the script as published by W. V. Spencer (Spencer's Boston Theatre, no. 11).

Concerning the popularity of these shows, see McGlinchee; Odell, vols. 5, 6; and Robert C. Toll, *Blacking Up: The Minstrel Show in Nineteenth-Century America* (New York: Oxford Univ. Press, 1974), 90–93.

32. Haskell, pp. 556, 561.

33. Ibid., p. 560.

34. As business-class audiences began going to minstrel shows in the 1850s, the norm against which minstrel characters were judged became the bourgeois man of principle. See Toll, pp. 65–103.

35. See especially Elizabeth Ammons, "Heroines in *Uncle Tom's Cabin,*" in *Critical Essays on Harriet Beecher Stowe,* ed. Elizabeth Ammons (Boston: G. K. Hall, 1980), pp. 152–65. Ammons's views have been widely accepted by other Stowe scholars.

36. Quoted in the preface to *The Drunkard, or The Fallen Saved,* Boston Museum Edition of American Acting Dramas, no. 1 (Boston: Jones's Publishing House, 1847).

37. Janis Stout, *Sodoms in Eden: The City in American Fiction before 1860* (Westport, CT: Greenwood Press, 1976), pp. 26, 21–42. See also David S. Reynolds, *Beneath the American Renaissance: The Subversive Imagination in the Age of Emerson and Melville* (New York: Knopf, 1988); and Stansell, especially on the literature of urban prostitution, pp. 171–92.

38. Quotations in Boyer, p. 72; and Stanley K. Schultz, *The Culture Factory: Boston Public Schools, 1789–1860* (New York: Oxford Univ. Press, 1973), pp. 229, 236. On the antebellum response to the Irish, see also Oscar Handlin, *Boston's Immigrants: A Study in Acculturation* (Cambridge, MA: Harvard Univ. Press, 1959); and Dale T. Knobel, *Paddy and the Republic: Eth-*

nicity and Nationality in Antebellum America (Middletown, CT: Wesleyan Univ. Press, 1986).

39. See Charles Glaab and Theodore A. Brown, *A History of Urban America* (New York: Macmillan, 1967); Rosenberg; Schultz; Handlin; Edward K. Spann, *The New Metropolis: New York City, 1840–1857* (New York: Columbia Univ. Press, 1981); and Sam Bass Warner, *The Urban Wilderness: A History of the American City* (New York: Harper, 1972), on the urban crisis at midcentury.

40. Norman H. Clark, *Deliver Us from Evil: An Interpretation of American Prohibition* (New York: W. W. Norton, 1976), treats nineteenth-century alcoholism as a response to modernization; and William Rorabaugh, *The Alcoholic Republic* (New York: Oxford Univ. Press, 1979), finds "significant underlying anxiety" (p. 146) as the cause of excessive drinking before the Civil War. On prostitution as a "choice" for urban women, see Stansell, pp. 171–92. In a review of Rorabaugh's book, Robert Hampel ("Review Essay: The Contexts of Antebellum Reform," *American Quarterly*, 33 [Spring 1981]) notes that another theory of alcoholism, which fits Rorabaugh's facts, "stresses the need of people with low inhibitions to have some feeling of personal power" (p. 96).

41. Haskell, p. 556.

42. Elder Olsen quoted in Angus Fletcher, *Allegory: The Theory of a Symbolic Mode* (Ithaca: Cornell Univ. Press, 1964), p. 307. On typological literature and its differences from nineteenth-century realism, see Jane Tompkins, "Sentimental Power: *Uncle Tom's Cabin* and the Politics of Literary History," in Tompkins, *Sensational Designs*, pp. 126–41.

43. Northrop Frye, *The Anatomy of Criticism: Four Essays* (Princeton: Princeton Univ. Press, 1957), p. 90; Northall, p. 167.

44. Fletcher, p. 302.

45. Walter M. Leman, *Memories of an Old Actor* (San Francisco: A. Roman Co., 1886), p. 223; Maude and Otis Skinner, pp. 71, 82.

46. Alfred Habegger, *Gender, Fantasy, and Realism in American Culture* (New York: Columbia Univ. Press, 1982), pp. 111–12. Michael Denning uses Habegger's insights on allegory to stress the powerlessness of antebellum working-class readers in *Mechanic Accents: Dime Novels and Working-Class Culture in America* (London: Verso, 1987), pp. 72–74. Denning's discussion of moderate-income and working-class readers' fondness for allegorical novels suggests that the print culture of these antebellum readers

may have helped to shape the predominately oral culture of their melodramatic theatregoing. On the reifying tendencies of antebellum northern culture, see Anne Norton, *Alternative Americas: A Reading of Antebellum Political Culture* (Chicago: Univ. of Chicago Press, 1986), pp. 33–63.

47. Lewis O. Saum, *The Popular Mood of Pre–Civil War America*, Contributions in American Studies, no. 46 (Westport, CT: Greenwood, 1980), p. 65. On revivalism, see William G. McLoughlin, *Revivals, Awakenings, and Reform: An Essay on Religion and Social Change in America, 1607–1977* (Chicago: Univ. of Chicago Press, 1978); and Wiebe, *The Opening of American Society*, pp. 273–82. In *Revivalism and Cultural Change: Christianity, Nation Building and the Market in the Nineteenth-Century United States* (Chicago: Univ. of Chicago Press, 1989), George Thomas links market penetration and Republican voting to revivalism.

48. R. Laurence Moore, "Religion, Secularization, and the Shaping of the Culture Industry in Antebellum America," *American Quarterly*, 41 (June 1989), p. 229. Charles Grandison Finney, "Sinners Bound to Change Their Own Hearts," in *Notions of the Americans, 1820–1860*, ed. David Grimsted (New York: George Braziller, 1970), p. 82.

49. Wiebe, p. 276.

50. Northall, p. 166.

51. Peter Buckley, "To the Opera House: Culture and Society in New York City, 1820–1860," Ph.D. diss., SUNY, Stony Brook, 1984, p. 495.

7. "How Her Blood Tells"

1. *Spirit of the Times* (October 26, 1861), p. 28.

2. It is likely that the French word *parquet* came to the American theatre via New Orleans. In his travels to New Orleans in 1833, Joseph Holt Ingraham reported in *The Southwest* (2 vols. [New York: Harper, 1835]) his visit to the American theatre:

> We passed across the first lobby, down a narrow aisle, opened through the centre of the boxes into the pit, or *parquette*, as it is here termed, which is considered the most eligible and fashionable part of the house. This is rather reversing the order of things as found with us at the North. The pews, or slips—for the internal arrangements were precisely like those of a church—were cushioned with crimson materials. (1: 223)

Critics and reporters used "parquette" and "parquet" interchangeably in the antebellum era.

3. *Ballou's Pictorial* quoted by Ben Graf Henneke, "The Playgoer in America (1752–1952)," Ph.D. diss., Univ. of Illinois, 1956, p. 15; playbill of the Boston Theatre in Eugene Tompkins and Quincy Kilby, *The History of the Boston Theatre, 1854–1901* (Cambridge, MA: Houghton, Mifflin, 1908), p. 15. Durham, "Boston Theatre Stock Company," in *American Theatre Companies, 1749–1887*, ed. Weldon Durham (Westport, CT: Greenwood Press, 1986), p. 94.

4. *Spirit of the Times* (November 20, 1856), p. 492; and (November 14, 1857), p. 390.

5. *Frank Leslie's Illustrated Newspaper* (December 18, 1858), p. 41. On Wallack's, see Rosemarie K. Bank, "Wallack's Theatre Company," in *American Theatre Companies, 1749–1887*, pp. 511–19; and Cecil D. Jones, "The Politics and Practices of Wallack's Theatre, 1852–1888," Ph.D. diss., Univ. of Illinois, 1959.

6. All quotations from the *Spirit of the Times*: (October 27, 1866), p. 144; (June 13, 1868), p. 308; (September 21, 1861), p. 148; and (November 2, 1872), p. 192.

7. On Daly's early theatres, see Marvin Felheim, *The Theatre of Augustin Daly* (Cambridge, MA: Harvard Univ. Press, 1956), pp. 1–13; and the two entries in *Documents of American Theatre History: Famous American Playhouses, 1716–1899*, pp. 19–201, 204–5; *Tribune* quotation on p. 204. Box 7 of the Augustin Daly file in the Brander Matthews Collection, Columbia University, contains a list of the auditorium furnishings and decorations of Daly's 1873 theatre.

8. On Daly's early career, see Albert Asermely, "Daly's Initial Decade in the American Theatre, 1860–1869," Ph.D. diss., CUNY, 1972; and Felheim, pp. 2–10. January 15, 1865, Joseph and Augustin Daly Correspondence, Robinson Locke Collection, NYPL.

9. The pseudonymous Nym Crinkle (critic A. C. Wheeler) commented on the financial success of *Gaslight*, clipping in Daly Scrapbook 143, Robinson Locke Collection, NYPL, p. 26. Reviewer for the *Leader* quoted by Asermely, p. 129. Joseph Daly, *Life of Augustin Daly* (New York: Macmillan, 1917), p. 77. In celebrating his brother's success, Joseph was surreptitiously praising himself since he probably played a part in the writing of *Gaslight*. As Felheim notes, "One can, on the basis of their disclosures [in letters

written to each other], discover that as long as Augustin lived, Joseph's part in their joint literary labors was great, and often more than halfway. Not only newspaper articles, but the adaptations of plays, writing of plays, composition of speeches, all went through Joseph's hands—without public acknowledgment" (p. 9). For the text of *Gaslight*, see *American Melodrama*, ed. Daniel Gerould (New York: Performing Arts Publications, 1983), pp. 135–81.

10. Joseph Daly, p. 88; Clara Morris, *Life on the Stage: My Personal Experience and Recollections* (New York: McClure, Phillips, and Co., 1902), p. 376. September 12, 1874, Joseph and Augustin Daly Correspondence.

11. Clara Morris, *Stage Confidences: Talks about Players and Play Acting* (Boston: Lothrop, 1902), p. 271; Winter quoted in Felheim, p. 30; John Rankin Towse, *Sixty Years of the Theatre: An Old Critic's Memories* (New York: Funk and Wagnall's, 1916), p. 121; Otis Skinner, *Footlights and Spotlights: Recollections of My Life on the Stage* (1923; rpt., Westport, CT: Greenwood Press, 1972), pp. 135, 136.

12. Morris, *Stage Confidences*, p. 271; Skinner, pp. 134–35. Daly's relations with the press were reprehensible even by the low standards of the Gilded Age. In 1874 he used invented quotations from newspaper reviews to advertise his production of *Oliver Twist* and was roundly condemned for his "Theatrical Charlatanism" by the *Dramatic News* (Felheim, p. 12).

13. Daly Correspondence, August 27, 1873, and July 2, 1874.

14. Mrs. G. H. Gilbert's *Stage Reminiscences* quoted in Felheim, p. 10; Morris, *Stage Confidences*, p. 271.

15. On midcentury business-class formation, see Stuart Blumin, *The Emergence of the Middle Class: Social Experience in the American City, 1760–1900* (Cambridge: Cambridge Univ. Press, 1989); and Michael B. Katz, Michael J. Doucet, and Mark J. Stern, *The Social Organization of Early Industrial Capitalism* (Cambridge, MA: Harvard Univ. Press, 1982).

16. See Karen Halttunen, *Confidence Men and Painted Women: A Study of Middle-Class Culture in America, 1830–1870* (New Haven: Yale Univ. Press, 1982); and John F. Kasson, *Rudeness and Civility: Manners in Nineteenth-Century Urban America* (New York: Hill and Wang, 1990). Kasson, p. 7.

17. For general studies of Boucicault, see Robert Hogan, *Dion Boucicault* (New York: Twayne, 1969); and Townsend Walsh, *The Career of Dion Boucicault* (New York: Dunlap Society, 1915).

18. William Winter, "Dion Boucicault: The Master of the Revels," *Saturday Evening Post* (May 18, 1907), p. 24; and Nym Crinkle [A. C. Wheeler] in the Townsend Walsh Collection, NYPL.

19. *The Poor of New York* in Gerould, *American Melodrama*, pp. 31–74. *New York Times* (December 10, 1857), p. 4; Boucicault quoted by Daniel Gerould, "The Americanization of Melodrama," in *American Melodrama*, p. 11.

20. *The Colleen Bawn* in *Selected Plays of Dion Boucicault*, ed. Andrew Parkin, Irish Drama Selections, no. 4 (Washington, DC: Catholic Univ. Press, 1987), pp. 191–255. *New York Times* (March 31, 1860), p. 8; New York *Tribune* (March 30, 1860), p. 8. Boucicault had already written two acts of *The Colleen Bawn* for Mr. and Mrs. Barney Williams, two Irish-American stars who had requested a piece from his pen, but he finished it quickly for the opportunity of producing it at Laura Keene's business-class theatre.

21. See the *Tribune* review for Boucicault's curtain speech. Boucicault's nervousness is evident as well in a program note, which announced: "Ireland, so rich in scenery, so full of romance, the warm touch of nature, has never until now been opened by the dramatist. Irish dramas have hitherto been exaggerated farces representing low life or scenes of abject servitude and suffering. Such is not a true picture of Irish society" (quoted in Walsh, p. 74).

22. See J. H. Amherst, *Ireland as It Is*, Acting Edition, no. 113 (New York: Samuel French, 1864). Several comedies written for the minor Irish-American star Barney Williams also included scenes of poverty and pathos, including *Shandy Maguire, or The Bould Boy of the Mountain*, Acting Edition, no. 143 (New York: Samuel French, [n.d.]); *Irish Assurance and Yankee Modesty* (1864; rpt., New York: Readex Microprint, 1967); and *Ireland and America, or Scenes in Both* (1856; rpt., New York: Readex Microprint, 1967), all by James S. Pilgrim. Regarding the politics of these plays, see my "The Cultural Politics of 'Paddy' on the Midcentury American Stage," *Studies in Popular Culture*, 10 (1987), 1–13; also Dale T. Knobel, *Paddy and the Republic: Ethnicity and Nationality in Antebellum America* (Middletown, CT: Wesleyan Univ. Press, 1986); and Kerby A. Miller, *Emigrants and Exiles: Ireland and the Irish Exodus to North America* (New York: Oxford Univ. Press, 1985), pp. 280–344.

23. Some of the other sensation melodramas popular at bourgeois theatres during this two-decade period include *The Life of an Actress, Pauvrette,*

Jessie Brown, or the Relief of Lucknow, The Octoroon, or Life in Louisiana, The Long Strike, After Dark: A Tale of London Life, Formosa, or the Railroad to Ruin, and *Flying Scud,* all by Boucicault; *A Flash of Lightning, Man and Wife,* and *Horizon,* by Daly; and *The Sea of Ice* (anonymous); *East Lynne,* by Tayleure; *Rosedale, or The Rifleman's Ball,* by Wallack; and *Across the Continent, or Scenes from New York Life and the Pacific Railroad,* by McCloskey.

24. Romantic love across class lines, which occurs as well in Boucicault's *The Octoroon,* also gives sentimental flexibility to the class divide. Boucicault, however, is not altogether consistent in his division of classes through language. When Anne Chute becomes excited near the end of the play, her speech takes on some of the characteristics of Eily's brogue. It may be that Boucicault was attempting to show through this that language would not be an insuperable barrier to Eily's marriage to Hardress. Yet language relates to gender as well as class in these plays. As I shall later argue, sensation melodrama characterizes women as more liminal and more natural than men. Anne Chute's broguelike speech at the end of the play, natural enough in a "changeable" woman, would not have fit in the mouth of a male character. Since men are the dominant carriers of class in these plays, Anne's outburst does not effectively alter the language/class alignment in *The Colleen Bawn.*

25. Although there are no true bourgeoisie in *The Colleen Bawn,* the business-class audience would have identified the Cregans as "one of us," since Hardress and his mother share the bourgeois values of self-control and rationality and they are attempting to preserve their respectability in the midst of hard times. On Boucicault's Irish plays, see David Krause, *The Profane Book of Irish Comedy* (Ithaca: Cornell Univ. Press, 1982), pp. 181–94.

26. On Freedley's books, see Rush Welter, *The Mind of America, 1820–1860* (New York: Columbia Univ. Press, 1975), pp. 160–62; Richard Sennett, *The Fall of Public Man: On the Social Psychology of Capitalism* (New York: Random House, 1976), pp. 138–39.

27. See Blumin, pp. 67–106, 149–86, 275–84. On the historical dynamics within the business world which created this new business class, see Alfred Chandler, *The Visible Hand: The Managerial Revolution in American Business* (Cambridge, MA: Belknap Press, 1977), pp. 50–133.

28. On the fear of extravagance among moderate-income families, see Blumin, pp. 185–86. Mary P. Ryan, *Cradle of the Middle Class: The Family in Oneida County, New York, 1790–1865* (Cambridge: Cambridge Univ.

Press, 1981), links the formation of a distinctive middle class to specific family practices, including the inculcation of respectability and prudence in the young. Blumin on "businessmen in training" and the "axis of respectability," pp. 76, 238. Welter notes that both political parties "shared the national predisposition to increase individual wealth by any acceptable means even if it meant sacrificing some of the scruples of the past" (p. 129). See also Eric Foner, *Free Soil, Free Labor, Free Men: The Ideology of the Republican Party before the Civil War* (New York: Oxford Univ. Press, 1970). Regarding the urban elite, see Frederic Cople Jaher, *The Urban Establishment: Upper Strata in Boston, New York, Charleston, Chicago, and Los Angeles* (Urbana: Univ. of Illinois Press, 1982), pp. 44–87, 173–250, 336–99. In Jaher's account, the midcentury elite of Boston and New York remained relatively open to arrivistes in part because they espoused the same bourgeois values as the rest of the business class.

29. Robert H. Wiebe, *The Segmented Society: An Introduction to the Meaning of America* (New York: Oxford Univ. Press, 1975), p. 66. Knobel, pp. 100, 68–103. Blumin concludes that "the intensification of ethnic differentiation and identification reinforced class boundaries" (p. 251).

30. Appleton quoted in Blumin, p. 108. See also Carl Siracusa, *A Mechanical People: Perceptions of the Industrial Order in Massachusetts* (Middletown, CT: Wesleyan Univ. Press, 1986), pp. 79–80, on "the image of the respectable worker." Lincoln quoted in Foner, p. 23. Wiebe, p. 323.

31. Gynecologist quoted in David G. Pugh, *Sons of Liberty: The Masculine Mind in Nineteenth-Century America* (Westport, CT: Greenwood Press, 1983), p. 72. John Frost, *Daring and Heroic Deeds of American Women* (Philadelphia: J. W. Bradley, 1854), p. iv. On the naturalization of women in the antebellum North, see Anne Norton, *Alternative Americas: A Reading of Antebellum Political Culture* (Chicago: Univ. of Chicago Press, 1986), pp. 55–58.

32. *Harper's* quoted in Blumin, p. 183. On the construction of masculinity in bourgeois culture, see Kasson; and David Leverenz, *Manhood and the American Renaissance* (Ithaca: Cornell Univ. Press, 1989), pp. 72–90.

33. Snorkey's line in the scene, "And these are the women who ain't to have a vote!" has provoked some interesting misinterpretation. Albert Asermely, for example, who reads *Gaslight* as twentieth-century liberalism, believes the play "shouts a cry for women's suffrage" (p. 141). The immediate context of the speech and the larger politics of the play, however, argue against this interpretation. Placed at the end of a very tense scene, Snorkey's line

is clearly intended as a throwaway remark to spark a laugh. Further, because it is said by the comic and not by the hero or heroine, it carries less dramatic weight. While some in the audience may have mused that such courageous women should indeed have more political power, others must have felt that such natural women had plenty of power already without the vote. Historically, the bourgeois practice of naturalizing women took them out of the public sphere and retarded the suffrage movement.

Courageous heroines were fairly common in English and American melodramas after 1850. According to Lyn Stiefel Hill, "Heroes, Heroines, and Villains in English and American Melodrama, 1850–1900," Ph.D. diss., CUNY, 1981: "Stage heroines who took an active part in extricating themselves from mental or physical pain were not viewed as any less feminine than their more passive counterparts" (p. 122). Hill's generalizations are based on fifty-four melodramas, mostly popular with bourgeois audiences.

34. According to Hill, the vacillating and occasionally even dissipated and cowardly hero was common in melodrama between 1850 and 1900 (pp. 20–76).

35. Hill points out that the traditional villain became less important in the plots of melodrama as the century wore on; indeed, some melodramas without villains gained popularity in the last quarter of the century (pp. 165–244).

36. New York *Tribune* (March 30, 1860), p. 8; *Herald* review quoted in Odell, *Annals of the New York Stage*, 7: 22; *New York Times* (December 10, 1857), p. 4. Walsh notes that "Lester Wallack . . . became the prime favorite of the town through his popular performance of Tom Badger" (p. 53).

37. For discussions of the well-made play, see Neil C. Arvin, *Eugène Scribe and the French Theatre, 1815–1860* (Cambridge, MA: Harvard Univ. Press, 1924); John Russell Taylor, *The Rise and Fall of the Well-Made Play* (New York: Hill and Wang, 1967); and Stephen S. Stanton, introduction, *Camille and Other Plays*, ed. Stephen S. Stanton (New York: Hill and Wang, 1957). Unfortunately, none of these critics makes clear, formal distinctions between the well-made play and the traditional melodrama.

38. Stephen Knight, *Form and Ideology in Crime Fiction* (Bloomington: Indiana Univ. Press, 1980), p. 44. See also John G. Cawelti, *Adventure, Mystery, and Romance: Formula Stories as Art and Popular Culture* (Chicago: Univ. of Chicago Press, 1976), pp. 80–105.

39. Arvin, p. 225.

40. Reviews from the *Citizen* (August 24, 1867), p. 8, and the *Express* (May 23, 1866), p. 2, both quoted in Asermely, pp. 148, 157.

41. Dion Boucicault, "The Art of Dramatic Composition," [1878], published posthumously by Arthur Edwin Krows (New York: Columbia Univ. Press, 1915), p. 1; Boucicault, "The Art of Acting," [1882], published posthumously (New York: Columbia Univ. Press, 1926), p. 29; "The Art of Dramatic Composition," pp. 5, 8, 10. Boucicault's dramatic composition article was apparently intended for the *North American Review*, but he never completed it. Regarding Boucicault and Scribe, see also Samira Basta, "The French Influence on Dion Boucicault's Sensation Drama," in *Literary Interrelations: Ireland, England, and the World*, ed. Wolfgang and Heinz Kosok, 3 vols. (Tübingen: G. Narr Verlag, 1987), 2: 199–207.

42. Kasson, pp. 54, 60.

43. Ibid., pp. 62, 165.

44. Ibid., pp. 115, 116–17. Kasson notes that the injunction to "mind your own business" propagated "an ideal of conduct that bound together propriety, privacy, and property" (p. 117). Sensation melodrama worshipped this same trinity.

45. Ibid., p. 150.

8. "Built to Endure"

1. John Higham, *From Boundlessness to Consolidation: The Transformation of American Culture, 1848–1860* (Ann Arbor, MI: William L. Clements Library, 1969), pp. 15–16.

2. See Bryan D. Palmer, "Social Formation and Class Formation in North America, 1800–1900," in *Proletarianization and Family History*, ed. David Levine (New York: Academic Press, 1984), pp. 254–65, for an overview of these processes in the 1850–80 period. The *New York Times* quotation and the percentages of workers employed in manufacturing are on pp. 257, 259, and 257 in Palmer. Regarding the origins and ideology of the Republican party, see Eric Foner, *Free Soil, Free Labor, Free Men: The Ideology of the Republican Party before the Civil War* (New York: Oxford Univ. Press, 1970). On the control of politics by the wealthy on the local level, see Amy Beth Bridges, "Another Look at Plutocracy and Politics in Antebellum New York City," *Political Science Quarterly*, 97 (Spring 1982), 57–71.

3. See Paul Boyer, *Urban Masses and Moral Order in America, 1820–1920* (Cambridge, MA: Harvard Univ. Press, 1978), pp. 85–161. Quotations in Boyer, pp. 92, 96. See also M. J. Heale, "From City Fathers to Social Critics:

Humanitarianism and Government in New York, 1790–1860," *Journal of American History*, 63 (June 1976), 29–41.

4. Adrian Cook, *The Armies of the Streets: The New York City Draft Riots of 1863* (Lexington: Univ. of Kentucky Press, 1974). Stoddard quoted in Paul A. Gilje, *The Road to Mobocracy: Popular Disorder in New York City, 1763–1834* (Chapel Hill: Univ. of North Carolina Press, 1987), pp. 285, 286.

5. Pintard quoted in Frederick Cople Jaher, *The Urban Establishment: Upper Strata in Boston, New York, Charleston, Chicago, and Los Angeles* (Urbana: Univ. of Illinois Press, 1982), p. 236. Olmsted and Brace quoted in Lawrence Levine, *Highbrow/Lowbrow: The Emergence of Cultural Hierarchy in America* (Cambridge, MA: Harvard Univ. Press, 1988), pp. 202, 203.

6. Strong and Henry quoted in Levine, pp. 181, 156.

7. See Levine, pp. 83–168, 227.

8. Daly's review in the New York *Sun* (February 18, 1867), p. 4. By 1886, Daly was more interested in sacralizing the theatre than elevating the masses. "The purification of the temple of drama has been so thoroughly effected that the worthiest people find it worthy of their affectionate regard. From the topmost gallery down, respectability reigns," he wrote in "The American Dramatist," *North American Review*, 142 (May 1886), 491.

9. Winter and Clapp quoted in Tice Miller, *Bohemians and Critics: American Theatre Criticism in the Nineteenth Century* (Metuchen, NJ: Scarecrow Press, 1981), pp. 85, 98, 30. On the "bohemian" critics of the late 1850s, see Miller, pp. 1–69.

10. Mari Kathleen Fielder, "New Chestnut Street Theatre Stock Company (1863–80)," in *American Theatre Companies, 1749–1887*, ed. Weldon Durham (Westport, CT: Greenwood Press, 1986), p. 211.

11. New York *World* cited by Charles H. Shattuck, *Shakespeare on the American Stage: From the Hallams to Edwin Booth* (Washington, DC: Folger Shakespeare Library, 1976), pp. 133–34. Quotation from the *New York Times* (September 7, 1865) review of Booth's Theatre in *Documents of American Theater History: Famous American Playhouses, 1716–1899*, ed. William C. Young (Chicago: American Library Assn., 1973), 1: 198. Winter quoted in Shattuck, p. 137.

12. *Evening Journal* quoted in Odell, 7: 470. For an overview of critical opinion on Keene's acting, see *Famous Actors and Actresses of the New York*

Stage, ed. William C. Young, 2 vols. (New York: R. R. Bowker, 1975), 2: 621–25.

13. Martin's reminiscence, published in 1886, quoted in *Famous Actors and Actresses of the American Stage*, 2: 981; *New York Times* (May 7, 1868), p. 4, and (May 8, 1868), p. 4.

14. *Herald* quoted in Odell, 7: 30; *Atlantic Monthly* in *Famous Actors and Actresses of the New York Stage*, 1: 588; *Times* in Odell, 8: 428.

15. George William Curtis, "Editor's Easy Chair," *Harper's New Monthly Magazine* (December 1863), 131–33. See Eleanor Ruggles, *Prince of Players: Edwin Booth* (New York: Norton, 1953), for an example of a history that does little to dispel the bourgeois myth of the great tragedian. Daniel J. Watermeier, ed., *Edwin Booth's Performances: The Mary Isabella Stone Commentaries* (Ann Arbor: UMI Research Press, 1990), and Charles Shattuck, in his *Shakespeare on the American Stage* and especially his earlier *The Hamlet of Edwin Booth* (Urbana: Univ. of Illinois Press, 1969), are considerably more balanced.

16. The reviews from the *Tribune* and the *Albion* quoted extensively in Odell, 7: 640, 641. The 1870 review in Shattuck, *The Hamlet of Edwin Booth*, p. 70.

17. See William D. Coder, "A History of the Philadelphia Theatre, 1856–1878," Ph.D. diss., Univ. of Pennsylvania, 1936, p. 142, for total performances of plays by author in Philadelphia. On the declining popularity of Shakespeare, compare Coder's figures to those cited by David Grimsted, *Melodrama Unveiled: American Theater and Culture, 1800–1850* (Chicago: Univ. of Chicago Press, 1968), in table 5, "Feature Plays, 1831–51," and table 6, "Afterpieces, 1831–51," pp. 254–56. Among the most popular 46 plays in Philadelphia from 1831 to 1851, the plays of Shakespeare had 644 performances and the three most popular contemporary playwrights only 190, 185, and 151. E. C. Stedman quoted by Shattuck, *The Hamlet of Edwin Booth*, p. 63.

18. *The Seven Sisters* quotation in Odell, 7: 311; *Spirit of the Times* review in Laurence Senelick, *The Age and Stage of George L. Fox, 1825–1877* (Hanover, NH: Univ. Press of New England, 1988), p. 143.

19. Quotations cited by Shattuck, *The Hamlet of Edwin Booth*, pp. 67, 60.

20. *Spirit of the Times* (February 18, 1854), p. 9; Henneke, "The Playgoer in America," p. 161; *Spirit of the Times* (September 26, 1863), p. 64; quoted in Henneke, p. 180; Olive Logan, *Before the Footlights and Behind the Scenes* (Philadelphia: Parmelee, 1870), p. 385. Kasson, in *Rudeness and*

Civility, notes that "salvos against rudeness" were discharged "most steadily in the playbills of minstrel theatres in the 1850s, '60s, and '70s" (p. 240) and cites several examples.

21. *Frank Leslie's Illustrated Newspaper* (March 1, 1856), p. 186; "Letter from Acorn," *Spirit of the Times* (April 24, 1868), p. 121.

22. *The Autobiography of Joseph Jefferson*, ed. Alan Downer (1890; rpt., Cambridge, MA: Belknap Press, 1964), pp. 42, 318–19.

23. *Black Crook* estimate in Odell, 8: 152.

24. On the number of actors in the Arch Street and Boston Theatre companies, see *American Theatre Companies*, pp. 62, 99–102. Davidge, *Footlight Flashes*, p. 238. "Slave market" quotation in John W. Frick, *New York's First Theatrical Center: The Rialto at Union Square* (Ann Arbor, MI: UMI Research Press, 1985), p. 122.

25. New York *Tribune* (July 12, 1864), p. 6.

26. Ibid.

27. *New York Times* (July 22, 1864), p. 8.

28. *New York Times* (August 1, 1864), p. 4.

29. *New York Times* (June 18, 1866), p. 4. The letter writer, who signed himself "Dramaticus" in good republican fashion, noted as well that actors fired in this way by the manager were also blacklisted. But it is difficult to know how widespread such a practice actually was. Davidge, whom one might suppose would have been a target, continued to work regularly despite his union activities. The evidence that Davidge was "Dramaticus" is wholly stylistic: both the letter and his book, *Footlight Flashes* (1866), are written in an orotund style displaying an eighteenth-century concern for the niceties of public discourse.

30. *New York Times* (August 19, 1864), p. 4.

31. See Frick, passim.

32. Davidge, p. 216.

33. New York *Herald* (September 6, 1859) quoted in *Documents of American Theater History*, p. 122; cited by Senelick, p. 103.

34. See G. L. Aiken, *Orion, the Gold Beater, or True Hearts and False*, MS, Players Library, New York [1857]; and John Brougham, *The Gun-Maker of Moscow*, French's Standard Drama, Acting Edition, no. 164 (New York: Samuel French, [n.d.]). Other plays in this genre included *Franklin* and *The Red Mask, or The Wolf of Lithuania* by John Brougham and *The Hidden Hand* by Robert Jones. Working-class passivity was pervasive during the

1860s throughout the industrializing West. See Eric J. Hobsbawm, *The Age of Capital, 1848–1875* (New York: Scribner's, 1979), pp. 228–52. On the other hand, another minor genre—plays of crime and punishment—may have enhanced images of working-class deviance during this period, but at a price. Spin-offs primarily of *Rookwood* by Nathaniel Bannister (MS, prompter's copy, NYPL) and *Jack Sheppard, or The Life of a Robber* by Jonas B. Phillips (MS, promptbook, HTC), these included *The Felon's Dream, The Spirit of Jack Sheppard, Dick Turpin in France, Handsome Jack, Dick Turpin, or The Highwayman's Ride*, and *Jack Sheppard and His Dogs*. Although copies of the spin-offs are no longer extant, the gothicism, dark adventure, and sexual desire (most featured a female bandit in a breeches role) which pervade the originals on which they were based suggest that these shows backed the apocalyptic and vengeful hopes of workers evident in apocalyptic plays into the political cul-de-sac of psychological anxiety and sexual release.

35. Alfred Bernheim, *The Business of the Theatre: An Economic History of the American Theatre, 1750–1932* (1932; rpt., New York: Benjamin Blom, 1964), pp. 30–31. Bernheim got his numbers from Harrison Fiske, publisher of the *New York Dramatic Mirror* (December 1, 1886), p. 7. See also Peter A. Davis, "From Stock to Combination: The Panic of 1873 and Its Effects on the American Theatre Industry," *Theatre History Studies*, 8 (1988), 1–9.

36. There are no completely reliable figures for the decline of stock and the rise of combination companies during these years. Harrison Fiske (in the article cited above) claimed that the number of combination companies was "over 100" in 1876. But as Rosemarie K. Bank ("A Reconsideration of the Death of Nineteenth-Century Repertory Companies and the Rise of the Combination," *Essays in Theatre*, 5 [November 1986], 61–75) notes, Fiske had reasons to exaggerate the demise of rep and the rise of the combination. Since Fiske was writing in 1886, his number of combos for that year (282) is probably close to accurate. Consequently, it is also probable that there were "over 100" combos in 1880, if not earlier.

Index

Burke, Kenneth, xi, 111

burlesque, 120–21

Burridge, Kenelm, 140

Burton, William E., 201, 203

business class, xii, 39, 66, 132, 186, 209; as spectators, ix, xii, 82, 94, 159, 164, 200–204, 209, 212, 217, 219, 228, 230, 235, 241, 244–46, 234; consolidation of, 221–35, 255–57; men of principle, 177, 178–80, 184, 185, 186, 187, 193, 194, 206, 208, 220, 238, 242; moralists, 67, 72–73, 121, 133, 157, 159, 177, 186–87, 217, 218, 219–20, 228, 230, 232, 233; problem of authenticity, 210, 225, 230; rise of, 66, 67–68, 95, 134–35, 158–60, 162, 165, 177, 186–87, 198–200, 217–18; social hypocrisy of, 160, 187, 196, 199, 210, 222, 223; women and families in, 71–72, 166–67, 208–209, 218, 220, 228–30

Butchers of Ghent, The, 142

Calvinism, 107, 137, 153, 154, 164, 172, 177, 180, 191, 193

Camp, George, 107

capitalism, 3, 6, 23, 27, 30, 32, 55, 59, 63, 65–68, 80–81, 82, 95, 133, 135, 158, 160, 177, 179, 187, 194, 196, 230, 232, 250

Carlyle, Thomas, 74, 76, 113

Carpenter of Rouen, The, 124, 126, 127, 128, 132, 134, 137–38, 142, 148, 163, 254; program illustration, 129

Caruthers, William, 107

catharsis, 140, 150, 165, 194

Catholicism, 40, 42, 55, 126, 139, 164, 186, 196. *See also* German-Americans; Irish-Americans

Cavaliers of Virginia, 107

Centlivre, Susan, 34

Chambers Street Theatre, 120

Chanfrau, Frank, 131

characterization in melodrama: African-Americans, 180–81; aristocrats, 37–38, 40, 45, 46, 51, 54, 98, 99, 103, 104, 105, 109, 116, 124, 126, 127, 139; comics, 44, 45, 128–30, 182, 215–16; fathers, 37, 38, 41, 42, 43, 44, 46, 52–55, 58, 98–100, 103, 180, 192, 226; heroes, 68, 92, 98–104, 105–106, 108–109, 112, 114, 117, 125, 126–28, 130, 138, 180, 192, 193, 199, 214–16, 221–22, 224, 225, 255; heroines, 37–38, 43, 44, 46, 47, 48, 50–51, 52, 53, 54, 68, 98, 127, 128, 137, 181–82, 183, 199, 206, 214–16, 221–22, 225, 226; men of principle, 179–81, 182, 254; Native Americans, 98, 100, 101, 102, 105, 108–109, 117, 127–28, 130, 137, 139; prophet-avengers, 125, 128, 133, 134, 137–38, 140, 143, 155; proto-detectives, 223–26, 227, 254; villains, 37–38, 40, 41, 42, 45–46, 51, 68, 112, 117, 119, 125, 126, 128, 136, 138, 153, 181, 196, 216–17, 222, 223, 225, 226

charismatic authority, 63, 68, 70, 74–75, 86, 90, 91–92, 102–103, 104, 105, 107, 110, 111, 118, 130, 136, 137, 148, 154, 184

Châteaubriand, René Francois, 40

Chatham Garden Theatre, 11, 12, 13, 14, 22; illustration, 17

Chatham Theatre, 120–21, 131, 148, 153, 173
Cherry and Fair Star, 36, 63
Chestnut Street Theatre, 3, 9, 11, 12–13, 18–19, 23–25, 26, 27, 46, 61, 93, 236–37
child-guidance literature, 57–59
Children's Aid Society, 233
Chinese Museum, 176
Cinderella, 35, 63
circus, 24, 25, 154, 243, 251, 253
citizenship, 66–67, 72, 89, 100, 125, 158
City Museum, 176
Civil War, ix, 32, 163, 167, 179, 194, 215, 218, 232, 233, 245, 248
Claflin, Horace B., 158
Clapp, Henry, Jr., 236
Clapp, William W., 7, 13, 163
Clari, the Maid of Milan, 35, 37–38, 41–47, 48, 52, 53–54, 55
Clay, Henry, 31, 33
Clifton, Josephine, 73, 77
code of honor, xiii, 66–67, 71, 72–73, 88, 89–90, 96, 125, 130–31; among workers, 95–96, 97, 119, 123, 130–32, 134, 143, 144, 150, 154–55, 165, 254; in melodramas, 68, 98, 100, 106–107, 126–28, 130–31, 140, 180. *See also* Forrest, Edwin
Coelina, or the Child of Mystery, 51, 52, 54, 55
Colleen Bawn, The, 211–16, 219, 221, 223, 227, 243, 254; illustration, 212
Collegians, The, 211
Colman, George, 36
Columbian Sentinel, 15
comedy, xii, xiii, 34, 35, 210, 237, 242, 252

Commerford, John, ix, 143
commodification of playgoing, 244, 246, 252
Concise History of the Life and Amours of Thomas S. Hamblin, A, 123
Conrad, King of Naples, 77
Conrad, Robert T., 77, 91, 97, 98, 99, 105, 108, 112
constables, 20–21
contractual relations, 67, 155, 177, 179, 187–89, 193–94, 220, 228, 249–50
conventions: acting, xi, 68, 112–14, 116, 117, 191, 239; audience, 15–17, 75–76, 83, 164; dramatic, xiv, 41, 51, 91, 164; literary, 98, 113, 125–26; oratorical, 112, 113; rioting, 20–21, 153; scenic, 142; theatre architecture, 204
Conway, Henry J., 178, 180, 188
Cooper, James Fenimore, 34
Cooper, Thomas A., 25, 28, 84
copyright laws, 124, 210, 252
Coriolanus, 84, 242
Corsican Brothers, The, 210
costumes, 6, 43, 51, 79, 93, 120, 181, 183, 192, 222–23, 248, 252
Cottin, Marie, 40
Country Wife, The, 34
Cowell, Joseph, 25
Cox, William, 47–48
Crock of Gold, The, 177
culture, xiii; alternative, 155, 254; dominant, 120, 159, 197, 220, 232, 255–57; emergent, xiii, 63, 155, 159, 162, 166, 197, 232; residual, xiii, 63, 66, 68
Cummings, Maria, 185
Curate's Daughter, The, 178
curtain speeches, 70, 75–76, 84

evangelical religion, 6, 67, 94, 143, 155, 193, 195. *See also* revivalism

Evening Journal, 237

Evening Post, 11, 146

extravaganzas, 242–43, 245, 247, 252

Eytinge, Rose, 238

fairy tales, 29, 36, 38–40

Faler, Paul, 95

families in audience, 158, 159, 163–65, 174, 175, 193

Fanchon, 242, 243

farce, xii, 175, 176, 210, 236, 238

Farquhar, George, 34

Farren, William, 144, 145, 148

Federal Street Theatre, 20, 21, 22

"feejee mermaid," 172, 175

feminism, xi

Fennell, James, 16

feudalism, 40, 41, 43, 56, 67

Fielder, Mari, 236

Fievée, Joseph, 40

Fifth Avenue Theatre, 205, 206, 208, 236

Finney, Charles G., 195

Fisher, Amelia, 47

Fisher, Clara, 47–51, 63; illustration, 49

Fletcher, Angus, 190, 191

floral tributes, 75, 76

folk tales, 29, 38–39, 40, 42

Forrest, Edwin, 192; as actor, 79, 82–83, 112–14, 116–18, 140, 141, 232, 239, 241; as American star, 25, 28, 63, 68, 81, 119, 120; as proto-capitalist, 77, 80, 82, 83–84, 93; audience for, 92–97, 239; belief in code of honor, 71, 72–73, 88, 89–90, 130; conflict with Macready, 86–87, 144, 145, 147, 150; curtain speeches, 70, 75, 84; early career,

81, 83, 84–85, 99; hero worship of, 69–71, 83–86, 88–90, 93, 94, 95, 117–18, 245; illustrations, 87, 115; marriage and divorce, 69–73, 106, 130; public image, 70–71, 84–90, 91–92, 239

Forrest Life Guards, 84

Forty Thieves, The, 36

Foster, George, 94, 133

Foucault, Michel, 61

Fourteenth Street Theatre, 251

Fox, George L., 63, 243, 253–55

Frank Leslie's magazine, 203

Franklin, Benjamin, 67, 165

Franklin Theatre, 120, 176

Freedley, Edwin T., 217

French Revolution, 226

Frost, John, 220

Fruits of the Wine Cup, The, 178

Frye, Northrop, 190

Fugitive Slave law, 188

Fuller, Margaret, ix

Gamester, The, 177

Garrick, David, 74, 241

Garrison, William L., 117

gas lighting: in auditorium, 11, 14–15, 160, 208, 245; on stage, 14, 36, 122, 142–43, 245

General Trades Union, 143

Genius of Christianity, 40

George Barnwell, 177

German-Americans, 132, 154, 164, 186

Gilfert, Charles, 81

Gilje, Paul, 146

Gladiator, The, 77, 78, 85, 91, 97–104, 105–106, 108–109, 114–17

Gleason's Pictorial, 174

Goldsmith, Oliver, 242

rehearsing, 27, 206, 207
reification, 194, 197, 210, 230
republicanism, xiii, 31, 59, 63, 72, 158; decline of in business-class culture, 158, 198, 228; in apocalyptic melodrama, 124–25, 126, 128; in heroic melodrama, 68, 89–90, 100, 103, 104, 106, 108, 109, 116; in yeoman culture, 65–68, 89–90, 96, 97, 104–105, 120, 134, 148, 151, 154, 155, 158, 250
Republican party, 219, 232
reserved seating, 175, 196, 200, 202, 203
respectability, 122; flouted by traditionalist workers, 150, 155, 187, 255; in business-class theatres, 201, 203–204, 205, 253; in business-class values, xiii, 68, 122, 157–60, 159, 165, 166–67, 187, 195–96, 198–200, 210, 217–20, 228, 238, 239; in moral reform melodrama, 179, 181–85, 189, 194, 198–99; in museums, 162, 167, 168, 173–75, 196–97, 200; in sensation melodrama, 213–16, 222, 223, 227
revivalism, 166–67, 172, 177, 194–95
Revolutionary War, 5, 33, 66, 144, 148, 179
Revolution of 1830, 226
Reynolds, David, 143
rhetoric, 113, 117, 125; Democratic, 107, 126; hortatory, 116–18; of charismatic authority, 111–12, 113, 114, 115–17, 126; of fairy-tale melodrama, 30, 41, 43, 54, 58, 61; of folk tales, 40; of humanitarian reform, 177, 179, 185, 193, 221,

228; of moral control societies, 59; of moral reform melodrama, 176, 182, 184, 189–91, 193–94, 199; of museum exhibits, 162, 168–73; of Pixérécourt's melodramas, 29, 51; of riots, 143, 144, 150; of well-made plays, 228, 230; Republican, 126, 134, 148
Rice, Thomas "Daddy," 145
Rich and Poor of Boston, The, 211
Richard III, 34, 47
Richmond Hill Theatre, 22
Rienzi, 125, 141
Riesman, David, 96
riots, 9, 120, 122, 155, 157; Astor Place, 68, 86, 88, 89, 92, 94, 144–54, illustration, 152; Boston (1834), 186; Draft Riots, 233; Farren, 144–52, 153–54; Kean, 9, 19–21; McKenzie, 12–13; Park Theatre (1838), 153; Philadelphia (1844), 132, 186; working-class, 143–55
Rip Van Winkle, 238–39
Ritchie, Anna Cora Mowatt, 77–78
Rivals, The, 163
Roach, Joseph, x
Robertson, Agnes, 210, 211, 238
Robertson, Tom, 242, 243
romanticism, 51, 74–75, 97
romantic literature, 91, 97–98, 107, 125–26
Romeo and Juliet, 242
Rosedale, 242
Rosina Meadows, 164, 178, 180–84, 185, 188–89, 192–93
Rothman, David, 60
Rudé, George, 144, 147, 149
Ryan, Mary, xi
Rynders, "Captain" Isaiah, 86

Sumner, Charles, 73
supernumeraries, 79–80, 110, 111, 116
symbolic act, x
symphony orchestras, 235

tableaux, 37, 41, 43, 45, 51, 55, 108, 127, 139, 140, 172, 191, 192, 227
Tale of Mystery, A, 52
Tammany Hall, 133–34, 145, 147, 151, 208, 251
Tappan, Arthur, 6, 146
Tappan, Lewis, 6, 145, 146, 148, 151
Tate, Nahum, 34
Taylor, Tom, 241, 242
temperance, 95, 158, 159, 164–66, 167, 172, 176–78, 179, 183, 185, 186, 188, 193, 194, 234, 254
Temperance Recorder, 166
Ten Nights in a Barroom, 178
theatre architecture, 1, 17; apron stage, 15; auditorium decor, 93, 174–75, 203, 236–37; balconies, 12, 200, 203, 205, 253; boxes, 9, 10, 11, 13–15, 93, 122, 175, 200, 201, 202, 203, 205; capacity, 13, 94, 173, 203, 204, 205; façade, 237; gallery, 10, 13–14, 94, 174, 200, 252; lobbies, 11, 12, 208, 237; orchestra, 174, 200, 203–204; parquette, 174, 200–204, 253; pit, 10, 13–14, 94, 122, 174, 175, 200, 201, 253; saloons, 11, 12, 122, 173, 176, 252; separate entrances, 12–13, 173; third tier, 8, 173, 200
theatre managers, xii, 1, 5, 6, 7, 11, 12, 17, 20, 21, 24, 25, 27, 28, 75, 79, 80, 123, 142, 154, 160, 164, 175–76, 192, 200, 205, 210, 243, 245, 247–51, 252, 254, 255–56.

See also Barnum, Phineas T.; Wood, William B.; etc.
theatre programs, 141, 191; illustration, 129
theatre seating, 17, 196, 201
theatrical benefits, 6, 21, 22, 24, 27, 77, 84, 123, 129, 144
theatrical formations, xii, xiii, 63, 159
Thérèse, the Orphan of Geneva, 35, 36–37, 38, 41–45, 48, 52, 53, 54, 63
Thirty Years, 177
Thomas, H. A., 17
Thompson, Edward P., 67, 143
Thompson, Lydia, 243
Ticket-of-Leave Man, The, 242
Todd, Rev. John, 186
Tom and Jerry, 19
Tompkins, Eugene, 202
Tom Pop's First Visit to the Boston Museum, 168
Tom Thumb, 170–71, 174
Tortesa, the Usurer, 77
tragedy, 91, 99, 102, 103–104, 177, 204, 227, 237, 242, 243
transportation, 8, 26, 32, 184
Tremont Street Theatre, 7, 9, 13, 22, 61
Trollope, Frances M., 8
Troy Museum, 176
Tucker, George, 107
Turner, Bryan, 75
Turner, Nat, 117

Uncle Tom's Cabin, 175, 178, 180–84, 188, 189, 192, 243, 253
Under the Gaslight, 206, 213–17, 221, 223, 226, 235, 245, 247, 254
Union Square Theatre, 251
Union Square theatre district, 247, 251–52, 256